THE DESCENT OF MANNERS

THE DESCENT OF MANNERS

Etiquette, Rules & The Victorians

Andrew St George

[handwritten inscription: For [name] & [name]]

[handwritten: with best wishes]

[handwritten signature: Andrew St George]

Chatto & Windus

LONDON

First published 1993

1 3 5 7 9 10 8 6 4 2

© Andrew St George 1993

Andrew St George has asserted his right under the Copyright, Designs and
Patents Act, 1988 to be identified as the author of this work.

First published in the United Kingdom in 1993 by
Chatto & Windus Ltd
Random House, 20 Vauxhall Bridge Road, London SW1V 2SA

Random House Australia (Pty) Limited
20 Alfred Street, Milsons Point, Sydney,
New South Wales 2061, Australia

Random House New Zealand Limited
18 Poland Road, Glenfield
Auckland 10, New Zealand

Random House South Africa (Pty) Limited
PO Box 337, Bergvlei, South Africa

Random House UK Limited Reg. No. 954009

A CIP catalogue record for this book is available from the British Library

ISBN 0 7011 3623 5

Phototypeset by Intype, London
Printed in Great Britain by
Clays Ltd, St Ives plc

For F. H. St. George

Contents

Acknowledgements

What follows is part of three year's work at Christ Church, Oxford and Columbia University in New York. The book represents one of my interests at that time and I have been fortunate to receive help from many quarters during the research and writing. I would like to thank these friends, colleagues and associates: Asa Briggs, John Burrow, Christopher Butler, Carmen Callil, John Carey, Peter Conrad, Stephen Gill, Kathy High, Ian Irvine, David Kynaston, J.H. Plumb, Christopher Ricks, Frank H. St George, Michael Sissons, Anthony D. Smith, Sohrab Sorooshian, John Swanzy, Jenny Uglow and Duncan Watt.

E.A.W. St George
Oxford 1992

Introduction

'The English, more than any other people, not only act but feel according to rule.'[1] John Stuart Mill wrote that in 1869. This book traces his insight through Victorian society, between 1830 and 1890. It is a social history which takes as its starting point Mill's observation that, in both a good and a bad sense, the nineteenth-century English were further from a state of nature than any other modern people. The English were a product of civilisation and discipline, of the imposition of codes of conduct and sets of rules. Mid-Victorian behaviour, manners, etiquette and the beliefs which lay beneath them were all about following rules.

England was a country in which rules and codes substituted themselves for nature. It was here that social discipline had most succeeded, not so much in conquering as in suppressing whatever was liable to conflict with society. Elsewhere, although the rules may have been stronger than nature, the nature was still there. According to Mill the greater part of life was carried on, not by following inclination under the control of rule, but by having no inclination but that of following a rule.[2] Rule-following provided the pattern for the Victorians' processes of thinking about themselves, for their feelings about their circumstances, and for the environment which made possible many of their achievements, both good and bad.

Prime Minister Disraeli combined the apt outlook of an outsider with the compromised vision of the party politician when he said in Manchester – that quintessential Victorian experiment of the mid-century – on 3 April 1872:

> . . . England has never experienced a revolution, though there is
> no country in which there has been so continuous and such
> considerable change. How is this? Because the wisdom of your
> forefathers placed the prize of supreme power without the sphere
> of human passions. Whatever the struggle of parties, whatever the

strife of factions, whatever the excitement and exaltation of the public mind, there has always been something in this country round which all classes and parties could rally, representing the majesty of law, the administration of justice, and involving, at the same time, the security for every man's rights and the fountain of honour.[3]

Disraeli knew England as a country governed by an unwritten constitution with laws based on precedent; with a crown which exercised a 'powerful and beneficial influence', as if influence were one of the most powerful forces for cohesion and government. The influence of the Crown, as Disraeli saw it, did not confine itself to political affairs:

England is a domestic country. Here the home is revered and the hearth is sacred. The nation is represented by a family – the Royal Family; and if that family is educated with a sense of responsibility and a sentiment of public duty, it is difficult to exaggerate the salutary influence they may exercise over a nation. It is not merely an influence upon manners; it is not merely that they are a model for refinement and good taste – they affect the heart as well as the intelligence of the people; and in the hour of public adversity, or in the anxious conjecture of public affairs, the nation rallies round the Family and the Throne, and its spirit is animated and sustained by the expression of public affection.[4]

How did this influence work, leading and following, being of the time and yet apart from them? Why did the Victorians, more than any society before or since, construct and adhere to strict rules and patterns of behaviour which in many instances were a substitute for thought and feeling about the things which daily confronted them? What Mill knew as a psychological leaning ('having no inclination but that of following a rule'[5]), Disraeli saw as an instrument of government, keeping at bay what the economist and constitutional historian Walter Bagehot – also in 1872 – called 'the supremacy of ignorance over instruction and of numbers over knowledge'.[6] Seven years later the historian T. H. S. Escott und a firm set of categories:

In the constitution of English society at the present day, the three rival elements – the aristocratic, the democratic, and the plutocratic – are closely blended. The aristocratic principle is still paramount, forms the foundation of our social structure, and has been strengthened and extended in its operation by the plutocratic, while the democratic instinct of the race has all the opportunities of assertion and gratification which it can find in a career conditionally open to talents.[7]

To look back from then to the 1832 Reform Bill was to see a road paved with good social intentions, what Escott called 'the accomplishment of great and undoubted good'. By this he understands the substitution of the prestige of achievement for the prestige of position; the fops and dandies, 'the glory of whose life was indolence, and who looked upon anything in the way of occupation as a disgrace, have gone out of date never to return'.[8]

The Victorians' consciousness of environment came through the consciousness of their social relations. Victorian society gradually developed a set of ideas which amounted to a mode of living – ideas about what was happening, what could be known, and what could be done: in a word, tradition. All forms of tradition are both presumptive and prescriptive. The importance of ideas which form a tradition is that those ideas transcend political life. They govern each transaction or encounter in the life of each individual.

What the Victorians knew was that the past could authorise the present by vesting it with continuity; what they did not know was that the steady hum of technology and the murmur of intellectual debate would gradually become the roar which drowned the quietude of their musings. The railway which threatened, as far as Thomas Carlyle was concerned, to bring the drunken hoards to the foot of Helvellyn also brought prosperity and comfort. The continuity of manners throughout the age was one of the most important forces for cohesion, and at the same time one of the most potent instruments of change.

Between 1832 and 1867 an extraordinary and growing social consensus emerged. This formed a pattern of behaviour that not only served a particular society but also left its imprint on the succeeding years. It had at its root the relations between people; 'all life,' thought Henry James, 'comes back to the question of our relations with each other'.[9] This consensus made manners, which both fixed and lubricated social relations, into something much more than mere precursor of the U *vs.* non-U debate.

Manners are social control self-imposed; and etiquette is class control exercised. Manners really amount to an unwritten social constitution. Between the two Reform Bills the notion and prosecution of manners combined the Victorian distrust of government with a devotion to legislation; they united the individuality of nonconformism with the community of belief; they stood as witnesses to the search for a workable culture; and they were the surest evidence of class emulation rather than class envy.

In the same period, Victorian thinking about the usefulness of legislation bore fruit with long series of parliamentary debates and action. These same impulses to regulate, impose and frame control reached out through the medium of the etiquette book and sermon into the area of social relations, and indeed beyond, into private meditation, creative thinking and writing. Because the prescriptions in these books appeared to have no political bias, the rules they promoted took on the vesture of natural law, or what some today see as 'ideology in its most powerful form'.[10] This unwritten social constitution *was* in fact inscribed in the pages of etiquette and manners books. The great paradox was that a recognised and learnable set of rules for conduct at several levels of society made society both ossified and organic, mobile and immobile. Mid-Victorian manners meant stasis with the potential for mobility, but above all structure. Manners books functioned as a check on the growing democratic impulse between the Reform Bills, but also held within them the potential for greater democratisation, the seeds of egality. As Henry Maine wrote, looking back in 1887, 'the immobility of society is to the rule, its mobility is the exception'.[11]

The idea of process, general historical shifts guided by an inexorable inner principle of movement, was familiar to the Victorians. Gladstone found it unobservable in detail, 'but as solid and undeniable as it is resistless in its essential character. It is like those movements in the crust of the earth which science tells us are even now going on in certain parts of the globe'.[12] The impetus of mid-Victorian process, the inclination to conduct political and social debate by thinking about resistless movements in history, found Mill struggling (in *Representative Government*, 1861) to escape his commitment to the idea that the form of society determined the form of politics. But what processes determined the form of society – or, rather, what did individuals operating together as social groups both desire and deplore?

The notion of the centrality of manners and their capacity to mollify the dictates of government stretches from Locke's 'civil society' through Hume to Leslie Stephen. The nineteenth-century Whig concept of working with rather than against the grain of society and manners allowed for complexity in the latter; it is not reducible to the individualism of market economics.[13] Moreover, the wide influence of de Tocqueville's *Democracy in America* had prompted the view that democracy itself could be seen in terms of manners as well as constitutions, with egalitarian public opinion as a vital factor in the process. As John Burrow rightly notes, 'the notion of American "democratic manners" called for an appraisal that was moral and aesthetic as much as sociological and political'.[14]

The advance of democracy, both in America after the Civil War and in England between 1832 and 1867, can be seen not only as a type of government but as a system of manners, a form of social life. 'Self-culture' and 'cultivation' came to stand as the opposite of eighteenth-century rudeness. If the poet Arthur Hugh Clough knew in 1849 that 'still, individual culture is also something',[15] Mill knew that the circumstances which surrounded different classes and individuals, and which shaped their characters, were daily becoming more assimilated; and this concern for individualism lies behind Mill's denunciation of provincial narrowness and middle-class manners in *Civilization* (1836) and *On Liberty* (1859).[16]

After 1867, or, rather, throughout the 1860s and 1870s, a strain of liberal intellectual pessimism emerged, a partial loss of confidence in an advancing civilisation. R. S. Surtees's John Jorrocks in *Handley Cross* may have been proud to be middle class in 1843; but Bagehot's great *English Constitution* found the English equivocally 'deferential' in 1867. The causes of this gradual shift are as much attributable to the decline in religious nonconformist fervour as to the more tangible effects of the American Civil War abroad or to the Lancashire cotton famine, Hyde Park Riots or the Fenian Conspiracy at home. By 1870 Anglicans asserted that a theological transformation had taken place: worldly Christian compassion had alleviated such stark evangelical doctrines as those of eternal and vicarious punishment.[17]

One of the social effects of evangelism had been to make puritan values (hard work, self-help) into a sense of duty. The ameliorative social schemes of the 1830s and 1840s (Poor Law, Committee on Inebriety, Health of Towns Committee, Sanitary Condition of Labouring Population, Public Health Act[18]) had as their object the spread of mental and moral improvement beyond the educated middle classes to the artisan and labouring classes: 'the overall aim,' writes J. F. C. Harrison, 'was the strengthening of a common culture, based on middle-class social norms, into which the working classes could be integrated'.[19] But while the 1840s had seen the Sunday School replace the cock-fight or bull-baiting, gradually the notion of improvement began to turn against those most in need of it. Self-help, made popular in 1859 by Samuel Smiles's book, had originally been a working-class means of glimpsing the material and cultural benefits denied them in the new industrial society. But by the 1860s 'self-help' became the rebuff of the privileged to the disadvantaged.

Social institutions were the expression of the moral values which ruled the lives of individuals. The period 1832–67 produced the British Association, the London and Birmingham Railway, the *Daily News*, the Evangelical Alliance, the *Daily Telegraph* and the Working Men's College. These institutions reflected the values of the mid-century, in general committed to progress and change. Almost invariably, the great thinkers of the age saw their times as 'transitional'.[20] Images of movement and environment abounded: Bulwer-Lytton, who knew that ideas travelled upwards and manners downwards, saw a country 'darkened by the shadow of change'[21]; Mill looked for principle in an age of transition and in an environment of quickening rates of change; and Carlyle, for whom Time itself was in the pangs of travail with the New, named his age 'the Age of Machinery, in every outward and inward sense of that word'.[22] Tennyson imagined an improving future hurtling down the ringing grooves of change. But most importantly, the process of evolutionary change entered the Victorian consciousness through Charles Lyell (1844), Charles Darwin (1859), and later T. H. Huxley and Alfred Russel Wallace.

In the 1860s and 1870s notions of social progress began to alter, not least because new notions of progress and evolution were already widely current by then, suggesting other and uncomfortable patterns of social development. The prevailing mid-century sense that what some were, all might be, was beginning to transform itself into a perplexing mixture of waning Protestant evangelism and waxing scientific discourse. The constant throughout this change was a concern for and a commitment to correct behaviour in as many spheres of life as possible.

The book of moral homilies, the sermon or the etiquette book governed social interactions where everyone agreed to behave in a certain way; but when technology changed the world by building a railway or by uncovering a medical problem produced by economic and military circumstances (in the case of prostitutes in garrison towns who suffered from sexually transmitted disease), the mid-Victorian impulse was to leap for the rule-book. Where there were no rules to suit the situation, the mid-Victorians searched for parallel situations or formulated new rules on old principles.

Where, then, do manners happen? Where did the mid-Victorians think they drew their standards? How far did the rule-bound thinking of the mid-Victorians extend beyond the realm of manners and etiquette books? The search for rules was the cornerstone of mid-Victorian thinking. This search was conducted across an extraordinary range of activities, more remarkable for being disparate, more understandable in light of anxiety about 'the right way to behave' in any given context. Manners were the clearest evidence of a mid-Victorian wish to do the right thing in society, at work, in religion, in legislation, and, indeed, in thinking about themselves. Manners were social control which kept others out, confined them to their place; and manners – in the form of refined, honed etiquette – were social emulation assiduously pursued.

The descent of manners throughout the century, in the sense of their origin and their decay, must be traced through several diverse yet contiguous areas of mid-Victorian experience. The key is the search for rules, thinking and feeling according to rule as a matter of instinct in any situation. That is what this book is about, and its diversity mirrors the diversity available to the nineteenth-century commentator. Seeing manners as an archetype, a way of thinking which most clearly emphasises the mid-Victorians' propensity to create rules about themselves, provides a compass of understanding for diverse areas of experience. Throughout books of morals, manners, etiquette, or through home design, health legislation and foreign attitudes, or within the thinking of poets and scientists, runs a common thread of knowing how to behave, how to play the game. In each area the Victorians reveal themselves in what they hope for or fear, how they plan and arrange, and how they deal with new and sometimes dangerous raw material.

The six sections of this book, therefore, are deliberately diverse and interdisciplinary. They cover morals, etiquette, home design, American manners, money and creative thinking in science and poetry; the broadening scope turns out to be a journey inward as well, to the creative springs of the mid-century, its energies and processes. The Victorian treasure house, always open to the social, cultural and literary historian, has many entrances and too many rooms to explore and alcoves to importune for an incontrovertibly complete haul to be made. But a clear picture does emerge.

The first section looks at the history of the manners book and books of moral and social instruction. The status and ethic of the self-help book, incarnate in the work of the self-help gurus Samuel Smiles and Martin Tupper, show how the mid-Victorian presented ideal versions of themselves both as a challenge and as an escape; it also shows how the principles of religious teaching and popular morals made themselves generally available. Above all, these guides to behaviour offered prescriptive rather than descriptive models for different levels of Victorian society. To know how and why individuals behaved as they did at home, at dinner or at the conversazione, is to know how their thinking on behaviour was shaped by their unacknowledged fears and assumptions, the beliefs the culture took for granted and which emerge best as processes within a system.

In the second section, the conversation manual listens to the mid-Victorians talking to each other with the aid of a bewildering variety of rules, maxims, tips and warnings. Above all, in matters of social import, the mid-Victorians agreed with Walter Bagehot's belief that the first duty of society was to protect society.

The home is the subject of the third section. This is important because it was an institution which the mid-Victorians evolved. While manners looked back to books of instruction, the home looked to models of design and taste, which provided the rules for its own behaviour. The domestic role of women in mid-Victorian society was linked to the Great Exhibition, the ideal which exemplified the procedures followed not only by home design, but by men's designs on women. The home needed to define itself against the outside, cherish the importance of here by recognising the importance of elsewhere. It was concern about correct behaviour which extended home values on to the streets in the guise of the Contagious Diseases Acts in the 1860s. The Acts' opponents also drew on the values of home and family to argue against them. The anti-Acts international public relations and lobbying campaign run by Josephine Butler showed an argument about Victorian legislation in which both sides appealed to notions of correctness and propriety.

By 1800 the etiquette book in Europe was already 400 years old. But in America, the focus of the fourth section of this book, manners were being made up as the country defined itself. Here was a situation in which people could rewrite the rules they disagreed with, recast the opinions which displeased them. If ever both Disraeli and de Tocqueville agreed on anything, it seems to be the cohesive effect of manners, the creation of a pattern of belonging and a means of thinking out a way of behaving. The progress of manners books, behaviour guides and etiquette books in nineteenth-century America showed a society amalgamating new forms of thinking and behaviour, those 'democratic manners' of de Tocqueville. Moreover, current differences in the arts of life between England and America emerged in the nineteenth century.

Section five looks at money. Financial behaviour is interesting because it combines intangible values related to worth, credibility and trust with stylised forms of commerce and palpable realities like wealth, ownership or debt. The rule of manners, and the kind of mid-Victorian thinking which lay behind it, stretched into finance, where the great financial frauds of the 1840s and 1850s showed how the fraudsters had used their understanding of the process of manners and behaviour in their society in order to operate successfully. On the one hand lay the imperatives of the divines, on the other, the small solicitations of circumstance.

The final section of the book traces the developments in poetry and science that made the idea of rule-following and adherence to strict codes obsolete. The will to behave and the will to believe stretched still further into the virgin land of the Victorians' creative and intellectual life. The age of the sermon and the novel generated the uniquely Victorian poetic procedure, the dramatic monologue. This enabled Victorian thinking to colonise new forms of life, exploring uncharted emotions; here, Browning, Clough, Meredith and the Rossettis made genuine advances by using new forms of writing and thinking. And the seismic impact of scientific thought on the Victorians' thinking about nature, natural behaviour and morals bore the imprint of one mode of thought on another in the 1870s and 1880s. As science came to account for behaviour, the behaviour book first reacted by trying to be scientific. But a complete account of human behaviour threatened to remove individual expression. What was unnatural when everything was nature and science had the confidence, and potentially the means, to explain all? Scientific process placed the Decadent movement in an intellectual rather than its usual social context, and showed how the last quarter of the nineteenth century has shaped relations between the arts and the natural sciences ever since.

Mill's certainties and perplexities about his age throughout the forty years he wrote were exemplary. Throughout his writing he showed a commitment to seeing life as a series of systems, a way of thinking that covered art and science alike. Mill was, in many ways, the last thinker in whom the two approaches offered by what was later to be called the Two Cultures, science and the arts, united. When he died in 1873 his *System of Logic* (1843) had been a Victorian staple for thirty years. The final book of the *Logic* explains the Victorians in terms of process and behaviour. Mill's lucid prose has the clarity of conviction:

> Whatever speaks in rules or precepts, not in assertions respecting matters of fact, is art; and ethics or morality is properly a portion of the art corresponding to the sciences of human nature and society.[23]

By 'art', Mill means how we get on with each other. What he is saying is that all forms of practical business compel individuals, in certain cases, to conform to pre-established rules; other circumstances charge individuals with finding or constructing the rules which will govern their conduct. Victorian society everywhere engaged in a perpetual search for such rules – scientific, religious, social, sexual – which it could then rely upon. This was the medium in which Victorian behaviour took place. Victorian society characterised the condition in which individuals conformed to pre-established rules, yet one in which they constantly sought to evolve new rules to govern their own conduct. Manners were the message of the century, the clearest indication of ideas applied to conduct.

1
Manners, Morals and Books of Instruction

The disposition of mankind, whether as rulers or as fellow citizens, to impose their own opinions and inclinations as a rule of conduct on others is so energetically supported by some of the best and by some of the worst feelings incident to human nature that it is hardly ever kept under restraint by anything but want of power.

John Stuart Mill, On Liberty[1]

Mill knew the kinds of pressure society in the 1850s brought to bear on the individual; his remark stakes out the territory colonised in the 1840s, 1850s and 1860s by the books of moral instruction which manifested that pressure. Thackeray saw the issue differently and less sharply in *The Book of Snobs* (1846), but recognised that pressure when he remarked: 'Society having ordained certain customs, men are bound to obey the law of Society, and conform to its harmless orders.'[2] Thackeray's language strays into the theological here, with 'ordained' and 'law', while Mill's leans more towards the scientific. Both typify a Victorian dilemma about the appropriate language for social commentary; about the right terms for talking about themselves. Commentators in the 1840s and 1850s sniffed the pace on the breeze; by the 1860s, the pace of social and economic change had quickened, and the commentator's view of the individual's role in a shifting society needed fixed points. These absolutes lay to hand in religious and increasingly in scientific method; these were the laws of construction for the books of morals and manners throughout the 1840s and 1850s.

The laws of the national character were the most important class of sociological rules. National character amounted to the power levied on the individual by the circumstances of society: artificial laws and customs. This character was fashioned by informal contact between individuals. John Locke was right to think that manners, 'about which children are so often perplexed, and have so many goodly exhortations made them . . . are rather to be learned by example than rules'.[3] For Locke, peer pressure rather than books of rules and instruction determined manners most effectively. This was true of the mid-Victorians, but the literature of improvement produced between the Reform Bills indicates that they were subsequently hijacked by the notion of rules to obey and instructions to follow for their own sake. Where had the idea of moral and manner instruction books come from? What made the period between the two Reform Bills so fruitful for purveyors of correctness to the burgeoning middle classes? What made these books peculiarly and particularly Victorian?

The history of the behaviour book, offering advice on morals to live by, manners to smooth social intercourse and etiquette to excise class blunders, stretches back to Erasmus and Della Casa in the sixteenth century. Manners are much more than a miscellaneous collection of changing social rules; there is a link between everyday norms of behaviour and the overall values of a society. There is never a precise correlation between the detail of rules and the detail of contemporary behaviour, although widespread literacy and increased numbers of such books in the nineteenth century diminishes if not dissolves the gap. Codes of manners, consistently observable from sixteenth-, seventeenth- and eighteenth-century manners books, were central to the mechanics and processes of power and prestige within society. In *The Civilising Process* (1939) the theorist of social history, Norbert Elias, identified a pattern of civility which places psychological constraints on impulse and instinct in such a way that society finds itself opposed to nature. There is what Elias calls a 'rising standard of repugnance' about the body: incivility is primitive, infantile and bestial; civility was civilised, advanced and social.[4] Elias finds in the progress of civilisation a process of increasing inhibition throughout twelfth- to twentieth-century Europe.

I The Etiquette Book

The earliest behaviour books were Erasmus's *De Civilitate Morum Puellum* (1530) and Della Casa's *Il Galateo* (1558). More important, however, these books established the tradition of courtesy writing in English. The first texts had appeared in fifteenth-century manuscripts;[5] these, like John Russell's *Boke of Nurture* (1450), tended to see manners as a domestic skill. But with the translation of Erasmus (by Robert Whytington as *A Lytell Booke of Good Manners for Chyldren*) in 1532 and of Giovanni Della Casa (by Robert Peterson as *Galateo: a Treatise of the Manners and Behaviours it behoveth a man to use and eschewe*) in 1576, the tradition which was to flower in the mid-Victorian summer had been planted. Della Casa and Erasmus dealt much more than their precursors with facial expression, control of the body, dress, behaviour for special occasions – the theatre, the bedroom, or at table. Erasmus has much advice on the proprieties of spitting, nose-blowing and tooth-picking. But it was in particular Della Casa who set out to codify the imperatives of social conduct by embarking on a theoretical investigation into their character.

The sixteenth century saw a march of courtesy books which were to divide over the succeeding centuries into books of parental advice, polite conduct, policy and civility. Everything was teachable, from how to carve a capon to how to rule a kingdom. The English equivalents of Erasmus and Della Casa in the 1520s and 1530s were William Harrington's *Comendations of Matrimony* (1528), Thomas Lupset's *Exhortation to Yonge Men* (1529) and Thomas Elyot's *The Boke Named the Governour* (1531). Lupset urged that virtue, health and riches should be sought in that order; Elyot's belief in liberty and rectitude found him valuing honour, responsibility, nobility and friendship. The start of a canon of polite conduct is observable in Elyot and in the *Institutio Oratorica* (Thomas Wilson, 1553), alongside shorter treatises on nobility. Less formal and ambitious discourses are seen in the work of Lupset, and in the private correspondence of Wyatt, Ascham and Sidney.[6]

What the sixteenth century shared with the Victorians was a sense of how society might be preserved by courtesy and humanity, or by standards of behaviour rigorously adhered to and universally acknowledged. After Elyot came a series of books of polity and politeness but not domestic manners: Thomas Hoby's wonderful translation of Castiglione's *Il Cortegiano, Boke of the Courtier* in 1561, followed by John Lyly's pedantic *Euphues* duet (1579, 1580); George Pettie's version of Stephano Guazzo's *Civile Conversazione* (1581), which left – along with Barnaby Rich – a deposit on the floor of Elizabethan literature; and Robert Greene's *Quip for an Upstart Courtier*, a fine 1592 parody of everything which Ben Jonson had railed against in the *Epigrams*. James I weighed in with the tedious *Basilikon Doron* (1599), originally advice to Prince Henry.[7] The whole genre was already established enough to be pilloried by Thomas Dekker in 1609 with his *Guls Hornebooke*.

Ten years on, in 1622, Henry Peacham's *The Compleat Gentleman* appeared in England, setting out and solidifying the connection between good manners and gentlemanly behaviour. This was the tradition which the Victorians were to look back on. It was consolidated by Robert Brathwayt in 1630 with *The English Gentleman* and *The English Gentlewoman* (1631) and then by the extraordinarily popular *Advice to a Son* (1656, 1658) by Francis Osborne and the vigorous *Gentile Sinner* (Clement Ellis, 1660). In Brathwayt and Peacham an encyclopedic picture of the English gentleman begins to emerge for the first time. Also revealingly popular were *The Whole Duty of Man* (1658) and *The Gentleman's Calling* (1660) from the Oxford divine Richard Alstree of Christ Church. Something comfortingly Chaucerian ('Seke out the good in every man, and speke of alle the best ye can') persists in this gentle insight: '[courtesy] does not only cast a glorious lustre round about, attract the eyes and hearts of others, but it also reflects with cheerful and confortable gleams upon ourselves.'[8]

Alstree's library, bequeathed to the College in 1688, contains wide available reading in history, geography, natural science and of course theology: Ralegh's *History of the World* sits alongside Foxe's *Book of Martyrs*; and Wanley's *Wonders of the Little World* alongside Bacon and Spenser. This promised an eclectic and broadening intelligence commensurate with the gentlemanly ideal Alstree had in mind. Rules alone could not impart good manners; experience of the broadest kind – within appropriate limits – was necessary. For example, Bacon's notion of good conversation in the 1623 *Advancement of Learning* turns on a notion of social relations, of maintaining an even balance of dignity between speakers, what Erving Goffman was later to call 'face-work'. Here is Thomas Wright's 1601 version in *The Passions of the Minde*; as Duncan knew in *Macbeth*, there's no art to find the mind's construction in the face:

> Neither do we holde it for good manners, that the inferior should
> fix his eies upon his superior's countenance, and the reason is,
> because it were presumption for him to attempt the entrance or
> privie passage into his superior's minde, as contrariwise it is
> lawful for the superiour to attempt the knowledge of his inferiour.[9]

The titles of these seventeenth-century books strive for manners in their entirety: *The Compleat Gentleman, The Whole Duty of Man.* They expressed various standards for the civilised life, but also provided a language of deference and social orientation. They represented standards of conduct and self-control as a flexible code allowing easy definition of one's place in the social hierarchy. Jean Gailhard's *The Compleat Gentleman* (1678) offers this on eating at table, showing how behaviour translates directly into social status:

> In England the manner is for the master of the house to go in
> before a Stranger. This would pass for a very great incivility in
> France: so here the Lady or Mistress of the House uses to sit at
> the upper end of the Table, which in France is given to Strangers:
> so if we be many in a company, we make no scruple to drink all
> out of a Glass, or Tankard, which they are not used to do: and
> if a servant would offer to give them a glass before it was washed
> every time they drink, they would be angry at it.[10]

In a world before specialisation, (or where generalism *was* the specialisation), in a world of thought peopled by Montaigne, Bacon, Elyot, Guicciardini and Castiglione, a certain type of society was preserved by courtesy and humanity. Machiavelli, that great generalist, never advocated bad manners, but just suggested that the nature of men necessitated a public morality which differed from and often conflicted with the accepted virtues fostered on Christian ethics. For Machiavelli, no ethical system had a place in the game of skill which was politics. On the one hand, those innocent of public engagement conducted their own lives, while on the other the experienced players got things done. Bacon knew Machiavelli was right, and Victor Hugo finally admitted in *Les Misérables* that Machiavelli was 'not an evil genius, nor a cowardly and miserable writer, he is nothing but the fact'.[11] The political element is one of the major aspects of conduct which the earliest conduct books stress, but which is blanched out of the mid-Victorian versions.

These sixteenth- and seventeenth-century imports to England coincided with an expanded Tudor court and an increase in the size of London to make manners an essentially metropolitan – or at least urban – matter. The succeeding century saw the gradual removal of relationships based in allegiance and service; a new urban society (universities, Inns of Court, Guilds, systems of commerce) emerged to impose itself on the rural environment. By 1642 Henry Peacham's *Art of Living in London* put the matter flatly and boldly, prefiguring the Victorian guides to the metropolis by seeing urban living as a particular kind of life-skill with the insight: 'It is a greater piece of skill to live in a populous place, where multitudes of people reside, than in a solitary place among a few.'[12] As the cities became more crowded throughout the nineteenth century (London in 1801 was 800,000; and by 1891 was 4,200,000), the Victorians sought, by means of codes of manners and behaviour, to re-establish the boundaries which had been eroded by the relatively fluid society of the seventeenth and eighteenth centuries with their gentlemen, courtiers, lawyers, poets and merchants. The notion of civility, a static model and a process of self-betterment in the urban environment of the sixteenth and seventeenth centuries, was reinvented by the mid-Victorians as politeness and correctness. The mid-Victorian equivalent of the poetry of Philip Sidney or John Suckling is a new literature of value.

By the end of the seventeenth century, manners had come to represent a form of personal culture responsible for the contracts and contacts made in civil society rather than the patterns of fealty and hierarchy of the feudal household. Models of political and cultural virtue were produced by the values of civility which also

bore on personal conduct, focusing aristocratic and political ideals
in private behaviour. Good manners meant communal integration
and ingratiation. But a strain of nonconformism saw good manners
as a form of insincerity. Here is William Gouge writing in 1622:

> Religion and Grace consisteth not in good manners: many that
> have not a sparke of Gods fear in their hearts are able to carry
> themselves very orderly and mannerly . . . Good manners are a
> hindrance to Grace: they who are the most diligent in teaching
> or practising the one, are commonly most negligent in the other.[13]

While the sixteenth and seventeenth centuries expressed social
participation as an aspect of self-control, sensitivity and courtesy
for others, a counter-movement is also apparent. Bad manners
prospered too; the 'roaring boys' and 'roysterers' of Nashe,
Greene and Dekker in Elizabethan England were encouraged by
the Civil Wars and their aftermath, the collapse of religious ideal-
ism and the tolerance of Charles II, to fashion themselves into
libertine bravados. The crossover point comes with the gentry-
beggars of Richard Brome's *The Joviall Crew* (1642) begging in
rhyming hexameters and experimenting with other moral codes.
Thomas Shadwell, the playwright pilloried by Dryden in *Mac-
Flecknoe*, focused on the rake and the libertine in his work, notably
in *The Virtuoso*, *The Libertine* and *The Scowrers*; his contemporary George Etheredge produced the anti-puritan rake *par excellence* in the 1676 *Man of Mode*. Later, the libertine transformed
himself into the scoundrel who crosses the pages of Smollett and
Gay in the eighteenth century. Bad behaviour was then – and
again, as it turned out, in the 1890s – a move beyond fashion
which took good manners into anti-manners, a view which saw
moral codes in a broadening world as geography misapplied. But
whereas bad manners were somehow seen as raffishly attractive
in Georgian England, mid-Victorian England regarded them more
seriously, and took a dim view of bad behaviour. If Beau Nash,
whose rules of engagement graced the Bath Pump Room in 1742,
was the point at which courtesy gave way to etiquette, then 1832
was the moment when etiquette gave way to manners and became
a class-based set of rules for admitting oneself and keeping others
out. For etiquette concentrates the sense of the ceremonial in

human affairs and actually becomes a means and a concept for the working-out of social rules.

The book of polite conduct reached its zenith in the mid-seventeenth century. Later writers on civility confined themselves to translations and excerpts from Erasmus, Della Casa and the Abbé Bellegarde.[14] Josiah Dare's *Counsellor Manners His Last Legacy to his Son* (1673) is really a reworking of Della Casa. Thereafter, eighteenth-century books tended to shelve off into abstractions and sententia, although there is a Hogarthian strain which makes itself long on retribution and short on forgiveness. Only Dr Johnson's *Rambler* essays – pure wine, he felt, alongside the water which was the rest of his work – maintained a serious, engaged moral conversation with the environment; but these were the products of a remarkable, driven melancholic, intimate with his personal fight against laxity and laziness, rather than a general exhortation to industry and productivity. The end of the century saw the beginning of the etiquette book which was to become so prominent in the mid-Victorian period:

> In the eighteenth century the book of polite conduct, with its comprehensive picture of the 'compleat gentleman', or 'compleat lady', gradually went out of fashion. Of it there survive, in the closing years of this period, only fragments and analogues: satirical pieces, didactic poems, sermons and homilies, or educational essays . . . After the close of the period, didactic fiction and bluestocking pronouncements carry the history of polite conduct into new and different domains.[15]

This ended a tradition which began with the sixteenth-century civility book. It argued for completeness, the well-rounded model to which the gentleman, as a politically and socially polished member of the ruling classes, aspired. The enduring values instilled by Castigilione – those of goodness, wisdom, manliness and temperance of mind – amounted to a complete lifestyle. Human conduct was everywhere discussed during the sixteenth and seventeenth centuries in terms of ideals rather than in terms of metaphysical absolutes. In the seventeenth-century behaviour books, the English gentleman emerged as an administrator, executive and public servant; the private life subordinated itself to public usefulness. The eighteenth century lived with the values and added little, save specific guidance from Defoe (*The Complete English-Tradesman*, 1725–7) and Swift (*On The Education of Ladies*, 1765). Genteel respectability became a profession too, as the business of society became more important both commercially and psychologically; so the 1780s and 1790s produced *Thoughts on the Importance of the Manners of the Great to General Society* (Hannah More, 1788), *Enquiry into the Duties of Men in the Higher and Middle Classes* (Revd Thomas Gisborne, 1794) and William Wilberforce's 1797 *Practical View*. These books fed the new ethos:

> . . . that of professionalism, 'improvement' being as much a
> psychological necessity as an economic calculation, and one that
> affected the new evangelical clergymen with their 'professional'
> interest in the saving of souls. Its moral tone was that of genteel
> respectability, as is clear from the numerous philanthropic
> associations compaigning 'for the restoration of public and
> private manners', for the 'suppression of vice', and the regeneration
> of the classes above and below themselves – the effete aristrocracy
> and the licentious rabble.[16]

Evangelism, with its close links to *laissez-faire*, free trade and self-help, began to shape attitudes in the early part of the nineteenth century. This was an ethic which easily adjusted itself to everyday commerce: the sacrifice of present pleasure for future gain and the pursuit of happiness through labour and suffering. The atmosphere among evangelicals at the end of the eighteenth century began to condense into clouds which blotted the Regency sun and fell as Victorian rain. The notion that one needed to improve was firmly fixed in the English psyche. This was paralleled in Adam Smith's discovery of the 'division of labour', in James Watt's invention of the steam engine, and in the rather smug sense that England was improving enough to avoid the revolutions which had latterly shaken France and America. By 1850, J. H. Newman was writing *The Danger of Riches*, as religious momentum divided from commercial (and just before Newman left the Anglican Church), but in the 1790s the sense of an evangelical mission to improve had entered the English soul. Nonetheless,

9

the late eighteenth-century behaviour book market was dominated by Chesterfield's *Letters to his Son* (written in 1737, published in 1774 and 1779); there is the usual advice on not being too familiar ('A gentleman is often seen, but seldom heard, to laugh'), fitting advice on dress (better to be a fop than a sloven), and curt advice on politeness ('Even your footman will sooner forget and forgive a beating, than any manifest mark of slight and contempt. Be therefore, I beg of you, not only really, but seemingly and manifestly attentive to whoever speaks to you.'[17]) Testimony to its influence comes from a letter of the hosiery manufacturer Jebediah Strutt to his eighteen-year-old heir. Strutt gave him Chesterfield's *Letters* in 1774:

> I need not tell you that you are not to be a nobleman nor prime minister, but you may possibly be a tradesman of some eminence. You may be assured if you add to the little learning and improvement you have hitherto had, the manners, the air, the genteel address, and polite behaviour of a gentleman, you will abundantly find you account in it in all and every transaction of your future life – when you come to do business in the world. It is impossible for you now to think how necessary it is to have these accomplishments as well as those of a more solid or more important nature – you may believe me in this, for I now feel the want of them by dear experience.[18]

What made the Victorians different was their decision to take the civility book down the highway of popular morals and stringent religious conformism, appealing to a system which lay outside that of class or social relations. In this, Hannah More's 1813 *Christian Morals*, bridging eighteenth-century evangelicalism and early Victorian prescription, set the tone:

> Even while we are rebelling against his dispensations, we are taking our hints in the economy of public and private life, from the economy of Providence in the administration of the world. We govern our country by laws emulative of those by which he governs his creatures: – we train our children by probationary discipline, as he trains his servants.[19]

Substitute 'Evolution' or 'Anglicanism' or 'Self-help' for Provi-

dence, and it can be seen that England in the early 1800s was ripe
for belief. The books of morals filled the gap; books of manners
and etiquette created new gaps to fill and new uncertainties to
allay.

The conduct books of the early 1800s also diverged from the
seventeenth- and eighteenth-century books by envisaging the civilising process as much more democratic, much more for every
man and woman to practice. And they were much more entrepreneurial in their advocacy of good manners: changing technologies,
new forms of transport, novel furnishings and advances in scientific, political and religious thinking all set the pace for those who
sought to guide others by prescriptive rules. With the 1820s came
the development of a public social world governed by rules recognised as necessarily but not corruptingly artificial. But the essential
mid-Victorian addition to the etiquette book was the idea of practical character.

The *OED* cites character as 'the sum of the mental and moral
qualities which distinguish an individual or race viewed as a homo-
geneous whole; the individuality impresses by nature and habit
on men or nation; mental or moral constitution'. The notion of
constitution, both political and personal, includes within it the
psychological and cultural assumptions which lend authority to
the moral ambitions it represents. As the moral and cultural primacy of leisure in the eighteenth century gave way to the moral
and cultural primacy of work in the nineteenth, the standards by
which men and women were judged, and indeed wanted to be
judged, began to change. Mid-Victorian England was becoming,
at many levels, an economic world in which reputation played a
powerful part: to be known as a man of character was to possess
moral collateral.[20]

II Victorian Practitioners

The great practical philosopher of the mid-Victorian age was
Martin Tupper. He sold as many books in England as his fellow
prophet of self-help, Samuel Smiles; many more in America. He
created a new literary form: it combined poetry, homily and
philosophy. The first series of *Proverbial Philosophy* was pub-

lished in 1838 (two years before the beginnings of Samuel Smiles's groundbreaking *Self-help*), when Tupper was twenty-eight years old and relatively fresh from the rigours of Charterhouse, Christ Church and the Inns of Court. He was called to the Bar in 1835, but an incapacitating stammer held back his career.[21] But in 1851 and again in 1876 he lectured and toured successfully in America, where he had sold over a million copies of his book by 1880. The lack of international copyright meant that Tupper received a paltry $400 from the Philadelphia publisher Herman Hooker.[22] By 1848 there were five stereotyped editions of *Proverbial Philosophy* actually in competition with each other throughout the United States.

Tupper pronounced with such authority and *gravitas* in his writing that the American *Home Journal* quoted him weekly, supposing him to be a forgotten Elizabethan, perhaps Thomas Tusser.[23] The mistake says much for Tupper's upholding of the tradition kept alive by John Florio's *Montaigne* and George Wither's homiletic pieces. Tupper's overall impact was evangelical; these Blakean rhymes open the fifteenth English edition of *Proverbial Philosophy*:

Thoughts, that have tarried in my mind, and peopled its inner chambers,
The sober children of reason, or desultory train of fancy,
Clear running wine of conviction, with the scum and the lees of speculation;
Corn from the sheaves of science, with stubble from mine own garner:
Searchings after Truth, that have tracked her secret lodes,
And come up again to the surface-world, with knowledge grounded deeper;
Arguments of high scope, that have soared to the keystone of heaven,
And thence have swooped to their certain mark, as the falcon to its quarry;
The fruits have I gathered of prudence, the ripened harvest of my musings,
These commend I unto thee, O docile scholar of Wisdom,
These I give to thy gentle heart, thou Lover of the right.[24]

The Tupper metaphor, resonantly Shakespearean ('the A and B

of C'), chases after and flirts with the realities it addresses, but never catches them. This was because Tupper necessarily wrote about abstract processes constituting a life of habit and outlook which ran parallel to the considerations of daily behaviour. In the trench between ideal behaviour and daily practice was a seed of mid-Victorian hypocrisy. Tupper advocated unceasingly what might be called the Victorian values: dutifulness, perseverance, patience, industry, moderation. But he never strayed from theory into practice: unlike Samuel Smiles in his idealised biographies; 'duties are all nows,' Tupper urged; 'redeem the time in little matters as in great'.[25]

Tupper's career, resonant with the kinds of advice he offered, was exemplary both in the way it mirrored the rise and fall of a particular kind of etiquette-instruction book. The success of his writing witnessed the popularity of the genre between the two Reform Bills. Even when aged ten, Tupper was setting himself targets for self-betterment. He wrote to his father from school at Brook Green on 3 July 1820:

> My dear Papa . . . As I wish this letter to be considered as a
> specimen of my writing, should you see anything in it to praise,
> you will allow me to observe that it is entirely my own, and not
> set off by touches of a master. Give my love to mama and
> brother.[26]

When Tupper progressed to Charterhouse, he met William Thackeray and John Leech; he was never far from contact with mainstream Victorian thinkers. Tupper's father, Dr Martin Tupper, was a doctor in a respectable firm which later became Tupper, Chilver and Brown. He had abandoned the idea of a degree at Exeter College, Oxford, gone to Guy's Hospital, and had tended Nelson's wounded at Yarmouth. Now he was running a lucrative West End practice; he was happily married to Ellen Devis Marris, the daughter of a landscape painter from Lancashire. As a child, therefore, Tupper wanted for little, either financially or emotionally; however, he hated the Tupper name, thinking it uneuphonious and ugly. He devoted himself in later life to tracing his maternal ancestors.

When Tupper arrived at Christ Church in 1828 he was already

engaged to his cousin Isabelle. He found time before matriculation to write a quick discourse on the life of matrimony which lay before him ('Seek a good wife of thy God, for she is the best gift of His providence'), and this was later prudently recycled as the first part of *Proverbial Philosophy*. Like the age he lived in, Tupper was quick to reuse old material, and hungry for new. He read theology; wrote poems; and abjured sugar as a protest against the slave trade. At Christ Church, he met Gladstone, with whom he shared an evangelical leaning; the two were brought closer together when Tupper beat Gladstone for the Theology Prize offered by the Regius Professor of Divinity. Tupper could look after himself intellectually; winning the Theology Prize also showed more than a professional scholarly interest in theology. When Tupper took his degree in 1832 he set about curing his stammer in preparation for taking orders. His letters to Gladstone at that time show exactly the religious zeal which enlivens the *Philosophy*:

> We live in a day of trouble, 'men's hearts failing them for fear', nation against nation and kingdom against kingdom – and the tide of public opinion roaring 'Where is the promise of His coming?' together with the tottering of governments, the national expectation of the Jews, the alarming crisis at which civilized society finds itself and other signs speak in no unintelligible tongue, the time of the end . . .[27]

Tupper's stammer, which was a genuine handicap for him until his mid-thirties, prevented a Church career. The introduction to the fourth series turns Tupperism on Tupper's speech difficulty:

> Not until he was growing grey did he become possessed of the full power of speech, and then he made good use of it; while the many books written in his days of enforced silence have testified by their wide usefulness to the wisdom of Providence in having silenced him so long.[28]

For silenced, read licensed. Tupper went into law chambers at Lincoln's Inn, and was called to the Bar in 1835. That year, on 26 November, the day after he became a barrister, he married Isabelle.

His father gave him a hefty £10,000, ample for a small house in St Pancras overlooking Regent's Park. There, Tupper's local chapel was the Hampstead Road establishment of the Revd Dr Henry Stebbing, former editor of the *Athenaeum*. Stebbing encouraged Tupper to write, suggesting a home could be found for his work at the *Athenaeum*. Tupper added 'On Matrimony' to the few other chapters that made up the first edition of *Proverbial Philosophy*; it was completed in ten weeks, and published by Joseph Rickerby of Sherborne Lane in the City on 24 January 1838. The Reform Act was now in force, the Poor Laws had been radically recast, the railway stretched between London and Birmingham, Gladstone had pronounced on Church and state, Dickens had published *Nicholas Nickleby* and the *Sirius* had crossed the Atlantic. England was ripe for guidance.

Tupper was to be a national institution. He offered in practical terms the ready-mixed 'moral cement' of evangelical religion. There was room for a work which told people how to conduct themselves morally, and one which rested on sound evangelical principle. Tupper appealed across the classes: to the upper class made thoughtful by the demographic changes around them, to the emerging middle class, and to the working classes safeguarded by the new Factory Acts and now with libraries and Working Men's Associations in their reach. The *Proverbial Philosophy* was the *Pilgrim's Progress* of the 1840s and 1850s. It made the ideal wedding or birthday present, and appeared in a bewildering variety of bindings and editions. The book reached its tenth edition in 1850, its twentieth in 1854 and its fiftieth in 1880. By 1866 Tupper had sold 200,000 copies in England to everyone from Crown to commoner. The book was challenged in popularity only by Keble's *Christian Year*.

The Tupper method was really to avoid complication and theory. This allowed him the luxury of saying whatever he pleased about *his* world. What he wrote became a kind of fiction with abstract qualities for heroes: ambition, circumstance, tolerance, experience. His letter to Gladstone showed that he felt society to be in crisis and in need of guidance. He wrote easily and earnestly. His popularity derived precisely from his ability to write verse which lived up to its own sententiousness:

The sting of pain and the edge of pleasure are blunted by long
  expectation,
For the gall and the balm are alike diluted in the waters of
  patience:
And often thou sippest sweetness, ere the cup is dashed from thy
  lip;
Or drainest the gall of fear, while evil is passing by thy dwelling.[29]

Tangible evils, real dwellings and felt pains fell outside Tupper's
ambit. The lure of the abstractions peddled by him witnessed and
encouraged the typical mid-Victorian move to see the world on
preordained terms. The Tupper world lay ready for the individual
to bustle in, without compromising either the world or the individuality. It was a habit of mind which the *Saturday Review* of
1867 reckoned with and deplored:

> We do not mean that silly picturesque platitude that the peasant
> in his straw-thatched hovel may be happier than the mighty
> monarch dwelling in marble halls . . . Nobody, except in a fit of
> spleen, pretends to believe that a peasant is particularly happy. The
> man is happiest who gets most out of himself on every side of his
> character; and if he is hard pinched on his back and in his belly,
> he gets nothintg out of himself on any side, except possibly a
> measure of animal fortitude. But without endorsing this Tuppery
> folly about monarchs and peasants . . .[30]

'Tupperian' had been coined in 1858, according to the *OED*, as
a pejorative,[31] and existed alongside 'Tupperish', 'Tupperism' and
'Tupperise' as the word settled into popular usage. 'Tuppery' is
not listed. So Tupper's sententia were not wholly accepted by
Victorian opinion; they were popular enough to be referred to
pejoratively. The *Saturday Review* objects to the Tupper platitude;
and that is exactly where Tupper's strength lies. For example, he
concludes 'Of the Smaller Morals' with a series of balmy clichés
issuing from the ideal world of the 'sturdy decalogue'; the image
is rewritten famously by the poet Arthur Hugh Clough, who
turned 'sturdy' into 'The Latest Decalogue' – a kind of Ten Com-
mandments for the lay person – written to show how compromise
and not absolutes have become moral laws: 'Thou shalt not steal,
an idle feat, when it's so lucrative to cheat.'

The platitude and the cliché represented a changing world in settled terms, conveying individual experience in the most general way. For Tupper, individuals were both fixed, in that they were easily identified, and malleable or apt for change – he predicated the *Proverbial Philosophy* on the individual's capacity for change. Tupper rarely probed into notions of nature or nurture; even the appearance of Herbert Spencer's 1851 *Social Statics*, in which the idea of the individual was set firmly in the defining context of what Spencer believed to be the natural order of things, left Tupper untouched.

Around the 1850s the relation between the individual and the environment was increasingly a matter of the single life within the context of the life of the species. Chambers and Lyell in geology, Tennyson in *In Memoriam*, Spencer in *Social Statics* and finally Darwin in evolutionary biology had pressed that argument. So in the 1850s, by ignoring these processes for change, Tupper necessarily addressed in social terms the same questions which Darwin and, later, Spencer and Huxley put in biological terms. Here, for example, is Tupper's version of habitat, the individual's role and function in society:

There is an outer world, and there is an inner centre;
And many varying rings concentric round the self:
For, first, about a man, – after his communion with heaven, –

I found the helpmate even as himself, the wife of his vows and
  his affections
. . .

Next of those concentric circles, radiating widely in
  circumference,
Wheel in wheel, and world in world, – come the band of
  children:
A tender nest of soft young hearts, each to be separately studied,
A curious eager flock of minds, to be severally tamed and tutored.
And a man, blest with these, hath made his own society,
He is independent of the world, hanging on his friends more
  loosely:
For the little faces round his hearth are friends enow for him,
If he seek others, it is for sake of these, and less for his own
  pleasure.[32]

Tupper's picture of the family dissolves into a group of assumptions about home life, wives, children's education and family unity. Beyond the family, Tupper found 'kith and kin', and an excuse for rare wit ('strangers, known and loved, or only seen for loathing') and even rarer psychological insight which showed his belief in familial collectivism in its rawest form:

> Friends are ever dearer in thy wealth, but relations to be trusted
>   in thy need,
> For these are God's appointed way, and those the choice of man:
> There is lower warmth in kin, but smaller truth in friends,
> The latter show more surface, and the first have more of depth.[33]

Beyond friends, 'the common crowd of social life buzzing round about'.

Tupper's categories presented an imprint of the anxieties and pressures which shape family life in a time of rapid social change. For him, the individual felt most at home within a family, the family within a circle of friends, and friends within the wider community. It was a lateral image: society for Tupper remained fixed. Social mobility would require a different metaphor, perhaps the vertical images which Samuel Smiles so happily provided when he wrote of upward social progress.

The connections between Tupper's work and other forms of Victorian social commentary stood out most clearly when he tackled the relations between individuals and circumstances. The Tupper world really amounted to the world of the poet Coventry Patmore in *The Angel in the House*, or the sentimental painting of Holman Hunt or Augustus Egg. Individuals found themselves stuck between severe behavioural imperatives and the tasks of moving forward in everday life. But the division was not peculiar to Tupper, for it underpinned *Self-help* as firmly as it did *The Origin of Species* or *On Liberty*. In literature, circumstance could figure as the web of connection in *Middlemarch*, or the operation of unavoidable and alien processes throughout *In Memoriam* ('The steps of Time – the shocks of Chance – The blows of Death'[34]). Tupper made no allowance for those whose circumstances proved overwhelming; to succumb was an individual fault. 'A wise man redeemeth his time, that he may improve his chances,' wrote

Tupper;[35] this involved – as Smiles's great hero Dr Johnson knew – letting no particle of time or knowledge fall uselessly to the ground, and, in effect, striking a bargain with the environment:

> Every one of us getteth his desert, somehow, somewhen,
>   somewhere,
> Penalties are earned as surely as rewards, pains alike with
>   pleasures:
> No man gathereth grapes of thorns, neither figs of thistles;
> Everything is consequent, and nothing by a chance.
> This thy torment of disease, this racking of a joint or of a nerve,
> Is due to thine own foolishness, and hath been well deserved.[36]

This was the Benthamite felicific calculus of profit and loss made palatable by means of a biblical account system of checks and balances; it suited Tupper well. But sometimes the system of biblical moral and world values was squeezed by another set of absolutes, and the most perplexing observations in *Proverbial Philosophy* issued from Tupper's struggle in the crossfire between science and religion, both severe masters. Tupper faced the difficulty by trying to argue a point rather than gently insinuate a set of values. For him, opening the Bible to sustained rational questioning was merely reading it the wrong way: 'It were derogation from the Bible, should it stoop to be the manual of science ... let Reason not expect, that the grand revelation of Religion / Will be liberal in answers to the questions our intellect would ask of nature.'[37]This showed the advantages and disadvantages of Tupper's limited, homey homiletics. He refused to be troubled by the fuller implications of the inconsistencies between the religious and the scientific accounts of the world. The result was a piece which resembles Browning's *Caliban upon Setebos; or Natural Theology in the Island*:

> He hath weighed the substance of the globe, exactly, as in a
>   balance;
> Holding it up by His omnipotence, the hollow of His hand:
> He sitteth on the circle of the world, guiding its career upon that
>   orbit,

And calleth out the stars by name, His worlds, His many
mansions.[38]

This confidence in an ordered universe categorised, named and
overseen by a guiding God was not, for Tupper, the result of
a victory over the inner naggings of spiritual uncertainty. His
conclusion lacked the troubling subtlety of Tennyson's fight with
the terrible muses, astronomy and geology, in *In Memoriam*, or
the contingent confidence of Browning's bluff negotiations with
the unknowable in *Caliban* or *Bishop Blougram's Apology*. Tupper's certainties set out in search of observable abstracts; they
become clearer when he writes on 'Success', an abstract with
practical implications. The most successful being imaginable for
Tupper is God; and the pursuit of success becomes a quasi-
religious matter:

> Often is there seen the youth, diligent rather than ambitious,
> Stop short in early mid-career by soon achieved success:
> The prize, the class, the local praise, have satisfied his yearning;
> His mind is not moulded of the highest, seeing thus he feareth for
>   his fame;
> Selfish glories have been gained, he will risk nothing further;
> And so that prudent whisper helped both indolence and pride.[39]

The view that success was an attitude of mind was familiar
enough from Browning's *Andrea del Sarto* and Tennyson's
Ulysses; as Tupper says, 'Alas! the many yearning souls that never
won Success, And yet have well deserved to win for diligence and
merit.'[40] This doctrine of Success overlooks the earlier 'every one
of us getteth his desert', for clearly Tupper believes that success
involves more than just being deserving. Success for the Victorians
entailed the wish to be other than one was. Smiles and Tupper
write well on this because they benefit from the hindsight which
occasions the short, uplifting biography. Everywhere there lurks
a kind of hysterical urgency that the successful person should
never talk of leisure because there really is none.[41] Success was an
attitude and a state of transformation; it allowed mobility based
on stability: 'Only strive, only deserve; and fear not thou a Failure;
Courage and constancy be thine, and thine shall be Success.'[42]

Tupper's career in the late 1850s was at a high point. He wrote in his diary for 23 June 1857:

> I judge it well to set down on paper for my children's sake an exact account of the unprecedented honour paid to my unworthiness by assembled Royalties the day before yesterday.
> Let me premise – that, from their infancy all the Royal Children have read and learnt by heart my Proverbial Philosophy; that it has been a frequent giftbook, one to another, among members of the Royal Family; that the Queen has several times most graciously commanded me to write tableaux in verse and other matters for Her Children, – has favourably received, and sent me kind messages for other like offerings personal to Herself . . .[43]

Tupper's books would also find favour as presents at the marriage of the Princess Royal and Prince Frederick of Prussia, whose uncle the King had read Tupper some ten years before and sent him a medal for science and literature. Now, attending the Queen's Levee (the largest known since her accession) on 18 June, Tupper was enjoined to present some of his books at Buckingham Palace the following day at one. However, it turned out that the royal party would be incomplete, and so Tupper was asked to attend after church that Sunday. This unusual royal manoeuvre caused some consternation:

> Wishing to know naturally enough what was 'usual on such occasions', and willing to get a hint as to etiquette, I found that such an occasion had never arisen . . . So, I had the course clear to act according to the light of Nature.[44]

This is nonconformism at its best; a search for and worry about rules before finally trusting to nature. But Tupper is still aware of duties, courtesies and courtliness here. This is the fascinating encounter of the spiritual guide with the temporal symbol of the nation:

> The Queen said, in a clear kind voice with a smile, 'I thank you, Mr Tupper, for your beautiful poetry: and my children are here to thank you too.' – Reticence being the duty of a subject, I could

only reply, 'it is most gracious of you your Majesty,' and bowed all round promiscuously.

Tupper then presents the books to the royals, and includes in his diary a small sketch like a battle plan marking their disposition in relation to him. He concludes:

> Seeing then that all was over – for it really was as if I had held a Court of Queens and Princes, – I said to Prince Albert – for I thought it only courtesy if not courtliness to say something – 'Sir, this is most gracious; and I humbly thank Her Majesty, and your Royal Highness, and the Royal Family' . . .
>
> I went out with the Court, – and a page – and then a lacquey escorted me out at the great entrance; where I suppose the gilded porters and footmen took me for an Archduke, – and among their bows I vanished.[45]

Tupper has treated the encounter like a piece of theatre: beauty and trim decays like courts removing or like ended plays; there is something uneasy and magical about his exit.

Tupper had yoked his star – and his familial values – to the royal wagon which pulled him across the prosperous 1850s into the ascendant. However, the Windsor *tableaux*, the 'Town and Country' eclogues at Osborne, or that Buckingham Palace visit were built around the image and actuality of the whole family of royals. When the Prince Consort died in December 1861, Victoria turned more towards *In Memoriam*, and Tupper's star gradually waned. When he fell on hard times in the late 1860s his decline coincided with the arrival of Hain Friswell the invalid, workaholic author of over forty books. The most famous of these was *The Gentle Life* (1864) which earned the Queen's commendations. Friswell was preferred to Tupper in the application for funds from royal bounty on the Civil List.

Success was not a permanent guest at Tupper's table. He had already been pilloried by the *Athenaeum* in 1854, but the 1860s – notwithstanding Tupper's sortie into military uniform design – saw the intensification of anti-Tupperism. The name became synonymous with folly, pomposity and incompetence. He began to put his verses 'No Surrender' and 'Never Give Up' into practice; the *Literary Times* offered this in 1863:

> There was an old rhymster called Tupper,
> Who of Pegasus mounted the crupper;
> But in spite of his 'Wisdom
> Proverbial', they quizz'd him,
> So precariously seated was Tupper.

Three years later the *Spectator* (27 January 1866) weighed in with this sarcastic tribute:

> Martin Farquhar Tupper has wrung for himself the vacant throne
> waiting for him among the immortals, and after a long and
> glorious term of popularity among those who know when their
> hearts are touched without being able to justify their taste to the
> intellect, has been adopted by the suffrage of mankind and the
> final decree of publishers into the same rank with Wordsworth,
> Tennyson, and Browning.

This turned out to be the case when the great poetry house, Moxon, published *Proverbial Philosophy* alongside Milton, Pope, Byron and Keats, in the Moxon's Popular Poets series edited by William Rossetti.

In 1868 a Keene drawing in *Punch* wishfully depicts a reading from 'Tupper's Last'. Lewis Carroll tried a few lines of Christ Church parody:

> Look on the Quadrangle of Christ Church, squarely, for is it not
>   a square?
> And a Square recalleth a Cube; and a Cube recalleth the Belfry;
> And the Belfry recalleth a Die, shaken by the hand of the
>   gambler;
> Yet, once thrown, it may not be recalled, being, so to speak,
>   irrevocable.

But it was Cholmondeley Pennell's vicious sonnet from *Puck on Pegasus* which stung Tupper – who knew with Dr Johnson that fame was a shuttlecock to be hit from both ends of the room –

into a letter of polite rebuke which exacted another, subtler sonnet.
Here is the original:

> 'Off! Off! thou art an ass, thou art an ass,
>   Thou man of endless words and little sense,
>   Of pygmy powers and conceit immense –
> Thou art a Donkey! – Take a bit of grass?'
>   Oh Martin! Oh, my Tupper! *thus* exclaims
>   A grov'ling Age, grown envious of thy fames, –
>   Thy boundless sonnets; and Proverbial bays:
> Blest Silence! loved silence! thou art Heav'n! –
> (See my remarks in 'Sonnet 47') –
>   *Yet* I will breathe my pleasant Poems forth
>   Innumerable. Hundreds more – ay tens
> Of thousands! Sweet etherial rhymes,
>   I hold ye here! and hug ye – all the lot; –
>   A monstrous pile of quintessential ROT!!

By 1870 even the *Daily News* felt that a truce might be appropriate, and urged:

> Disparaging allusions to Mr Tupper . . . have long ago lost the
> merit of freshness, and whether fair or unfair, regarded as a means
> of repressing that gentleman's energies, it must be acknowledged
> that they have proved to be useless . . . There seems to be a class
> of persons who really do admire Mr Tupper's works, and who
> ought to be allowed to enjoy them in peace.[46]

All this goes to show that Tupper's fame was not universal and
that praise for him was not automatic. But Tupper was far more
than an emotional and spiritual panacea to the middle classes. His
works shaped themselves and cleaved to the forms of evangelical
religion. Tupper was known as 'the Shakespear of the Church',
was widely cited by divines like Canning, Spurgeon and Newman,
and managed to be much more profound than his contemporary
Eliza Cook.

III Proverbial Philosophy and Self-Help

Why did Tupper's popularity fade? What had happened to mid-
Victorian society to turn it from the wholesome sentiment and
moral mainstream which Tupper represented? The answer was
that Tupper failed to integrate his sentiments with one of the great
and most typical processes of the age – religious debate. The mid-
Victorians had evolved a 'religious method', an approach to life
which turned to scripture for moral certainty; when, increasingly
during the 1860s and 1870s, this method came under assault,
religion ceased to be regarded as an absolute. George Eliot had
worried, after the 1,500 pages of *Das Leben Jesu* by D. F. Strauss,
which she had translated for Charles Hennell in 1846, that the
book would undermine the simple faith of people who had nothing
to put in its place. Her fears were played out not in the professional
scepticisms of Mill or the writers of *Essays and Reviews*, but in
the decline of Tupper's appeal. The will to believe had atrophied.

Evangelism of the sort readily found in the *Evangelical Magazine* (1793–1904) or the *Record* (1828–1923), and which had flourished in the 1820s through Catholic Emancipation, the constitutional crisis and the great cholera epidemics, was beginning to
lose touch with the new processes of scientific thinking – not
necessarily the thought, but the method. The result was that,
divorced from the most fruitful of the mid-Victorian forces for
change, evangelism found itself not exactly exiled but stranded in
a world of its own making, one which could not be remade anew
as fresh evidence arrived from the empirical science, philosophy
and, at the end of the century with Bain and Spencer, psychology.
The mid-Victorian belief that art must be connected to morality
both promoted Tupper's books and helped integrate them into
the penumbra of formal and semi-formal edifying works surrounding the sermonisers and homiletic essayists. Moreover, the 1860s
saw a decline in the ranks of upper-middle-class people from
which Tupper himself had emerged, and at the same time a growth
in the manufacturers and financiers with social and commercial
ambition. The man who fitted himself to their needs was born in
1804, one of eleven children of a Haddington paper-maker, gram-
mar-school boy, student of Edinburgh University, medic, journalist, railway administrator and biographer. His name was Samuel

The Descent of Manners

Smiles, and his five books were a pentateuch for mid-Victorian moral thought: *Self-help, Character, Thrift, Duty* and *Life and Labour*.

Self-help appeared in 1859, the year that saw the publication of J. S. Mill's *On Liberty*, Darwin's *Origin of Species*, and also of George Eliot's *Adam Bede* and Alexander Bain's much-overlooked *The Emotions and the Will*. Each of these books exerted an influence down the century in its own field: morals, politics, science, literature and psychology. Their resonance as records of their time derived from their ability and readiness to borrow and interchange terms: so in each the language of social, political and scientific discourse drew on and informed the others. And behind each lay a belief in the guiding influence of principle as the first and last resort of moral, political, scientific or artistic practice. Smiles's *Self-help* opens by stating that 'The origin of this book may be briefly told', and proceeds to deliver a martyrology of inventors and entrepreneurs who personalised and popularised Mill's notions of the relation between the state and the individual (whatever crushes individuality is despotism). Smiles adopted a scientific approach to success by thinking inductively about the general rules ('self-culture, self-discipline, and self-control'[47]) and arriving at provable conclusions from testable facts. He struck an evolutionary tone in his obvious interest not only in the origins of those whose biographies he wrote, but in their procedural abilities to fit themselves best for the society in which they functioned. Origins remained important, the more so as a check on the extent of the progress.

The simple difference between the origins of Smiles's *Self-help*, born out of a collaborative and ameliorative working people's association, and Tupper's *Proverbial Philosophy*, the ten weeks' work of a divine and lawyer, shows how mid-Victorian society was moving. The energies and mobilities set in motion by Smiles were far from the settled platitudes of Tupper's world. Society stretched to accommodate and encourage the Smilesean values. Eight years on, the *Saturday Review* complained of the tendency of self-help books and sententious novels to revisit the origins of their subjects: 'the conduct of society is constantly being brought back to the first principles, not of society, but of a state of nature,' adding, 'The inconsistency is plain.'[48] The men (almost invariably) who have made a mark are pictured 'revisiting the scenes of their youth, and moralising over them with a gushing and hateful complacency'.[49] But at the same time, the *Review* asserted the values of continuity by warning of the dangers of becoming divorced from one's own past.[50]

Self-help, along with Smiles's other homiletic works (*Lives of the Engineers* and *Industrial Biography* (1863) *Character* (1871), *Thrift* (1875) and *Duty: with Illustrations of Courage, Patience and Endurance* (1880)[51]), mapped out the territory of mid-Victorian high-mindedness in the matter of individual development. Each reader found something to answer in Smiles: for example, reviewing *Duty*, *Harper's Monthly* found the good which Smiles's books had done to his millions of readers beyond computation; the *Church Review* found useful sermon material; and the *Pall Mall Gazette* preferred it to 'the lighter productions of the time'. Smiles's appeal was the broadest possible. His homiletic biographies, the best in the genre, treated an extraordinary range of human concern, and witnessed a kind of eclecticism in service of a few guiding principles: a shopping-list of virtues for a banquet of success. That breadth of concern exactly paralleled the function of the books of etiquette and behaviour which existed alongside Smiles; for as behaviour touched dealings with all other people, the behaviour guide was licensed to rove anywhere decency allowed. The range of material available for exhortation bears witness to the Victorians' sense of the reducibility of all experience to a few main principles. Smiles recalls:

> Twenty-four years since I wrote 'Self-help'. It was published three
> years later, in 1859. The writing of that book was occasioned by
> an apparently slight circumstance. I had delivered a few lectures
> at Leeds to some young men, in a place that had been used as a
> temporary cholera hospital. I endeavoured to point out to them
> that their happiness and well-being in after life depended very
> much on themselves – upon their diligent self-culture, self-
> discipline, and self-control; and, above all, upon the honest and
> upright performance of individual duty, which constitute the glory
> of manly character.[52]

Smiles set out absolutes. The history of the behaviour book in

27

the mid-century was the history of applied principles. These books showed the mid-Victorians grappling with the tensions which those principles generated when they met with the practical difficulties of life; and their negotiations with the language of religion and science which yielded these principles.

One typical popular author of the 1850s, T. Binney, listed the essentials for a happy life as HEALTH, CHEERFULNESS, COMPETENCE ('along with this, for most men, I should put the feeling and consciousness of *getting on*, – of success and advancement'), REPUTATION, and THE CULTURE OF THE INTELLECT. He continues, 'and, underlying all, I require *some source and spring of consolation and strength equal to the pains and pressures of inevitable sorrow*'.[53] His language is at once biblical in its search for consolation and scientific in its urgency for fundamental truth; and it is measured in its search for an inner balance, depicting a typical Victorian anxiety to set the individual and the social impulses in equilibrium. Where the social commentary of books which urge moral improvement, almost invariably fixed in a moral register, met practical concerns, the language of engagement at this period carried the responsibility of scientific rigour, and mixed it with social, economic and personal concerns. So the *Saturday Review* drew on the Mill of *On Liberty*, the Clough of the '*laissez-faire, laissez-aller*' *Amours de Voyage*, the free-trade analyst, and the social critic:

> The moral influence of political doctrine on social doctrine is
> always very important; and the notion that you ought to see
> your neighbour march off to perdition, if he chooses, without an
> effort to keep him back, is sure to find favour in an age when so
> many spurious forms of *laisse aller* obtain credit in the wider
> sphere of public affairs.[54]

These books chose the language of science, of the examination of causes, effects and origins, as the most persuasive discourse available to them; but elementary discussions of facts, proofs, theories and principles still had a religious colouring. That word 'perdition' lingered on.

Smiles's contribution was to show how some model individuals had behaved and set out in broad terms how the reader should emulate them. So he became famous for his exhortations to application, industry, perseverence, energy and courage in all walks of life. His brilliance was to capture a cultural moment which allowed him to write of success and industry in terms which the age had framed and which spoke to a variety of cultural experience. He found a voice which mediated between the individual and the nation, between religion and science, and between phylogeny and ontogeny. His achievement was to invent a set of criteria for rendering personal and social experience understandable in new terms. He spoke to the working classes, and to those of the middle class who continued to strive for self-improvement. His popularity persisted because his ethic of 'self-culture, self-discipline, and self-control'[55] changed with the age. Perhaps the enduring strength was Smiles's identification of the personal with the public good (again the anxiousness of melding the individual to the public). He subscribed to Mill's observation that the worth of a state was the worth of the individuals composing it. His fervent advocacy that steady application to work trained the individual and disciplined the state put the work ethic and profit motive in service of a sense of nationality.

The spirit of self-help was, for Smiles, the root of all genuine growth in the individual; and constituted the true source of national vigour and strength. Smiles was the ideal popular psychological heir to the demotic success of the Great Exhibition; what the Crystal Palace did for the Victorian public by putting on show the accumulated wonders of design and industry, Smiles achieved for the mid-Victorian by showing moral exemplars and models for endeavour. While Smiles was not, like so many of his heroes, self-taught, he was self-motivated and vigorously independent. So he could be critical of his models, and maintain a steely presence in face of the disapproved great. He dismissed Coleridge with the resonant 'infirm of purpose';[56] and the French poet Benjamin Constant for high thinking and low living. His criticisms, like his praises, always returned to consistent principles, and he frequently condemned by citing a lack: so he found Coleridge wanting the 'gift of industry' and 'averse to continuous labour'.[57] He fails to allow that the fragmentary nature of Coleridge's work, the medium itself, is the message.

Smiles voiced Victorian thinking on individual action in and out of the public gaze. Really, this amounted to a kick at hypocrisy; and in 1859 Smiles probed a dichotomy which the decadents and aesthetes of the 1890s were to live *in*, rather than worry over. He advocated consistency in character as a guard against temptation:

> Without this dominating influence, character has no protection,
> but is constantly liable to fall away before temptation; and every
> such temptation succumbed to, every act of meanness or
> dishonesty, however slight, causes self-degradation. It matters
> not whether the act be successful or not, discovered or concealed.[58]

Finding someone to watch over you was easy for, as Mill had pointed out, the age was morbidly self-conscious. The better-known Victorian prophets ranked consistency high: Matthew Arnold's culture, T. H. Green's ethics, John Ruskin's economics and Thomas Carlyle's heroes all depended on consistency. Its opposite, as George Eliot showed with Lydgate's 'spots of commonness', could be more than a social handicap; it could be spiritual, too. While Dr Johnson and the eighteenth century made litte distinction between bodily and mental health, the nineteenth created separate categories for both: so the mountebanks and quacks prospered alongside those who ministered to the uneasy Victorian mind.

It was precisely where the arguments presented in books of practical morals threatened to dissolve in face of an awkward discrepancy between principle and practice – where Duty cut across Kindliness, or Honesty across Prudence – that they became most vigorous. Uncertainty generated stridency, a kind of protesting too much. Smiles avoided this problem by writing in the exact science of biography, where to cite an event was to construct a lifetime's chain of cause and effect. He wisely wrote only about those who succeeded winningly or failed heroically; his Preface to the second edition of *Self-help* reconnoitres the territory mapped out by his critics: 'a record of mere failure would probably be found excessively depressing as well as uninstructive reading'.[59] Failure was felt to stimulate to new effort, and push the individual to new levels of self-culture and self-control in the move toward elevation of character. But Smiles's view that those who failed were readiest to whinge about their lack of good fortune persisted into subsequent editions of *Self-help*.

Smiles's own success depended on avoiding those situations where giving advice would become difficult, where, as George Eliot knew, a structure of ideas can be muddied by that which opposes it. So he kept his discussion abstract by creating new forms: the structure of *Self-help*, a series of biographies and homilies, presented a society comprised of individuals; the heroes like John Heathcote (industrial designer and manufacturer) or Hugh Miller (self-educator and geologist) were cast as proto-self-helpers so that Smiles could present a new outlook in the form of an old recognition. He did concede that trade and commerce tried character more than any other pursuits in life, but he eschewed specifics; trade and commerce fall to other pens.

Writers like Tupper and Smiles injected a tonic of popular certainty into the 1860s. Mill had predicted the difficulty of seeing too many sides to the question in his diary of 13 January 1854, where he lamented the fact that there were few 'in the educated classes' who seemed to hold any opinions, or placed any real faith in those they professed to have. These guides to behaviour answered Mill's difficulty:

> It requires in these times much more than intellect to marshal so much greater a stock of ideas and observations. This has not yet been done, or has been done only by very few; and hence the multitude of thoughts only breeds increase of uncertainty. Those who should be the guides of the rest, see too many sides to every question.[60]

Reserving judgments may have been a matter of infinite hope, but not where behaviour waited on them. Mark Pattison, radical theologian and Dean of Lincoln College Oxford always alert to the more abstruse leanings of British intellectual life in the mid-century, wrote in the *Quarterly Review*, *Westminster Review* and *National Review* in the 1850s and 1860s of the disdain of the educated for the littlenesses of ordinary life, and lamented the retirement of superior mental endowments from the field of action. Tupper and Smiles provided certainties in that field. In place of intellect, the Victorians used as their basis for thinking about the world around them the very principles which these behaviour books advocated.

As well as Tupper's certainties and Smiles's examples, more practical urgings constituted a growing religion for the Victorians, which developed from the 'Work is Religion' message of Carlyle's *Past and Present*. As religious belief itself started to feel the pressures of science and to look powerless in face of social misery in the 1850s and of a creeping disillusionment in the 1860s, it became more worldly. Other discourses – poems, novels, autobiographies – began to experiment with more sentential forms and to fill the moral ground left open by religious uncertainty. Matthew Arnold had predicted the rapprochement of poetry with religion in a letter to his friend and fellow poet Arthur Hugh Clough in 1853, the very year Arnond defended the classics in the Preface of his *Poems*. Poetry, he wrote to Clough, could progress only 'by becoming a complete *magister vitae* as the poetry of the ancients did: by including, as theirs did, religion with poetry, instead of existing as poetry only'.[61] Poetry for Arnold came increasingly to apply moral ideas to the business of life. The differences between Arnold and Tupper were first that Arnold was a better poet, and second that Tupper maintained a different view about what the business of life might be.

IV Self-culture and Plain Living

By 1880, Smiles's terms of self-help and self-culture had grafted themselves on to the language of moral improvement *and* the language of practical instruction. W. H. Davenport Adams's *Plain Living and High Thinking or Practical Self-culture: Moral, Mental and Physical* (1880) showed exactly how pervasive and widely applicable notions of self-help had become. The dedication to Gladstone indicated Adams's feelings about the book's general acceptability. Adams first shelved the need to reiterate the 'usual copybook maxims in praise of industry', for 'no one would undertake the work of self-culture who was not prepared to pursue it diligently'.[62] But he then incorporated the Smiles methods by urging readers to adopt a 'science of biography'[63] which accumulated biographical facts of candidates for emulation. Adams divided *Plain Living* into discussions of moral, mental and physical self-culture. The shortest of these, 'Physical Self-culture', offered little unusual. Adams took the *'mens sana in corpore sano'* path, suggesting that all bodily functions should be subject to the habitual strong control of a disciplined will. But the previous sections harboured insights which were typical in their assumptions and typically perplexed in their worries about the nature of the advice they gave.

The first of these sections, moral self-culture, involved questions of conduct at home, advice on how to begin 'the noble labour of self-culture', the dangers of growing weary of home life, and – borrowed straight from Francis Bacon – the usefulness of realising that conversation makes a 'ready man'. Moral self-culture extended to social life, and Adams advised on choosing friends, on the honour of work, and gave examples in the art of politeness. The chapter on 'Character' exhorted moral courage, moderation, self-restraint, independence, self-reliance and self-sacrifice; while 'Conduct' pressed the virtues of punctuality, patience, thrift, method and purity. Behaviour meant character:

> 'The world judges us by our conduct; it has neither the time nor the inclination to study our character; moreover, it assumes that our conduct is necessarily the reflex of our character.'[64]

All of mid-Victorian social life rested on this assumption. The Victorians emphasised the steady link between conduct and character in a changing world because both were at the same time individual and universal. The relation between the two allowed for moral judgment to be made on social grounds. The righteousness of the equation suited both the nonconformists whose self-reliance resisted stricture, and the social conformists who used others' conduct as a social weapon. In literature, judging others became an abiding mid-Victorian concern: Browning's poems were novel because they worked counter to this insight, while depending on a dissent from a version of it. A Browning dramatic monologue refused to judge, and advocated instead that the smallest circumstance which denoted character was true. George Eliot's novels sought an account of character which probed beyond conduct and, until William James and the beginnings of psychoanalytic enquiry, furnished the Victorians with their most complete accounts of character, the stirrings of behaviourism.

Adams's second section in *Plain Living*, mental self-culture, amounts to a reading course in poetry (Chaucer to Tennyson); history (Henry II to George IV); biography – particularly those books which 'stimulate the moral and intellectual nature', for 'every man lives that others may benefit from his having lived, and most truly is this the case when the man has taken his life in earnest, has thought great thoughts or done great deeds';[65] fiction (Marryat, Galt, Peacock, Michael Scott, Gore, Charlotte Brontë, Kingsley, Disraeli, Lever, Eliot, Thackeray, Dickens and Bulwer), with muttered warnings against desultoriness in reading and the snares of versatility; travel; theology, philosophy and metaphysics, where he praises F. D. Maurice who was 'practical rather than dogmatic . . . dwelt upon points of duty rather than upon difficulties of doctrine';[66] and science, including a brief account of Darwinism, which

> has seized hold upon the public mind, and awakened a widespread and permanent interest, so that Darwinism is one of the prevailing 'isms' of the day, and the battlefield of critic and theologian.[67]

He came up to date with the 1874 edition of Darwin's *Descent of Man* but refused to follow the 'enthusiastic evolutionists' who traced all forms of life to a primordial protoplasm, for 'it is quite possible to accept the *principle* of evolution and to part company with these speculative minds before so low a depth is reached'.[68] So Adams steered the reader away from T. H. Huxley's *Man's Place in Nature* towards St George Mivart's *Contemporary Evolution* (1876), which maintained a distinction between humans and other animals.

The most remarkable facet of Adams's enterprises was that discussions of natural history and theology should have entered into them at all. He spent considerable effort in advocating *The Unseen Universe*[69] to show that the ultimate conclusions of science 'tend to confirm the doctrines of revelation'.[70] His project committed him to a notion of progress and perfectability which he took only so far as a belief in self-improvement. But the individual needed to base the regimen of improvement on substrata of solid character. In 1867 Adams had written this to conclude *The Boy Makes the Man: Anecdotes and Examples for the Use of Youth*:

... the habits adopted in youth – the modes of thought cultivated
in youth – remain with us in our manhood, cling to us in our
latest years, are never wholly thrown off or forgotten. Take heed,
therefore, O reader, how your youth is regulated, and what
theory of conduct inspires it; for all biography proves – at least
the exceptions are so few as to confirm the rule – that THE BOY
MAKES THE MAN.[71]

Adams believed both in the fixity and the changeability of the individual; his outlook in 1867 amounted to a form of individual determinism, which he was keen to correct in *Plain Living* by widening the application of the forces for change and opening the individual to new kinds of influence. So by 1880, in the roll call of Victorian commonplaces which preface *Plain Living*, he found himself making claims for self-culture on a broader scale: 'it treats of Self-Culture in its widest range, follows it into society, into business, into the home circle; illustrates the laws of health as well as those of duty; it is scarcely less concerned with the manners than with the mind'.[72] The awkward last clause gropes towards the division which Adams wanted to make between manners and mind, between social culture and self-culture; it was a division maintained by the mid-Victorians as useful both personally and socially.

What Adams, alongside many Victorians, stood most in fear of was failure. His 1880 *Wrecked Lives: Or Men Who Have Failed* enumerate failures visited upon and emanating from the individual. Failure built character. But force of character was itself a way of avoiding failure, steering clear of shipwreck. In June 1882, Disraeli's executor, the lawyer Sir Philip Rose wrote to his fellow executor, Lord Rowton. His *memorandum* concerned Disraeli's affair, during 1833–34, with Lady Henrietta Sykes[73]:

Very Private and confidential
For Lord Rowton's Eye alone — and then to be destroyed

The letters in this dossier relate to the intimacy that existed, from 1833 to 1836, between D. [Disraeli] and the writer, Lady Sykes, wife of Sir Francis Sykes Bart, which materially affected D's health, and nearly shipwrecked his career; – few other men could have had the necessary force of Will to escape from such an entanglement.[74]

The undated letters showed Rose 'the nature and progress of the Connection up to its final denouement, and the disgraceful exposure of the Lady'[75] as if the threat had a logic and momentum all its own.

In the same vein, the *Saturday Review* suggested that one might be a failure and not know it; either through scant self-knowledge or through ignoring popular judgments of one's performance:

The world is full of people who, either consciously or without knowing it, have failed; that is, have fallen a vast way short of the point to which their qualities and their circumstances alike seemed certain to raise them.[76]

It added the caveat that often passion exceeds capacity. But in the Victorian register, failure was not the sudden cataclysm so beloved of Victorian chroniclers of natural disasters, earthquakes and shipwrecks, but rather the steady drip of indolent afternoons inexplicably wasted. Later in the century the Decadents were to treat time itself as a commodity for conspicuous consumption, reliving the state of youth not because youth was unenduring stuff, but because at that phase of life time stands still. This contrasted with George Eliot's view in *Adam Bede* that 'even idleness is eager now';[77] the 1890s made eagerness idle.

As Tupper's sad career from 1835 to the late 1860s shows, by the 1870s the whole notion of the relation of social to private conduct had begun to change. This was principally due to the decline of evangelism, but can be partly traced in the technological changes wrought by science, and the social changes wrought by the second Reform Bill. The social cement had become commercial, not moral:

Social evolution follows the law of organic modification. It is the exercise of the feelings we wish to predominate that alone will strengthen them and increase the size of the organs with which they are connected. The commercial age in which we live . . . is making all men better off . . . When a man is well off and happy he desires to make others so, exercising his benevolence.[78]

Questions put throughout the first half of Victoria's reign pressed more urgently as the religious basis for both personal and social behaviour began to lose ground. Taking the long view from the end of the century, Theodore Roosevelt looked back. This from the *Century*, October 1990:

> In Mr Lecky's profoundly suggestive book, 'The Map of
> Life',[79] . . . he emphasises the change that has been gradually
> coming over the religious attitude of the world because of the
> growing importance laid upon conduct as compared with
> dogma.[80]

William Lecky's *Map of Life* had embarked from the notion that 'heredity and circumstance make us what we are',[81] each individual coming into the world with given moral and mental constitutions. He admitted a schism in the Darwinian school on the heredity transmission of character, but called the character one is born with 'one of the most powerful molding influences in life'.[82] However, he quoted approvingly Burke's notion that it is man's prerogative to be a creature of his own making, and set about analysing the necessary and sufficient conditions for self-improvement. New habits and feelings passed into the individual and the race, reproducing themselves by force of heredity; Lecky continued chillingly: 'If this be true, it gives a new and terrible importance both to the duty of self-culture and to the duty of wise selection in marriage.'[83]

V Gentlemen

The issue of heredity bore exactly on the debate between inward self-culture and outward appearance, because both originated in a view of the raw materials the individual starts out with. Mill was right in his observation that the individual was no longer born to his place in life; but he left undiscussed the criteria for how the individual might decide where the starting-out place was. Victorian anxiety about failure, the beliefs in personal progress and success, and the debate between heredity and environmental influence bore on the question which every Victorian asked and which was put by Thackeray in 1846: 'What is it to be a gentleman?'[84] He went on to answer his own question:

> Is it to be honest, to be gentle, to be generous, to be brave, to be wise, and possessing all these qualities, to exercise them in the most graceful outward manner? Ought a gentleman to be a loyal son, a true husband, an honest father? Ought his life to be decent, his bills to be paid, his tastes to be high and elegant, his aims in life lofty and noble? In a word, ought not the biography of a First Gentleman in Europe be of such a nature that it might be read in young ladies' schools with advantage, and studied with profit in the seminaries of young gentlemen?[85]

The wit here depends on exactly the situation of the word in the opening sentence, where 'be' means either to behave as a gentleman, or to be in the state of gentlemanliness; and it works through to the vision of young gentlemen learning how to be gentlemen in the seminary.

The precise meaning of what it was to be a gentleman haunted the Victorians in the expanding mid-century years because it marked both a passage of progress, personal and social, and also a gathering of stable concepts in a changing world. The whole history of this quintessential Victorian dilemma resounded with the difficulty of origins and personal advancement; it took the perspective of the great Hippolyte Taine, writing on England in the 1860s, to frame the issue; he has wisely been reading Mrs Craik for enlightenment:

> ... a real gentleman is a real noble, a man worthy of commanding, upright, disinterested, capable of exposing himself and even sacrificing himself for those whom he leads, not only an honourable man, but a conscientious man, in whom generous instincts have been confirmed by straightforward reflection, and

who, acting naturally well, acts still better on principle. In this you recognise the accomplished chief; add to it the English varieties, empire over self, continuous coolness, perseverance in adversity, natural seriousness, dignity of manner, the shunning of all affectation or boasting; you will have the superior model who, copied closely or vaguely discerned, here rallies all who aspire and all who serve. A novelist has depicted him under the name of 'John Halifax, Gentleman'; the subject is a poor abandoned child who ends by becoming the respected leader of his district. A single phrase will show the tone of the book: when, after great misadventures, John attains independence, buys a house, and keeps his carriage, his son exclaims, 'Father, we are gentlefolks now!' – 'We always were, my son.'[86]

Taine balances 'generous instincts' with 'straightforward reflection', and having 'acting naturally well' improved by acting 'still better upon principle'. He offers a picture of Carlyle's hero Victorianised, where the picaresque of *John Halifax* becomes an 'Origin of Social Species' mediating between how one behaved and where one was born. Taine's acuteness found the debate about gentlemanliness worthwhile because he saw it recurring constantly, comprising 'a mass of ideas wholly English'.[87]

Taine knew that, for the English, the question 'Is he a gentleman?' or 'Is she a lady?' was irreducible and vital. It was often asked in matters of personal probity; and the differences in scope expected in the answer reflected the mid-Victorian attitude to the social scope of men and women: for women, being a lady had as much to do with sexual history as social acceptability, the more so in those situations where the two were synonymous; and for men, gentlemanliness as a description of behaviour often signified proficiency in social and business commerce. Taine suggested that a workman, peasant or shopkeeper could not cross the line of demarcation. Then he put the question which every behaviour guide tried to answer: 'But how is it recognised that a person belongs to the superior class?'[88] France offered nothing comparable; but 'these three syllables' of the word gentleman 'so used across the Channel', he wrote, 'summarise the history of English society'.[89] Taine's nationality offered means of speculation: for in France in the nineteenth century, *gentilhomme*, the nearest equivalent, implied elegance, delicacy, tact, exquisite politeness in the salon; and tender honour and prodigal liberality on the boulevard. Thomas Arnold, that single-handed creator of English gentlemen through the public schools system, famously found no English gentleman in France, in either education or manners.

The cogency and accuracy of Taine's observations were borne out by the career of the word 'gentleman' in the 1860s. The *OED* charts a move through the century from a man possessing chivalrous instincts[90] to a man not engaged in trade, or able to make his way without earning a living:[91] the 1834 and the 1879 citations distinguish 'gentleman' from 'lawyer' and from 'tradesman', respectively. But the *OED* leaves unmentioned the more pressing implications and usages of the word for the Victorians. The *Cornhill Magazine* offered this in 1862:

> The characteristic moral divisions by which society is, as it were, divided into two halves, are summed up in the one word, 'gentleman'. The division between those who are and those who are not entitled to this appellation, is as real and important as it is indefinite.[92]

If an observer writing at the time, immersed in the context which defines the usage of the word, can offer only 'indefinite', then contemporary usage spoke more of the user than of the much that might be said about the word. G. P. Marsh's lectures in language, the same year, felt the pressure of correct usage, finding that using the word correctly necessarily entailed a clear social idea of its meaning; so that, according to Marsh, to speak of the low-minded or grovelling as gentlemen was either to miss the concept which the word professed to describe, or to shun belief in the possibility of such a concept. The burden of unbelief weighed heavy. The admiring readers of a writer who misused the word 'will end by adopting his incredulity, and renouncing the effort to develop and cultivate qualities which, in every virtuous community, have formed the highest objects of social ambition'.[93]

The end of the decade brought no clearer views; in 1873 J. A. Hessey's perplexity rested firmly on shifting social sands: 'Take the standard of "gentlemanly". It is a term of fleeting and variable meaning. Many things have been considered to be becoming a gentleman at one stage of society, which at another have been condemned.'[94] This dual testimony made the indefiniteness of 'gentleman' certain; the concept more complex and appealing. In 1862 the *Cornhill* tried a little social history, pre-empting Taine by invoking *gentilhomme* and suggesting that:

> As people came to perceive that the moral and intellectual qualities were far the most important and distinctive, they learned to attribute the word a moral rather than a personal meaning. Hence, in the present day, the word implies the combination of a certain degree of social rank with a certain amount of the qualities which the possession of such rank ought to imply; but there is a constantly increasing disposition to insist more upon the moral and less upon the social element of the word, and it is not impossible that in the course of time its use may become altogether dissociated from any merely conventional distinction.[95]

Smiles and the practical peddlers of wisdom answered Victorian anxieties about gentlemanliness by setting up a parallel universe where the qualities most associated with a gentleman were both the prerequisite for and the means towards wordly advancement. So as late as 1886, W. R. Browne was able to write in 'The English Gentleman' for *The National Review*: 'A gentleman is one to whom discourtesy is a sin and falsehood a crime.'[96] In the light of Mill's thinking on the difference between social and legal sanction in *On Liberty*, it was hard to gauge the force of Browne's notion of falsehood as a crime.[97]

Discussing the word allowed writers like the Ruskin of *Modern Painters* to enlarge their thinking on class relations – where the 'so-called higher classes' loaf while the 'lower classes, denying vigorously and with reason that a gentleman means an idler, and rightly feeling that the more anyone works, the more of a gentleman he becomes',[98] – and to find a definition of the word which works for them. As usual, Ruskin placed a parting kick by remarking 'the lower orders, and all orders, have to learn that every vicious habit and chronic disease communicates itself by descent'.[99] Divines like J. H. Newman and Charles Kingsley, at odds in theological debate in the middle years, shared a common language and discourse when they discussed the social virtues of the gentleman. In the 1852 *Idea of a University*, Newman had favoured the man who refined himself to the point of non-existence without seeming too refined, and was, like the awful troupe in *Loss and Gain*, 'tender towards the bashful, gentle towards the distant, and merciful towards the absurd'.[100] The three qualities which showed the gentleman tender, gentle and merciful led him, by the tripartite steps of Newman's prose, to be 'patient, forbearing, and resigned, on philosophical principles', and to submit to pain 'because it is inevitable, to bereavement because it is irreparable, and to death because it is his destiny'.[101] While Newman's clauses led inexorably to a conclusion, Kingsley's led to conclusiveness:

> A wise ancient has said, 'It is virtue, yea virtue, gentlemen, which maketh gentlemen; which maketh the poor rich, the weak strong, the simple wise, the base-born noble. This rank neither the whirling wheel of fortune can destroy, nor the deceitful cavillings of worldlings separate, neither sickness abate, nor time abolish.'[102]

Kingsley created Amyas Leigh in *Westward Ho!* three years later, and gave him the recalcitrance of spirit to allow him to take pride in believing it the finest thing in the world to be a gentleman.[103]

The whole career of the concept of the gentleman, and the Victorians' confusion about it, aptly illustrated Mill's sense of the forces that shape an individual's dealings with society. The word and the concept formed a ready-made social career path for the ambitious, and a comfortable resting-place for those already there. The anonymous *Quite a Gentleman* in 1878 complained of an instance where the 'varnish' of polite manners wears off, exposing the shabbiness beneath.[104] That metaphor of varnish, of surface, called upon Dickens's more thoughtful usage in *Great Expectations*: 'no man who was not a gentleman at heart, ever was, since the world began, a true gentleman in manner ... no varnish can hide the grain of the wood ... the more varnish you put on, the more the grain will express itself',[105] where 'express' makes the wood eloquent in making the origins speak. Mrs Craik's 'a Christian only can be a true gentleman'[106] put the definition in the hands of the divines, and connected with the theories put forward by Tupper and Adams. As early as 1847 Lieber had urged a definition which subjected 'refinement of feeling, and loftiness of conduct' to

42

'the rigid dictates of morality and purifying precepts of religion',[107] while in *The English Gentleman* of 1849, 'Christian gentleman' represented the highest possible praise.[108]

The ease with which the idea of a behaviour pattern absorbed other forms of belief and other sets of principles bore witness to the co-optive way in which mid-Victorian society worked. Notions of progress tended to make the community move centrifugally as individuals took on new roles and responsibilities. The enquiry into origins occasioned by the debate between Darwinism and orthodox religion made the community move centripetally back to a fixed point of all origins. In social terms, the behaviour book mediated between these two competing forces; it presupposed the fact of change, while it asserted the notion that certain principles remain fixed, allowing an appeal to social authority. The developing idea of the gentleman from the 1850s to the 1870s illustrated exactly the tension between these two forces. In Mill's terms this tension showed itself as the clash of inner belief with outer conformity; the result was refreshingly radical:

> In our times, from the highest class of society down to the lowest, everyone lives as under the eye of a hostile and dreaded censorship. Not only in what concerns others, but in what concerns only themselves, the individual or family do not ask themselves, what do I prefer? or, what would suit my character and disposition? or, what would allow the best and highest in me to have fair play and enable it to grow and thrive? They ask themselves, what is suitable to my position? what is usually done by persons of my station and pecuniary circumstances? or (worse still) what is usually done by persons of a station and circumstances superior to mine?[109]

A social, religious and moral set of concepts like those required by gentlemanliness exerted pressure on three fronts. The question of origins in the Victorian novel – Bulstrode's past, Pip's inheritance, Jem's planned emigration to Toronto – became the question of process. Each venture was a new beginning, another chance to avoid failure by drawing selectively on one's own past and, through biography, on the pasts of others. So as the century advances, a social fund established itself in the writings of Tupper,

Smiles, Adams, Hain Friswell[110] and Peter Bayne, the journalist, author and leader-writer for the Presbyterian *Weekly Review*.[111] Knowledge became hereditary, and individual social progress depended on collective social know-how.

The pervasiveness of rule-following and the reign of the conduct book stretched far beyond the scope and enterprise of Tupper and his popular successors. Every aspect of mid-Victorian life came to need rules to follow and – like Tupper's unconventional encounter with Victoria – a set of principles to fall back on when the rules simply had not arrived to govern the situation. In every aspect of their lives, the mid-Victorians faced the potential and the actuality of rule-governed activities. Appropriate conduct became a habit of mind, in conversation, design, commerce and in creative work; this was exactly Mill's observation, that the mid-Victorian disposition was to impose opinion and inclination as a rule of conduct.

2
Etiquette and Other People

> In conversation, as in life, there is much tyranny, the strong and
> unscrupulous invariably overpowering the weak and retiring;
> hence the necessity for something like a code of well-understood
> rules to protect the weak from such oppression, just as laws
> are required in national and social communities for a similar
> purpose.
>
> Roger Boswell, *The Art of Conversation*[1]

This was written during the countrywide social agitation of 1866
and published in 1867, the year of the second Reform Bill. The
ubiquitous question of others' rights bridged the public and the
private in mid-Victorian social life. Relations with other people
were the measure of personal and social advancement, and meeting
others was the intersection of two cultures, the personal and the
social. Mid-Victorian public space was changing, providing new
forums for development in both the personal and the public
sphere: libraries, museums, railways, working men's associations.
The etiquette book became the informal social legislation which
governed the way people thought about meeting and communicating with each other.

Through the influence of the etiquette book, the period between
1832 and 1867 saw the development of personality as a social
category. John Stuart Mill had originated the science of Ethology,
essentially the business of deducing character from the minutiae
of everyday behaviour; the popular versions of this, phrenology
and graphology, were part of a continuum which included Darwin's *The Expression of the Emotions in Man and Animals* and
Carlyle's *Sartor Resartus* on clothing:

> All visible things are emblems; what thou seest is not there on its
> own account; strictly taken, is not there at all; Matter exists only

spiritually, and to represent some Idea, and *body* it forth. Hence *Clothes*, as despicable as we think them, are so unspeakably significant.[2]

In a world where appearances were clues to the self, one was what one appeared to be. The mid-Victorian impulse was to construct personality through the control and moderation of the desires; through checking and identifying feelings; and through well-known and familiar feelings which came to constitute the personality. The freedom to feel different almost invariably came over as a disruption of the social norms. Hippolyte Taine wrote of the mourning English that the custom of reserve led to a kind of stoicism:

> There is no confiding, no letting go, even with one's nearest and dearest. In a family which has just lost a near relation, a father or a son, there is never an outburst of grief, no noisy crying or loud mourning. On the day following, everyone comes down as usual in the morning; all take their places at table in the usual way and at the usual time. There will be a little less talk than usual. One may be grief-stricken, but that does not mean one must not get on with one's job, and do it well and as conscientiously as ever. When, after the death of Prince Albert, the Queen shut herself up in solitude and seemed to be giving up the business proper to her position, the newspapers, after letting several months go by, began to censure her conduct, and informed her that a private grief excuses nobody from fulfilling public obligations.[3]

As the Queen's reading of Tennyson showed, poetry and religion were the great escapes from the dolours of grief or the pressures of everyday life. They provided for the very feelings and emotions which the English tended to excise. Decent behaviour, especially in conversation with others, was often a matter of concealment and understatement; as Taine said, 'What we display and exaggerate, they conceal and attenuate. It is necessary to discount part of what we say and add something to what they say.'[4]

The broader, high Victorian version of this came up in the anonymous *Modern Etiquette in Private and Public* (1871), which isolated the category 'manner' as a social entity:

Etiquette means a code of social laws regulating the external
conduct of that order of society which is emphatically styled
'good' – that is, well-bred. Now, the word 'well-bred' at once
shows us that 'manner' is a thing to be acquired or taught, since
it depends on the 'breeding', or bringing-up; and good breeding
is taught from the nursery days amongst the wealthy or
aristocratic classes.[5]

This writer believed, as did almost every Victorian, that manners
could be taught – a belief greeted eagerly by the classes of self-
improvers intent on refining themselves into existence. The etiquette book was principal among the tools for the self-helper;
belief in unseen codes was the law of its construction, and a
willingness to think, act and feel – in public at least – according
to rule was the energy which kept these rules in force. As the self
became a construct of various forms of behaviour, the balance
between public and private began to fluctuate, for the public
persona could be learned and practised in private. The influence
of the mid-Victorian home, centrifugally felt in the gentlemen's
club and centripetally concentrated in the *idea* of home, was
another mutually sustaining interchange between public and private.

Balzac's Paris, central to his work,[6] and Thackeray's London
were the models of nineteenth-century urban consciousness in
which the mid-Victorian social personality was formed. The etiquette book simply looked at the conceit from the other side: if
character could be deduced from externals, then externals might
represent character. First among the set of social constructs which
the mid-Victorians valued was the ability to converse well.

Victorian thinking about conversation, especially in the improving years between the first and third Reform Bills (1832–84),
reduced itself to a series of maxims broadly identifiable together
under the idea of accomplishment. The mid-Victorian made his
or her contribution as expertly as possible; kept in mind the
objects of conversation; prepared for conversation; respected the
claims of others; and treated conversation as a matter of performance – practised, learned, and used for improving others as well
as oneself. These socially determined imperatives, along with other
adjacents such as 'Improve others', or 'Maintain class', gave social

intercourse a purpose other than the mere conveyance of information.

Conversation as the ultimate social attribute appealed to the rigorous ethic of self-help and self-improvement embedded in early Victorian evangelism. The fact that it could be practised at home and then carried abroad answered the evangelical impulse. Interest in conversation was underpinned by the growing mid-Victorian application of scientific ideas and techniques to linguistic enquiry. This in turn rested on a burgeoning popular and academic interest in language, dialect, accents and slang, from Max Müller to William Barnes. The issue of communication also engaged scientists of the natural world, notably Charles Darwin:

> The power of communication between the members of the same tribe by means of language has been of paramount importance in the development of man; and the force of language is much aided by the expressive movements of the face and body. We perceive this at once when we converse on an important subject with any person whose face is concealed.[7]

Or as the etiquette book *Manners and Rules of Good Society* put it, 'The usages of good society relate not only to good manners and to good breeding, but also to the proper etiquette to be observed on every occasion.'[8] The observer of the natural and the observer of the social world shared an interest in what it was to communicate; and they emerged with an emphasis on behaviour.

The mid-Victorian etiquette books were the first to tackle the issue of how one conversed with a view to self-advancement. While Castiglione told one how to laugh without vulgarity, and while the eighteenth-century rationalism of Locke or La Rochefoucauld recognised that there were rules of engagement for conversation, only the mid-Victorians made the matter of *how* one conversed into a general concern. What could be more personal than conversing? What could be more political than conversing correctly? The mid-Victorians were the first to put conversation in service of a vision of society, whether for personal advancement, for religious purposes, or for political control.

The notion of 'conversation' roamed across distinct and discreet meanings, gradually, throughout the nineteenth century narrowing, its earlier recorded sense. The word's beginnings were social, including dealing with others, commerce, society, intimacy. At one time the meaning encompassed intercourse or intimacy, through to 'the condition of acquaintance or intimacy with a matter',[9] to mean a circle of acquaintance, a company or society. The meaning fluctuated as the notion of what it was to be a conversant member of society altered. The nineteenth century muddled matters decently, with 'manner of conducting oneself in the world or in society; behaviour, mode, or course of life,' and the citation from Morley[10] alongside 'interchange of thoughts and words; familiar discourse or talk'.[11]

The start of the nineteenth century had seen the arrival of three crucial terms. The first, 'conversazione', from around the end of the eighteenth century, was often used to describe assemblies of an intellectual character, in connection with literature, art or science;[12] this broadened into one of the staples of nineteenth-century social life: 'Now chiefly used for a soirée given by a learned body or society of arts at which the society's work is illustrated by the exhibition of specimens, experiments, or demonstrations.'[13]

The second term, 'conversationalist', came into the language, according to the *OED*, in 1806, and then meant 'one who converses much, or is addicted to conversation; one who practises the art of conversation'. Conversation stood as an objective accomplishment; the term did not yet include someone who was an expert at conversing: it registered the quantity rather than the quality of the devotion to talking. Nathaniel Hawthorne in *The English Notebooks* wrote of Bayard Taylor as 'a brilliant conversationist',[14] and had to slip that adjective in. However, the concept of someone who specialised in conversation had become familiar by the time Hawthorne wrote this.

The third of these terms, 'conversationalist', arrived around 1836. The meaning given to it by the *OED* – 'one who is conversational; one who excels in conversation' – traces the vital Victorian addition of the notion of competence. The word moved closer to 'conversationist' throughout the period, but never came close enough to be synonymous. Browning was described as 'one of the most entertaining and instructive conversationists at dinner in London',[15] but this was still a discreet distance from the poised observation of F. Arnold, 'A Middle-Aged Englishman'. Arnold dined at the high table of a Cambridge college, where he anticipated meeting 'with a professed conversationalist. In those days', he wrote in 1857 of the 1830s, 'there were professional conversationalists, as at the present time there are professional beauties.'[16] Arnold here wanted 'professed' and 'professional'[17] kept close, raising an eyebrow and a question, courting a disappointment. One earnest mid-Victorian commentator calculated that his contemporaries spoke for around five hours every day; the consequent number of volumes of talk produced by each talker ran to some 27,300 volumes of 520 octavo pages over a lifetime.[18] This seems excessive by modern standards in the electronic age. But so much of Victorian social intercourse came down to talk, gossip, tales retold and retailed. The Victorians' great capacity for self-publicity and for cataloguing others' conversations resulted in the great legacy of memoirs, biographies, autobiographies and essays which drew on this world of talk.

Talk was social currency, real conversation the gold standard. Writers, artists and politicians at leisure fitted into a context of competence, of professionalism in their talk. Robert Browning and the painters Millais and Leighton, at dinner with the John Lehmanns in Half Moon Street, were a typical conversational troika of London worthies: 'though each of the gifted conversationalists loved to take the lead, they all subdued their inclinations so courteously that no one of the three usurped more than his fair share of public attention'.[19] This was an ideal Victorian situation: people of pitch and moment agreeing to share the glory of the evening, and the term 'conversationalist' hovers close.

The conversation guide for the Victorians made talk and the techniques of conversation much more demotic than they had been in the eighteenth century. It amounted to social grace professionalised. Bridging the eighteenth and nineteenth centuries, the wit, raconteur, conversationist and orator Sydney Smith always knew what to look for in the talk of others, and how to frame courteous, ironic objections. He said of Macaulay, whom he met at the home of the poet Samuel Rogers, that he was certainly more agreeable since hs return from India. Smith wryly noted that some might be tempted to accuse Macaulay of having talked too much, 'but now he has occasional flashes of silence that make his conversation perfectly delightful'.[20]

When Smith later called Macaulay that 'book in breeches',[21] he showed that he could listen to others in a way which made talk continuous with the written word. Smith, no mean talker himself, perfectly caught the good-natured pique of a man with something to offer but prevented from offering it:

> 'Oh yes! we both talk a great deal, but I don't believe Macaulay
> ever did hear my voice,' he exclaimed, laughing. 'Sometimes,
> when I have told a good story, I have thought to myself, Poor
> Macaulay! he will be very sorry some day to have missed hearing
> that.'[22]

Smith lived during a time when conversation increasingly came to be one of the registers of status.[23] His own conversation can be heard as far down the century as 1898, in a remark by G. W. E. Russell, who lamented the decline of parliamentary oratory and wondered whether conversation ought to be included in the same category:

> To answer with positiveness is difficult; but this much may be
> readily conceded – that a belief in the decadence of conversation
> is natural to those who have specially cultivated Links with the
> Past; who grew up in the traditions of Luttrell and Mackintosh,
> and Lord Alvanley and Samuel Rogers; who have felt Sydney
> Smith's irresistible fun, and known the overwhelming fullness of
> Lord Macaulay.[24]

Here it was taken for granted that conversation itself could be a subject for analysts; that conversation had somehow changed over the years, and that it therefore had in some sense a set of qualities which allowed it to be defined.

I Talking to Each Other

The rise of the quintessentially mid-Victorian conversation guide matched the changes in the urban environment in the mid-century.

While political and social legislation throughout the 1840s and 1850s attended to the improvement of urban conditions, parallel movements in evangelical religion and in self-help ministered to the inner life. But the etiquette and behaviour book negotiated between the outer and inner life of the individual. Conversation could be practised at home, prepared for alone, and then put to use in company.

The scope and diversity of daily contact also increased exponentially in the cities: between 1801 and 1831 the population of Greater London grew from 865,000 to 1.5 million; Glasgow from 77,000 to 200,000; Manchester from 95,000 to 238,000; Birmingham's population doubled, Liverpool's increased two and a half-fold. Patterns of work, particularly in London, meant that people were more mobile, both geographically and socially: clerks, messengers and domestic servants travelled to work, like Dickens's Mr Jaggers, Mr Mallard or Mr Wicks, from a London which had spread out laterally. This was no longer the city of Dr Johnson or Christopher Wren or Samuel Richardson. Middle-class mid-Victorian work and leisure were more equally balanced.

The 1849 *Manners and Customs of the English*, written by Percival Leigh depicted the endless round of pleasures and distractions unfolded by the city, like the ranks of houses in Wordsworth's sonnet 'Composed upon Westminster Bridge'. Lunch was taken in a public space when the press of people was at its greatest; evening entertainment presented itself at the throng of theatres in Drury Lane or along Shaftesbury Avenue; something less taxing was available at the Panorama, Leicester Square, the Diorama in Regent's Park, the Egyptian Hall (where Tom Thumb topped the bill) or Madame Tussaud's waxwork museum. *The Times* for 9 June 1841 reported the destruction of Astley's Theatre near Westminster Bridge on the previous morning. This was the worst London fire since the Royal Exchange burned down in 1838. It was the crowd which caught the reporter's attention:

The crowd that assembled last night round the scene of desolation was immense. There could not have been less at one period than 20,000 persons. Owing, however, to the admirable arrangement of the police, we heard not of the slightest accident occurring.

Beneath all this lay the need for order. Engels and de Tocqueville had despaired about the new urban environment in Manchester, where they – unlike Disraeli's Coningsby – felt civilisation had been turned back into savagery.[25] In urban London, Peel's uniformed police were instituted in 1829, but between 1830 and 1848 the threat of armed and violent disturbances was real. 'Looking back,' muses the historian R.H. Mottram, 'one catches one's breath to see the risk that we ran during a period untouched by general education, stated leisure, and the rising tide of prosperity that changed the complexion of affairs after the half-century.'[26]

Social space for meeting others was changing in the 1850s: on the newly macadamed London roads, recently cleared of livestock, on railway platforms at the new termini, at the new department stores in Piccadilly. These places provided social space for encountering people of different work, if not class, backgrounds. The urban experience was maturing. Respectable families felt the pressure of the rising middle classes, and gradually disappeared from public spaces to make dinner at home the social apogee. Only in the 1890s was there provision for respectable women to meet in public places outside their own homes, in cafés and tea houses.

But in the mid-century, tea gardens, outdoor entertainments, zoos and circuses catered to the need for escape within defined urban limits. The synchronic culture spread out laterally, allowing increased access to greater numbers. *The Times* found an apt symbol combining collective technology with personal need in the unveiling of London's first public drinking fountain on 21 April 1859. A large crowd attended:

Yesterday afternoon the interesting ceremony of opening the first public drinking fountain was performed by Mrs Willson, the daughter of the Archbishop of Canterbury, in the presence of a large concourse of people. The fountain is situated at the corner of Giltspur-street and Skinner-street, by St Sepulchre's Church. The hour fixed for the ceremony was three o'clock, and long before that hour a vast number of people of all descriptions assembed in the vicinity . . . Lord Radstock then briefly addressed the assemblage, pointing out the great good that must result from the erection of these fountains . . . The assemblage then dispersed, and a number of people partook of the refreshing liquid.[27]

Middle- and lower-class society was becoming more fluid in its requirements and enjoyments. Although the lower classes were prevented for the most part by economic and time constraints from frequenting the venues beloved of the middle classes for recreation and instruction, the 1840s and 1850s saw government and local legislation creating a leisure and educative environment for them. The Museums Act (1845), Public Libraries Act (1850) and the Great Exhibition (1851) gradually broadened the area, and conditions, in which people met. The way they spoke to each other was paramount, and was regulated by the sets of informal and often unspoken rules which the mid-Victorians evolved for social exchange. This was one aspect of a growing political consciousness of class defined not by occupation but through meeting others of palapably different interests and values.

At home, furnishings created the environment in which manners and customs functioned. The double-ended sofa, the sociable, the late-Victorian Chesterfield or the Hepplewhite-style sofa, all provided speakers with defined and obvious seclusion; the tête-à-tête chair held two speakers together and apart at the same time, allowing proximity while maintaining distance. It was unusual to have a tête-à-tête with another person of the same sex without choosing one's companion and seeking out the opportunity; however, two people of different sexes often found themselves brought together and ordered, so to speak, to converse, for no other reason than the command of society.[28]

II The Art of Conversation

Above and before anything else, mid-Victorian models of social interaction owed much to middle- and upper-middle-class practice. Here is what one typical commentator thought 'the proper objects of conversation' should be:

These are, to make the time pass agreeably, for others as well as for ourselves.

To make people like us and think well of us.
And, when suitable opportunities occur, to instruct and improve
ourselves and others.[29]

Hugo Reid wrote that in his 1867 *The Art of Conversation*,
under the name Roger Boswell. By then Reid had written books
under his own name, including self-help guides and books on
mathematics. The fact that he was a non-specialist and that he felt
able to pronounce on conversation showed what a general concern
it was becoming. His pseudonym kept his life discreet from itself,
like a well-ordered party. He tackled his subject with a prescriptive
pragmatism, and set out a series of rules which he felt would
necessarily produce fine conversation.

Reid subtitled this book 'Cultivating and Promoting Pleasant
Social Intercourse'. It was based on the calm assumption that,
since much of life was spent conversing, a guide or manual on the
subject could scarcely fail to be useful. His introduction systemati-
cally set out those rules which, 'if attended to, may, at least, point
out what to avoid, and assist in rendering conversation pleasant
and harmonious'. Reid thought himself a pioneer:

> In the absence, so far as the author knows, of any popular work
> specially devoted to the Art of Talk, he ventures to submit the
> following, which he hopes may prove of service not only to the
> young, who should cultivate the graces of conversation for
> purposes of their own advancement and the uses of society, but
> also to many of maturer years by whom the various matters
> suggested in this small volume are too frequently overlooked or
> disregarded.[30]

Conversation filled in the gaps between the fatigues of business;
accounts of mutual friends in the day's news combined with anecdote, narrative, 'curious traits of character, sallies of wit, humour,
or sprightliness, jest and repartee', along with occasional useful
information and 'discussion of a solid and improving character',
to supply a 'mental cordial that "cheers but not inebriates"', and
make time fly quickly and agreeably'.[31]

Reid's work framed a set of rules independent of the world they
sought to influence, yet which had to return habitually to that

world for practical testing. He gathered his considerations – 'in reality, a sort of A,B,C of social intercourse'[32] – under the heading *Hints for Talkers*. His first tip, *Previous Preparation is Necessary for Conversation*, played on Victorian worries about the relation of hard work to success in the world. He probed the mid-Victorian fear of insufficiency by warning against thinking too lightly of conversation or neglecting it; he inveighed against those who supposed that it required no thought or preparation, 'that every one is provided by Nature with sufficient conversational gifts, and will easily find out any rules necessary for his guidance'.[33]

Once conversation was brought under the heading of something to be worked at, each individual was held responsible for personal social success or failure. Reid's advice to talkers echoes the register of popular mid-nineteenth-century moral virtues: 'prepare for conversation by laying in a stock of caution, self-control, patience, forbearance, good humour, kindly feeling, and,' he advocated, supposing that being in possession of all these heady qualities at once might distort one's sense of oneself, 'if possible, a little modesty'. Occasionally Reid 'modestly' put his own wide reading on show, invoking the nation's favourite playwright: 'Conversation is truly the balm of life. Like mercy, it is twice blessed – it blesses him who gives and him who receives, and is one of the most beneficent products of civilization.'[34]

Reid knew that while the rules of the game could be isolated, they were never just rules:

> Independently of the desirableness of rendering conversation –
> from which we anticipate, and should derive, so much of our
> happiness – as pleasant, instructive, and useful as possible, there is
> another consideration which should lead all, especially the young,
> to study carefully the exercise of the art – this is, the effect our
> behaviour in conversation may have on our interests: no doubt,
> a view of the subject connected with an inferior class of motives,
> but still too important to be altogether passed over.[35]

The poised anxiety of this typifies the middle-class mid-Victorian concern about getting on while seeming not to do so. Everyday hypocrisy it might not be, but rather a sudden anaesthesia of the political sense of fair play. Everywhere Reid related his set of conversation rules to the notion of a system of national and international law. He was preceded in this by the 1856 *Talking and Debating*, which mentioned the 'law which requires us to listen' under the heading *The Laws of Conversation*.[36]

Reid differed from twentieth-century thinking about conversation typified by J. L. Austin, Paul Grice or John Searle[37] in maintaining that conversing involves bringing the homework to class: in this he was quintessentially Victorian. The Victorians also had a strong sense of propriety about the available subjects. Ten years earlier, in 1857, the voice theorist and conversation guru Edwin Drew had defined conversational competence in terms of the subjects prepared and covered by the conversers. The refinement he envisaged was intimate with a kind of social poise which put literature at a premium:

> What subjects are best? Plainly those that belong to the elegancies
> of life, and which are not likely to strike deep at personal
> prejudices, or to beget contentions or sectarian differences: –
> Nature, as seen abroad and at home – the varied aspects of human
> society, as witnessed during foreign travel – History, in its various
> unfoldings of human character, and its record of the greatnesses and
> failings of nations – Science, in its applications to the wants of life,
> and its revealings of natural laws and economies – and, above all,
> Art and Literature – pictures, sculpture, and books.[38]

It was an essential mid-Victorian move to define a particular area of human life and fence it off into a manageable field. In the midst of good conversation sat the arts and humanities. Literature, which served up conversations in novels, poems and plays, maintained a fertile and doubly-bound relation to the conversations which took it as a subject for discussion. Material had to be gathered for conversation, as if each Victorian were to become their own imaginary museum of conversational artefacts: just as Pitt-Rivers scoured the empire to create a collection of the unusual and the incongruous, so the ordinary Victorian was expected to cull the arts, science and literature for the conversational banquet:

> Prepare, then, for conversation by storing the mind with
> interesting matter on subjects calculated for general discourse.

Amongst the principal of these are, History, not forgetting the history going on at the present time; Biography, particularly of recent celebrities; Anecdotes and curious traits of human nature; Remarkable Crimes and Trials; Adventures; Voyages and Travels; Manners and Customs of different Nations; Antiquities; Geography; Curious Facts in Physical Science; Natural History; Commerce and Manufacturers; Inventions; Statistics; and, above all, a knowledge of the Lives, Works, Opinions, and Sayings of the Great Men of all ages.[39]

This taxonomy of Victorian staples represented the ultimate popularisation of hard-won philosophical and social concepts: Physical Science, Natural History, Commerce, Statistics. The ease with which these concepts entered the conversational arena contrasts sharply with the difficulties they caused for other and more famous commentators of the period. These coolly-formed categories burned at the centre of heated nineteenth-century polemical controversy: Carlyle on History; Mayhew on the manners and customs of a different nation within England; Arnold and Spencer on what *could* be called worthwhile knowledge; Morris and Ruskin on commerce; Dickens, Gaskell and Thackeray on manufacturers; Butler, Chambers, Huxley, Lyell and Wallace on natural science; Charles Booth on statistics in Liverpool. The exaltation of History fitted neatly with popular intellectual sentiment in the 1870s and 1880s: with Morley's claim in 1881 that Macaulay's essays had done more than any other writing of the generation to settle the direction of historical interest and curiosity, and with the revived sense of Carlyle's assertion that History was not only the fittest study, but that it included all others.

The conversation etiquette book was the communicational equivalent of Henry Cole's prescriptive register of good taste and design, which he established in 1848 under the pseudonym Felix Summerly as Summerly's Art Manufacturers. Where the arrival of the morally earnest rich coincided with new developments in manufacturing techniques, as it did in the 1840s and 1850s, a measure of taste was required. The popular commonplace books which filed into the pages of mid-Victorian novels gathered and stored the information required by this rigid view of conversation.

So too when people found themselves conversing across classes and in new situations. What, then, was to be avoided?

OBJECTIONABLE SUBJECTS – But there are certain subjects that should never be introduced in general conversation, however fit they may be for the consideration of friends' tête-à-tête. Religious matters are at all times unfit, though it is common enough in middle-class life to find a whole company at loggerheads about some question of Popery or Protestantism, some refined point in church discipline, or doctrinal peculiarities. In a mixed assembly it is next to impossible to express an opinion on any religious topic without stirring up the bile of some dogmatist, or wounding the sacred feelings of some devotional heart. Leave the Pope alone, let Dr Cumming have his way, never mind the 'Eclectic Review' and the 'Hymn Book' controversy, we want to be happy, and we can't when our deepest and most cherished sentiments are assailed, or when some one would convince us that his opinion is the soundest.[40]

This shows how ideally divorced the popular etiquette book was from the intellectual debates of the age. But then, writers immersed in the culture can also write against it. So much of value in Tennyson or Meredith issued from their reaction to the assault on deeply cherished sentiments. Moreover, the atheism of Charles Bradlaugh, the agnosticism of T. H. Huxley and the biological rigour of W. H. Clifford carried the debate between science and religion into the late nineteenth century, at one remove from what the etiquette books were prescribing. Mid-Victorian intellectual debates on education, evolution or manufacturing turned on exactly the belief that one opinion was sounder than another. The injunction 'we want to be happy', albeit ironically, allowed a rigorous social diction to operate; the unpleasant or the confusing was kept out of the drawing room and away from the dining table.

Along with this squeamishness about certain kinds of exchange in conversation came the notion that different forms of assembly required different forms of talk. Advice from *Talking & Debating* presumed: 'Of course, in little family circles, where the parties are old friends, the case is quite different', as if one needed absolution to talk about what one liked among friends.

Instructions to conversers resembled the moral imperatives of sermons or self-help books – 'Do not suppose that all is right because you succeed in silencing others and getting a monopoly of the conversation'[41] – which exemplified the workings of an economic social model built on the relations between individuals and monopolies. There was, however, a law of natural selection among conversers: 'There may be occasions when you are beside persons who have no talent for conversation, or who perceive that the company prefer to hear you, and, having the good sense to refrain from obtruding themselves, give way to you.'[42] Other instructions followed: do not interrupt anyone, never contradict anyone on trivial matters and rarely on any important point, seldom argue.[43] Agreement for the mid-Victorian talker meant recognising that those one talked to were also forms of life: the participants realised they were playing the same game. This communication below the surface of what was said typifies not only the mid-Victorian tendency to maintain face and live an inner, secret life, but also to stress the manner rather than the content of the conversation. The etiquette books advised against entrenched opinion: 'Avoid being positive, very confident, dogmatic', 'Do not obtrude Opinions, nor give them out uncalled for' and 'Never quiz, ridicule, nor make game of anyone.'[44]

The anonymous *Talk & Talkers* of 1859 surveyed the field of 'reprehensible' talkers: 'Liars, Braggarts, Hypocrites, Flatterers, Small-Talkers, Gossips, and Scandal-Mongers.'[45] That these social types should be offered up for scrutiny in a book on talk shows how close concepts of moral behaviour came to spilling over into descriptions of competence. *How To Shine in Society; or the Art of Conversation; containing its Principles, Laws, and General Usage in Modern Polite Society* (1867) stressed that conversation was not limited to talking only, but embraced general conduct as well. The tongue colonised an empire of its own; but *How to Shine* it echoed the thought, on which it depended for its force and its beauty.[46] Loose habits of thinking and of talking 'will make but a sorry conversable member of society'.[47]

The fact that conversation could be talked of in these terms – social, intellectual, moral – set it aside as a subject in its own right. 1856 saw the publication of the anonymous *Talking & Debating: or Fluency of Speech Attained Without the Sacrifice of Elegance*

and Sense: a Handbook of Conversation and Debate. The book
set out the 'Laws of Conversation' and advised 'How to Make
Conversation'. *Talking & Debating* made clear where such skills,
once acquired, necessarily led. It spoke plainly of a person's conversation marking the state that person has attained in intellectual
and moral culture. The merest word of the most taciturn could
be as expressive as the banter of the garrulous: 'to talk well is
everywhere the ambition of persons moving in refined circles,
or aspiring to such circles for the qualification of honourable
ambition'.[48]

Conversation in its uses and practice naturally focused other
forces – 'intellectual and moral culture', 'ambition' and the desire
for those 'refined circles'. *Talking & Debating* moved quickly
from exhorting the benefits of listening to this, its second Law of
Conversation:

> SELF-POSSESSION must be cultivated by the conversationalist, that
> he may not run away headlong, and say many things that he may
> afterwards regret. This is the source of that gentlemanly reserve
> which distinguishes the man of refinement from the mere bore,
> and begets that patience in listening, and that generous spirit of
> appreciation, which makes a speaker feel as much pleased with
> his hearers as with himself.[49]

The grim prospect of a world of talkers, each as pleased with
one's hearers as with oneself, eluded the author of *Talking &
Debating.* But the book did sound a note of caution, in case the
talkers were enjoying their sense of themselves or their hearers
too much. It warned with typical Victorian trepidation that the
hour of general merriment deserved the greatest caution: 'under
strong impulse many things may escape from the tongue that the
speaker would afterwards gladly recall'. This was also true of high
literary circles, 'where the brightest wits and most profoundly
learned men assemble, that the perfection of nonsense is talked',[50]
and gestured towards the literary tradition of table-talk, reminiscences and memoir which gradually diluted the great – even
Johnson and Coleridge – into characters whose every word was
not a high-octane fuel for the culture.

The English abroad were subject to the same imperatives and

injunctions. The *Punch* almanack for 1858 (a year in which, ironically, passport troubles made foreign travel less easy) cut an ironic swathe through English behaviour in 'Why Englishmen are beloved upon the continent':

> Because they are always so careful to abstain from either word or action, which, in any way, might hurt the feelings of a foreigner.
> Because they speak so fluently in any continental language, and are always so affable when publicly accosted by a stranger, and so ready at all times to enter into conversation with those they may be travelling with.
> Because they don't bawl for beer at a first-class table d'hôte, nor make wry faces at the wine as though it disagreed with them.
> Because whatever provocation they may think they have received, they are so careful not to let strong language pass their lips; and so far from making extracts from the Commination Service, are never heard to use an exclamation more forcible than 'Dear me!' or 'Now really, how provoking!'[51]

III Conversation and Morals

Into the 1870s and 1880s, after several decades of conversation manuals and guides on form and content in conversation, there was a move away from instruction towards intuition. This may have been because the environment was so strong an influence by then, or it may have been because advances in the 'art for art's sake' movement (initially from France in the 1850s) had reached England in the form of social self-assertiveness which in turn took the form of social misbehaviour. While French decadents destroyed themselves by over-indulgence, the English sought to disrupt the order nearest at hand, the social order.

A comparison of the 1860s and the 1890s points up the difference in view. Mid-Victorian received opinion felt this:

> The talker, like the poet, is born, not formed by art. Still, a good deal may be done by one who will take pains to examine his own talk and that of others, to improve his style and render his conversation more acceptable and more likely to be attended

to . . . Brevity and clearness are the essential points; these, with the use of plain familiar language (the homely Saxon rather than the latinised English), and a distinct, impressive manner, will succeed when there is really anything in what you are going to say; if there is not, you had better not say it.[52]

At the end of the century, thirty years after mid-Victorian self-improvement had refined itself into the improved selfhood of decadence, Beatrice Knollys in *The Gentle Art of Good Talking* (1899) put the counter-case firmly:

A good conversationist, unlike the poet, is made, not born, and, as with the best port, each year adds, up to a certain period, to its richness.[53]

However, the notion that conversation could be worked at, improved, and that conversational competence could alter one's chances of success in the world made conversation and etiquette a specifically mid-Victorian issue.

By 1882 Robert Louis Stevenson envisaged conversation as an easy social encounter between consenting equals. Behind the etiquette books which crowded the market in the 1860s lay the notion that the ease of manner which Stevenson noticed in his *Talk and Talkers* had to be worked at, learned, acquired by following a set of rules:

Natural talk, like ploughing, should turn up a large surface of life rather than dig mines into geological strata. Masses of experience, anecdote, incident, cross-lights, quotation, historical instances, the whole flotsam and jetsam of two minds forced in and upon the matter in hand from every point of the compass, and from every degree of mental elevation and abasement – these are the material with which talk is fortified, the food on which the talkers thrive.[54]

Most mid-Victorian theorists of conversation were worried by the issue of whether principles could be laid down for the activity called conversation; advances in the natural sciences, archaeology and geology and astronomy from the 1840s onwards suggested the possibility of a set of theories which stood in relation to a discipline.

By 1887 J. P. Mahaffy's *Principles of the Art of Conversation* marked the maturity of the discipline. Mahaffy's talents spread themselves wide: he was by turns a Professor of Classics at Dublin, editor of Walter Savage Landor's *Imaginary Conversations*, a man of letters and indefatigable correspondent; and, most famously, tutor of Oscar Wilde. When he tackled the principles of conversation, he felt his subject was both novel and complex. 'There can be no doubt,' he wrote, 'that of all the accomplishments prized in modern society that of being agreeable in conversation is the very first.'[55] His work typified much of the writing of the 1860s and 1870s on social conduct, and absorbed its preoccupations and ignorances. Above all, he stressed the notion of accomplishment, where social contact becomes an acquired skill.

But the fascination was that Mahaffy wanted to make principles from what he called 'a Protean impalpable acquirement'.[56] He tackled it like this:

> The whole system of human reasoning in all its wonderful intricacy
> is built up from a few general principles in themselves perfectly
> and necessarily obvious, just as the prose of Ruskin and the poetry
> of Browning are expressed in combinations of twenty-six letters.
> But as in this case the theory of composing words is easy enough,
> and yet the art a mystery, which only very few can ever attain
> in perfection, – each, too, after his own fashion, and stamped with
> his own genius, – so the theory of conversation may be reduced
> to a small number of general observations, and yet the perfect
> practice of it is a mystery, which defies analysis – one of the
> myriad manifestations of human genius which all can admire but
> no one can explain.[57]

The issue of accomplishment in conversation for nineteenth-century talkers depended on notions of class, morals, good behaviour, good taste in dress, and a range of related concerns. The attraction of the profound moral uses of conversation, which Mahaffy saw as the main vehicle of good education and religious teaching, was balanced by the fact that conversation was *the* social skill. Conversation fascinated the Victorians simply because it represented an area of private life open to the dictates of self-improvement which was also an area of public life where progress could be tested against contemporaries. As the anonymous *Modern Etiquette* (1859) had put it: 'study at home, then, if you would converse well in society'.[58]

Mahaffy found a commercial and then religious vocabulary to put social veneer over knotty rules:

> The best kind [of conversation] is when the subject is discussed
> by the company as at an informal council, in which each member
> gives his opinion and contributes something to the common stock;
> where each is not only listened to in turn, but is expected to
> speak; and where the variety of views and of the expression of
> them constitutes the very charm of the company. The more
> people succeed in adopting this form of discussion, the more
> successful their society will be. The most perfect host and hostess
> are those who induce all their guests to talk, and elicit even from
> the silent and the bashful some stray sprinkling of intelligence,
> which gives additional flavour to the spiritual repast.[59]

The commercial metaphor allows itself a pun on 'company'; but this was liable to be limited ('some stray sprinkling of intelligence') in a way that the recently created (1855 and 1862 Acts of Parliament) limited liability company was not. Mahaffy expected everyone to perform, to have something to say. Even the usually tolerant George Eliot remarked that silence did not always sit brooding on a clutch of eggs, dissipating the awe surrounding one who chooses not to talk.

Shyness was a social disease to be excised gradually by correct instruction or good husbandry. When this applied to children, Mahaffy's thinking typified the mid-Victorians' dilemma over whether to create childhood for the child, whether to treat the child as a small adult, or whether to take a third, Wordsworthian view about childlike wisdom. Mahaffy warned against allowing children to run away whenever a stranger appeared, 'as if nature were a state of war, and man the natural enemy of man':

> Such children will require training to be cured of their own and
> their parents' stupidity, and must be taught that every stranger
> is not a bogy. But this is mere domestication, such as we apply to
> the lower animals.[60]

Domestication took many forms. Mahaffy had in mind a form of social acclimatisation, learning the rules of the game.

The preparation of children, and oneself, for social encounter was seen as a duty on which worldly and personal success depended. Moreover, the pressure to talk, and the imperatives to enable others to do so, formed one set of social duties for the mid-Victorians. Lady Greville wrote coolly in *The Gentlewoman in Society* of dinners or dances at which no enjoyment was expected or received, but in which 'a duty to Society is simply fulfilled'.[61] Failure to talk counted as a failure of nerve; and not to encourage others to talk a lapse in social duty. Mahaffy everywhere stressed the duty to say *something*:

> Every civilised man and woman feels, or ought to feel, this duty;
> it is the universal accomplishment which all must practise, and
> as those who fail signally to attain it are punished by the neglect
> of society, so those who succeed beyond the average receive a
> just reward, not only in the constant pleasure thy reap from it,
> but in the esteem which they gain from their fellows. Many men
> and many women owe the whole of a great success in life to this
> and nothing else.[62]

The notion of success for Victorians in the 1880s was intimate with notions of moral virtue. So Mahaffy added this caveat at the foot of the page: 'Of course I do not mean to say that there are not moral conditions required, the absence of which would make social talents perfectly useless.' He concluded, banishing all doubt, that if one were immoral, one deserved to fail, and almost invariably did so; whereas if one were moral one may or may not succeed, 'according as he is agreeable or not'.

Sometimes what counted as moral virtue yielded social vice. Modesty in moderation works well, but modesty without simplicity 'is always a social vice, and therefore highly detrimental to conversation, for as soon as modesty becomes conscious, it assumes one of two forms – the parade of apology or the cloak of reserve'.[63] The key was accomplishment; no matter how shy the speaker, if he or she were accomplished, then all was not lost.

Mahaffy believed that, while there had been an increase in the means of acquiring knowledge, and while his world had seen 'great inventions to save time in so doing',[64] there had been no corresponding moves in the art of conversation. Mahaffy's second edition of *Principles*, newly subtitled 'A Social Essay', had a clearer sense of the discipline it promulgated, and rang with the confidence based on sure sales. His writing on conversation became theoretical; in the 1888 second edition Preface to *Principles* he maintained that there was no object to human life, however serious, which did not depend on exposition and discussion; and that in most cases conversation was a means, but that when it became an end in itself and was conducted for recreation's sake, that is, for its own sake, the theorist at last had some purchase on describing it: 'Then all the higher interests of life become in their turn means, and means for the purpose of recreation.' But for Mahaffy the practice of conversation cut across other precepts: even a consummate liar, though generally vulgar and therefore offensive, could attribute more pleasantly to a conversation than the scrupulously truthful man, weighing every statement, questioning every fact, and correcting every inaccuracy.[65]

Mahaffy always moved deftly from what he called the intellectual to the 'moral conditions' of conversation. He produced this rationale for his discussion:

> It is, of course, certain that these qualities are frequently congenital
> or constitutional, and that, therefore, the owner of them deserves
> no credit for possessing them. But as they are qualities enjoined
> upon us by moralists, and are in any case analogous to moral
> virtues, we may in this book, which does not affect precise
> philosophy, class them as moral.[66]

This seemed extraordinary in a book about conversation, but it was representative of the kind of enquiry which searched for moral origins and sought to apply the processes of natural science to the register of moral discourse:

> . . . the instinct of sociality, which is really the same as the
> gregarious instinct in birds and animals, is not the same as the
> love of our neighbour enjoined by the Gospel, but is closely
> connected with it, for to be social without being civil is not
> possible . . . This, too, appears to be why a class of social instincts

is so agreeable to men, and so honoured in society – their close
relationship to moral virtues.[67]

Social manoeuvres were also moral manoeuvres. The business of
maintaining moral purity involved abstaining from certain forms
of talk, avoiding those occasions on which impurities might easily
disgrace the lips; or an upright individual of tested moral worth
could be trusted to prevent the conversation from degenerating
into the profane, ribald and indecent.

The mid-Victorian social institution which revelled in exactly
those aspects of life which the conversation manual enjoined
against was the music hall. This form of popular entertainment,
reputedly started in 1852 by Charles Morton at The Canterbury
Arms, Lambeth, provided a repository of the undesirable and a
lexicon of the lewd, dressed in that most unbecoming of suits,
popular slang. The etiquette guides spoke out with a singular voice
against what they termed slang.

What slang was, and when it could be used, severely taxed the
Victorians. The man who was preferred over Martin Tupper for
royal favour, J. Hain Friswell, in 'The Great Question of "Slang"
in Writing and Conversation' from *The Gentle Life*, felt slang was
the great question of the day, 'when a female novelist calls *delirium
tremens* "Del. Trem.", and gets praise for her facility in using
mannish phrases and cant terms by one's Pet Review; and it may
be worth while gossiping [sic] about the use of that fanciful
verbiage which is spoken everywhere, which dwells upon the
tip of every tongue, and which in town and country is equally
understood and used'.

Friswell lamented the fact that everybody spoke slang, that high
and low life indulged in it, and yet that its name was 'a vulgar
one, nothing less than "slang".'[68] Mid-Victorian slang filled the
drawing room from many quarters, mostly in connection with the
activities which mid-Victorian society allotted to men: warfare,
sport, gambling, finance and popular journalism. For the upper
classes slang was a double-barrelled social weapon: a dangerous
sortie into low life to prove they knew the difference, and a refined
redefinition of language to exclude the unwary *arriviste*. Wilde's
Dorian Grey turns that downmarket impulse into a physical metaphor as Dorian visits the stews of East End London; Browning's

The Inn Album (1873) teems with upper-class card-playing slang which maintains gentility. *Punch* has a fine cartoon exchange from the 1860s:

> HOST: Nice party, ain't it, Major Le Spunger? 'Igh and low, rich
> and poor – *most* people are welcome to *this* 'ouse. This is 'Liberty
> 'All', *this* is! No false pride or 'umbug about *me*! I'm a self-made
> man *I* am!
> THE MAJOR: Very nice party, indeed, Mr Shoddy! How proud
> your mother and father must feel! Are *they* here?
> HOST: Well, no! 'Ang it all, you know, one *must* draw the line
> somewhere![69]

Friswell's worries were fed from situations like this. As the burgeoning forms of discourse – advertising, press, travel literature, science, novels, sermons – pressed in upon the mid-Victorians, their lives became more linguistically diverse than they had been thirty years earlier.

The mid-Victorians, in a pre-homogenised society, proudly and deliberately kept regional accents, some well into the 1880s. Most notable were the self-conscious ministrations of William Barnes in Dorset to mark out a provincial accent and imbue it with literary decency. But regional accents were felt to mark the speaker as provincial; that, for Mahaffy, could entail a great deal:

> [local accent] marks a man out as provincial, and hence is akin to
> vulgarity and narrowness of mind. It suggests too that the speaker
> has not moved much about the world, or even in the best society
> of his native country, in which such provincialism is carefully
> avoided, and set down as an index of mind and manners below
> the proper level.[70]

Examples of mid-Victorians with regional accents who succeeded in public life easily spring to mind: Gladstone with his Liverpool accent, Lord Derby with what Disraeli called his 'Lancashire patois', and Peel with his blend of Staffordshire and Oxford. By 1898 the government Education Department was prescribing to teachers the correct method of teaching vowel sounds;[71] this prescription was helped by the new science of elocution which had established itself in college appointments and university professorships, among them the great Professor Plumptre at King's College, London. So the Victorians of the 1870s and 1880s had an ear attuned to regional differences which translated easily into class differences.

After delighting in hearing in others' voices the very class differences which maintained his distance from them, Mahaffy wrote:

> . . . any one who hears the lower classes discussing any topic at the corners of the streets, may notice not merely their coarseness and rudeness in expression, but also the loudness and harshness of their voices . . . Contrariwise, nothing affects more at first hearing than a soft and sweet tone of voice.[72]

The street noise in Victorian cities was constant and intrusive, abating only rarely to let those soft and sweet tones pipe through. Mahaffy kept a sociologist's distance with his language of observation. He wrote as if the purpose of the voice were to affect and nothing more. He catalogued the minor slips and quirks which could mar a conversation, and concluded that the effect of these trifles was like the effect of other personal habits upon general reputation: 'If he be untidy, and neglect to wash his face or brush his clothes, he will require very sterling virtues to counteract the dislike which his appearance creates.' On the other hand, Mahaffy mused, 'if a man or woman be overdressed, and ostentatiously neat, the public at once infers triviality or shallowness of character'.[73] This recalls Carlyle's reaction on first seeing Browning, who was wearing lemon-yellow gloves. Lapses in sartorial or social diction involved a great deal. G. M. Young suggested that an unguarded look, a word or a gesture 'might plant a seed of corruption in the most innocent heart', and that the same word or gesture might betray a lingering affinity with the class below.[74]

Talking & Debating warned against politics and religion in matter, and provincialisms and cockneyisms in manner.[75] For if the subject matter fitted, then the accent (although nowhere near the uniform standardisation which radio, television and video have negotiated in twentieth-century 'received pronunciation') had to be free of regional dialect incomprehensible to one's fellows. Provincial accents translated directly into an attitude of mind (even

then one defined by others) essentially provincial. Yet a concept
of provincialism only works inside and alongside a concept of
nationalism. The intimacy of national identity with conversational
behaviour was glancingly noted by Frederick Jenner,[76] but more
directly by W. H. Griffiths in *The Human Voice*, which, for all
its scientific treatment of the voice as an instrument subject to the
proper functioning of the body, gives this:

> For conversational purposes also, the language is very characteristic
> of the solid determination and bull-dog tenacity of the English
> people, and it is probably this peculiarity which helps to make it
> such a universal and widespread mode of conversation.[77]

Mid-Victorian conversation displayed in its forthrightness and
surety the force of a national character as well as the personal.
The Revd J. P. Sandlands regarded public speaking, for him close
to conversation,[78] as an exercise in exactly this kind of force of
character, a national affair typically resting with the individual; he
compared the speakers of the 1880s with Demosthenes and Cicero:

> But we are no less than they are. We have the same, or at least an
> equal force of character, and we possess the same, or at least
> equal, mental powers. It remains, then, for us only to do as they
> did to produce the same results. We must feel that we possess
> powers and we must labour to make a way for them to display
> themselves.[79]

This strange relevance followed directly: 'We live in days of progress. Every art and science is advancing. Civilisation makes rapid
strides.'[80] The society he envisaged was all display, performance,
assertion, possession and power; the advance of conversational
standards was part of the process.

At this point, writings about conversation gave scope for speculation about the respective claims of various members of society
to talk to one another. The criterion of conversational competence
occasionally ceded to that of social standing. L. A. Tollemache on
'Literary Egotism' wondered whether the ordinary man or woman
talked too much about himself or herself, and whether, 'by one
of society's by-laws, certain classes of persons are not privileged

to do so more even than is usual'.[81] This was an informal disruption of an unwritten code. Good listeners made good conversers:

> It would be premature to lay aside our plea on behalf of
> conversational, or, if we may christen it by a shorter name, social
> egotism, until we have mentioned a case in which even persons of
> very ordinary attainments may sometimes be pardoned for
> talking about themselves – the case, namely, when they have
> nothing better to talk about.[82]

This was snobbishness wrapped in a smug cocoon of complacency.

Those whose talents could not find a scale for measurement outside their class were given some rights to speak in the novels of George Eliot and Elizabeth Gaskell. Other authorities warned that one should not suppose that all was right because others were silent: 'Numbers of modest, unobtrusive persons, who are able to converse pleasantly and well in a quiet, easy style, give way to loud, rapid, boisterous talkers, who haste always to snatch the first word, and hate them all the while.'[83] This amounted to social policy on the hoof, part of de Tocqueville's democracy of manners.

But in the performance society envisaged by Tollemache, it must have been strangely off-putting to talk well, like Disraeli or Gladstone or Milnes or Browning, in the knowledge that some people considered it the social duty of the eloquent and interesting to speak of themselves. Mahaffy wrote of the benefits:

> When the company comes together for the purpose of hearing
> some remarkable person, who is held out as the attraction of the
> party . . . this is truly the epideictic or *show off* style, in which the
> solitary speaker is supposed to delight and display himself
> without a rival, or with a rival silenced before him.[84]

Politics, publishing and social life all shared this combative style. G. W. E. Russell quoted Disraeli's talk in the *Spectator* for 5 August 1882:

> He talked like a racehorse approaching the winning-post – every
> muscle in action, and the utmost energy of expression flung out
> into every burst. Victor Hugo, and his extraordinary novels came

next under discussion, and D'Israeli, who was fired by his own eloquence, started off, *à propos des bottes*, with a long story of impalement he had seen in Upper Egypt . . . no mystic priest of the Corybantes could have worked himself up into a finer frenzy of language.[85]

In this company, the risk of disappointment loomed. One could disappoint by not talking, or by deliberately saying the wrong thing. Mrs Humphry Ward remembered a Kensington dinner party 'in '84 or '85' at which Browning, exasperated with the talk of the guest opposite, 'which was damping the conversation', began to quote Molière to his neighbour: 'the recitation lasted through several courses, and our hostess once or twice threw uneasy glances towards us, for Browning was the "lion" of the evening'.[86]

IV Conversation: its Uses and Abuses

When the influences broadened, the need for discrimination between them increased. Hain Friswell advised:

> Certainly he who endeavours to lead the Gentle Life, will not
> allow his tongue to catch up every idle trick of expression, and
> thus introduce into the drawing-room that which came from the
> gutter. Slang lames thought and clogs it with unmeaning
> repetition; if we think of what we are speaking, that mind must
> be a poor one which does not furnish its owner with language
> far better than slang.[87]

The drawing room and the gutter faced each other across a barricade of social poise. But the nineteenth-century secular world not only faced up to itself across the divides it had created; it also faced the moral imperatives of the sacred world. A stern religious vein ran through all strata of Victorian society and Victorian social practice.

The search for a set of regulatory principles for conversation stopped, for some, at the church door:

> If language be the gift of God, should it not be employed so as to

honour Him? and that, looking at it in this particular sphere, in its ordinary use in conversation? and, most of all, when employed for the expression of our highest thoughts upon the most sacred subject – religious conversation?[88]

Some theorists maintained that Christian values should regulate 'the whole of our conversation'.[89] This view left room for personal improvement along Christian lines, and, returning again to the issue of accomplishment:

> Without abandoning any of our sober good sense, or destroying
> the distinctiveness of our national character,[90] we may yet become
> more conversable if we will only turn our attention more to the
> rhetoric of conversation.[91]

Typical of the late nineteenth-century line on moral conversation was the Revd G. S. Bowes's *Conversation: Why Don't We Do More Good By It?* of 1886. Bowes gathered nineteenth-century religious musings about the moral potential of conversation. What interested him was the use of conversation for religious purposes. Conversation was for him a distinct branch of Christian usefulness, whereby Christians 'may glorify God, and be constantly helping to make life happier, brighter, better!'[92]

Bowes asked around his Christian friends, and found himself surprised to find how few had given moral conversation serious thought.[93] But while he was unclear what they should be serious about, attitude counted for everything; this specific religious seam surfaced well before Bowes in G. W. Hervey's *The Rhetoric of Conversation: With Hints Specially to Christians on the Use of the Tongue*. Hervey's book was introduced by yet another churchman, the Revd S. Jenner of Camberwell:

> 'The Rhetoric of Conversation' is a novel subject, attractive by its
> very title. We do not remember ever to have met before with
> any treatise on the use of that most important organ of our social
> existence – the tongue – in its relation to our social converse.[94]

Jenner's preface to Hervey maintained that the conversationist 'should be a man of high principle, if not of evangelical piety'.[95]

For the evangelical, the purpose of talking was clear: 'one end for which our tongues were given us was, that we might correct and improve each other'.[96] Here was the belief in the primacy of conversation and its role in communicating with others. Divines such as Bowes and Jenner pointed to a particular role for conversation in Christian conduct; this alone made it central to Victorian culture, but the issue of conversation and its uses spread further. Conversation was put to use:

> I have also carefully watched the general character and tone of conversation in ordinary life in the social intercourse of many people, in the home circle, in travelling, in social gatherings, &c., and it has struck me very forcibly how little is done, speaking generally, to redeem the opportunities of usefulness which are so frequently occurring every day.[97]

From the late 1870s even the most ardent nonconformists, short of social or constitutional grievance, were finding it hard to keep the redemptive spirit alive. Much of their zeal channelled itself into self-help manuals and books of conversational behaviour, its 'general character and tone'. This was clearest in advice on what to avoid. Jenner listed among the moral pitfalls of conversation 'Flattery & Praise', 'Detraction & Scandal', 'Interrogations & Impertinence', 'Egotism & Boasting' and 'Wit & Pleasantry'. Lapses in conversational technique became aberrations of character in a society of surfaces, where performance determined standing; lapses in conversational technique during a religious discourse revealed cracks in moral probity.

'By a well-ordered conversation,' wrote Bowes, '*we glorify God*.'[98] Bowes distinguished four planes for the well-ordered conversation: the Informational, the Cheerful, the Helpful and the Spiritual. But cheerfulness depended on 'good conscience', 'the spirit of thankfulness' and 'loving spirit'.[99] Helpfulness issued from the ability, in Bowes's words, 'to be continually leading others to see the value of right principles to follow out through life, and to be commending such principles when opportunities occur, in our ordinary conversation'.[100] The fact that these concepts were contiguous with Bowes's idea of 'ordinary conversation' showed how far the mid-Victorians had moved the notion of what it is to

The Descent of Manners

converse on to moral and spiritual ground by the latter part of the century. Therefore, speaking in the semi-public drawing room or at the soirée entailed a great deal. Much was at stake: one represented oneself by one's conversation.

The secular voice of *The Habits of Good Society* put it well: 'Since language is the exponent of character, it is necessary to refer to its abuse, as if it does not in all cases show a vulgar and pretentious mind, it is apt to render it so.'[101] Guarding against the corrosive effects and disastrous results of the abuse of language entailed a moral effort; a flickering anaesthesia of the conscience could entail serious consequences. Because of this constant watchfulness, many of the Victorians' most cherished notions of self-improvement, hard work, diligence, endeavour and accomplishment were put in service of the practice and conduct of a conversation. The vital mid-Victorian word 'improvement' still animated the late-Victorian thinking of Beatrice Knollys in *The Gentle Art of Good Talking*:

> It is a very educational age this – we are all bent on mutual improvement; and if we can acquire something like accuracy and elegance in our written and spoken expression, we feel a just pride in having subdued some of the roughnesses that beset our moral life, and of having required in their stead the polish that bespeaks refinement.[102]

This has accuracy and elegance refining moral roughnesses out of existence. The uneasy relationship between how something was said and its moral implications was another staple of the mid-nineteenth century. Since being polished and refined depended on avoiding those situations in which it would be possible to be otherwise, much rested on the choice of subject.

In 1886 J. P. Sandlands introduced his book *How to Develop General Vocal Power*:

> The book will be useful to the General Public. It will serve to brighten and sharpen articulation, and render conversation generally more intelligible. The careful observer cannot fail to notice the numerous and great deficiencies in this respect. The

76

reason is obvious, and may be expressed, – How should people speak well, having never properly learnt?[103]

Conversation was regarded not only as a way of helping others, but as a focus for self-improvement. One way of improving the delivery of the rigorously prepared material was to practise by studying the ultimate of all social and self-helps, elocution. The soirée, salon or 'at home' owed much to studies in elocution. Part science, part art, elocution produced terms and diagrams for the way the voice worked, and indicated how and where it could be improved. It also promised widespread social advantages for the individual.

The conversation and elocution guru Edwin Drew wrote in the *The Elocutionist* annual for 1889 that the real beauty of elocution lay in its availability for practice, wherever one went; a kind of portable gymnasium for self-improvement.[104] Drew certainly set conversation close to elocution, and both close to social competence:[105] 'the elocutionist,' writes Drew, 'can be always on show'. He struck a vital note when he touched on the aspect of performance in conversation; the delivery of anecdotes mattered as much as the content: 'It is said that writing is now become a common art . . . Let speech become a common art; for men should be taught the delights of delivery, and to this end all able elocutionary teachers should be sincerely encouraged.'[106]

Notions of what it was to converse shelved into notions of what it was to hold forth, and from there into matters of technique in public speaking. The grand rhetoric of the assembly hall waited at the end of the enterprise which began in the drawing room. Once communication with each other was seen in the terms of a public performance, then public performances shared common ground. *The Public Speaker's Vade Mecum* typified the writing of those who combined the techniques of elocution with the practice of reading aloud; it offered this advice to the intending speaker:

Another important rule to be observed in elocution is *Study Nature*, that is, study the most easy and natural way of expressing yourself, both as to the tone of voice and the manner of speech. This is best learnt by observations on common conversation, where all is free, natural, and easy, where we are only intent on making ourselves understood, and conveying our ideas in a strong, plain, and lively manner, by the most natural language, enunciation, and action. And the nearer our enunciation in public comes to the freedom and ease of that which we use in common discourse (provided we keep up the dignity of the subject, and preserve a propriety of expression), the more just, natural, and agreeable will it generally be.[107]

The parenthesis contains a notion of diction more familiar in literary discussion; reading itself became closely linked to conversation. Other forms of communication which privileged the speaking voice drew on conversational practice. George Vandenhoff in *The Art of Reading Aloud* applauded the 'merely natural or conversational style, for common-place subjects and occasions';[108] this raised the question, in the behaviour, elocution and etiquette books of the period, of what exactly it would be to speak in a conversational style.

Concerns bearing on the practice of conversation pressed on the Victorians from several directions: the writers of conversation manuals treated it as an art to be acquired; divines and teachers as a means of instruction; and elocutionists or public speakers as a model for delivery.[109] One of the foremost high Victorian theorists and practitioners of voice production, Charles Lunn, claimed in *The Philosophy of Voice* that voice production 'affects the pulpit, the platform, the forum, and the stage'.[110] All of Lunn's areas (and his differentiation of the stage and the platform showed a mind apt for accurate distinctions) figured large in the life of the nation during the second half of the century. The Victorians valued the oratorical and the public – talkers, public speakers and preachers. They also valued the attempt to discover a scientific grounding for the business of voice production; so Lunn asserted with assurance in 1880, 'It is *Fait Accompli*, I have founded a New Profession standing midway between the Musical and the Medical worlds, with Art on its one side, Science on the other; firm and irrefutable.'[111] His relief stemmed from the uncertainties he had undergone on the way to being able to say just that; for uncertainties and disappointments wait on most new discoveries, and final presentations conceal the pains of formulation. Lunn commented uncharacteristically on the essays in *Vox Populi*, 'they were wrung from my pen as a duty during a time of intense intellectual depression'.[112]

The science of elocution moved forward with Manuel García's development of the laryngoscope – enabling visualisation of the larynx – during the 1850s. Max Müller mentioned it in 1868; and by 1892 W. H. Griffiths commented in his *Human Voice* that, due to García, 'the human voice is no longer a sealed book to the student'. García was more famous for coaching the great Jenny Lind, but his technical achievement put him in the history of science books. So the growth in technical and professional interest in conversation coincided with the growth of the science of elocution. As more became known of the way humans made sounds, articles and pamphlets[113] appeared putting elocution in truly inter-disciplinary territory by giving diagrams of the vocal apparatus, hints on how to use the diaphragm for breath control, medical tips for singers,[114] comments on the nature of language,[115] and poems to read as part of a regimen in the drawing room or on the platform.

As the study of elocution and of conversation became more widespread, so the custom of reading aloud came under closer scrutiny in the home and at the theatre. At home, the evening or Sunday reading formed a vital part of the social process of the household. The great appeal of elocution for the mid-Victorians was its capacity to put conversation alongside literary, dramatic and musical expression as another way of using the voice. Some poems, for example, asked to be read aloud. In July 1876, the *Athenaeum* recommended:

> To properly enjoy this ['Hervé Riel'], as is indeed the case with almost all that Mr Browning has ever written, we must read it aloud, and then – to use a phrase as abominable as 'numpholeptos', or 'Aischulos' – the 'onomatopoeia,' or lilt of the thing, becomes not so much evident as infectious.[116]

The *Athenaeum* pleaded special attention for Browning's poems, a criticism which begins with the reading aloud of the matter in hand.

The Victorians were adept and habitual readers; a world before television, radio or widespread telephone and recording made

room for the speaking voice in the drawing room. Browning
provides a fascinating case. His own poems, for example, became
part of this aspect of Victorian social behaviour, first because some
of them – 'How They Brought the Good News from Ghent to
Aix', or 'Incident of the French Camp' – came to be read much
more than others; and second because they were less widely read
aloud than those of Tennyson. For a sense of what had become
canonical in elocutionary readings, the mid-Victorians turned to
one of the many elocution books which reprinted passages for
reading.

One such book, 'a standard work on the elocutionary art',[117]
*Voice, Speech, and Gesture: A Practical Handbook to the Elo-
cutionary Art*, showed three aspects of the elocution genre. There
were 'many works on the subject'; although in places execrable,
this comprises sections written by different authors, indicating
that there were several writers (as well as reviewers) interested in
the subject. According to one of them, Clifford Harrison:

> Perhaps no form of entertainment, or expression of dramatic art,
> has been so well abused and so mercilessly caricatured as has
> Recitation over the last few years . . . For who has not suffered
> from its evil and desolating claims to silence and a hearing at 'At
> Homes' and social gatherings?[118]

Harrison wrote of 'the over-strained popularity of *The Charge
of the Light Brigade*, or of *How They Brought the Good News
from Ghent*', and attested to 'the welcome an audience invariably
gives to *Amphion, The Brook, A Toccata of Galuppi's*, and *Abt
Vogler*'.[119] The 1870s and 1880s witnessed a growth in the recitation – in reading aloud to those who could read for themselves,
rather than for those who could not; reading had become performance. Trollope's journal gives an inventory of what he read aloud
to the family. Trollope obviously enjoyed longer poems, for the
list from 1876 includes Browning's vast poem *The Ring and the
Book*, as well as *The Faery Queen, Aurora Leigh, The Excursion,
The Odyssey* and *The Iliad* (both Homer and Pope, in both cases)
and *The Task*. But *The Ring and The Book*, unlike any other
entry, received two exclamation marks in the manuscript; even
Paradise Lost was listed without comment.[120] Browning's poem

presented a daunting challenge and represented a considerable investment in time; yet Trollope's reading aloud should not look unusual or aberrant.[121]

He also read prose to his family (Gladstone's *The Bulgarian Horrors and the Question of the East*[122]), and in this too he kept company with practice elsewhere.[123] Even professional academics allowed themselves to drift with the tide of change. For understanding a poem often depended on reading it aloud, just as part of the impact of poems such as Herbert's 'Easter Wings' or William Carlos Williams's 'The Right of Way' depends on seeing them. Hiram Corson, one of the early academic appreciators of Browning in America, read *The Ring and the Book* to his Cornell classes each year, and in doing so, reported Elizabeth Porter Gould 'reached a high opinion' of the poem.[124] James Stuart recorded a similar experience in a reminiscence of the Cambridge mathematician W. P. Turnbull:

> He had an extraordinary memory, and it was a specially good verbal one, so that he could repeat whole poems without a single misplaced word. He was the only person who ever made me understand Browning. When he repeated any of his poetry at all it seemed quite plain.[125]

Stuart found Browning not by discussing poetry but by recalling an individual reading style. Professional readers like Browning himself, Dickens, or Carlyle were frequently enjoined to read not in public but in semi-public. Mark Twain used to spend three days preparing for an hour's reading, indicating by underscore the shades of emphasis to be brought out. Twain said, 'I don't wish to flatter anybody, yet I will say this much: put me in the right condition and give me room, according to my strength, and I can read Browning so Browning himself can understand it.'[126]

Browning himself was a keen reader, of his own and others' poems. These readings belonged, as F. T. Palgrave suggested, in the natural social context of talk: 'Latterly he now and then dined with us. At this last house I had some long talks with him, when he spoke enthusiastically, and much, of his wife; and one day read over passages to me from *Troilus and Cressida* on love, with much warmth.'[127]

Browning also read aloud frequently to his family.[128] He regarded reading as a kind of *métier*, rather like a singer's performance: 'he was always pleased to read his poems aloud, and he also knew how to say the nice thing. "I will read to you, and in turn you shall sing to me." '[129] He read *Asolando* to Fannie Barrett Browning in Asolo: 'One evening before dinner he read from the "Asolando", and I remember how delightfully he read "The Pope and the Net" . . .'[130] However, he did not always read his own poems, or even poems. He frequently used to read out police reports – 'comparisons of these delinquencies with those of similar columns in other lands was really a source of delight to the poet'.[131] He also read sermons. On the penultimate Sunday of his life he read his own poems, but began the afternoon by suggesting the work of someone else. Fannie Barrett Browning again:

> But the Sunday before the last one of his life stands out alone from all the times I ever heard him read. All the household, everyone but he and I, had gone out and I was lying on the sofa when he came into the room and said he would sit with me a little while, and would read aloud if I wanted him to do so, suggesting one of Canon Melville's sermons.[132]

Before sermons could be read, they had to be gathered, written or transcribed. The collection of sermons represented one of the most enduring forms of Victorian literature; in that these collections were read aloud, on Sunday, just as Browning proposed, the reading of them became a social and political act in face of the parliamentary sabbatarianism of Sir Andrew Agnew, whose annual proposals to prohibit Sunday working fuelled the debate on the role of the Sunday in the life of the nation.[133] Browning's wish to read to his daughter-in-law was a typical Victorian impulse.

Collections of sermons suited Sunday reading because they dealt with devotional subjects; and reading aloud, because divines wrote them to be heard. Browning wrote:

> I am informed that a collection of sermons by the late Rev. Thomas Jones, of Bedford Chapel, has been made and will shortly be published. Among them may probably appear some of those I listened to a long while since, and I shall have curiosity as well

as interest in ascertaining how far the surviving speech – whether preserved by a reporter or printed from the author's own notes – will correspond in effect with the original extempore utterance, of which I retain a sufficient memory.[134]

Browning knew the difference between speaking and writing, while remaining fully aware of how the two interacted in a book of the written versions of spoken works. Speech could be preserved, but never exactly. When recitation put the written into the realm of the spoken, according to Clifford Harrison in *Reciting and Recitative*, 'It touches the material it uses, not only with the bare truth of an interpreting voice, but also with a force and delicacy that are its own,'[135] and introduces the reciter's distinct contribution.

Conversation, marked the point at which abstract moral codes interacted with social realities. The guides to etiquette functioned best where the codes were realities, where social practice loaded itself with moral cargo. Victorian notions about conversation depended on models of how people as members of a moral order interacted. Henry James in *The Question of Our Speech*:

All life therefore comes back to the question of our speech, the medium through which we communicate with each other; for all life comes back to the question of our relations with each other. These relations are made possible, are registered, are verily constituted, by our speech, and are successful in proportion as our speech is worthy of its great human and social function; is developed, delicate, flexible, rich – an adequate accomplished fact.[136]

3
At Home with the Great Exhibition

> Another chief characteristic of the English would seem to be
> their love of domesticity. Although in part the product of their
> climate (the damp cold of his native land doubles the English-
> man's desire for a comfortable home), this love is also one of
> their most commendable virtues and the basis of their achieve-
> ments as citizens.
>
> *Illustrieter London-Führer*

This was written by a German visitor in 1851, the year the Great
Exhibition defied the climate by creating its own under an enormous glass dome; it was also the ideal home. The claim that
the English love of domesticity was the basis of English civic
achievement showed how rooted the notion of home had become
by 1851, how central to the English ideal. Families, houses and
the national identity were intertwined. On 8 October 1853 the
Illustrated London News reported the laying of the foundations
at Balmoral:

> After a short prayer by the Rev. Archibald Anderson, of Craithie,
> for the welfare of its future inmates, a glass cylinder was placed
> by her Majesty in the cavity of the foundation, containing
> specimens of the current coin of the realm, and a parchment
> document describing the nature and date of the commencement of
> the building, signed by all the members of the royal family
> present, and the ladies and gentlemen in attendance. Her Majesty,
> having spread the mortar, the stone was lowered under the
> superintendence of the contractor for the works. Her Majesty then
> applied the square, level, plummet and mallet, and having
> ascertained that the stone was correctly placed, poured over it
> some corn, wine and oil. Immediately after the ceremony, the
> whole of the workmen employed on the new works, with their

wives and families, sat down to a dinner, prepared for them by her Majesty's command, in the temporary iron ball-room, where they danced afterwards in the evening.[1]

While twentieth-century America sent human artefacts to outer space, the Victorians in 1853 put their time-culture capsule in the foundations of a home. A semi-pagan libation ceremony and a big familial party crowned the event. The *Illustrated London News* created a news story out of the values which the anonymous author of *London-Führer* had made specific.

The *London-Führer* added that the English love of the home was likewise 'the basis of the marital fidelity which may be found in England, especially in the countryside. In no land,' the writer observed, 'are violations of marriage vows so severely and inevitably punished as in England.' The judge, jury and agents of the domestic scene were stern authorities: 'Neither rank nor wealth can protect against the penalties imposed both by law and social convention.' Home was always associated with ideas, environment with lifestyle, bricks and mortar with moral injunctions.

The Victorians turned marriage into a creed and the home into a domestic shrine. The ideal home, the 1851 Great Exhibition, was fittingly a vast transparency: the nation exposed the workings of its own most private imaginings, encouraging an inward gaze which at the same time was the most flagrant form of economic and imperial tourism. England's most magnificent public architectural achievement was a home pretending to be a public thoroughfare. The food consumed under the glass dome was consumed by middle-class visitors who felt at home. If café society flourished, and continues to flourish, on continental Europe in comparison with English domestic society, it speaks a different attitude to public space. Boulevard society never existed in England, even in the days of Dekker's *Guls Hornebooke*, in the early 1600s.

Mid-Victorian England was the last environment capable of building public spaces commensurate to the task of social cohesion and division, but chose the different, domestic route. If the idea of home reached its zenith in the 1850s and 1860s, then design for the home flourished in the 1870s and 1880s. William Morris used the home, as the Great Exhibition had before him, as a keyhole to a plenitude of elsewhere: medieval design in the Manchester labourer's cottage, crafted furniture in an age of increasing mass-production.

The home modelled Victorian thinking about the world, a pattern of behaviour imposed on what lay readiest to hand. That was the key to domestic life. Even if the rank and circumstances of a woman relieved her in a measure from the cares of superintending a household, she still faced the management for the whole family of its intercourse with others – what was called society; the less the call made on her by the duties of home, the more onerous the calls of society: the dinner parties, concerts, evening parties, morning visits, letter-writing, and all that went with them. This, thought Mill, was added to 'the engrossing duty which society imposes exclusively on women, of making themselves charming'.[2]

The home made an impact on three areas of mid-Victorian thinking: home values and values concerning women; domestic etiquette; and moral values seeking to make the rest of the world continuous with home life. These three broader concerns floated on the fluid social milieu in the 1850s and 1860s. Home was a way of thinking as well as a place to return to.

I Women and the Home

> What I should wish to see above all things is, not a race of learned women, but – what is necessary to their husbands, their children, and their households – intelligent, judicious women, capable of sustained attention, well versed in every thing that it is useful for them to know, as mothers, mistresses of households, and women of the world.[3]

This was written by a French commentator, Monseigneur Dupanloup, in 1868. A woman should, he argued, confine herself and her training to that which was necessary to the husband. This extraordinary statement followed:

> . . . the rights of women to intellectual cultivation, are not only rights, they are at the same time duties. This is what renders them inalienable. If they were only rights, women might sacrifice them; but they are duties. The sacrifice, therefore, is not possible without a dereliction of duty.[4]

86

The forces of social convention which shaped the lives of Victorian women worked through the agency of society and social custom, always pressing, always providing what the Victorians regarded as principled answered to everyday questions. Social conduct bore directly on the mid-Victorian woman in two ways: first on her role as the guardian and proprietor of the home and its values; and second on her role as an individual for the most part pushed to the side of her own life by the control of men over her. These pressures applied markedly to women of the mid-Victorian middle classes, for their welfare depended on the economic and social stability of the household.

The home provided mid-Victorian England with a concept wide enough to outflank the realities which challenged it. In a changing society, it offered the hope of stability and poise. Yet at the same time the omnivorous domestic scene absorbed dissent, continually re-created itself as technologies (mass production of furniture, gas and then electric lighting, integrated plumbing) required the household ethics to change as the house evolved technologically. The protean quality of the home forced its inmates to change with it, or stand out. So often with the mid-Victorians, values existed in ideal worlds created in parallel to the social and economic world.

Throughout the century public life became gradually more domesticated, as did, if George Augustus Sala can be believed, public space, with the rise of the club, another home from home created for men by professionals.[5] Homes, clubs and other institutions developed sets of elaborate rules in response to the growing social chaos beyond their doors: behaviour within set itself against misbehaviour without.

The Exhibition constructed a series of ideal worlds; the world of the perfectly furnished home was one of them: at its centre, the middle-class woman. It was an image which persisted into the 1870s. Mrs H. R. Haweis, who dissolved the gap between personal and environmental beauty by writing on both in the 1870s and 1880s, cites an 'Eastern Lady' pitied for dull harem life who in turn pitied the English women whose husbands 'locked them up in a box'.[6] But women – wives, daughters, mothers – were contained not only by the household they lived in, but by being associated with the things which both facilitated and circumscribed their social function: the furniture and decoration of their homes.

What was celebrated were the social processes hidden behind the exhibits; the conversation possible only at the tête-à-tête, the dance enabled only by the sofa that collapses into a brass bedstead, or the new dry-cleaning process that prolonged the life of carpet or tapestry. These were patterns of behaviour made palpable. The Exhibition's effect was of overwhelming plenty. A troubled Dickens found too many things there, a sensory overload. He complained of being 'used up' by it: 'I don't say there is nothing in it – there's too much. I have only been twice; so many things bewildered me. I have a natural horror of sights, and the fusion of so many sights in one has not decreased it.'[7] The Queen, however, a frequent and enthusiastic visitor throughout the 140 days of the Exhibition, wrote at Osborne in her diary for 9 August, 'At the Exhibition everything is brought together in a small space and one has all the advantage of seeing the different exhibits together.' Dickens's discomfort and the Queen's delight in what she called 'all that is useful or beautiful, in nature, art and science', derive from the same source: a temple to things.

The story of Joseph Paxton's design for what *Punch*'s Douglas Jerrold christened 'The Crystal Palace'[8] has become part of Victorian engineering folklore: the chance design meeting with Robert Stephenson on 25 July 1850 on the Derby-London train going south; the kindness of Isambard Kingdom Brunel, a rival for the contract, letting Paxton have the tree-heights in Hyde Park. Then followed 3,300 columns, 2,300 girders, and, in the year of window-tax repeal, the 1 million square feet of glass which made up the building. When the 14,000 exhibitors and 6 million visitors crammed into the Crystal Palace, Paxton had achieved his metamorphosis. From foreman in the Chiswick Gardens of the Royal Horticultural Society he had become Sir Joseph, cultural consultant and man of society. His success illustrated not only the Smilesian principles of hard work, self-culture and self-dependence, but also the Victorians' passion for technical achievement which subdued nature.

Ruskin's description of the building as a 'cucumber frame' saluted, albeit critically, the process behind Paxton's achievement. Paxton's models for the Crystal Palace – first the conservatory at

Chatsworth, then the Lily House (built on the ridge and furrow principle) – rested on the notion that a roof could regulate light and heat, that columns could channel water like drainpipes, and that a floor could be both a ventilator and a dust trap. The processes of nature were canalised and used in the construction of a building which was not just an engineering feat, but a triumph of nurture.

Under that blazing arch of lucid glass, the Victorians had evolved a new environment, a sparkling network of connection and inter-relation. This new, connected, autonomous environment consumed people and things throughout its summer's lease in Hyde Park. John Davidson disapproved:

> But come; here's crowd; here's mode; a gala day!
> The walks are black with people: no one hastes;
> They all pursue their purpose business-like –
> The polo-ground, the cycle-track; but most
> Invade the palace glumly once again.
> It is 'again'; you feel it in the air –
> Resigned habitués on every hand:
> And yet agog; abandoned, yet concerned!
> They can't tell why they come; they only know
> They must shove through the holiday somehow.
>
> In the main floor the fretful multitude
> Circulates from the north nave to the south
> Across the central transept – swish and tread
> And murmur, like a seabord's mingled sound.[9]

The amused, annoyed drone of Davidson describing the Victorians at play can still be heard above the ocean's long withdrawing roar.

The Exhibition championed inclusiveness; it set a cultural value on clutter and collection; it depended on categories which spilled 6,000 pounds of ink over nearly half a million volumes of the 2,000-page catalogue, 'a record of the most varied and wonderful objects ever beheld . . . a book of reference to the philosopher, merchant, and manufacturer'.[10] Mid-Victorian visitors returned home to reconsider their own environments. The Exhibition speeded the perceived process by which the old organic arts gave way to the new manufactured products, noticed with such concern by Francis Palgrave in 1840.[11] By 1880 the cultural critic and designer J. L. Stevenson echoed the design wisdom of the cognoscenti by writing, 'The Great Exhibition of 1851, it has been not untruly said, destroyed the last remnants of art in England. Everywhere, the old traditional arts are perishing.'[12] Traditional arts required no manuals, but new manufacturing techniques created new markets and demands as the organic ceded to the industrial and commercial. Just as there were guides to behaviour, so there were guides to buying, to accumulating, to servicing. In place of traditional arts, the Victorians opted for a bewildering array of shop-made extravagance without selection or meaning which yearned to be arranged.

Guides to household management and etiquette addressed the question of arrangement for them, but the crowding of Victorian things into jumbles of disunity left the field open for a unifying principle. It was found in the autonomy of the home, which contained the cacophony of things. The chief unifier was the woman. When men came to take pride in their 'interiors' the stereotyped image made them effeminate – in the case of Wilde and Charles Ricketts, appropriately so: Wilde lived up to his china, Ricketts decorated his Chelsea house (he and his partner, Charles Shannon, were known as 'the sisters of the vale') with lettuces.

Society had built the dream and the actuality of Paxton's Crystal Palace on the sound values which came to belong to Samuel Smiles later in the decade: self-reliance, self-help, self-dependence. The Victorians treated the Exhibition itself like a large home: well run, crammed with objects, and financially independent. *The Times* reported and shared the Royal Commissioners' delight in the non-intervention of government in the Exhibition:

> Those who have had experience only of the continental systems of exhibitions, which are managed and paid for wholly by their Governments, find it difficult to understand the self-supporting and self-acting principle of the present Exhibition, which has hitherto depended wholly upon the voluntary subscriptions of the British people; the heavy liabilities which still hang over the undertaking rest wholly upon individuals in their private capacity, and not upon the Government.[13]

Here at the height of national unity, as the century swung past its mid-point, that mid-Victorian distrust of government which shaped politics up until the second Reform Bill made itself felt.

In *English Traits*, Ralph Waldo Emerson noted that the conservative, money-making, lord-loving English still loved liberty; and through the Englishman's 'personal force' the nation resisted the immoral action of the government, wishing neither to be commanded nor to obey but to be kings in their own house.[14] In fact the Great Exhibition collectively affirmed the value of domestic self-help, and of home as well as national industry; it did so through affirming the value of household possessions.

The Exhibition section which bore directly on the home, and therefore on the woman's environment, was Class XXVI, which offered all species of decoration for churches, palaces and houses; upholstery, paper hangings, japanned goods and papier-mâché. In the 1850s, at a time when changes in art and manufacturing made new design quickly available, furniture could speak volumes; it did so famously in *Barchester Towers*,[15] where the Archdeacon lamented the intrusion of that 'almost irreligious' chintz sofa in the Palace; the sofa made a statement about the role and power of the Bishop's wife, who placed it there: modern, uncompromising, powerful. Dr Grantly found something 'democratic and parvenu in a round table . . . the most abominable article that was ever invented'; he suggested that dissenters and calico-printers chiefly used them, 'and perhaps a few literary lions more conspicuous for their wit than their gentility'. That was certainly true of the famous round tables at Punch and the Beefsteak Club (and later, Whites).

Influence through things engaged G. R. Porter in *Progress of the Nation*, which celebrated the 1851 middle-class home stuffed with paintings, engravings and the fruits of domestic labour, 'full of evidences that some among the inmates cultivate one or more of those elegant accomplishments which tend so delightfully to enlighten the minds of individuals and sweeten the intercourse of families'.[16] The notion of entertainment and cultural elevation underpinned the Exhibition's success, making its enterprise continuous with that of the home; the word 'inmates' seems awkward, because that describes exactly the role and status of women in the home in the 1850s, just as the royals at Balmoral were to be 'inmates' in their own palace.

The Descent of Manners

As 1830s Georgian interiors gave way to the clutter of the mid-Victorian house, work and maintenance increased in proportion to the bulk of objects to care for. In 1845 Tennyson wrote of Sir Walter Vivian's *objets* at his ancestral home; in 1864 Browning's 'A Likeness' caught the clutter of the dining room presided over by the woman:

> Some people hang portraits up
> In a room where they dine or sup:
>   And the wife clinks tea-things under,
> And her cousin, he stirs the cup,
>   Asks, 'Who was the lady, I wonder?'
> ''Tis a daub John bought at a sale,'
>   Quoth the wife, – looks black as thunder.[17]

This toyed nicely with the notion of what control of the household purse entailed; but it also imagined a disorder contingent on a wife's absence:

> Or else, there's no wife in the case,
> But the portrait's queen of the place,
> Alone 'mid the other spoils
> Of youth, – masks, gloves and foils,
> And pipe-sticks, rose, cherry-tree, jasmine,
>   And the long whip, the tandem-lasher,
> And the cast from a fist ('not, alas! mine,
>   But my master's, the Tipton Slasher'),
> And the cards where pistol-balls mark ace,
> And a satin shoe used for a cigar-case,
> And the chamois-horns ('shot in the Chablais')
>   And prints – Rarey drumming on Cruiser,
>   And Sayers, our champion, the bruiser,
> And the little edition of Rabelais.

Between the dates of these poems, 1845 and 1864, the mid-Victorian passion for filling available space continued unabated. In the 1850s the typical striped or trellised wallpaper, brocade curtains (sometimes with tartan pelmets, in tribute to the Balmoral vogue) and Brussels carpets were the backdrop to hour-glass ottomans, back-to-back settees alongside wax flowers and fruits under glass cases, clock and mantel ornaments *en suite*. All had to be cared for, orchestrated. Later in the century the pattern of domestic tasks became a basis for the middle-aged upper-class woman to erect a vast structure of time-consuming devices to conceal from herself how much time she had on her hands.[18]

The domestic domain had been cleared, colonised and allocated by the Great Exhibition to the woman. While the men attended to commerce and manufactures, to railways and steamships, the women took on the responsibility not only of the dispersal of furniture in the home, but, much more importantly, the interpretation of what the furniture *meant*. Life with a sofa or without an ottoman could be sharply different.

The taxonomic arrangement of the Exhibition catalogue provided, as if in anticipation of Darwin, an account of the role each piece played in the domestic hierarchy, its genus and species. Each had a name and use: the 'day-dreamer' chair, the 'bachelor' sideboard.[19] But furniture at the Exhibition could change roles: it witnessed an inventiveness in which men figured actively and women passively – men as designers and woman as end-users. J. E. Townsend exhibited a bedstead for invalids which converted into an armchair;[20] White & Parlby offered a ladies' work-table which could double as a writing-desk;[21] John Everest's ottoman switched into a chair (with commode enclosed);[22] and Elizabeth Rose's embossed screen into a chess-table.[23]

Just as individuals equipped themselves for change in the 1850s, so the furniture was determined to be flexible, multi-functional: Jennens and Bettridge exhibited 'The multum in uno' *papier mâché* loo table.[24] Pictorial furniture, popular in the mid-century but deplored by the 1870s, tried to be other than it was: so coal scuttles bore pictures of Warwick Castle; hearthrugs, dogs after Landseer; and screens, Melrose Abbey by mother-of-pearl moonlight. And if the furniture could not achieve inclusiveness by changing its shape, by becoming all things, it tried instead to arrogate all things to it: so a chromatrope table by Nye contained 129,500 pieces of wood;[25] while Arthur Jones's extraordinary teapoy (a lockable free-standing holder for tea), like the mid-Victorian England of Empire 'a receptacle for foreign produce',[26] daubed itself with scenes of Dublin's commercial, military, literary and scientific genius. Where the furniture could not change function its designers tried to alter the environment: for example, Sowerby & Castle made a geometrical ottoman couch 'constructed so as to assume various forms of drawing-room seating':

> It may be placed against a straight wall or round a corner, to form a semicircle round the tea-table or fire-side, or to make a central circular ottoman.[27]

Here, form suited social function; but function depended on the correct deployment of space in the Victorian home so that there was a tea-table and fireside to gather around. The impact of furniture and technology on ordinary domestic life was simply noted in 1842 by John 'Orlando Sabertash' Mitchell, who reported the French sense that English conversation was a languid silence broken by monosyllables, and by the water flowing every quarter of an hour from the tea-urn.[28]

Often it was social purpose, rather than strict domestic utility, that defined Victorian furnishing. The Chippendale was banished to the servants' attic in the mid-century. Furniture was developed which did not metamorphose, but subsumed many cultural functions in one piece. This cultural form kept faith with the long novel, elongated poem and the etiquette book in its ethic of inclusiveness. When a piece of mid-Victorian furniture had only one function, it tended to be wantonly specialised: either over-ornamented or oversize. The cult for vast furniture, best exemplified by the *Kenilworth Buffet* sideboard, inscribed after Scott's *Kenilworth*,[29] persisted in the examples of sideboards from Poole & Macgillivray,[30] Jackson & Graham,[31] or in Charles M'Clean's enormous ornamented console table and looking-glass.[32] While the mid-Victorian home made the love of objects into a creed of household ethics, it also made the woman chief among those objects, as it were, continuous with the furnishings she carefully maintained.

Training for the job started young. Lady Barker's *Bedroom and Boudoir* set out a bewildering variety of rules and principles for behaviour in household management. Prescriptive patterns lurked among the Morris Kidderminster carpets and the bedroom chintz. Each aspect of the house and of the running of it conformed to rules. In the bedroom, where ventilation reigned supreme, 'no soiled clothes shall ever, upon any pretence' be kept there, and the sleeper should leave the windows open:

> It is also an excellent rule to establish that girls should keep their rooms neat and clean, dust their little treasures themselves, and tidy up their rooms before leaving them of a morning, so that the servant need only do the rougher work. Such habits are valuable in any condition of life. An eye so trained that disorder or dirt is hideous to it, and a pair of hands capable of making such conditions an impossibility in their immediate neighbourhood, need be no unworthy addition to the dowry of a princess.[33]

The language here linked the patronising with 'their little treasures' and the moral with 'unworthy'. But the figure of the little girl in her own room persisted into the little girl's adulthood:

> How many of us mothers have taken special delight in preparing a room for our daughters when they return from school 'for good' – when they leave off learning lessons out of books, and try, with varied success, to learn and apply those harder lessons, which have to be learned without either books or teachers.[34]

The 'special delight' showed mother in her role as organiser and provider; the daughter trapped in hers as organised and provided for. The daughter's return, perhaps for a single life in the middle-class home, was anticipated by an arrangement of household effects. The house became a forum for self-assertion and for ratifying the functions which society asked women to fulfil.

As the high individualism of the early Victorians ceded to the conformity of the 1870s, self-expression turned inward. The textbook for the 1860s and 1870s, Robert Kerr's *The English Gentleman's House*, simply advised, 'take me as I am, and build my house in my own style'.[35] The nonconformism of this mediated the wish for individuality and the wish for correctness. Private life began to impinge on social process in architecture. The Loftie school advocated an integrated middle-class house, one in which everything happened as a consequence of divided use; while Robert Kerr, the first president of the Architectural Association (1847–8), urged a separatist view of the functions of rooms. Both originated in social behaviour: the former in an upwardly mobile middle-class design concept, the latter in a settled upper-middle-class context. In Loftie's parlour, grown-up sons and daughters could be given 'a little corner of their own . . . a place to write or draw, or read, or put by their work'.[36] In Kerr's drawing room, family members met after coming from private rooms.

House design, unlike poetry or art, was not individually driven, could not be accomplished by one agent; architecture yielded groups of ideas from bodies of opinion. More complex lives called for commensurate complexity in the home, and in its functions. So in 1880 J. L. Stevenson set out a series of principles for design which owe much to process and use within the house. He advocated the union of *multifariousness* with *isolation*; the century's demands for a house of 'a number of separate bedrooms, at least three public rooms, and a complicated arrangement of servants' offices' nonetheless had to negotiate with the principle of isolation which required separate communication to each room:

> With us, from our love of seclusion and retirement, each room
> must be isolated. A room loses its value to us if it is a passage
> to another. The dining-room must be capable of being shut off
> from the rest of the house, communicating during dinner only
> with the kitchen. The dinner should not have to be carried past
> the drawing-room door, or through the hall and public passages,
> and the kitchens must be so placed that their smells and noise do
> not invade the house.[37]

The house itself had an etiquette about its arrangement; certain parts of it kept aloof from others in functional terms. Hippolyte Taine's psychological observation that every Englishman and woman 'holds some part of himself or herself back, has a corner of forbidden enclosure which is respected by everyone', dovetailed with the physical layout of the Victorian house.[38]

Stevenson also advocated *unity* and *convenience*; the one to ensure the house's integrity, the other to make life easier for the occupants. However, convenience rarely figured as a major consideration, for the middle-class family needed rather to find tasks for its servants than to save them labour. London houses frequently situated the pantry on a floor different from the dining room: the arrangement gave life to the social metaphor of the lower classes, but in practical terms it meant that a request and its implementation entailed the climbing of two flights of stairs. Stevenson then urged *Compactness and Simplicity* in planning, which removed obvious expedients such as cut-off corners and steps down into rooms. *Light and Air* had to be adequately managed, like all other processes within the house, and *Heat* was to be deployed sensibly and without waste. Stevenson's final principles were purely aesthetic: the house's *Aspect and Prospect*, and the overall *Architectural Effect*.

Stevenson's useful book enumerated the various rooms properly belonging to a family house. Here was domestic architecture in social terms; the architectural ethic was in keeping with Stevenson's predecessor in these matters, Robert Kerr, who advocated in *The English Gentleman's House* 'no style at all, except the comfortable style if there be one'. The very environment which the mid-Victorian woman inhabited, in the predetermined social categories of daughter, wife, mother or spinster, was itself a dedicated environment with a range of special uses which excluded the woman.

As so few women architects worked to create houses for individual women, and as the exteriors of houses expressed the style and taste of owner and architect, who were usually men, this left little scope for the woman with designs. Dorothea Brooke in *Middlemarch* busied herself in designing labourers' cottages, albeit according to the injunctions of sanitary and health necessity. Mrs Haweis approved of Alma-Tadema's Townsend House in Regent's Park because individuality, she noted, asserted itself in every nook. She approved of the design work of William Wallace, praising him for stretching the space within the house by making features of structural fixities and deft use of colour.[39]

Questions of taste for the Victorians kept close company with facts of social status. Aesthetics, where debates hovered between proof and opinion, and yet where nobody thought a debate rested on *just* a matter of opinion, gave way to etiquette, where a raised eyebrow or inflected voice stood as both proof and opinion. Lucy Orrinsmith archly placed 'perchance' here to imply its impossibility, no-chance:

It becomes a social duty to strive to attain some guiding principles which may prevent an exhibition distressing to a visitor of, perchance, more educated taste than our own.[40]

In the house, as in personal appearance, trivial detail counted. Orrinsmith felt it impossible to overstress details which showed 'personal care for, and interest in, the decoration and embellishment of our homes'.[41] Bad taste, although sometimes apparently intuitive, derived from perverted taste, from habituation to the wrong models. William Bellars's *The Fine Arts and their Uses* put the matter simply enough:

The very fact that we speak of 'good taste' and 'bad taste', and generally conceive ourselves to be possessed of the former, shows that we do practically recognise some criterion, although we may theoretically deny its existence, or at least may profess ourselves unable to define it.[42]

However, the bases on which the Victorians made aesthetic decisions were often social and behavioural. And aesthetic judgment tended to become a register of education and social training; in the 1880s and 1890s the exclusivity of aesthetes depended on others' sense of standing in face of superior education. Orrinsmith dismissed a popular advertisement for a typical drawing room:

FINE ITALIAN WALNUT DRAWING-ROOM FURNITURE, comprising a luxurious lounge, lady's and gentleman's easy and six well-covered chairs upholstered in rich silk, centre table on massive carved pillar and claws, the top beautifully inlaid with marquetrie, large size chimney-glass in handsome oil-gilt frame, chiffonière with marble top, lofty plate-glass back and three doors; lady's work-table lined with silk, occasional table on spiral supports, two papier-mâché chairs and coffee-table to match, five-tier what-not, pair of handsome ruby lustres, and gilt and steel fender and fire-irons, with ormolu heads, & c., & c., & c.

'It may be safely affirmed,' she observed, 'without even seeing the particular furniture in question, that all the articles mentioned in the foregoing advertisement are objectionable from an aesthetic point of view.'[43]

The 1870s, perhaps responding to the influence of Morris, reacted against the heavy mid-Victorian interiors celebrated by the Great Exhibition; design books warned against over-ornament, and suggested the futility of making any material or thing into something it was not. *A Looking-Glass for Landlords*:

> However cheap, whate'er is bad eschew,
> Let all be real, all be strictly true;
> Shun all excess, avoid all vain expense,
> True taste is founded upon common sense.
> What most offends, what most the whole will damn,
> The sin no beauty can redeem, is SHAM.[44]

The subtle and less riotous interior structure mirrored the more settled social scene of the 1870s. The 1850s had seen a commercial feeding frenzy, an urgent desire to equip the home for a long journey through an uncertain life, but the 1870s were more sedate. The Hyde Park Riots of 1866 were a memory; the last of the great commercial crises had evaporated in 1867; the new Reform Bill had given society a sense of its own extent – of where the boundaries lay; the famine and railway mania of the 1840s lay beyond a lifetime's experience for many. Legislation in the 1870s was of an ameliorative rather than a remedial kind: the 1874 Public Worship Regulation Act, the 1875 Acts for Improving Artisans' Dwellings. The action was abroad: the Franco-German war of 1870, the Indian famine and the Ashantee war of 1874, the Bulgarian atrocities of 1876 and the Afghan war of 1878.

At home and abroad, as the Victorians divided and categorised everything, their lives became more specialised; this held true in house management – where Taine noticed that every servant had his duties defined,[45] and that no territory overlapped another – and for house decoration. In 1878 Rhoda and Agnes Garrett advocated, for a middle-class family, a professional decorator who also decided professionally on the colours and configuration of a room. The Garretts warned against over-ornament in furniture, the *en suite* chintz-covered chairs, the silk-panelled piano, the damask curtains in stiff folds. They treated the room as a frame or background best designed to set off the picture it contained. This was in design terms the social view that life in the home took place

against the stage provided by the rooms and furniture. They advocated harmony, simplicity and the decorative treatment of design.
Bedrooms in particular needed to be rooms fit to grow old and
die in: restrained patterns, movable carpets, plenty of ventilation.

In the 1860s and 1870s, the home was both the museum and
the laboratory for social intercourse. The curator of both was John
Ruskin. His *Sesame and Lilies* appeared in 1865, midway between
Mill's writing (1861) and publishing *On the Subjection of Women*
(1869). Ruskin's polemic for home values, for the situation which
Mill called 'domestic slavery', made itself heard just after the
passing of the first of the Contagious Diseases Acts (1864), and
at a time when Meredith's anti-domestic *Modern Love* had etched
itself on to the public consciousness.

Ruskin thought that education could not fit women for wider
duties 'until we are agreed upon what is their constant duty'.[46] If
women could be kept in the home and made to feel they naturally
belonged there, then society needed a set of principles for women's
behaviour. Ruskin provided those in a piece which has, for some
social commentators, displaced Mill's sane, liberal polemic as the
final utterance of mid-Victorian man's opinion on women:

> The man's power is active, progressive, defensive. He is eminently
> the doer, the creator, the discoverer, the defender. His intellect
> is for speculation and invention; his energy for adventure, for war
> and for conquest . . . But the woman's power is for rule, not for
> battle, and her intellect is not for invention or recreation, but sweet
> ordering, arrangement and decision . . . By her office and place, she
> is protected from all danger and temptation. The man, in his rough
> work in the open world, must encounter all peril and trial – to
> him therefore must be the failure, the offence, the inevitable error;
> often he must be wounded or subdued, often misled, and always
> hardened.[47]

The home preserved from outside threat a set of values which
Ruskin enumerated as the true nature of home. It was the place
of peace; the shelter, not only from all injury, but from all terror,
doubt and division. Ruskin kept the outer world at bay, for if
its anxieties penetrated, and the inconsistently-minded, unknown,
unloved or hostile society was allowed 'by either husband or wife

to cross the threshold it ceases to be a home; it is then only part of the outer world which you have roofed over and lighted fire in'.

The mid-Victorians were most afraid of the idea of non-home: the street, the workhouse, the shame of not belonging. Home itself provided a tangible representation of the values of married life.[48] Ruskin saw it as 'a sacred place, a vestal temple, a temple of the hearth watched over by household gods, before whose faces none may come but those whom they can receive with love – so far as it is this, and the roof and the fire are types only of a nobler shade and light, shade as of the rock in a weary land'.[49] The woman's role in this ethical drama of abstracts was paramount:

And wherever a true wife comes, this home is always round her.
The stars only may be over her head, the glow-worm in the
night-cold grass may be the only fire at her foot, but home is
wherever she is; and for a noble woman it stretches far round
her better than ceiled with cedar or painted with vermillion,
shedding its quiet light far for those who else were homeless.[50]

Popular versions of this persisted into the 1880s, with E. J. Hardy's *Manners Makeyth Man* laying down lines of behaviour for women to travel along: 'Sweetness is to woman what sugar is to fruit. It is her first business to be happy – a sunbeam in the house . . . it is not every woman who remembers that her *raison d'être* is to give out pleasure as a fire gives out heat.'[51] The woman faced with living up to these metaphors was circumscribed by society's images of her scope and capacity.

The power implicit in seeming to give all power away was the power exerted by the Victorian husband or father over his partner and children. Two years after Ruskin, this, from *The District and Parish Helper*, 1867:

A judicious wife is always snipping off from her husband's moral
nature little twigs that are growing in wrong directions. She keeps
him in shape by continual pruning. If you say anything silly, she
will affectionately tell you so. If you declare that you will do
some absurd thing, she will find means of preventing your doing
it. And by far the chief part of all the common sense there is in this

world, belongs unquestionably to woman. The wisest things a man commonly does are those which his wife counsels him to do. A wife is the grand wielder of the moral pruning-knife . . . steady; they are the wholesome, though painful, shears, snipping off little growths of self-conceit.[52]

The castrating energies of this, from one of the more innocuous periodicals of the period, show the man's sexual identity under threat. 'In shape by continual pruning' strikes the twentieth-century ear strangely; it sounds painful, but it also represents a vivid metaphor of moral process.

Women themselves, contented or discontented with their domestic lot, made great sacrifices. Eldest daughters and elder sisters were advised by Mrs William Fison in 1850 to lead by example and to 'curb your own spirit; to watch every outbreak, and to see to it that the youngest member of your circle, are all treated with the courteous and gentle bearing which belongs to your character as a follower of your meek and lowly master'.[53]

As the home milieu became more important throughout the century, its widening scope demanded commensurate management styles to run it. The absorption of new felicities of taste meant that new forms of help became necessary to maintain the home: cleaners, cooks, engineers, maids, nursemaids. The home always revolved around the ideal of the woman. And the ideal woman stood in relation to the mid-Victorian woman as the hero stood in relation to Carlyle's worshipper. The womanly ideal filled the lack of practical ambition with a plethora of practical advice. So in the 1860s, middle-class women were trained in one or two languages, the piano, drawing and fancy-work. These, with light reading, filled the days, months and years until they were eighteen, 'and then they are turned into the world to devote their time and talents to trimmings, novels, and tittle-tattle disseminations in morning calls'.[54]

By 1867 the *Saturday Review* thought that this state of affairs encouraged a woman to think no further than marriage, made her indifferent to politics and literature, 'in a word, to anything that requires thought'.[55] While the education issue raged in Eliot, Dickens, Kingsley and even Newman, little illuminated the problem of women's education, for questions about women's education raised

questions about their educators. In 1886 Charlotte Mason asked
'a question sufficiently puzzling to the heads of households: What
is to be done with the girls? About the boys there is less difficulty
– they go to college, or they go to learn their profession.'[56] Mason
arrived at this question after setting out a programme to educate
mothers to educate children which read like a version of Samuel
Smiles fallen short. She put her faith in a system in the home:

> System – the observing of rules until the habit of doing certain
> things, of behaving in certain ways, is confirmed, and, therefore,
> the art is acquired – is so successful in achieving precise results
> that it is no wonder there should be endless attempts to straiten
> the whole field of education to the limits of a system.[57]

Mason recited the litany of Victorian ideals for children and the
mothers who educated them: 'out-of-door geography', 'out-of-
door games', good nourishment, pure air and free perspiration
figured large. But she insisted that children should be confronted
with the most Victorian of all things, things themselves. So 'we
owe something to Mr. Evans for taking his little daughter Mary
Anne with him on his business drives among the pleasant War-
wickshire lanes',[58] even if Robert Evans bequeathed to another
daughter the set of Scott which Eliot had read to him.

Mason's project fitted perfectly with the ethic which animated
all books of instruction, educational and social: 'the formation of
habits *is* education, and *Education is the formation of habits*'.[59]
Games such as cricket, tennis and rounders shaped the muscle,
sharpened the eye, but above all served the moral purpose of
'bringing the children under the discipline of rules'.[60] Here, the
belief in the power of rules to affect behaviour combined with the
sense that 'exactly anything can be accomplished by training'.[61]
Theory was brought to bear on practice.

This exactly matched the ethic of the etiquette book. The process disclosed itself in Mason's move from 'moral qualities' to
'training':

> Certain moral qualities come into play in alert moments, eye-to-
> eye attention, prompt and intelligent replies; but it often happens

that good children fail in these points for want of physical training.[62]

Infant habits, cleanliness, order, neatness were the vanguard of moral qualities, affections and passions – 'so too,' wrote Mason darkly, 'of conscience, the sense of duty', neatly internalising the one guiding rule – duty – to make social behaviour bear directly on the operation of the conscience.

Later, Mason urged 'obedience' as the 'whole duty of the child'; but it was also the 'whole duty of man – obedience to conscience, to law, to Divine direction'. The interplay between behaviour and moral standing everywhere informed Mason's thinking. She championed the habits of attention, application, thinking, imagining, remembering, as moral habits;[63] she recognised the link she forged between morals and conduct: 'rewards should be dealt out to the child upon principle: they should be the *natural consequences* of his good conduct'.[64] As the child grew, habits became the 'outworks[65] of character'[66] where character was both worked out and worked outwards. Mason stated plainly, '*character* is the result of conduct regulated by will'.[67]

In America, the same questions of women's education presented themselves in the same terms: Thomas Higginson speculated on the benefits of recognising 'that girls as well as boys need strength of will'.[68] But the English orthodoxy was that what girls stood most in need of was instruction in how to behave. The etiquette book came to be seen as a version of self-education or self-help for women, as if to know how to behave was to know everything. Hippolyte Taine knew something of this, and noted that in the English household, rules and discipline were more strictly kept than in the French: the 'social fabric loosely woven in France, firmly woven in England'.[69]

The user's manual for the home was the book of household management and the etiquette book. Both were forms of platonism; while novels tended to dissent from social rules by providing a gradually sharpening psychological account of behaviour *at the same time* seeming to reflect and ratify forms of behaviour, the etiquette book simply delivered society's dreams in a pocket-sized form: the reader could take the book anywhere, and the book could take the reader anywhere. Moreover, because etiquette books appeared to have no political bias, they seemed to represent the world as an agglomeration of ideals. They were the 'self-help' books of the domestic scene. *How I Managed My House on Two Hundred Pounds* (1864) by the prolific and influential Eliza Warren, started *in media res*: 'My children were all around me,' she wrote, 'before I had devised any certain method of managing my household affairs.'[70] But what were those household affairs? The social fabric of one part of mid-Victorian life was woven on threads which stretched from parties, visits and offices of society which took place in the home. This was the place for social manoeuvrings, a comfortable environment in which to put the etiquette to use.

II Home Etiquette

Books of household management, etiquette and memoirs between the Reform Bills showed men and women advancing towards a division of labour which in itself was a labour of division. The home environment, physical surroundings, dress and modes of behaviour available to the mid-Victorian set out the rules by which individual personality became a social category.

Books of etiquette sat politely alongside books on household management, for the two were intimates at this period. Following Margaret Dodd's *Cookery Book*,[71] Eliza Acton's *Modern Cookery in all its Branches* was popular in the 1840s; it resulted from her frankness about market forces to her publisher, Longman: 'Give me the subject of a book for which the world has a need,' she wrote, 'and I will write it for you. I am a poet but I shall write no more poems. The world does not want poems.'

Acton's book was a lifestyle guide to social process across the dining table. But the most enduring of the cookery-society books continues to be Isabella Mary Beeton's 1861 masterwork, which gathered far more than just recipes; Beeton herself ran a tight household, and fitted in four children as well as the cookbook before her death in her late twenties. Her husband, Sam, edited *The Englishwoman's Domestic Magazine*, dishing out advice to the timid and admonition to the bold. Both Beetons thought dining was the first privilege of civilisation. Isabella claimed that the rank which people occupied in the grand scale could be gauged by how they took their meals, as well as by their way of treating women.

For example, the vexing question of the point at which the ladies should retire from the table was not just a matter of the men no longer drinking themselves to incapacity, but an issue of an increased delicacy of conduct in keeping with the levels of esteem in which Beeton felt women were held. The nation which knew how to dine had learnt the leading lesson of progress. Discussion of these matters fell under the ægis of household management, for behaviour at table formed part of the household environment. After Beeton, the cookbook faced up to its broader responsibilities, reflecting this in the title; Mrs Rundell's *New System of Domestic Cookery, formed upon Principles of Economy and Adapted to the Use of Private Families* caught the Victorian sense of the reducibility of all experience to a set of principles at the same time as broadening the available experience.[72]

Cookbooks were sensitive to changes in eating style: the Epergne for dispensing fruits at table; the popularity of service *à la russe*, which required few plates, not general until the 1870s, which cut the number of dishes from service *à la français* which required separate plates for each dish. This speeded the meal, and reduced the paraphernalia at table. These seemingly small alterations had a palpable effect on Victorian lifestyle. Thackeray predictably, had commented on this in *Snobs*:

> If I had my way, and my plans could be carried out, dinner-giving would increase as much on the one hand as dinner-giving snobbishness would diminish . . . the 'dinner at home' ought to be the centre of the whole system of dinner-giving. Your usual style of meal – that is, plenteous, comfortable, and in its perfection – should be that to which you welcome your friends, as it is that of which you partake yourself.[73]

Thackeray further related the plate – 'mere shiny Birmingham lacquer' – to the hospitality, making the link between dining paraphernalia and dining behaviour even clearer. Mrs Loftie used part of Thackeray's castigations in rearranged form in *The Dining-*

Room (1878), showing how these concerns stretched down the century to Loftie's wider social public.

Beeton's recipes and Thackeray's plates had to find the appropriate setting. *The Dining-Room* offered an exacting blend of practical and moral advice: the room should contain the facility for boiling water, heating soup, making coffee by fire, spirit-lamp or gas; the table should be of solid wood, not easily marked by hot dishes, 'but of late years,' Loftie pronounced, 'since the old habit of taking off the cloth after dinner has gone out, it does not much matter except on high moral grounds, whether the top is of mahogany or deal'.[74] Chairs too varied with women's fashion, affecting and affected by their behaviour, for the wearers of wider crinolines needed a different kind of support from that 'on which the well "tied-back" lady of the present day [early 1870s] can sit comfortably'.[75]

The dining room and drawing room remained sensitive to fashion – and in particular women's fashion – because they remained pre-eminent as the arenas for social exchange: 'as conversation is supposed to belong especially to the dinner-table, it will be well in this case to give our fair readers,' urged *Modern Etiquette*, 'some hints on the subject'.[76] From the standpoint of conversation training, J. P. Mahaffy found matters of social ordering depended not only on the determination of manners and customs, but on the disposition of the furniture.

Carlyle visited the Queen on 11 March 1869. Another visitor was Mrs George Grote, famous for wearing men's clothes, showing her ankles, and never having felt shy. After the introductions and acknowledgments:

> ... coffee (very black and muddy) was handed round; Queen and three women taking seats in opposite corners, Mrs Grote in a chair *intrusively close* to Majesty, Lady Lyell modestly at the *diagonal* corner; we others obliged to stand, and hover within call. Coffee fairly done, Lady Augusta called me gently to 'Come and speak with her Majesty.' I obeyed, first asking, as an old and infirmish man, Majesty's permission to *sit*, which was graciously conceded. Nothing of the least significance was said, nor *needed*; however, my bit of dialogue went very well ... Whereupon Mrs Grote rose, and good naturedly brought forward her Husband

[the philosopher George Grote] to her own chair, *cheek by jowl* with Her Majesty, who evidently did not care a straw for him, but kindly asked 'Writing anything?' and one heard 'Aristotle, now that I have done with Plato,' etc., etc. – but only for a minimum of time.[77]

The solecism lay in the proximity: what shocked Carlyle was the redoubtable Mrs Grote's literal forwardness. Sydney Smith had, after all, always claimed Mrs Grote as the originator of the word grotesque. The disposition of the room, the layout of the chairs, was an image of the social relations between the characters in the drama. Just as the Barcelona or the Vassily chair in the 1920s imposed a certain kind of behaviour on their occupants, so Victorian furniture was intimate with Victorian etiquette.

The proximity and manner of being seated was all-important. John Mitchell kept behaviour and furniture close together when he complained of the vogue for lounging:

> . . . by *nonchalant* airs of affected ease and freedom from restraint, which I must here denounce as a breach of good manners . . . I mean the practice of lounging in graceless attitudes on sofas and arm-chairs, even in the presence of ladies. All these vile and distorted postures must be reserved for the library-couch, or arm-chair, and should never be displayed in the society of gentlemen, and still less in the society of ladies.[78]

The Victorians favoured furniture which kept people at a distance: the ottoman, the tête-à-tête chair, the chaise-longue for one. Moreover, on public occasions they arranged themselves on their furniture in order to keep their own distance; people deployed themselves in the same way that the objects around them were deployed. It was not usual to have a tête-à-tête with another person of the same sex without actively choosing your companion and seeking out the opportunity; two people of different sexes were often brought together and ordered (so to speak) to converse, 'for no other reason than the command of society'.[79]

That 'command of society', its social and economic realities, dictated the behaviour of the courting couple. The home was one of the principal venues for courtship. Etiquette guides tended to treat the matter and manner of engaging the opposite sex in conversation as, initially at least, part of the social mechanism surrounding conversation. In matters of courtship, the rules of home applied first, regulated the meetings and the duration of visits. Privacy was the premium, as Robert Browning's assignations with Elizabeth Barrett at 50 Wimpole Street in 1845 and 1846 showed.

The etiquette of courtship amounted to a subset of the etiquette of social relations invariably based in the home. Everything came back to conversation, the first contact between individuals. The language of courtship differed little from the language of polite conversation, for the etiquette guides were always advocating consistency across all social relations. The whispered hints and guesses between men and women after dinner *a quattr' occhi* were more a matter for the novelist than the social scientist.

The mid-Victorian attitude to courtship as a social act was consistent with the overall approach which evolved in the rapidly-changing 1850s and 1860s.

The mid-Victorians reinterpreted all acts as social acts, and this included the act of furnishing a room. This was a preparation and groundwork for the social etiquette which was to take place there, a meticulous preparation of the scene beforehand. The broadening religion of the home made almost anything acceptable if the woman performed it. But success, when it arrived, was defined in men's terms. The *Saturday Review* made the issue serious by refusing to take women seriously:

> Women are universally admitted to be the adroitest masters of the
> diplomatic art. They play the part in the comedy of modern life
> which was allotted in the drama of less civilized ages to Davus and
> to Syrus, and they play it much better. The heroine of 'Vanity
> Fair' is more entertaining than Davus or Syrus, because she works
> naturally and easily, and without resorting to the coarse
> expedients of lying, or stealing, or worse. All is effected by real
> finesse; and, above everything, women are perfect in what has
> been justly called the most subtle of all forms of finesse – 'de
> savoir bien feindre de tomber dans les pièges qu'on nous tend'.
> The skill of the diplomatist can go no further than this. Whether
> it is artifice or tact is one of those nice questions which it is

perhaps not consistent with the rules of gallantry to examine too closely.[80]

This clearly set out standards for success and failure in social life, even if it did flirt with the fear of women's capacity in 'she works naturally and easily'. By supporting an ethic which balanced success and failure by weighing behaviour, the etiquette book shared the presuppositions of other quintessentially Victorian activities which depended for their outcome on the judgment of others: just as business, entrepreneurial and manufacturing projects all fled from failure as much as rushed to success, so the social world fortified itself against the chaos of everyday life by building ramparts which limited the boundaries of success and failure, and also set limits on the extent to which failure might be felt by the individual. Rarely do these guides advise departure from the crowd; instead, propriety comes to be just another form of conformity.

The knowledge and education habitually given to men became one route of dissent for the women who challenged home values, either through their work in art, literature or science, or through their lifestyle – and this meant dissenting from their fathers. The family circumstances of Barrett Browning, Brontë and Eliot showed these writers confronting paternal disapproval, encouragement, possessiveness or pride, and bear witness, for a particular kind of commentator, to 'the extraordinary dependence of female talent on male direction'.[81] Barrett Browning felt that the evil lay in the system, and that her father simply took it to be his duty to rule.[82] On seeing her son, Penini, in London for the first time, he commented, 'Whose child is that, pray?' Father and daughter were unreconciled at his death in 1857; he had encouraged her when she was young, stifled her when she was grown up, and ignored her middle age.

The Victorians' male heroes either rise above the hostility or indifference of their home environment, or react hostilely or indifferently themselves; the well-known case of Samuel Smiles, one of eleven children; George Stevenson, second son of a fireman at Wylam Colliery; Alfred Tennyson, whose father indulged in drunken, violent outbursts; Trollope, whose useless father and dynamic mother left little room for him; Disraeli, whose father never understood him; Palmerston, whose parents died before he was twenty-one; Gladstone and his overpowering father, or Macaulay and his; and of course John Stuart Mill and his rigorous father. F. C. Anstey's *Vice Versa* played the now familiar role-reversal trick in 1882 where father and son swap places but not minds.[83]

Men had the choice of leaving home, setting up another. (Some, like Browning, had the choice, but scarcely left.) All women, young, middle-class and mid-Victorian, either stayed and conformed as ageing daughters, or left as new wives; the alternative to those options was the unpleasant prospect of becoming – according to class – a governess or factory worker. Men survived the ordeal by being programmed to leave the family, or allowed by society to live without it. They may, like railway pioneer Daniel Gooch, have been subject to an intensely ambitious parent. His mother used to say each day as he left for work, 'Ever remember, my dear Dan, that you should look forward to being some day manager of that concern.' But men rarely suffered the daily rigours of rules governing their behaviour not only in the home, but in the arrangement of home affairs.

The mid-Victorian woman's role in the middle and upper classes was rooted in two sets of social relations: the family and 'society'. There was an acute problem of 'redundant women', and no one made the redundant feel more vestigial than her helpers, who were invariably other women. In 1851 there were 750,000 female domestic servants, and 25,000 women in the curious situation of governess (a woman who taught in school, lived at home and travelled to her employer's to teach, or who lived in as a teacher).

The treatment of the governess was the test of etiquette. Good manners required that she be included; etiquette that she be reminded that she was not one of her employer's family. The proximity of the relationship eroded the economic fact of the governess's life. The discomfort of a governess's position in a private family arose from the fact that it was undefined; she was neither relation nor guest nor mistress nor servant, thought the proto-feminist Elizabeth Sewell in 1865, 'but something made up of all. No one knows exactly how to treat her.'[84] Foreign governesses in England fared better, not because of any alteration in their station, but largely because of their ignorance of English customs.

The Descent of Manners

It came down to etiquette. Elizabeth Eastlake saw the problem on the horizon in 1848:

> The real definition of a governess, in the English sense, is a being who is our equal in birth, manners, and education, but our inferior in worldly wealth. Take a lady, in every meaning of the word, born and bred, and let her father pass through the gazzette [bankruptcy], and she wants nothing more to suit our highest *beau idéal* of a guide and instructress to our children.[85]

Sarah Stickey Ellis, in her 1843 *The Wives of England*, had warned against 'the loss of character and influence occasioned by living below our station'.[86] The difficulty was felt by all, including the governess:

> She is a bore to almost any gentleman, as a tabooed woman, to whom he is interdicted from granting the usual privileges of the sex, and yet who is perpetually crossing his path. She is a bore to most ladies by the same rule, and a reproach, too – for her dull, flagging bread-and-water life is perpetually putting their pampered listlessness to shame.[87]

The appearance of a free radical in the settled formula of home life could produce volatile results. This from *Governess Life: its Trials, Duties and Encouragements* (1849):

> Frightful instances have been discovered in which she, to whom the care of the young has been entrusted, instead of guarding their minds in innocence and purity, has become their corrupter – she has been the first to lead and to initiate into sin, to suggest and carry on intrigues, and finally to be the instrument of destroying the peace of families ... This kind of conduct has led to the inquiry which is frequently made before engaging an instructress, 'Is she handsome or attractive?' If so, it is conclusive against her.[88]

Home etiquette helped, via a set of easily observed rules, to police the conduct of all the women in the household. Yet the etiquette at the same time appeared to be originated by women themselves. Women's home etiquette also established a division between men's behaviour in and out of the home. Mill had observed that men's lives were more domestic than ever before; as popular opinion had turned against the rougher amusements which had hitherto occupied most men outside the home, it threw the man back on the resources of the home and its inmates for personal and social pleasures.

Frederick Warne published a representative guide to etiquette for women in 1871 which issued from and pointed towards the stability of upper-middle-class home life: 'the nurse takes care that the children get nice habits and are civil and courteous; the governess, at home, or at school, gives *her* share of the same training, and the habits of the home society complete the formation of the young lady's manner, under the *surveillance* of the mother'.[89] *Modern Etiquette* recognised both a 'grammar' of society and the necessity of learning it.

That year, 1871, population returns for England and Wales listed 11,058,934 men and 11,653,332 women; the surplus of women had commentators writing until the end of the decade on the necessity for women to present themselves well-shod for the inevitable journey down the aisle. Real social mobility belonged to men; their women travelled with them. The growth of status groups and the obsession of the aristocracy with access to their ranks witnessed the threat of new wealth and new forms of life; but access could occur and maintain itself only through the upkeep of forms of manners: a middle-class yen for a fish-knife at an upper-class dinner in the 1860s or 1870s could return the miscreant to the lower stratum in an instant, for especially at the dinner table social solecisms were obvious, and irredeemable.

Matters were serious enough to be parodied by Mrs Loftie, who cited the battle of the forks, three or four prongs: 'The "three-prongians" hold their own against the "four-prongians", except in the matter of young peas.'[90] In this world of self-furtherment, achievement, geographical mobility, the home was the only place where practising the skills for regulated social life made consistent sense; and in such a highly formalised society, women become the stable centre. As distinctions in rank became less marked, responsibilities devolved to women:

... the circles of good society are so constantly receiving into
themselves the man who has risen from the cottage or the
workshop, a knowledge of these social laws becomes important
for his wife and daughters; and can best be acquired, we
believe ... from a book than from a living teacher.[91]

The principles which underpinned the advice directed at women
invariably came from an interpretation of Christian morality
applied to the home. Charles Kingsley spoke for many mid-Victorians when he found religious observance in the very conduct of
everyday social relations and family duties, especially for women.[92]
This meant that the mid-Victorian precepts which yielded love,
joy, peace, long-suffering, gentleness and goodness for society
were readily applied to the smallest of social transactions.

The elaborate etiquette of morning calls illustrated this simply.
The practices of visiting and the leaving of cards figured as highly
structured forms of social exchange, the participants indicating
their own complicity by devising rules of gathering complexity.
The complexity rolled down the century like a runaway train
gathering speed. *The Lady, a Magazine for Gentlewomen* hinted
at these complexities; in the late twentieth century only the options
available from a combination of telephones, portable telephones,
answering machines and secretaries have begun to rival calling-
card rigour:

> There is very strict etiquette in this matter of cards and calls and
> there is one essential difference between *calling* and *leaving cards*.
> It is usual on paying a first visit merely to leave cards without
> inquiring if the mistress of the house is at home. Thus Mrs. A.
> leaves her own card and two of her husband's cards upon Mrs. B.
> Within a week, if possible, certainly within ten days, Mrs. B.
> should return the visit and leave cards upon Mrs. A. Should Mrs.
> A., however, have 'called' upon Mrs. B. and the latter returned
> it merely by leaving cards this would be taken as a sign that the
> latter did not desire the acquaintance to ripen into friendship.
> Strict etiquette demands that a call should be returned by a call
> and a card by a card.[93]

Exact fences make exact neighbours. In 1894, in Edinburgh, a
mourning Margaret Oliphant declared herself 'shy, and not clever

about society – constantly forgetting to return calls, and avoiding invitations'.[94]

Women, or rather ladies, never called on gentlemen unless professionally or officially. This limited the scope for the impropriety of a social visit. Social networking fell to the women because time played an important part in the process; women had plenty of it:

> Leaving cards is the first step towards forming, or enlarging, a circle of acquaintances. A lady's visiting card should be printed in small, clear, copper-plate type, and free from any kind of embellishment. It should be a thin card, 3½ inches in depth or even smaller. The name of the lady should be printed in the centre, and her address in the left-hand corner. It is now considered old-fashioned for husbands and wives to have their names printed on the same card: they should have separate cards of their own. Leaving cards principally devolves upon the mistress of a house; a wife should leave cards for her husband as well as for herself. The master of a house has little or no card-leaving to do, beyond leaving cards upon his bachelor friends.[95]

The card itself presented few difficulties, but the etiquette of calling was a minefield for the unwary:

> Mostly cards should be delivered in person, and not sent by post. A lady should desire her man-servant to inquire if the mistress of the house at which she is calling is 'at home'. If 'not at home', she should hand him *three* cards: one of her own and two of her husband's; her card is left for the mistress of the house, and her husband's for both master and mistress. If the answer is in the affirmative, she should, after making the call, leave *two* of her husband's cards on the hall-table, and neither put them in the card-basket nor leave them on the drawing-room table, nor offer them to her hostess, all of which would be very incorrect.[96]

This depended on a recognisable home environment: a hall table, drawing room table, even the snare of the card-basket. Calls were generally made between three and five in the afternoon, and rarely exceeded half an hour; etiquette never permitted a visitor to wait in line, as it were, for the departure of previous visitors – as in the phrase to 'sit them out'. The etiquette of calling cards typified both the woman's different – not necessarily subordinate – social position, and her importance as a social connector and networker. Further nuances awaited the *arriviste*; this was etiquette at its most powerful, policing the class boundaries to keep out the interloper and admit the *bona fide*; this from 1871:

> If the lady on whom you call is not at home, you must leave your card. If she has grown-up daughters or a sister living with her, *two cards*; or you may slightly turn down the corner of your card, which signifies that the visit is paid to all.
>
> Very frequently now the names of the daughters who are introduced into society are printed on the same card as their mother's. It is a saving of expense and trouble, and is in good taste, we think, as implying the protection under which the young ladies visit.
>
> A card left at a farewell visit has P.P.C. (*pour prendre congé*, i.e. to take leave) written in the corner.[97]

Requests for attendance at parties rigorously reinforced the social strata; thus 'request the pleasure' for equals, and 'request the honour' for those of higher social status. This preserved the Victorian process of keeping the lower echelons below while concentrating on climbing to the higher: the elaborate and subtly changing system of etiquette kept the unwanted at bay. Letters to tradesmen and sometime servants addressed them in the third person, keeping a neat grammatical distance between the participants in the exchange.

Timekeeping meant distance-keeping. The century had begun to measure time more accurately and portably ('Never look at your watch during a morning visit; it is very rude to do so'[98]); and had discovered the social uses and value of time. The 1850s and 1860s cluttered middle-class lives inside the home with watches, clocks, gongs and house bells; outside with timetables and postal deliveries. Time became a social weapon as society allocated specific units for social functions: the tea, the visit, the dinner. Handling time correctly required a knowledge of process and access. Women as social agents deployed their minutes with apt parsimony. The working classes, tradespeople or servants were, by definition, always available, and had no private time to themselves.

Etiquette books clamoured to advise on lunches between one and two (until the 1860s, without coffee, for lingering after the lees of the meal with the hostess might be considered improper); in the social round of the 1830s and 1840s, cake and wine at three in the afternoon gave way to afternoon visits until five, or parties from three until six, then dinner; or the *thé dansant* (black satin and very thin boots *de rigueur*); or the evening dinner which became later as the century progressed.[99]

Dissenters from usual patterns of etiquette were noticed and noted. Sometimes they achieved collective popularity. Sometimes foreignness alone sufficed, as in the case of the 'downright Swede' and brilliant coloratura soprano, Jenny Lind:

> She liked 'intimates'. And 'Society', therefore, in admitting her, never felt that it had done her a great kindness, or that she hung on its favours. Rather it knew that something was there in her, which made all social distinctions become very small matters indeed. For the standards, which her presence forced to the front, were not 'social' but moral and spiritual: and it was impossible to have intercourse with her, without becoming conscious of this . . .[100]

Proof of this came from Lind's life-long friendship with A. P. Stanley (the Dean of Westminster), who was 'absorbed under the sway of her personal fascination'.[101] And her qualities cut through the conventions of a self-conscious soirée in Stockholm in 1839, recorded by the periodical *Dagny* (Fredrika Bremner Association, which furthered the cause of women anxious to make their own living):

> The beauties of the season are forgotten and, what is more, they forget about themselves; flirtation is suppressed; etiquette is sinned against unpunished . . . and a crowd of the high assembly gathers round the plain-looking young girl [Jenny Lind] . . .[102]

This pointed to the kinds of licence allowed to artists and performers in society; the latitude persists in the late twentieth century, which applies different standards of public behaviour to, say, an accountant and an actor.

To look back on the earlier part of the period from the relatively cool 1870s was to see how far mid-Victorian civilisation in the form of the etiquette book had come. William Taylor was a footman in the 1830s. He recorded a party in his diary for 18 May 1837:

> The company comes jenerally about ten or eleven 'clock and stays until one or two in the morning. Sweet hearting matches are very often made up at these parties. It's quite disgusting to a modist eye to see the way the young ladies dress to attract the notice of the gentlemen. They are nearly naked to the waist, only just a bit of dress hanging on the shoulder, the breasts are quite exposed except a little bit comeing up to hide the nipples. Plenty of false hair and teeth and paint. If a person wish to see the ways of the world, they must be a gentleman's servant, then they mite see it to perfection.[103]

At the other end of the social spectrum from the same period, Julian Charles Young, son of the great tragedian Charles Mayne Young, recalled in his diary for 20 October 1834:

> Dined with Lord and Lady Winchester . . . Lord W. told me that, three years ago, he was at a party at Lady Hertford's at Manchester House, when lady of high *ton* entered the room in the latest fashion from Paris, the gown being rather high in front, and extraordinarily low at the back, so as to expose the blade bones. [Joseph] Jekyll [wit and raconteur], who was there, and saw it, and was standing next to the noble marquis, at once delivered himself of this impromptu:
>
> > Les Elégants, who used to bare
> > Their snowy bosoms to the air,
> >   A new device have hit on:
> > For now they wear their gowns so low,
> > 'Tis thought they soon intend to show
> >   The very parts they sit on.[104]

Etiquette books for the mid-Victorian woman maintained and promulgated the fear of vulgarity; but that fear turned the mid-

Victorian woman away from those situations where vulgarity would be easy. To be gaily dressed in the morning or when walking in the streets was first vulgar, and second indicative of a moral life which ran counter to conventional expectation. Jewellery worn in the early morning, with the exception of habitual rings, indicated a racy life; when they were worn, the style of choice for brooches and earrings was plain, since pearls or diamonds might betray a hidden life. Dubious-looking gifts were never apt for display, but the wedding-ring was always on show.

The ethic of understatement and restraint in all matters of women's dress pervaded: 'it is always better to be *too little* dressed than *too much*',[105] the penalty being the sanction of awkwardness which the assembled company levied on the offender. The anti-vulgarity rule illustrated Mill's observation that society imposed its own ideas and practices as rules of conduct. But it still seems hard to understand why kid gloves should be preferred, on grounds of vulgarity rather than design or taste, over cotton or silk, both 'very vulgar'.[106] Dress etiquette had a social and a moral edge: never dress above your station; never appear to be thinking about your dress; tone down bright colours with black; and never spend more than you can quite afford on dress.[107]

In 1878 Margaret Oliphant found changes of principle behind changes in dress, so 'that which we wore placidly, or even with a little complaisance and sense of superior good taste twenty years ago would fill us with alarm and horror now. The change which has taken place is more than a change of fashion, it is a change of principle.'[108] She thought fashion in the 1860s and 1870s left margin for individual fancy undreamt of even twenty years before – 'Not to speak of a more distant past, the immediate difference between that date and this is quite enough to tell for a century.'[109] Fashion dealt more discreetly with men, chiefly haunting their legs, and as Oliphant charted the changes between the bright gowns of the 1850s enabled by new dyes and processes, to the softer, restrained shades of the 1870s, she passed over the changes in men's dress as an evolutionary adaptation of use to purpose:

The change is chiefly visible in feminine apparel, yet even in the case of men, the morning clothes, in which so many look their best, and are most entirely at their ease, may be said to be the

creation of the last quarter of a century. The black frock coat,
which is now the solemn uniform of town, the semi-state dress of
morning assemblies, afternoon teas, the Park, and society, was
then a common garment of all-work, without which no man could
go abroad; and this of itself is a revolution. But in the dress of
women the change has penetrated still deeper.[110]

Oliphant searched for a 'sensible dress' in which women 'could
walk easily, take reasonable exercise, and do reasonable work'.[111]
The fitting of clothes to functions had been achieved for men,
whose attire reached an exemplary degree of suitableness and
appropriateness:

> In itself it is ugly; there is no abstract grace in the garments all
> men wear – but it is convenient, it leaves the wearer free for
> exertion, and gives him, except when he happens to be very
> specially interested in his appearance, the minimum of trouble.[112]

The French Revolution had committed man to a black,
trousered future, only the waistcoat remaining aristocratic, absorbing all the bright colours leeched from the other garments; Disraeli
wore chains on his, the bearing of one who tried too hard. The
upper-class man could dress for every emergency, changing for
boating, cricket, tea, dinner and smoking. This used up much of
the time and leisure which made these activities possible in the
first place. The working middle-class man had no time. But his
wife did.

Oliphant's *Dress* advocated a fashion which combined good
sense, use and art; she left the theorising to adroitly placed
citations from Carlyle's laborious *Sartor Resartus*, which spoke of
clothes as 'vestural tissue', 'the grand tissue of all tissues', and 'the
outermost wrappage and overall' of man's soul. But in practical
terms, dress could speak wardrobes about a wearer. Oliphant
approved of the long skirt indoors on the grounds that it had the
poetic and symbolic qualities necessary to her 'noble and fine ideal
of dress';[113] but outdoors, the long, trailing dress became 'a very
evident and easy symptom of social inferiority'. Why?

The woman who lets her gown trail through the dust behind her,

will, in all likelihood, not even be a pretty housemaid. She will
belong to a class more independent, less well-mannered, with more
money to spend. It is doubtful even whether she will be a
dressmaker, for dressmakers have a greater respect for the dresses
which cost them so much labour. But one thing is certain – that
she will not be a lady; and on this point we speak without
hesitation or doubt.[114]

Ruskin objected to the same behaviour because he blamed it for
causing his loss of faith in women's commen sense and personal
delicacy. When they allowed their dresses to sweep the streets, he
underwent a momentary spiritual amnesia.

In the 1880s, *The Science of Dress* (by Ada Balin), to be read
'chiefly by the wealthier portion of the community',[115] enforced
the sense that, among the exhortations to younger women to dress
in wool with high necks and long sleeves, dress styles nonetheless
divided along class boundaries. The words 'portion' and 'community' looked back to a society divided by wealth:

In the Dress Department of the International Health Exhibition
were several dresses adapted for tricycle wear. Of special dresses
which would be exceedingly comfortable and suitable I noticed
one or two, but these could hardly be worn in towns unless the
wearers were hardened to a considerable amount of staring and
comment from the younger and dirtier portion of the community
as they passed along the streets.[116]

Singers and violinists could have elastic dresses, as society had
sanctioned their movements; but developments in fabric and in
style often waited, as Amelia Jenks Bloomer's hostile reception in
1850s England showed,[117] for the right activity to introduce the
clothing to a wider group of wearers.[118] *The Times* reported on
21 October 1851 from the theatre in Dean Street, Soho, where 'a
representative of the American press' was lecturing on 'bloomerism':

A very modest portion of her oratory, however, was devoted
particularly to the dress in question, but it served more as a
rallying, or central point, round which to group long disquisitions,

medical, legal, political and moral . . . But through all the phases of serious, lively, grave, or gay, the audience laughed. It did not matter to them what was said or what effect was meant to be produced; they had come for a lark to see a 'Bloomer' lecture on 'Bloomerism', and to prove their enjoyment of the spectacle cheered and laughed at every full stop . . . Our American instructress sometimes thought the laughter was ironical, and that she had unwittingly said something susceptible of a *double entendre*, and then, by apologising for her unknown offence, called down fresh roars.[119]

Bloomer's famous campaign was targeted principally against the tyranny of the corset. Along with the crinoline and the bustle, the corset attracted scathing ridicule from a various array of commentators: medics, satirists, feminists. One 1867 issue of the *Englishwoman's Domestic Magazine* claimed that 20,000 women annually were injured through the direct or indirect agency of tight-laced corsets. So Victorian women waited for archers[120] or croquet and tennis players[121] to soften the edges of a harsh sartorial régime.

Dress reform persisted from Bloomerism in the 1850s. By 1887 there was the National (later, Rational) Dress Society founded by Lady Harberton. At one Westminster Town Hall lecture chaired by Mrs Oscar Wilde, she wore Turkish black satin trousers, black velvet jacket clasped over a waistcoat of satin and lace; she delivered her peroration by cracking a riding-whip between sentences. But the Rational Dress Society based its discussions on what it thought men might think, and on how women's dress related to that of men, rather than by asking women what they really wanted to wear.

For those women who felt that the hoop and farthingale was little more than a ball and chain, one way out was the lightening of fabrics hoped for by Margaret Oliphant;[122] another was a change in style of the kind shown in Sargent's picture of Madame Brackhard, dress on hips. Because women's activities tended to be more circumscribed – the effects predicted and their consequences allowed for – commentators worked within the strict boundaries society set out by offering systems, principles, sciences of codified behaviour. So in Balin's *Science of Dress*,[123] Mill's notions of individual autonomy and Smiles's of self-help shaped themselves into the idea of 'self-care' which, thought Balin, 'ought certainly to occupy a considerable amount of the thought and attention of every individual . . . it is only by such care that the condition of the community can be improved'.[124] Balin added that once this principle of caring for the self was accepted, no item, 'however seemingly trifling', which concerned the individual's well-being could be thought unimportant.

This brought self-help, a rigorous regimen for the 1850s and 1860s, into the dangerous waters charted by Decadents and Aesthetes in the 1880s. Yet while Decadents like Huysmans or Pater looked beyond nature for their principles of beauty, Balin recognised that the natural world arbitrates taste, for she returned to 1738 – the *Gentleman's Magazine* – for guidelines on dress sense: anything that forced, constrained, over-ornamented or was out of character with nature was simple false taste.[125]

Balin's book, however, strayed easily from matters of dress to matters of social relations. By thinking about the rules which governed female dress, she succeeded in explaining in physiological terms why some principles harmed and others benefited the wearer. She urged women to think for themselves on the issue of clothing, and concluded, almost without realising it, that the time had come for women to think for themselves in every aspect of life, not in opposition to their male relations, but 'in order to be able to be true helpmeets to them, and not mere dolls to be looked at, admired, and petted, but not consulted in difficulty or trouble'.[126] She uncovered a social bedrock by digging down beyond the principles of dress; but no sooner had she exposed it, than she covered it over: 'I cannot now discuss this question at any length, but it is of great importance in regard to the present subject, for the dictates of reason are never more neglected than in matters concerning dress.'[127]

Changes in dress, as Virginia Woolf pointed out in 'Modes and Manners of the Nineteenth Century', a review of *Modes and Manners*, call up the connection between dress, character and behaviour:

A woman's clothes are so sensitive that, far from seeking one influence to account for their changes, we must seek a thousand. The opening of a railway line, the marriage of a princess, the

trapping of a skunk – such external events tell upon them; then
there is the 'relationship between the sexes'; in 1867 the Empress
Eugénie, wearing a short skirt for the first time, went for a drive
with the Emperor and Empress of Austria. As the ladies stepped
into the carriage the Emperor turned to his wife and said, 'Take
care, or some one may catch sight of your feet.'[128]

The Emperor's warning went unheeded in the 1880s and 1890s,
when feet were in fashion, boots were beautiful, and the skirt
had begun to rise. The Empress herself had already in the 1850s
inaugurated the *coiffure à l'impératrice* by wearing gold and silver
dust in her hair.

III Moral Values: Home and Abroad

Dress was everything; it went everywhere. The less substantial the
home, the more important the dress outside it. In 1869 James
Greenwood's *Seven Curses of London* made the vital link between
dress, lifestyle and home values. Greenwood was writing about
prostitutes:

> They are infinitely worse off than the female slaves on a nigger-
> plantation, for they at least may claim as their own the rags they
> wear . . . But these slaves of the London pavement may boast of
> neither soul nor body, nor the gaudy skirts and laces and ribbons
> with which they are festooned. They belong utterly and entirely
> to the devil in human shape who owns the den that the wretched
> harlot learns to call her 'home'.

Two years later, Alexander Lowry, Chaplain to Portsmouth
Hospital, was questioned by the Royal Commission upon the
Administration and Operation of the Contagious Diseases Acts;
Commissioner Cowper-Temple asked simply about the 'fallen
women' under Lowry's charge: 'Do you find that the love of dress
is often an impediment to a change in life?' Lowry replied:

> Of course when any young women mean to reform or go home I
> take my gauge of their probable intentions by the way in which

they dress themselves after they give in that resolution, and I
always see, when I observe earrings or hair adornments, which
way the current runs . . . And I have found it a most certain
criterion, a very good thing to judge by, if a girl means to do
what is right she generally does her hair and dresses in a respectable
way, and as soon as ever she begins to give up the intention she
commences to decorate and adorn herself.[129]

When the etiquette of home went out on to the streets, it was
part of a system of behaviour derived from moral – usually Christian – ethics. This foundation allowed newcomers with the right
tools to build from ground level; but these same principles easily
supported more ambitious moral projects which sought to dictate
how people behaved.

That year, 1871, was the seventh year of the notorious Contagious Diseases Acts.[130] They were an example of opinion
imposing itself as a rule of conduct pushed forward into legislation: the result was a series of acts legislating women's behaviour
on the streets in much the same ways as their husbands legislated
their behaviour at home.[131] On 13 May, the forty-fifth day of the
Lords Commission hearing on the Administration of the Acts,
John Stuart Mill answered Question 19,993, put by the Commission Chairman, The Right Honourable William Nathanial
Massey:

– The principal Act now in force is entitled 'An Act for the better
prevention of contagious diseases at certain naval and military
stations'. And are you aware that the policy which dictated this
legislation in the first instance was a desire to maintain the health
of soldiers and sailors whose physical efficiency was reported to
be very seriously affected by the disease which they contracted at
garrison and seaport towns, those towns and garrisons being the
resort, in a peculiar manner, of common prostitutes?

– [Mill] Yes, I am aware of that.[132]

That explained the purpose and function of the Acts from the
Commission's viewpoint. The next question allowed Mill to
explain his:

– Do you consider that such legislation as that is justifiable on principle?

– [Mill] I do not consider it justifiable on principle, because it appears to me to be opposed to be one of the greatest principles of legislation, the security of personal liberty. It appears to me that legislation of this sort takes away that security, almost entirely from a particular class of women intentionally, but incidentally and unintentionally, one may say, from all women whatever, as it enables a woman to be apprehended by the police on suspicion and then taken before a magistrate, and then by that magistrate she is liable to be confined for a term of imprisonment which may amount I believe to six months, for refusing to sign a declaration consenting to be examined.[133]

Both Mill's analysis and his facts were right. These Acts remained on the statute until 1886. One of their fiercest opponents was Josephine Butler, who well knew what 'the advancing force of public opinion' in the form of committees and commissions was capable of doing.

Throughout the 1860s, 1870s and 1880s, Butler pressed for the repeal of the Acts[134] by a radicalism which conformed entirely to the Victorian norms around her. The values which allowed her to dissent worked two ways: they helped shape her protest against the Acts from 1869 to their repeal in 1886[135] by concentrating both on their iniquities and on the causes of prostitution; but at the same time, while having the effect – if not the intention – of greater liberty for certain women in the 1870s, they reinforced the role of the woman in the home. Butler's protests relied on exactly those values which kept women under men's domestic subjugation. If the home was a place for the Victorians to keep some women in, it was also the place to keep other women out.

In Butler's *The House Before the Dawn*, her 1876 appeal to men who used prostitutes (although proprieties dictated that her language left this to the reader's divination: 'the language of this appeal will be incomprehensible to many'[136]), she introduced the work of her publisher in this instance, the Social Purity Alliance:

The Social Purity Alliance is designed to promote the practical application of two radical principles – namely, the sacredness of the home, and the duty of men to live and to suffer women to live in purity.[137]

In the light of the practical application of these principles, Butler's values here remained staunchly non-radical. Her entire appeal was based on 'the sacredness of the home'. She advocated social relations between men and women which kept women in the home.

But in the 1860s and 1870s venereal disease brought street life into the mid-Victorian home: a moral punishment for the unfaithful which brought matters of practical morality to bear on personal conduct by providing tangible evidence of trangression. Later in the century, probably around 1890, the now famously public writer of *My Secret Life*, made public in *The Other Victorians*, returned home to his wife after visiting a prostitute involved with a drunken sailor:

> Then a dread came over me, I had fucked a common street nymph,
> and in the sperm of a common sailor; both might have the pox
> – what more probable. I could feel the sperm wet and sticky
> around my prick, and on my balls . . . Fear of the pox kept me
> awake some time. Then the scene I had passed through excited me
> so violently, that my prick stood like steel. I could not dismiss
> it from my mind. I was violently in rut.[138]

He raped his wife. The terrible mixture of fear, guilt, lust and anger makes this episode painfully typical of a Victorian attitude to sex; but it also puts the issues of self-esteem and responsibility in play, and in the context of the home.

The patterns of belief in the Acts' supporters and critics[139] depended on categorising prostitutes as 'fallen' or 'wandering' women. They had fallen through the domestic net, were no longer part of a home. They were unconnected with the processes which checked and balanced the function of daily society. Josephine Butler again:

> One main cause of the existence of a large amount of prostitution
> in this or other countries is the total estrangement between the
> prostitute class and all other classes of society . . . The present

resistance to these Acts is, above all else, a humble and bitter confession that men and women, singly and in society, have hitherto grossly offended in their duties to their wandering sisters.[140]

In these circumstances, women were estranged from the support and security of home; William Cobbett, cited in *The Friendly Counsellor* (1876), showed the domestic version of Butler's insight:

> Women are a *sisterhood*. They make *common cause* in behalf of the *sex*; and indeed this is natural enough, when we consider the vast power that the *law* gives us over them. The law is for us, and they combine whatever they can to mitigate its effects.[141]

The year before the Acts' inception, Dinah Craik wrote this in *Mistress and Maid,* the story of the Misses Leaf and their choice of a new maid, Elizabeth Hand:

> A household exclusively composed of women has its advantages and its disadvantages. It is apt to become somewhat narrow in judgement, morbid in feeling, absorbed in petty interests, and bounding its vision of outside things to the small horizon which it sees from its own fireside. But, on the other hand, by this fireside often abides a settled peace and purity, a long-suffering, generous forbearance, and an enduring affectionateness, which the other sex can hardly comprehend or credit. Men will not believe what is nevertheless the truth, that we can 'stand alone' much better than they can: that we can do without them far easier, and with less deterioration of character, than they can do without us.[142]

As a vision of women without men, unlike the lesbian fantasy of Christina Rossetti's 1862 *Goblin Market* (a journey out from home into sexual and commercial discovery), Craik's writing balanced the probabilities sensibly, persuading without appealing. Behind it lay a moral vision: peace, purity and forbearance.

It was exactly these moral qualities which underpinned Butler's attack on the Acts. She put moral vision in service of a rare acuity about publicity,[143] and shaped a public debate[144] to an end which allowed her chronicler, W. T. Stead, radical editor of the *Pall Mall*

Gazette, to write in 1888 that she had roused the great revolt of 'the human conscience, which forms one of the most encouraging features of the moral development of our day'.[145] She wrote in her *Reminiscences*:

> Our fathers to their graves have gone;
> Their strife is past – their triumph won;
> But sterner trials wait the race
> Which rises in their honoured place –
> A moral warfare with the crime
> And folly of an evil time
>
> So let it be. In God's own might
> We gird us for the coming fight,
> And, strong in Him whose cause is ours,
> In conflict with unholy powers,
> We grasp the weapons He has given –
> The light, and truth, and love of Heaven.[146]

The language remained military, liturgical, almost anything but medical. She wisely kept her 'abolitionist' issue-based movement discrete from the great 'Woman Question' in as astute an act of argumentative etiquette as the nineteenth century produced:

I never myself viewed this question as fundamentally any more a woman's question than it is a man's. The legislation we opposed secured the enslavement of women and the increased immorality of men; and history and experience alike teach us that these two results are never separated.[147]

Butler took a non-party line and based her argument on principles recognisable to her contemporaries – 'the Ethics of Christ'[148] – and, principles straight from Mill's thinking: the worth of the individual, of liberty, and of the sacredness of the human person. Looking back, she analysed her mid-Victorian environment precisely by perceiving 'an approaching revival of moral faith and spiritual energy, simultaneously with the rapid advance of a materialism . . .',[149] using 'materialism' in a sense which mediated between the new Victorian usage in theological debate and the modern consumerist sense.

Butler's ministry worked in practice.[150] She nursed prostitutes in her Liverpool house, and recalled the work in *The Beehive* of 18 January 1872. Here the ethics and etiquette of hospitality work to make each visit a homily. The home was again central:

> . . . we have received into our houses and tried to restore again to hope and to society many a cast-off mistress of men of fashion, and many a despairing mother of a bastard child, ignored and forsaken by her father . . . I have sought out not only women, but the most miserable of men, suffering from humiliating disease, poor sailors – Norwegians, Spaniards, Greeks & C. – who arrive at this great seaport . . . No loathsome attribute of this disease ever kept me and other ladies away from this labour of love.[151]

Butler's campaign fitted exactly with Victorian habits of fact-gathering and problem-solving; she wrote, spoke and visited to press her case.[152] W. T. Stead reported her public speaking début, and makes the scene continuous with crowd scenes in *Alton Locke*, *North and South*, and even *Felix Holt*, where crowdedness denotes a kind of interest:

> The red light shone on the sea of upturned faces for the first few ranks, and beyond them the crowd was seen dimly in the light of the silver moon. The labourers, puzzled and curious, crowded around the strange lady, and listened not untouched by the pathos and fervour of her eloquence. She had their attention; and, having that, she soon gained their support. She spoke simply, earnestly, passionately, of the wrongs of the poor fallen women . . . [153]

Her successes relied on her sense of timing and perseverance in public relations. She called for an *Uncle Tom's Cabin* for the cause, hoping to raise awareness of the 'ghastly truth'.[154] She began the social investigation based on evidence from the great 1861 census to bring an awareness of the pace of social change to bear on a social problem: 'Formerly muscles did the business of the world, and the weak were protected by the strong; now brains do the business of the world, and the weak are protected by law.'[155]

The census had found 5,782,983 women (wives 3,488,952; widows 756,717; spinsters over twenty 1,534,314); when spinsters

under twenty joined the figures the census lists 3,436,749 women
who worked for their subsistence. Butler's search for a solution
to the prostitution problem led her to argue for a system which
counteracted employers' prejudice, defective education and closed
shops which prevented women's advance in employment. She
observed coolly:

> When it is urged upon them [men] that the women who do and
> must stand alone are counted by millions, they are perplexed,
> but only fall back on expressions of a fear lest a masculine race of
> women should be produced, if we admit any theories respecting
> them apart from conjugal and maternal relationships.[156]

Butler knew economics lay at the root of practical morality,
and lamented the tears shed over sentimental works of fiction
which might better be bestowed on pressing social reality.
Throughout *Before the Dawn* she returned to social and economic
theory to explain prostitution. Custom and usage produced the
prostitute.

Butler's campaigning typically took the form of arduous European tours. Her famous December 1874 Paris visit to the 'Service
des Moeurs', the French equivalent of the Acts' administration,
made prostitution seem even more a matter of custom. Writing
home, Butler rechristened it the 'service de debauche'.[157] In 1875
she helped form the British, Continental and General Federation
for the Abolition of Government Regulation of Prostitution
(3 March); and the book *The New Abolitionists* charts her visits
to the St Lazare Hospital and the famous 'warfare amongst foreigners' tour starting in Naples, and taking in Rome, Florence,
Milan, Geneva, Lausanne and Berne. Returning to England in
March, Butler summed up: 'I have poured out my life for this
cause. The feeling of exhaustion induced by the efforts I had to
make is such as I never before experienced in my life ... It was
no holiday work.'[158]

However, Butler's brilliance was to make the issue continuous
with matters of decency and moral standard; in short, to make
the campaign against the Acts one which caused society to look
at its actual behaviour and the codes which underpinned it. Here
again the idea of the centrality of manners and their capacity to

mollify the dictates of both government and individual need found a practical application in mid-Victorian England. The nineteenth-century Whig concept of manners as an aspect of politics, a control over behaviour was strongly evident here.

Butler writes of 'the *unequal standard of morality* for the sexes',[159] touching in social terms on arguments put forward in literary terms by Meredith, Hardy and, most notably, by Shaw in the 1894 Preface to *Mrs Warrens's Profession*. But Butler went further. By aligning her complaints with one of the Victorians' passionately-held positives, she integrated her argument with the moral world:

> The 'new world of progress' among us is clear; and while contending on every hand against all the unmistakable proximate *causes* of prostitution, we shall wage a spiritual warfare against its ultimate *cause*, – the permission and sanction of the double standard, the doctrine that impurity in man is a slight and excusable offence, while in woman it is a deadly and unpardonable sin.[160]

Butler always brought her arguments back to bear on how people actually behaved. In July 1886, three months after the Acts' repeal, she addressed the Congress of the Ladies' National Association. She found, as many thinkers continue to find, that Mill was waiting for her when she arrived at her conclusion:

> I am reminded, as I stand here, at the close, so to speak, of one chapter of the history of our cause and the opening of another, of the noble words of John Stuart Mill: 'fear not,' he said – 'fear not the reproach of Quixotism or of fanaticism; but after you have weighed what you undertake, and are convinced that you are right, go forward; even though you do it at the risk of being torn to pieces by the very men through whose changed hearts your purpose will one day be accomplished.' That man, John Stuart Mill, had discernment to recognize what is the fountain-head of all true energy to bring about real reformation – namely the changed hearts of men.[161]

Mill himself had pronounced in 1869 on the activities of women like Josephine Butler. Writing about philanthropy in *The Subjec-*

tion of Women, he found the class apt and equipped to help others in a particular way:

> A woman born to the present lot of women, and content with it, how should she appreciate the value of self-dependence? She is not self-dependent; her destiny is to receive everything from others, and why should what is good enough for her be bad for the poor? Her familiar notions of good are of blessings descending from a superior.[162]

Ideas of conduct radiated out of the middle classes, themselves uncertain about how to behave, shoring up their own identity by pressing it upon other classes.

Ideas fostered in the home had currency abroad. The *London-Führer* struck on two quintessentially English home-based concepts, 'gentleman' and 'temper'; it concluded: 'only the English have understood how to identify in society those points of equilibrium at which one is neither common nor noble, neither unfeeling nor oversensitive'.[163] The idea of temper was key, particularly when the writer turned to Englishwomen in the home:

> . . . they generally possess that agreeable trait which one calls 'good temper' in England. It means something like quality of character; this is so expressed in the English idiom that when one does not specifically refer to the good qualities one signifies the bad. If one says 'she' or 'he has a great deal of temper', that means something like 'she' or 'he has a very bad temper'; in German: he or she has a temperamental nature. The word 'temper' therefore denotes a mind that is irritable, excitable and changeable. The expression 'good temper', on the other hand, refers to a mind that because of an unusual air of calm, even phlegm, is less sensitive to impressions from the outside and that in the face of all the vicissitudes of life remains more or less stable.[164]

Here was an English paradox: temper, which suggested mental balance, composure, moderation and command over the emotions, meant something only when it was clear that those qualities were *not* being shown. 'Ill-temper' – that 'heat of mind or passion, showing itself by outbursts of irritation or anger upon slight

133

provocation' (*OED*) – arrived in the language in the 1820s; but by the 1880s the prefix had atrophied. Later, in 1892, Richard Church wrote in *Cathedral and University Sermons* of 'what we all understand when we speak of a man "showing temper" '.

In mid-Victorian England the medieval origins of 'temper' (connected with conduct, measure and restraint) vied with the new notion of temper as a contagious irascible condition, so in 1884 John Hall's *A Christian Home – how to make and how to maintain it* hinted that 'Servants sometimes suffer from the ill-temper of their employers.' The word itself and the ideas it represented were out of control. In *Theophrastus Such*, George Eliot knew exactly what was happening to the slipping usage: 'What is temper? Its primary meaning, "the proportion and mode in which qualities are mingled" is much neglected in popular speech.' The concept of temper had embarked *en route* for temperance: 'self-restraint or moderation in action of any kind' and 'the avoidance of excess in eating and drinking'. A form of behaviour peculiarly English and specifically domestic: *The Ladies' Treasury* from 1867 advocated care for the servant's health and comfort, but warned, 'indulgence is not apt to improve her health, temper, or manners'.[165]

IV Home and Duty

Home was where important social and behavioural changes were taking place, a crucible of chemical transformation. Hippolyte Taine canvassed his friends and came up with six causes for the good temper of middle-class Englishwomen. First, they controlled their own behaviour; second, they banished romantic dreams and illusions; third, they reinforced their natural common sense through sensible novels and charity work with the poor; fourth, they lived for eight or nine months of the year in the country, out of temptation's way; fifth, they had children sufficient to occupy them, with the nursery staff of maids and governesses under constant supervision; and sixth, they undertook all manner of additional work which allowed them to 'keep the world at their finger tips'.[166]

Taine's thinking typified mid-Victorian views on women and their environment. He recognised the exigencies both of convention and of physical setting. The Victorian environment brought physical condition and pressure to bear on ordinary behaviour: a well-tempered environment. The enduring value of the home for the Victorians was its capacity to bond the physical and the ideal in one setting. The home fixed the ethic of wifely or daughterly or sisterly duty to the woman by means of its, and her, physical conditions.

The design and use of furniture, the wearing of clothes, kinds of drawing room behaviour, the etiquette of visiting and calling cards, as well as the flat transgression of a dangerously-cut dress or an exposed ankle; all these affected the ways a mid-Victorian middle-class woman behaved. Typically, mid-Victorian men set the scope and tenor of the domestic scene but left the running of it to their wives, daughters or mothers; they made the household into a social, economic and, more importantly, psychological unit. But the influence stretched beyond the home. The great British male institution, the club, was really a stab at an ideal home, a place where comfort and security mixed with the cut and thrust of conversation. By 1837 there were twenty-five clubs in Pall Mall and St James's Street; many had been extant for fifty years. These were not wholly homes from homes for the idling rich, but often – in the case of the Carlton and the Reform – places of intellectual exchange and political intrigue, made to look like homes. As a vehicle for mixing physical, psychological and social pressures, the idea of home took Victorian women into a rich cultural dead-end; while many women were encumbered, their husbands travelled fast and light without hindrance.

Taine mixed in select circles. The Englishwomen he knew took physical exercise and cultivated their talents, with the result that every family had one or two watercolourists; and that all the ladies of every family rode at least once a day. These occupations, Taine felt, kept the mind busy, filled up time, and barred the path of unwholesome ideas. Behind them lay a principle:

> Such are the auxiliaries of the moral principle, but we also take account of the principle itself. In France it is based on the feeling of honour; in England on the idea of duty.[167]

Nothing better explained the woman's situation in mid-Victorian

England than the notion of duty: to the parents when young, to the husband when married, to the children and family when mature; always to the good of the home; never to her own development.

Duty recognised the satisfaction of something to be lived for beyond the satisfaction of self, and was to the moral life what 'the addition of a great central ganglion is to animal life'.[168] The sense of duty ran through the house: one of Taine's friends thought it fundamental in an Englishman, and believed the feeling to be supreme in the kitchen and antechamber: 'there is nothing like this feeling for reconciling a subordinate to his subordination'.[169]

While objects and occasions for various kinds of duty forced themselves into men's consciousness, little presented itself to women. Middle-class men exercised duty in areas of life to which women had no access: work, politics, the club. Henry Sidgwick found duty 'as real a thing as the physical world, though it is not apprehended in the same way'.[170] But for women, Sidgwick's implied distinction meant nothing, for duty *was* the physical world of the home and family, beyond which many women had nothing but their charity work; even this lay within the purview of their husbands or fathers. Few role-models existed for Victorian women. George Eliot's biographer, the poet Mathild Blind, listed an uninspiring selection, even though she looks back through English history: Elizabeth I, Fanny Burney, Jane Austen, the Brontës and Elizabeth Barrett Browning;[171] no mention of George Sand, Harriet Martineau or Florence Nightingale.

Eliot herself was an ambiguous role model for Margaret Oliphant, who placed the intelligent woman in a familiar situation; she opened her autobiography on 1 February 1885 with this:

> I don't quite know why I should put all this down. I suppose because George Eliot's life has . . . stirred me to an involuntary confession. How have I been handicapped in life! Should I have done better if I had been kept, like her, in a mental greenhouse and taken care of? This is one of the things it is perfectly impossible to tell. In all likelihood our minds and our circumstances are so arranged that, after all, the possible way is the way that is best; yet it is a little hard sometimes not to feel with Browning's Andrea, that the men who have no wives, who have given

themselves up to their art, have had an almost unfair advantage
over us who have been given more than one Lucrezia to take care
of.[172]

Oliphant had written an episodic life of her mother, Mrs Wilson,
for Blackwoods in 1853; she knew the pressures from within and
from observance. A clever woman of the middle classes had to fit
her other activities around family duties; Margaret Oliphant wrote
to the publisher John Blackwood in 1857:

We set off on Saturday for Birkenhead, and I have innumerable
babies' frocks to look after, begging your pardon for postponing
the dignified demands of literature to such small considerations.[173]

A clever woman of the higher ranks, with domestic matters
under wraps, could devote herself elsewhere. Success for the
woman within the middle-class and upper-class lifestyle depended
greatly on her ability to negotiate domestic social encounters of
all kinds, both intimate and public. Mill thought that only the
upper-class society woman found sufficient employment of her
talents in cultivating the graces of manner and the arts of conversation. Oliphant had to shift for herself.

4

American Manners and
Transatlantic Attitudes

In England, 1859 produced *Adam Bede, Self-help* and *The Origin of Species*. In America, 1859 produced Randolph B. Marcy's *Prairie Traveller, a Handbook for Overland Expeditions*:

> After a particular route has been selected to make the journey across the plains, and the requisite number have arrived at the eastern terminus, their first business should be to organise themselves into a company and elect a commander. The company should be of sufficient magnitude to herd and guard animals, and for protection against Indians.
>
> An obligation should then be drawn up and signed by all the members of the association, wherein each one should bind himself to abide in all cases by the orders and decisions of the captain, and to aid him by every means in his power in the execution of his duties; and they should also obligate themselves to aid each other, so as to make the individual interest of each member the common concern of the whole company.[1]

That year, nearly 40,000 settlers travelled West to Oregon, California and Utah; there had been a quarter of a million since 1849. Everywhere along the trail, for each individual and each family and each company, identifying individual with collective interest was the rule of the journey; without such a commitment, many more settlers would have perished. The blurred boundary between public and private life was one of the lasting results of the transient experience. The distinction had been prominent in European life and political thought in the early nineteenth century. The American experience dissolved the distinction between the realm of the individual and the realm of the official group.[2]

The three great nineteenth-century American experiences were collective: the journey West, the Civil War, the post-war reconstruction. Yet all fostered a hearty individualism, often in service of the wider community, but always committed to the self. Before the law, beyond the injunctions of government, de Tocqueville's sense of 'democratic manners' was a milder but no weaker version of the contracts which had bound the travellers together *en route* for California and Oregon.

Throughout the 1850s and 1860s settlers formed self-help groups and gathered themselves into organised mining districts. These were informal assemblies: at the same time legislature, judiciary and executive. They relied little on outside authority. In 1866 there were five hundred self-organised mining districts in California, two hundred in Nevada, a hundred each in Idaho, Arizona and Oregon. Congress passed the Mining Act on 26 July 1866, recognising 'the force of local mining-customs or rules of miners wherever not conflicting with the laws of the United States'. Those laws were the subject of an 1866 Senate committee:

> By this great system established by the people in their primary
> capacities, and evidencing by the highest possible testimony the
> peculiar genius of the American people for founding empire and
> order, popular sovereignty is displayed in one of its grandest
> aspects, and simply invites us, not to destroy, but to put upon it
> the stamp of national power and unquestioned authority.[3]

This was the West speaking to the old East and hearing its sentiments echoed back. An uneasy relationship reigned between the two: Horace Greeley was to urge the young man to go West in the 1860s, but in the 1840s, as reports of deaths on the Oregon trail reached New York, he pronounced it 'palpable homicide to tempt or send women and children over this thousand miles of precipice and volcanic sterility to Oregon'.[4] Between the two lifestyles lay what in 1843 the *Edinburgh Review* called 'a howling wilderness of snow and tempests'. A New York commentator in 1844 saw a westward march of 'migratory legions leading all the trail of social and civil virtues out into the wilderness, to adorn and beautify its desert places'.[5] Etiquette was East Coast, manners West Coast, survival between.

The Descent of Manners

I 'We pledge ourselves to stand by each other . . .'

The country which was a nation of equals could make up the etiquette rules, start over. Matthew Arnold saw this tendency as a disadvantage in 1888: 'Everything is against distinction in America . . . The glorification of the "average man", who is quite a religion with statesmen and publicists there, is against it. Above all, the newspapers are against it.'[6] Why? The origins of this sense of legality were strewn out along the 150-day east-west trails to Oregon and California in the 1840s and 1850s.

America spawned cities with no history. It promised quick growth and high hopes. In a new country, where laws did not – and could not – necessarily protect the pioneers, it put community before government. As settlers embarked on their journey West, which between 1840 and 1860 might take anything from 107 to 157 days (California) or from 125 to 169 (Oregon),[7] they formed companies to protect themselves. These frail travelling coincidences forged strong agreements. The Green & Jersey Co. of emigrants to California adopted this resolution on 9 May 1849:

> . . . we the subscribers . . . now rendezvoused at St Joseph; in view of the long and difficult journey before us, are satisfied that our own interests require for the purpose of safety, convenience, good feeling, and what is of the utmost importance, the prevention of unnecessary delay, the adoption of strict rules and regulations to govern us during our passage: and we do by our signatures to this resolution, pledge ourselves each to the other, that we will abide by all the rules and regulations that may be made by a vote of the majority of the company, for its regulations during our passage; that we will manfully assist and uphold any authorized officer in his exertions to strictly enforce all such rules and regulations as may be made. And further, in case any members of the company, by loss of oxen or mules, by breaking of wagon, robbery by the Indians, or in fact from any cause whatever beyond their control, are deprived of the ability to proceed with the company in the usual manner, we pledge ourselves never to desert them, but from our own resources and means to support and assist them to get through to Sutter's fort, and in fact, we pledge ourselves to stand by each other, under any justifiable circumstances to the death.[8]

The wagon trails set up a dialogue between East and West, the Civil War set North and South at odds, and the post-war reconstruction forced the new out of the old. Everywhere the continuity, like that in 1830s England, was the continuity of change; the pace of transition was quickening. Manners, the way one American treated another, became a matter of national identity, something to hold on to in a world which was itself undergoing a process of becoming American. William Alexander Alcott's *Young Man's Guide*, which had reached its sixteenth edition (1844),[9] included a copy of the US constitution, as if to suggest that to behave well was to know how to be a fine citizen.

Manners and etiquette had national implications for nineteenth-century Americans; a break with the past did not necessarily always entail a break with the continuities implicit in the manners of the past. As the country expanded west, so the population increased, growing from 4 million in 1790 to 8 million in 1814, 31 million in 1860, 50 million in 1880, 63 million in 1890. More investors (9 million) lost in the market crash of 1929 than there were Americans in America in 1814. Growing American society had little else but an appeal to national sentiment to bind it together until the arrival of the railways gave the country a metaphor and a means for its own progress.

Out on the trail west in the 1840s and 1850s a relatively small number of Americans conjured a drama which represented the rise of the nation. For the non-travellers at home, the image of the drive made the mind return on itself, contemplate the horrors avoided, relish the advances made; they found gratitude for present comfort and a shudder of admiration (in the repeated 'their own') for those who eschewed it:

> Only think of it: men, women and children, forsaking their homes,
> bidding farewell to all the endearments of society, setting out on
> a journey of over two thousand miles, upon a route where they
> have to make their own roads, construct their own bridges, hew
> out their own boats, and kill their own meat; and undergoing
> every diversity of pain from agues, chills, sprains and bruises;
> where twenty miles is an average day's travel, exposed to every
> variety of weather, and the naked earth their only resting-place!
> In sickness they have no physician; in death there is no one to

perform the last sad offices. Their bodies are buried by the wayside, to be exhumed and defiled by the Indians, or devoured by the wolves.[10]

What required the greatest measures of tact in England, sickness and death, was a struggle with the environment on the trail.

Pioneers, by definition, had no precedents. The American nineteenth century had few recognisably English totems to sustain its etiquette – no royals, no aristocracy, no concentrated forms for society. The year 1859 also brought worries about the language itself; while philologists like Max Müller in England were searching for origins, Dr Alfred L. Elwyn's *Glossary of Supposed Americanisms* regretted their lack in American language culture:

> The chief reason why we have, and continue to have, the various strange and odd modes of using language and of utterance is, that we have no standard for either. The people of England have Parliament, filled with men of the best education, to be their standard; the people of this country will hardly look to their National Legislature for an example in the use of language or of national refinement.[11]

This was a tradition of worry that continued through Walt Whitman's 1888 *November Boughs*, which exalted American slang, and Henry James's *The Question of our Speech* (1905), which urged that all life came down to the question of our speech, our relations with each other.

In the Indian cultures the settlers found systems of belief and behaviour not only foreign to their own but sternly resistant to the new. Communication with Indians required a breaking of all manner of rules of etiquette and good behaviour. In 1846 at Hastings Cutoff, west of Salt Lake City on the route which lined the Humboldt River, Heinrich Lienhard, having eaten too many roots offered him by the Indians, and wanting to convey why he refused more, sketched his digestive condition like this:

> Since I could explain why only by signs, I bent over forward, held my stomach with both hands, and groaned as if I had severe stomach pains. Then I imitated a certain sound with my lips that

could come only from another part of the anatomy, and at the
same time made a quick gesture to my behind. The Indians
understood completely, and they all burst out in a storm of
laughter. My friend laughed loudest of all, and threw his roots at
my back. We naturally joined in the laughter and parted as good
friends in spite of all.[12]

This had nothing to do with politeness and everything to do
with expediency. The residual embarrassment ('my lips' but 'the
anatomy') betrayed the old New World squeamishness, but this
was an essentially novel situation. New rules for behaviour were
being formulated; a new country was being formed.

II American Visitors: Trollope's Folly

Behaviour and citizenship shared a partnership which helped over-
throw the British in 1781; they heightened the twin piques of
Fanny Trollope's 300-page attack on American manners in 1832,[13]
and Fanny Kemble's in 1835[14] and 1863.[15] The fight for independence itself took on the air of a social encounter. The English and
French fleets flirted with each other like regatta hopefuls at Rhode
Island in 1778. Sir John Burgoyne, playwright and general on tour
at Saratoga in October 1777, caused his aide-de-camp to comment
on the offensive as on a day's hunting: 'This campaigning is a
favourite portion of Life: and none but stupid Mortals can dislike
a lively Camp, good Weather, good Claret, good Musick and the
enemy near.'[16] Burgoyne's British surrendered that month to the
Americans under William Gates, who thought the setback would
teach England, 'the obstinate old slut', some manners. It did.

The victory put individual Americans in service of a collective
dream. Faced with the cruelties of the infamous butcher Banastre
Tarleton, or the stupidities of the British regulars, the Americans
consistently showed a high reasonableness as private citizens dril-
led as professional soldiers. This individualism in service of a
community later helped the drive West as America discovered
itself. But the War of Independence highlighted American traits
in a context which made their origins understandable. Principled
faith in the law was scrupulously upheld by Adams and Quincy,

who defended the British troops accused of the 1770 Boston Massacre; and by the First Continental Congress of 1774, of which lawyers formed half the membership.

Nineteenth-century American manners, in the absence of a state religion, and in the midst of an expanding country, explored fewer class avenues and more highways of individual and national identity. British manners sought to inculcate a sense of propriety and decency based on religious codes adapted to social usages and implemented by homiletic, hortatory texts; American manners relied on no firm consensus. In the West they came second to survival, but were important in the absence of other codes of conduct such as business or law. In the East they assumed a disproportionate importance because they became the only common ground between new Americans and their European forebears. Trollope realised this in her preface:

> Although much has already been written on the great experiment, as it has been called, now making in government, on the other side of the Atlantic, there appears to be still room for many interesting details on the influence which the political system of the country has produced on the principles, tastes, and manners of its domestic life.[17]

America represented the experiment in all forms of human interaction, but particularly those governed by political expedient. This explained the obsession of American manners books with the Washington scene, for difficulties emerged where native Americans interacted with foreigners in Washington diplomatic society at home, and with other English-speakers abroad.

Nineteenth-century America looked across the Atlantic to the régime which they had cast off, and for a set of social codes to help make sense of their protean society. On this axis, drawn between the rejection and the need for the past, the co-ordinates of anglophilia and anglophobia first appeared. The ironic, tight-lipped preface to the first American edition of Trollope's swingeing *Domestic Manners of the Americans* plotted them exactly:

> In presenting to the American public the following work, the publishers cannot refrain from congratulating their countrymen

on the appearance of so just and happy a delineation of American characters and manners. Moderate, conciliating, and good humoured, it cannot but astonish us with the display of our own virtues, and fill us with a proud gratification at finding ourselves so much better than we expected. Coming from the source it does, we had reason to anticipate the usual quantity of prejudice, ignorance, and misrepresentation which has heretofore distinguished most English travellers in the United States; but the reader will be surprised and delighted to find that the good-natured author has actually, on several occasions, omitted some capital opportunities of introducing various picturesque incidents . . .[18]

Trollope's *Manners* was a kick at misery, a piece of remedial action to salvage three and a half wrecked years in the United States. She had arrived in New Orleans, travelled to Cincinnati with entrepreneurial intent and established a bazaar – known to the locals as 'Trollope's Folly' – which had become a physico-medical institute by the time Anthony Trollope visited thirty years on. The 1830s yielded the novel *The Refugee in America* and the anti-slavery polemic *The Life and Adventures of Jonathan Jefferson Whitlaw, or Scenes on the Mississippi*; but it took until the 1843 novel *The Barnabys in America* for it to distil into the liquor of strong caricature – the tobacco chewer and the revivalist minister; while 1849 brought the acute *The Old World and the New*.

However, the *Manners'* thirty-four chapters of colonial vitriol etched a name for Trollope. It achieved four editions by the end of 1832, made the remarkable middle-aged Trollope into a literary lion, and set her on the way to her 130-volume writing career. The book caused a stir in London, but a storm in New York; E. T. Coke, a British lieutenant, recalled:

At every table d'hôte, on board of every steam-boat, in every stage-coach, and in all societies, the first question was, 'Have you read Mrs. Trollope?' And one half of the people would be seen with a red or blue half-bound volume in their hand, which you might vouch for being the odious work; and the more it was abused the more rapidly did the printers issue new editions.[19]

Trollope made between \$130,000 and \$140,000 from the book which contempory American papers felt – combining economic envy with national sensitivity – had libelled the United States. Her criticisms operated on the ground of cultural process, the very area in which Victorian England excelled. The American nation Trollope saw found itself in the midst of a process of self-definition against, and at the same time with, the grain of English behaviour. Her Europe, different from the chauvinist states of the 1850s, traded in manners and behaviours to produce the best possible 'eurocharm', as individuals from different nations 'note it a mark of fashion and good taste to imitate each other in all the external embellishments of life'.[20]

The long peace, Trollope thought, had provided the perfect nursery for the exchange in customs and manners, with a consequent advance in refinement and, as she puts it, general information. The *Illustrated London News* crowed on the same theme in its Great Exhibition pronouncement, claiming that London had become not simply the capital of a great nation, but the metropolis of the world; and that the Exhibition rendered its local character no longer English merely, but cosmopolitan. The *News* also mentioned the peace, suggesting that the post-Waterloo hordes of English upper-middle and upper-class sightseers had wooed the foreigner with prodigious accomplishment, quaint eccentricity and hard currency:

> But our Continental friends have not returned our visits. They
> have seen us abroad, and not at home; and have, for the most
> part, been slow to understand what inducements we could have
> for travel. While it has been rare to find an educated Englishman
> who did not speak French, or perhaps German and Italian, more
> or less perfectly, and who did not know by personal inspection
> the main features of the most celebrated of the Continental cities;
> it has been still more rare, among the same classes in France or
> Germany, to find a man who personally knew anything about
> London or who could speak, or even read, the English language.[21]

The *News* mixed respect for foreign knowledge with contempt for foreigners; this mixture functioned in matters of information and education – knowledge of Paris or Heidelberg, and the acquisition of French or German.

Trollope's Americans failed to sip this cultural cocktail: they lacked examples; they lacked the education which produced accomplishment in Trollope's terms. The pattern of her criticism gradually mapped itself out over her American stay. *Manners* ranged across an expected landscape: theatre, the country, farming, weather, religion and the great British anti-American issue, slavery: 'The effect produced upon English people by the sight of slavery in every direction is very new, and not very agreeable, and it is not the less painfully felt from hearing upon every breeze the mocking words, "All men are born free and equal." '[22]

On the drift up the Mississippi from New Orleans to Cincinnati, Trollope stepped ashore to write of watermelons, pigs, children, literature, schools, elections, women, money, dress, sleighing, stage-coaches and church-going. She unearthed the community's nonconformist roots in churches which resembled cafés and theatres, parades of fashion and of clerical influence. She dug for its political roots in 'the want of interest, of feeling, upon all subjects which do not immediately touch their own concerns', so that 'all the enthusiasm of America is concentrated to the one point of her own emancipation and independence'.[23] And she found in American energy and ambition the reason for the coarseness she detected in their manners: while they knew that any individual could rise, this was also a spur 'to that coarse familiarity, untempered by any shadow of respect, which is assumed by the grossest and the lowest in their intercourse with the highest and most refined'.[24]

Trollope blamed America for lacking the hierarchy of manners within which mid-Victorian England flourished; until the later century provided America with its class system based on money, and in the absence of the lifestyles of the rich and famous to inspire, the country had no behavioural models outside the legal and political personalities of its founders. Perhaps its easy adoption of the flamboyant Lafayette in the 1780s had witnessed the paucity of role models. Trollope noticed the lack of court:

Where there is no court, which everywhere else is the glass wherein the higher orders dress themselves, and which again reflected to

them from them to the classes below, goes far towards polishing,
in some degree, a great majority of the population, it is not to
be expected that manner should be made so much a study, or
should attain an equal degree of elegance; but the deficiency, and
the total difference, is greater than this cause alone could account
for.[25]

This showed Trollope's accurate view of how manners tended to
work in English society. But she could not account for American
society as a whole, principally because of its demographic dispar-
ateness; she found the vast continent mostly 'in the state which
nature left it, and a busy, bustling, industrious population, hacking
and hewing their way through it'.[26] For Trollope, money united
and untied Americans in groups: 'I know,' she observed, 'not a
more striking evidence of the low tone of morality which is generated by this universal pursuit of money, than the manner in which
the New-England states are described by Americans.'[27]

At home, Trollope found women's behaviour circumscribed by
the lack of money entrusted them; this confinement, she felt,
preserved American society from an outbreak of the relaxation in
manners and behaviour championed by women. Moreover, middle-class American home culture kept women attending to the
home to an extent that precluded their becoming elegant and
enlightening companions: America's ladies were too actively
employed in the interior of their houses to permit much parading
in full dress for morning visits; this home role accounted for the
large numbers of men in Washington, whose wives had stayed at
home to mind the estate in other parts of the Union.

Trollope found female society chiefly among the families of the
foreign ministers, those of the officers of state, 'and of the few
members, the wealthiest and most aristocratic in the land, who
bring their families with them'.[28] Here, Trollope made a non-
distinction of one of the major Victorian distinctions, that between
wealthy and aristocratic, as if sensing an America already on the
road to its wealth-based hierarchy.

Elsewhere, Trollope exposed the fissures which ran through
American attitudes to modesty, to personal space, and to the
treatment of slaves within that structure. In literature, these issues
met in Melville's mythic, American archetype 'Benito Cereno',

Frederick Douglass's slave narratives, or the inevitable *Uncle Tom's Cabin*. For Trollope, one illustration served all three issues:

> I once saw a young lady, who, when seated at table between a
> male and a female, was induced by her modesty to intrude on
> the chair of her female neighbour to avoid the indelicacy of
> touching the elbow of *a man*. I once saw this very young lady
> lacing her stays with the most perfect composure before a Negro
> footman.[29]

Where prurience adjoined racism and both bordered a code of behaviour which ratified them, manners emerged as the political instruments they were elsewhere. Trollope's misfortune was that she rarely produced examples which gave point to her arguments and observations. Throughout *Manners*, the specific grounds of her dislikings remained unclear.

Her most compelling opinions issued from her look at England through the American lens. She thought the American education system wider and less confiningly scholastic than the English, but applauded an old-fashioned school of discipline in the latter; when school ended, money-making started: 'When the money-getting begins, leisure ceases, and all of lore which can be acquired afterward, is picked up from novels, magazines, and newspapers.' Then the vital question: 'At what time can taste be formed? How can a correct and polished style, even of speaking, be acquired?'[30]

None was more anxious for applause, nor less inclined to make sacrifices to obtain it, than the American:

> To doubt that talent and mental power of every kind, exist in
> America would be absurd; why should it not? But in taste and
> learning they are woefully deficient; and it is this which renders
> them incapable of graduating a scale by which to measure
> themselves. Hence arises that overweening complacency and self-
> esteem, both national and individual, which at once renders them
> so extremely obnoxious to ridicule, and so peculiarly restive under
> it.[31]

The English in America from Trollope and her predecessor Basil Hall onwards[32] pictured England through the New World's eye, saw themselves through what they were not.

The mid-Victorian English represented themselves to each other not only through prescriptive manuals, homiletic stories and heavy sermons, but also through the very processes by which they felt the country was advancing: progress, self-education, self-betterment. In America through the earlier part of the century which Trollope recorded, no Horace Greeley had come forward with his westward urgings, no Russell Conwell crying 'Get rich, get rich!',[33] no goldrush concentrating the greed, and no railway to make the country whole enough to divide itself into conscious parts. Trollope issued her criticisms from a settled, middle-class English – at times European – prejudice that a system of manners and etiquette necessarily depended on a hierarchical social structure.

In America in the 1830s manners were more of a national concern, and less of a class concern. Faced with a demotic society which had yet to evolve is own brand of materialism, Trollope made flat, brutal claims. She concluded forthrightly:

> I speak . . . of the population generally, as seen in town and county, among the rich and the poor, in the slave states and the free states. I do not like them. I do not like their principles, I do not like their manners, I do not like their opinions.[34]

Trollope's voice made itself heard further down the century in American anxieties about the influence of her book. It pressed on many areas of American life, and left an imprint on both the etiquette book and the popular culture, showing the close association between the two. According to the ingenious, if not altogether veracious, Trollope, women in the boxes of American theatres were to be seen nursing their babies, men to be squirting tobacco juice at random over the playhouse. One guide ruefully recalled Trollope on an occasion where national self-chastisement was also a form of social disapprobation:

> We have seen men put their feet over; but the sovereigns of pit and gallery never neglected to give the admonition of 'Boots!' while ladies and gentlemen, wanting somewhat in their manners, turning to sit on the railing, with their backs to the pit, were saluted with the cry of 'Trollope!' which soon brought them to a sense of propriety.[35]

Ten years after Trollope, Dickens arrived. What struck him first on visiting Boston was that 'in all the establishments of America, the utmost courtesy prevails';[36] and what struck him second, as he toured the Perkins Institution and Massachusetts Asylum for the Blind, was the spirit of self-respect, of self-help, which the institution fostered, a spirit, he felt, 'common to all the Institutions at South Boston'.[37] Both observations took institutions and not individuals or classes as the basic unit.

Dickens indulged a favourite and justified concern in his comments on the parpahernalia of the English legal system as against the comparative simplicity of the American. This was one of the few areas of life where, ideally, an individual could represent an institution, and where concepts of the two placed themselves in sharp mutual distinction:

> . . . there is undoubtedly a degree of protection in the wig and
> gown – a dismissal of individual responsibility in dressing for the
> part – which encourages that insolent bearing and language, and
> that gross perversion of the office of a pleader for The Truth, so
> frequent in our courts of law. Still, I cannot help doubting whether
> America, in her desire to shake off the absurdities and abuses of
> the old system, may not have gone too far into the opposite
> extreme; and whether it is not desirable, especially in the small
> community of a city like this, where each man knows the other,
> to surround the administration of justice with some artificial
> barriers against the 'Hail Fellow, well met' deportment of everyday
> life.[38]

Dickens chose the issue to isolate the dilemma of American institutional behaviour in the face of a population of egalitarians. An institution dealing with official business negotiated with a society whose own rules were not hierarchical.

Moving south, Dickens followed the received wisdom that there was no place in the United States where ceremony was so much observed and practised as at Washington,[39] which he described as 'the headquarters of tobacco-tinctured saliva'.[40] On his arrival he launched immediately into a discourse on tobacco-chewing and spitting, a practice which cut across the strata of American life to a degree that all but tempted him to write a Carlylean spittoon history of America. He described how in the law courts the judge, crier, witness and prisoner, the jurymen and the spectators, each had a spittoon to themselves. With a nod towards Fanny Trollope, Dickens ventured further:

> . . . in some parts, this custom is inseparably mixed up with every meal and morning call, and with all the transactions of social life. The stranger, who follows in the track I took myself, will find it in its full bloom and glory, luxuriant in all its alarming recklessness, at Washington. And let him not persuade himself (as I once did, to my shame) that previous tourists have exaggerated is extent. The thing itself is an exaggeration of nastiness, which cannot be outdone.[41]

The move from observed detail to apt generalisation typified the travelogue technique, a way of representing a culture in the fewest details.

Elsewhere, Dickens attuned his ear to the subtler differences in vocabulary between English and American coachmen or porters. He compared the English 'All Right!' with the American 'Go Ahead!': emblems of national characteristics.[42] These local felicities, and the weighty diatribe against slavery (taken from a Washington paper's slave-sale advertisements), contributed to Dickens's enjoyment in writing up *American Notes* at Broadstairs with the encouraging conversation of the ubiquitous Captain Marryat. However, the scope of the book's success extended to its making a thousand pounds and famously escaping being savaged in the *Edinburgh*, for the reviewer, Thackeray, thought it vulgar, flippant, frivolous and dull; and refused to review it.[43]

Three years earlier, the Frenchman Michel Chevalier issued his *Society Manners and Politics in the United States*, a sheaf of letters gathered from his travels there in the 1830s. He conformed with other travellers in meeting the national character of the individual American close to the surface of daily affairs. Chevalier brought a European perspective to bear on the American character: while a Frenchman preceded apprenticeship with professional training, 'The American learns by example merely; we must learn by general principles; we stand more in need of them, and we have a greater aptitude for mastering them, than they.' He related this practicality to the systems of political liberty established by Anglo-American societies, for he saw public liberties as the means to wealth. In France, the process worked in reverse: 'other nations, and we, I think, are of the number, must arrive at political franchises by the progress of national wealth'.[44] Chevalier also allowed himself the luxury of speculating on the status of the hereditary principle – whether applied to an aristocracy or not – which assumed in general terms the 'sentiment of the family' so lacking in his America.

Chevalier touched an obvious difference between European and American society in the mid-nineteenth century – the comparatively weaker status of the family in America: 'As soon as they have got their growth, the Yankees, whose spirit now predominates in the Union, quit the paternal roof never to see it again, as naturally and with as little emotion, as young birds desert forever their native nest as soon as they are fledged.' Settlers regarded it as unmanly for sons to settle too close to their parents. The English mid-Victorian middle-class family established itself as a boundary within and against society. Chevalier felt the American weakness in family sentiment only temporary, since it necessarily resulted from the general dispersion of individuals which accomplished the colonisation of America in the first instance.[45]

At the height of English domestic fervour over the Great Exhibition, one of the most influential men in America was dining at the White House with President Millard Fillmore. The date, 8 May 1851; the man, Martin Tupper:

Altogether this evening could not have been surpassed for quiet, telling, lasting, influence and success: I have met here all the chief men of America, and every one of my personal book friend and lover . . .

There is no style, or ceremony, or restraint in any way at the President's house or table, beyond what you would meet at every private dwelling. This was almost a state occasion, the cabinet dinner before the President's departure on some public errand northward; but all was ease, affability, and absolute practical equality. The President is a portly nice-looking respectable man in black clothes and grey hair, well-bred, affable, dignified, and so kind that it's impossible to be otherwise than quite at your ease before him. His wife is a homely body, very plainly dressed, and with not too much to say: a motherly good sort of woman.[46]

The contrast with Tupper's visit to Windsor six years later could not have been greater. Windsor was to be compared only with the houses of the New York 'merchant princes' Astor, Ruggles, Strong, Hayte and Parker: 'all marble, and silver, and thick velvet carpets, and rich hangings'. Tupper's New York visit made him sensitive to a distinction which Fanny Trollope had missed, and which came down to a combination of behaviour and ancestry:

> There is more exclusiveness and aristocratic feeling here, among
> the select few, than in the old country; wealth is *not* the passport
> to it, – but *ancestry*! – and old world respectability! . . . There is
> a good deal of fashionable female-dominion here: and all the
> fairy-land of the Hayte and Parker suites of gorgeous rooms cannot
> attract the best people; – who in their knickerbocker plainness
> and pride look down upon these luxurious parvenus.[47]

Martin Tupper sailed in the *Asia* from Liverpool (on 1 March), arriving in New York fourteen days later. He was in America because of the runaway success of *Proverbial Philosophy*, which by 1848 had run to five stereotype editions and, together with *Probabilities: an Aid to Faith*, was competing for the public attention and purse. Tupper's home at Albury had become a place of pilgrimage by 1847. Why was Tupper such a success in America? The New York *Literary World*, 1 January 1848:

> The circulation which the works of Tupper have in this country,
> is truly astonishing. A circulation, not confined to cities, towns,
> or villages, but embracing the entire population. The 'Proverbial
> Philosophy' is found upon the centre-table of the metropolitan,
> in the scanty library of the student, and has gone hand-in-hand
> with the 'Farmer's Almanac', into the dwelling of the humblest
> tiller of the soil.

Not only there would Tupper have found his hortatory maxims, but in the Philadelphia Hospital for the Insane, where his ballad 'Never Give Up' was placarded in almost every room. On visiting the institution as part of his American tour, Tupper was delighted to learn, 'That appeal to their hope, the doctor told me, was the most efficient medicine he knew after religion. When I told them I would send them the music of it, they were overjoyed!'[48]

Tupper's visit compassed many of the great and good: Daniel Webster, P. T. Barnum, Washington Irving, Henry Longfellow; he even dropped off a copy of *Proverbial Philosophy* for Jenny Lind who was singing at Castle Garden, New York, under the auspices of the great P. T. Barnum. Tupper then discovered that Lind had already read his 'Pro. Phil.' and found it immensely comforting. As he embarked on the *American Arctic* out of New York on 24 May 1851, a paper was pressed into his hand on the gangplank. It read:

> Poet, philosopher, and sage,
>   Farewell, Farewell to thee,
> Oh may thy life, through every stage,
>   a path of pleasure be,
>
> And when Eternity's blest morn
>   Shall dawn upon thy soul
> Thine be the palm branch and the crown
>   While ceaseless ages roll.[49]

III Stepping Eastward

Eastward travellers held England in awe. Cleveland Coxe's 1855 tour account, neatly aligned with the establishment by its dedication to an Oxbridge cleric, re-created London in the 1850s through a language of religious ecstasy. Coxe enjoyed 'the social pleasures of a brilliant capital', where 'so sacred are even the most public of domestic civilities, that whatever goes on under a private roof, seems necessarily invested with a character, to which types cannot do justice, without, at the same time, becoming sacrilegious'.[50]

Coxe breakfasted at ten or eleven and dined between five and eight on a round of social engagements which exposed his foreignness in his punctuality, and which gave him republican pause when he heard children announced formally. He marvelled at the understatement. This society consisted of 'cultivated persons, male and female, whose accomplishments are not displayed, but exist as a matter of course, and as essential to one's part in the duties and civilities of life'.[51] That put him deep in Castiglione country, where *sprezzatura* lent ease to the greatest accomplishment and absolved the accomplished from perpetual trial of their gifts.

Later in the century, S. J. Ransone, an 'American resident', wrote of the portfolio of social graces called 'good form', impossible to reduce to its constituents. Instead, the anonymous writer listed professions, hunts and clubs – every one from the Albemarle to the York, from 1760 (White's) to 1885 (the Beaufort and the Wellington) – as if these externals represented and constituted the practice of good form. For the visiting American, there was useful advice on tipping – advisable but not necessary on public occasions when dealing with cabmen, railway porters, railway guards, crossing-sweepers and waiters ('the least deserving of all'[52]), vital for private dealings with others' servants. ('A week's stay should entitle the footman or maid to the tip of a sovereign', although gamekeepers might sneer at anything under a 'paper' or five pound note[53]). Ransone's editor warned with a caveat, 'The question of tipping in English country houses is a complex one.'[54] On no account should customs-house officials be tipped, for 'it will not only get you into trouble, but be an exhibition of very "bad form" '.[55]

As late as 1911 the American traveller could still thrill to the 'icy servility' of an Englishman of the servant class, and wonder why 'the men who have made America great at home, and respected abroad' could find little on offer in the American salon, while great Englishmen fitted unobtrusively into the drawing room: 'they go . . . because they meet men there of their own calibre'.[56]

These two accounts bore witness to the cautious approaches of those who felt inferior yet reluctant to admit it. The observers saw only upper-middle-class English society even as they visited the London of Mayhew and Butler. However, the redoubtable European feminist and journalist Fredrika Bremer, who toured in 1849 and again in 1851 for the Great Exhibition, found only a mass of population in a society without religious or moral care, lacking contact with the harmonising effects of higher mental cultivation.[57] The internationalisation of mid-Victorian middle-class English social life brought middle-class values into contact with and under the scrutiny of other forms of life.

American worries about the relative status of American politesse showed how close observable forms of behaviour were to what others perceived to be the national character. This was not to say that the English always behaved in one way, the Americans in another; it was rather to show that Englishness or Americanness defined itself not by the way business was conducted, newspapers run, women emancipated or children taught but most of all by the conduct of manners. So this American aim set itself against English models in 1855:

> It used to be our ambition to get rich, or be President; but these
> things are now become so common and so easy, that they lose
> their charm. Probably the best ambition just now is to be
> distinguished as an eminently tasteful and accomplished lady or
> gentleman. As hereditary aristocracies are losing *prestige*, we had
> best create a pure and genuine aristocracy, of the finest blood,
> the best breeding, and the noblest action and endowment.[58]

And it further enlisted a science which flourished as the American brand of self-help – in scientific terms as a theory of evolution, where 'breeding' and 'culture' were both social and biological:

> The scientific principles of breeding and culture, now understood
> and practised with respect to vegetables, fruits, and the lower
> animals, would, if applied to the human race, in three generations
> change the whole aspect of human society, by the elevation of
> the whole human character.[59]

When the American visited mid-Victorian England, the model of a functioning, literate society presented itself. Yet this model failed to translate westward.

As late as 1888 Thomas Higginson wrote of 'a tendency to Anglomania which is said to prevail just now in American society, or at least in a few cities and watering-places along the Atlantic shore'.[60] However, anglomania confined itself to a limited class: 'It does not exist, for instance, among our men of science, inasmuch as they go to Germany in shoals for study, and rarely visit England since the death of Darwin.'⁶¹ This split the professionals from the socialites, and Higginson recognised that the borrowing from England furnished the 'accessories of high-bred life' which fostered comfort, convenience and the organisation of a large household with its routine of social life:

> The key to this alleged Anglomania, therefore, is simply this: that the American habit of mind is essentially cosmopolitan, and goes to each nation for that which it finds best of its kind. As unerringly as it goes to Germany for its scientific instruction, or to France for its cooks, so it goes to England for what is not so well to be found in France or Germany – the minor conveniences or facilities which belong to a highly trained leisure class.⁶²

Higginson thought manners, embedded in the traditions and habits of society, were 'funded or accumulated good feeling', the result of years of experience in avoiding awkwardness and simplifying all procedure. This introduced the element of longevity as a nation, the English advantage, and the source of the American sense of inferiority. English manners grafted on to American stock produced hybrids.

Dickens had an answer for this in 1842. He approached Mill's formulation for English social life (the 'transactions of social life') when what Dickens later called the 'stern utilitarian joys of trade'⁶³ strayed into the enclosure normally reserved for social interchange. The model for American social intercourse could not be aristocratic, or hierarchical, but financial and political. Nineteenth-century American etiquette books searched for models of behaviour to stand in relation to social life as, say, mathematics stood in relation to science.

IV Civil War, Civil Conduct

At the time of the American Civil War, the Union was subjected to a tremendous strain. There was a threefold antagonism; there was the oppostion between the interests of some individual States and that of the Federation; between emancipation and slavery;

and between Free Trade and Protection. Over these three dangers the Union triumphed.

Lionel Tollemache, *Talks with Mr Gladstone*[64]

Gladstone was right. While Lincoln was destroying his enemies by making friends of them, Carlyle muttered darkly, 'There they are, cutting each other's throats, because one half of them prefer hiring their servants for life, and the other by the hour.'[65] The Americans' problem in the 1860s was how to get along with each other after the war, and how to present a united front to the world.

England had stood aloof, ever since Peel had coped with America's claims on Texas, California and the North Pacific coast by treading a pacifist line. In the late 1840s England had eschewed interference about Texas and California, which the United States annexed after the Mexican war. In the 1860s opinion was divided in England over the Civil War:

Tollemache. – Do you suppose that the condition of the slaves was as bad as might be gathered from *Uncle Tom's Cabin*?

Gladstone. – So far as the physical suffering is concerned, I think the picture is too darkly coloured. Mrs Beecher Stowe has combined all the worst details which were reported in various quarters. I will not say that she was morally to blame for this exaggeration; it was probably necessary for artistic effect. But I hold the great evil of slavery to have been, not physical suffering, but moral debasement. *It degrades God's human creatures below the human level.*

He also spoke of the bad effect on the masters, who were sinking lower and lower.[66]

The uneasy alliance of Whigs and Liberals under Palmerston, Russell and Gladstone (1859–65) had to cope with the crisis over Italian unity (1859–60) on liberal principles, and the American Civil War on no principles at all. Gladstone's support of the South at Newcastle in 1862 (he later described this as a 'mistake of incredible grossness') was made to seem untenable in October of that year by Lincoln's proclamation of the freedom of slaves in the rebel states. From then on, pro-South was made to seem pro-slavery. But if the origin of the Civil War was the quarrel over freedom against slavery, the final form was the Union against Secession. England faced the prospect either of the emergence of a powerful Union, or of a Southern power predicated on slavery.

Southern sympathisers in England, mostly from the upper echelons of society, were more articulate and more vocal than the Northern supporters, generally from the lower classes. America appealed more to the cottage than the country house. The lower classes were more in touch with grass-roots American opinion, often related to recent emigrants, avidly receiving letters home. The emergence of a democratic Union also concentrated English minds on the prospect of political reform at home. Lincoln's victory in 1865 challenged the domestic conservatism which Palmerston had imposed on English Liberals.

English reformers such as John Bright or Richard Cobden sided with the North, while anti-reformers sided with the Confederacy: after Palmerston died came the deluge, American democracy, feared by Whig and Tory alike:

> The issue was greatly influenced from overseas. The colonies had just been granted self-government without any limitation on the suffrage – a powerful argument against the restriction of the franchise at home. And now the principle of democracy as a practical form of government was undergoing ordeal by battle in the United States.[67]

In 1865 England had tested the goodwill of the North and failed to gain friends in the South; the gradual rapprochement between America and England throughout the 1840s and 1850s had cooled. The gulf between the nations concerned, at one level, how their citizens organised themselves: politically and socially. American manners were different, egalitarian, democratic. American behaviour was intimate with the American's sense of national identity. Not only was this the new country, but after 1865 this was the home of a new democracy.

The classic American behaviour book was George Washington's *Rules of Conduct* made popular in Jared Sparks' edition of Washington's *Writings* (1834–37). It withstood countless reprintings and illustrated the standard of good manners and morals among those who had Washington's training.[68] But the search for an exact science of behaviour took the etiquette and manners book into strange byways.

Cecil B. Hartley's 1860 *Gentleman's Book of Etiquette and Manual of Politeness* covered conversation, table etiquette, calling, street behaviour, ballroom manners, dress, exercise, travel, church etiquette, parties, home etiquette, weddings, letters, and etiquette for places of amusement. The grasp at comprehensiveness made by the last 'Miscellaneous' chapter showed how thinly these books spread themselves, producing weak opinion strongly held. What emerged was a series of advisings which Dogberry would be proud to have given to the Messinan watch: 'If you are invited to drink with a friend, and do not drink wine, bow, raise your glass of water and drink with him.'[69] Yet alongside these inanities, this: 'Avoid any air of mystery when speaking to those next you: it is ill-bred and in excessively bad taste',[70] where notions of ill breeding (hereditary connotations) sat uneasily with notions of bad taste (cultivation connotations) in a demotic society.

The American etiquette book of the mid-century searched for its own identity by casting wide and trying to apply itself to a range of issues. A book on 'gentility' advised on beauty, piano-playing, dress, 'treatment of the hair, use of the brush, removal of scurf', dentifrice, the offices of domestic social interaction (calls, dinners, visits, invitations). This advice rubbed shoulders with 'the whole art of correct and elegant letter-writing' and tips on lappets, herring-stitch and the effect of tight lacing. It came from 1857 in Emily Thornwell's *Lady's Guide to Perfect Gentility*.[71]

Such books colonised new areas of experience, and defined the ways in which the familiar could stay familiar. Thornwell had the woman reader in mind, for little pertained to men's dress or activities conventionally defined by society for men. Hartley's typical book for men, advocated exercise (sailing, hunting, skating), or counselled on etiquette in places of amusement (theatre, opera, concert). Its language refined the woman companion out of existence: 'In a crowd, do not push forward, unheeding whom you hurt or inconvenience, but try to protect your companion, as far as possible, and be content to take your turn.'[72]

The state of the Union's manners in the mid-century were

intimate with nationalism, and therefore maintained an equivocal relationship with mid-Victorian England. ' "Young America",' wrote Samuel Wells in his 1857 *Book of Republican Etiquette*, 'can brook no restraint, has no conception of superiority, and reverences nothing. His ideas of equality admit neither limitation nor qualification.' The same social democracy took behaviour at face value, for as Wells knew, 'True Republicanism' required every person to have an equal chance to become as unequal as he or she could.[73] The uniqueness of American turned out to lie in its readiness to remove uniqueness.[74]

The etiquette of America in the mid-century was the etiquette of the city, a product of metrophilia in the writing which matched the shifting demographics of the period. Between 1815 and 1847 the population of the United States grew from 8 to 17 million; the vast immigration of the non-English races was only just beginning. For the most part America was a rural nation. The 1860 census classified five of every six Americans as rural dwellers, and took a liberal view of what a city was. But as the century discovered ways of turning more of the virgin land into commutable property, the metropolitan lifestyle became more prominent. Preserved foods, packaged meats, standardised sizings and demotic travel put the urban experience in touch with the rural setting. Manners followed.

As Americans changed their homes and work, the city and its manners came to set the tone for all; by 1890, 15 per cent of Americans lived in one of the twenty-eight cities with a population of over 100,000. Cities represented not only the confluence of social forces, but places where, with an instantly usable and easily recognised code of manners, vital social information could be imparted or registered. Here was the point where individual and community met, in a country where each was in the process of defining the other. M. C. Conkling wrote in 1857 that manner itself, the adjunct to expressiveness in words, should be 'in a degree modified by circumstances – be *individualized*'.[75] In America intercourse with others limited individual scope:

> Democratic friction has necessarily broken up and rubbed off a
> good deal of the original crustiness of our nature. Casual
> intercourse between strangers in America is much freer than in

England. The American, perhaps, is wanting as the Englishman is abounding in reserve.[76]

This was an environmental account of individual behaviour.

The quintessential American civil institutions of the 1860s and 1870s were the railway and the hotel: pieces of achieved culture *en route* to the unknown. The American hotel showed social circumstances interacting with individual proclivities (themselves resulting from national learning). Many etiquette books proffered hotel advice, timetabled alongside travel behaviour, and the 1878 *Laws of Etiquette* suggested a strict arrivals and departures routine, as if trying to make sense of new possibilities not yet overrun by rules.[77] The idea of the American hotel was itself exactly on the frontier of civilisation, for it represented the first inroad of gentility and also contained within itself the potential for gentility in its furthest extreme.

The hotel as an institution oscillated precisely between the moving poles of individual and social behaviour. As early as 1836 Charles Day was able to pronounce that, while in England befriending a coffee-house or boarding-house acquaintance showed lack of respect and self-respect, 'In America, this must be taken with some allowance; boarding in hotels, and living much in public, being the custom of the country, but which is contrary to English prejudices. Besides, in the United States, there is at least a profession of equality, however chimerical may be the reality.'[78] By 1870 the *Bazar Book of Decorum* felt self-conscious enough to define the process: 'That great caravansary, the American hotel, is a characteristic expression of the national protest against individual separateness.'[79]

In England railways spawned hotels, but in America the hotel often preceded the railroad. Anthony Trollope caught the ethos in 1862 with his 'American Hotels' from *North America*:

The American inn . . . is altogether an institution apart, a thing of itself. Hotels in America are very much larger and more numerous than in other countries. They are to be found in all towns, and I may almost say in all villages . . . In the States of America the first sign of an incipient settlement is an hotel five stories high, with an office, a bar, a cloak-room, three gentlemen's

parlours, two ladies' parlours, a ladies' entrance, and two hundred
bedrooms . . . Whence are to come the sleepers in those two
hundred bedrooms, and who is to pay for the gaudy sofas and
numerous lounging chairs of the ladies' parlours? In all other
countries the expectations would extend itself simply to travellers;
– to travellers or to strangers sojourning in the land. But this is
by no means the case as to these speculations in America. When
the new hotel rises up in the wilderness, it is presumed that
people will come here with the express object of inhabiting it. The
hotel itself will create a population, – as the railways do. With
us the railways run to the towns; but in the States the towns run
to the railways. It is the same thing with the hotels.[80]

The mobile American population of the 1860s was much less
domestic than its fixed Victorian counterpart in England. The
English 'home' became the American 'house'. More fluid patterns
of employment encouraged workers to go where the jobs were; a
general atmosphere of hope and enterprise encouraged couples to
marry earlier, often without substantial means, but with enough
short-term support to enable them to live in a hotel – it was, as
Trollope said, not imprudent, but 'the way of the country'; and
hotel life actually suited many Americans of the period.

The hotel required rules. It took Trollope's English eye to
discern a pattern of manners there:

One is in a free country . . . and yet in an American inn one can
never do as one likes. A terrific gong sounds early in the morning,
breaking one's sweet slumbers, and then a second gong sounding
some thirty minutes later, makes you understand that you must
proceed to breakfast, whether you be dressed or no. You certainly
can go on with your toilet and obtain your meal after half an
hour's delay. Nobody actually scolds you for so doing, but the
breakfast is, as they say in this country, 'through' . . . They
begrudge you no amount that you can eat or drink; but they
begrudge you a single moment that you sit there neither eating
nor drinking. This is your fate if you're too late, and therefore as
a rule you are not late.[81]

The hotel was the resting place for a transient population, but
also a way of life for the urban dweller. As the century wore on,

and America became more urban, hotels flourished, but they took their origin and their style from the frontier. Like the railroad and the stage-coach, they provided occasions and opportunities for meeting others. This had always been the case, for according to one etiquette book of the 1830s the stage-coach was almost the only place where discussion should *not* be avoided, although the traveller always risked being seated next to an English noble *incognito*.

The railroad brought with it its own set of rules and manners, so by the end of the century guides like Isaac Peebles's *Politeness on Railroads* found an audience to which it explained first the values of politeness: thoughtfulness and care for others, self-denial and the self-sacrifice of one's own comfort for another's; and then the situations in which politeness might be at issue: with the ticket agent ('a decided smile would not hurt him'), on boarding ('avoid boarding the train with dogs of any kind'), and in transit ('whistling, loud talking, immoderate laughing, and singing should not be indulged by any passenger').[82]

With the stage, and then the railroad, a new environment of prolonged proximity came into being, and social rules took on the appearance of psychological principles: 'Passengers should not gaze at one another in an embarrassing way, and yet none should look as if they dislike to see one another at all.'[83] Peebles's prescriptive book failed to mention or give any indication of the different classes of passenger travel, an omission recognising the perceived breadth of the American middle class.

The first American railroad, the Baltimore & Ohio, was founded on Independence Day 1828; it was closely followed by the Charleston & Hamburg (1829–33), the railway built for steam. By 1840 there were 2,816 miles of track; the figures increased through the century: 1850 (9,015 miles), 1860 (30,600 miles), 1880 (87,801 miles). The great Union Pacific west from the Missouri River at Omaha opened in 1869. In England, Charles Kingsley hailed the 'great railroad age. Who would exchange you, with all your sins, for any other time?' The railway fired the Victorian imagination in a world hurtling down Tennyson's 'ringing grooves of change' to an improved future. The railway needed money. Railway speculation in the 1840s found the Victorians' beliefs in machinery, progress and self-help united in the figures of railway engineers and entrepreneurs. Each used the railway for his own end: Brunel's London-Bristol line started a personal transatlantic journey ending in the *Great Western*; George Hudson, MP, the 'Railway King', loved the power and money which railway investment yielded; and Samuel Smiles used railway engineers as subjects for inspiring biography.

British and American alike left the shape of their rail networks to the market and individual promoters. In America, while the railway preceded the roads west, its function on established routes was to make money: by the 1890s, twenty-one routes connected New York to Chicago and ninety New York to New Orleans. But nineteenth-century Europe saw the railways as symbols of national unity and international conncection: in France, the historian Jules Michelet rejoiced that the railway brought 'Lyons and Paris into communion with one another'.

English railways spelled class mobility and proximity; American railroads meant discovery and freedom. The cars themselves were differently constructed. Railroads not only reduced distances between places, but between different classes. Dickens had noticed the absence of 'class' cars on railways (although there were some apartheid cars in the South); and Tupper noted the open interiors, 'like long omnibuses, with the seats arranged as the aisle of a church'.

The railways spawned the desire and measurement of change: looking back over his century, Alfred Russel Wallace crooned over them as one of its great cultural developments. In England, Ruskin was scared of mass mobility – 'I don't want them to see Helvellyn while they are drunk'; in America, they were the instrument of discovery.

V The Domestic Scene

Since 1851, when England celebrated the Great Exhibition, America had absorbed great shocks to the political system: civil war, one president murdered, another impeached, and three political parties split (Whigs, 1852; Democrats, 1860; Republicans, 1872). The forces for cohesion were the new national entrepreneurial spirit, the drive westward, and the growing sense of national identity. America offered more opportunity for social intercourse between equals, but fewer rules to legislate over these interactions.

Throughout the century American manners depended crucially on the comparative lack of social consensus; they began to rely on a growing body of books of instruction. English mid-Victorians could draw on a system of etiquette books, moral essays, homiletic novels and poems, and multi-media sententia on envelopes, railway timetables and advertisements. English mid-Victorian society had means of self-representation to hand, but the more volatile and mobile society of mid-nineteenth-century America lacked the density of connection in established formal and informal institutions. As young America grew it formed its railways, lending libraries, working-men's societies or philanthropic societies; but it formed them laterally rather than vertically.

Accounts of American behaviour related not to other forms of behaviour but directly to interpretations of the American character: this explained the damaging nature of the remarks from Dickens and Trollope. The early set of the American etiquette book was more aligned towards the immediate implications of the behaviour it advocated than its English counterpart.

The voice of American etiquette, heard here in 1829, modulated between the legal and the pragmatic: 'Every act of politeness is, or ought to be, produced from some cause, and done for some special motive, that some end may be accomplished';[84] the language of act, cause, motive and end implied a much more practical view about what a set of manners might achieve than most English books offered.

The place where the most American etiquette occurred was in the newly created environment of the street: gentlemen walked on the outside when with a lady and allowed women, the elderly, priests and parcel-bearers to pass on the inside; they refrained from smoking in the street before nightfall. While *American Etiquette and Rules of Politeness* remained undecided in 1882 about which side of the sidewalk a man and woman should take, it returned to the rule that the woman's preference should be honoured, 'or that [side] on which she will be least exposed to crowding – usually the side toward the wall. On having crossed the street, to unlock arms and interchange positions is too formal.'[85]

While Mrs Admiral Dahlgren's *Etiquette of Social Life in Wash-*

ington (which cites a range of divergent opinions on many points of etiquette) and the Home Journal's *Social Etiquette in New York* urged the man to offer his left arm to the lady and keep her on the inside of the sidewalk, the formidable Mrs Ward (Clara Bloomfield-Moore) dissented on the grounds that the woman might be right-handed and need to hold her dress or parasol, and claimed that the women near the wall rule applied in cities with narrow streets, and not in modern America.

These dissonant opinions signified little until Mrs Ward, who followed her technique of drawing on a dozen of so of the more popular books and six dozen or so popular writers,[86] admitted their unimportance but said:

> as the non-observance of just such trivial points creates confusion
> where harmony should reign, and inconvenience where the
> comfort of all should be regarded, we shall try to show which of
> these rules is best suited to our mode of life in America, without
> reference to the customs of any other country.[87]

Beneath Ward's project lay the need for rules in an environment not yet properly cultivated. Conflicting customs were explained by accounting for their usefulness in context; the aim was a uniformity and fixity of social usage essential before America could be said to have what questing foreigners called society.

The Nation, in debate with *The Galaxy* ('What Constitutes American Society?'), worried about exactly this point: 'From our want of fixed society, then, and of a fixed national type, it follows that whoso seeks among us fixed society usages will always be liable to mistakes.'[88] *The Galaxy* felt itself outflanked by the subject's universality, and shrugged towards the March 1873 edition of *Lippincott*. This yielded one Mrs Moore, regretting the diversity of manners in America, sensing that where no fixed rules obtained misunderstanding must follow, perplexing both the giver and taker of the offence. Ward sums up by expressing the perplexity of the putatively well-behaved American of the 1870s:

> What our society needs is '*fixed society usages*', not various customs
> laid down as actual laws, where there is no general understanding
> as to the origin of, and reason for, the customs, – where, in fact,

only a few hold them in observance, the majority knowing them to be contrary to prevailing ideas, and in some cases antagonistic to the spirit of our institutions. A knowledge of etiquette is not merely a knowledge of common politeness, but *of the general customs of society at its best*, and obedience to it is to social life what obedience to law is to political life . . .[89]

This state of affairs contrasted with Victorian England, where class etiquette distinguished itself largely by its inexplicability in practical terms. The English manners myth trapped them inside an organic institution where dissent dropped the dissenter not into a waste of lower quality manners, but into a vacuum of no-manners. Ward's shrewd pronouncement came from doggedly following one path of energy through the American anxieties about correct street behaviour: 'we do not wish to be told only what customs are, in American society, but what they ought to be'.[90]

Ward's enquiry into street manners led her to discuss street traffic in the Black Hills and in Deadwood, the wedding ceremony (the bride stands on the bridegroom's left, the better to stand on his right when they turn round to process out through the congregation), and the custom in French dining rooms. The breadth of her reference showed how apt American manners thinkers were to reach for precedents while at the same time trying to keep an individual voice.

In a society where encountering others as they went about their business was the only way of meeting them, street behaviour took on a particular importance. In nineteenth-century urban America the street represented the commercial and social forum where all met equally, but some more than others:

If walking with a female relative or friend, a well-bred man will take the outer side of the pavement, not only because the wall-side is the most honourable side of a public walk, but because it is generally the farthest point from danger in the street . . .
Courtesy and manly courage will both incite him to this line of conduct.[91]

The anxiety about rightness turned walking into a matter of

breeding, and part of the setting into an 'honourable' area. This typified the nineteenth-century American approach to environment: the New World had to be colonised by more than homesteads and staked claims. It had to be ethically assimilated to the American mind. So the Americans evolved non-ownership terms which nonetheless appropriated the landscape: the West, the Prairie, the Midwest.

The 1830s witnessed the greatest American nervousness about the status of Union manners. No set of works more clearly draws the line between manners – the way we relate to everyone else – and etiquette – the way an individual relates to others in the same class or narrow 'society'. The 1838 *Ladies Pocket Book of Etiquette*, published in Liverpool and handy for the New World steamer, required all society's participants to know social observances and the reason for them. The book meant something less than an entire community when it referred to etiquette as the set of laws which governed what was commonly called *society*.[92] The divisions upheld by etiquette and the community implied by a system of manners continued through the 1840s, when, faced with a mercantile, movable society, Charles Day (mistakenly thought to be Count D'Orsay by a New York bookseller), said the unsayable:

> Etiquette is the barrier which society draws around itself as a protection against offenses the '*law*' can not touch – it is a shield against the intrusion of the impertinent, the improper, and the vulgar – a guard against those obtuse persons who, having neither talent nor delicacy, would be continually thrusting themselves into the society of men to whom their presence might (from the difference of feeling and habit) be offensive, and even insupportable.[93]

Day's language of defence and offence snubbed the community beyond the 'society' twice mentioned, with sharpening focus (first 'society' and then 'society of men' of a particular kind). The abstract phrasing here create a hesitancy about the status of 'the impertinent, the improper, and the vulgar': the qualities and the persons who bring them become indistinguishable and loiter on the edge of being recognised.

In terms of strict social intercourse and interplay, Day was right, for etiquette developed to ensure that a social environment, like a contained fluid in dynamic equilibrium, neither expanded nor condensed, remaining free from outside influence. This separatism explained his view on English social mobility in the 1830s, highlighting the English aristocracy's perpetual, easy self-rejuvenation:

> The English are the most democratic aristocrats in the world; always endeavouring to squeeze through the portals of rank and fashion, and then slamming the door in the face of any unfortunate devil who may happen to be behind them.[94]

Forty years on, a Baltimore dance manual put the matter even more plainly by finding in the superior manners of an aristocracy its securest defence and safeguard against insurrection from the unmannered.[95] And at the century's end, the ubiquitous Mary Sherwood described London society as only a confident, separated outsider could: 'London possesses a regular system of society, a social citadel, around which rally those whose birth, title, and character are well-known.'[96] This separateness started early and ran throughout the century.

The anonymous 1836 *Laws of Etiquette* looked back to English models by looking back at Chesterfield; but it yearned for a hierarchy not yet established across all America. It found society in England intimately connected with the government, where 'the distinctions in one are the origin of gradations in the other'; it also found society in America one in which 'there is distinction . . . but there are no distinctions'.[97] Here, American individualism maintained the balance between the notions of separateness and exaltation in 'distinction', without necessarily making one the reward for the other; by 1850 the word shoulders the full weight of its ambiguity: 'in this free land, there are no political distinctions, and the only social ones depend upon character and manners'.[98]

Etiquette made clear that any distinction should be earned, deserved and approved by the wider community; so the earned 'respectable' replaces the undeserving 'genteel'.[99] Conformist individualism, fostered by manners books in the 1840 and 1850s, saw America through the 50 per cent rise in population between 1870 and 1890, and directed the expenditure of the 132 per cent increased national income over the same period, before the market panic of 1893. Moreover, as the poet Will Carlton poignantly recalled,[100] the agricultural crash of 1887 weighed severe droughts and disastrous winters in the mortgage balance, and helped to cut the 1820 proportion of agricultural workers (73 per cent in 1820) to 43 per cent by 1890, leaving them to make their own way in the newly created urban areas which, by 1890, contained 35 per cent of the population.

Etiquette books quickly inculcated the national sense that manners constituted a code to be learned for successful living. This development occurs parallel to the nationalism which makes space for it to expand. As the century advanced, American etiquette books took leave of the image thrust upon Americans by Fanny Trollope, and started to explore the society itself through the medium of etiquette. Charles Leland's *The Art of Conversation* plotted the changes:

> Social intercourse, even in royal circles, is every day being based
> more and more on the laws of common sense, of kindness and
> of respect for the innate dignity of every man, than on the accidents
> of rank, and on a conversational Japanese-like etiquette. The laws
> which lend grace and a charm to life are, in other words, becoming
> more distinctly intelligible, and more capable of being defined as
> something real, even in a book.[101]

In 1860, *Advice to Young Men on their Duties and Conduct in Life* advocated the reading of other etiquette books so that the reader could 'thereby acquaint himself with the laws that are observed in polite society'.[102]

Gradually the books formed a system of social standard related to but independent of society. Mid-Victorian English etiquette books had reached this procedural watershed long before the American manners books, mostly by their assumption of shared values, usually Christian. In 1852 G. W. Hervey, who published in both England and America, wrote multi-denominational and non-sectarian series of hints and observations for Christians gathered as his *Principles of Courtesy*,[103] which he felt reached beyond the *secular* customs of polished society, and which balanced matters of common decency – manners – with those of temporary, local etiquette. Hervey's tripartite guide originated in moral discourse, and dealt first with matters of humility, gravity, gentleness, delicacy, propriety, sincerity and zeal; secondly with forms of courtesy in religious society, deportments for hymn-singing, posture in prayer and behaviour at a range of ceremonies; and thirdly with the secular society which inhabited the familiar territory of social calls, visits and travels.

Hervey's book, along with others in the same genre,[104] began to turn manners into etiquette, a specialised set of rules pertaining to a particular situation. This move produced a series of guides to Washington in particular, as America created an environment in which manners interacted with politics. This coincided with the rise of men who did not speak nationally: Jefferson Davis (1809–89) of Mississippi, Stephen A. Douglas (1813–61) from Illinois. New manners came to the capital.

Washington guides attended to the minutest and most telling details: style of dress for a presidential audience, calling etiquette for members of Congress. One 1866 guide recalled smugly that nowhere 'are the advantages of education and polished manners more conducive to happier results than they are among the *beau monde* of the Federal Metropolis'.[105] This marked the nexus of manners with politics; here, the language of advantage and result met the language of polished manners among the *beau monde*.

By the mid-century matters of government became matters of behaviour under certain particular rules. The city quickly created precedents for its own past, particularly in social-political life. The Washington lobby, which it was thought arose while General Jackson was waging war against the last United States Ban, from 1830 to 1836, was a a case in point. 'Lobbying,' claimed Horace Greeley's biographer, James Parton, 'is as ancient as governing', and maintained its necessity on the grounds of the governing power's need for the special knowledge which a lobby properly supplies. 'It is only when the governing power is weak or corrupt or too transient,' Parton reflects in his 1870 'Log-Rolling in Washington', 'that there is a danger of the lobby laying aside its modest office of supplying information, and assuming the mastery.'[106]

From the start the Washington visiting routine represented social patterning overlaid by political expedience:

A private citizen may make a member of congress, ten visits; but
the citizen must not think it any thing extraordinary if the
member should not return . . . them, for it is not very common
for them to return visits, or calls, unless they have been former
friends, or that the citizen is a very distinguished person.[107]

Washington etiquette also brought demotic republicanism into
contact with a rapidly developing high society; this contact engen-
dered the feeling that something more than access or wealth was
needed: 'even amongst us republicans', wrote Louis Tasistro in
1866, 'the exigencies of polite society require something more
commanding to entitle a man to admission to the enchanted circles
of what is called fashionable life than the mere attributes of
wealth',[108] trying to set the trap both ways by equivocating the
value of what he advocated.

With the notion of a separate Washington society, other groups
were free to develop their own separatisms; what was fashionable
on Fifth Avenue or Madison Square did not necessarily suit the
salons of Washington. So the later part of the century proliferated
the *Metropolitan Culture Series* (including 'Social Life' and 'Good
Manners'),[109] a recognition of the importance of urban dwellers,
and their anxieties about what correct behaviour might be.

American individualism, nationalism, provincialism and metrophilia all worked to produce the brand of American behaviour
book typified by the popular 'Mrs Manners', whose reputation as
'the highest authority we can possible quote on such matters'[110]
derived from the 1853 *At Home and Abroad*.[111] This was into its
second thousand by the following year. The book set out from
declared Christian principles – *'all things whatsoever you would
that men should do to you, do ye even so to them'* – to cover table
manners, church behaviour and travel (steamers and trains). Two
chapters, 'How to Choose and win Friends' and 'Directions for
Letter-writing', turned manners into pragmatic interchange
between people, and etiquette into the conduct of specifically
defined social relationships. 'It is considered polite, in ordinary
letters of friendship, to write to the middle of the fourth page,
leaving that part of the letter, which will be outside when folded,
a blank; but this is a mere matter of etiquette.'[112]

As manners books became more sophisticated, and as an American voice started to make itself heard, these books arrogated more activities and brought more of the middle-class American's daily life under the regimen of written but unspoken rules. The substantial 500-page *Illustrated Manners Book and Manual of Good Behaviour and Polite Accomplishments*, which sold by post from New York for One Dollar, admitted the increasing incidence of occasions which required some knowledge of the etiquette or style of behaviour appropriate to 'and necessary in a well-regulated society'.[113]

Everywhere the American manners book rested on the notion that manners aided social achievement in the land of freedom, ambition and energetic self-hood. Whereas the mid-Victorian English etiquette book took everything for granted by taking its models from an aristocratic class, the American version typified the American approach by arguing a code of behaviour from first principles. This from the *Illustrated Manners* explains exactly the American attitude:

> . . . all that makes up a Science of Behaviour, will appear hereafter, and need not be stated in the form of abstract propositions. There is no rule of life which is not based on science, and which may not be referred to some principle or law. Doubtless there may be observances of etiquette which seem purely arbitrary and capricious, but they are few, and of no consequence. Even these, if carefully examined, may be found to have, or to have had, some good reason. But every genuine and valuable rule of behaviour may be referred to some principle of natural law; so the observance of what may seem at first glance a matter of trifling etiquette, may be a moral duty; and a breach of decorum a crime.[114]

By the 1870s the status of the American manners book mirrored the growing cohesiveness and inclusiveness of American society; for in the American etiquette book, comments ranged from the pious to the practical.

In keeping with mid-Victorian orthodoxy, the American woman shouldered the family responsibility for the moral tone of the house, for 'the very presence of a respectable female will often restrain those from evil whose hearts are full of it'.[115] She also took the moral and intellectual training of the children as her task.[116] The American family unit, the instrument rather than the obstacle of social change, operated under a wider range of circumstance than its mid-Victorian counterpart. For the middle class, advice on house building, drainage and animal husbandry (aimed at men) sat alongside tips on baking, moral instruction for children and housekeeping.

The American model valued practicality and was less squeamish about the tasks of daily life than its transatlantic equivalent:

> The more closely you examine the work of any woman who is a successful housekeeper, the more evident it will become to you that, like the woman we have been following through the duties of the day, she is orderly, systematic and thorough in all her habits . . . the work of each day is arranged so that nothing is left to chance.[117]

Unlike her English sister, the American set her agenda, and behaved as if in business. The very notion of examining the work of a middle-class Victorian woman affronted her status, but not so the American's.

The Englishwoman as wife and mother still owed her allegiance, energies and duties to the home, but the American woman was less confined by the confinement. As *Our Manners and Social Customs* suggested: 'if the wife have her duties, so has the husband his . . . the privilege . . . of making the home happy is not the wife's alone'.[118] A spirit of partnership emerged, reaching towards the independence and assertiveness which Marie Corelli so applauded in American women when they dealt with the stolid British. The bestseller and cultural pundit wondered why American women were so popular in England:

> Why is her charmingly assertive personality acknowledged everywhere? Why is she received by knights and earls and belted churls with such overpowering enthusiasm? Surely something subtle, elusive and mysterious, clings to her particular form, nature and identity, for more often than not, the stolid Britisher, while falling at her feet and metaphorically kissing the hem of her garment, wonders vaguely how it is that she manages to make such a fool of him![119]

Corelli considered the issue in terms of chromosomes rather than conditioning, but her assumptions mediated between the national and the sexual. The male Britisher stood no chance with the 'charmingly assertive personality' of the American woman. Marion Leroy's *Good Manners* leaves the man in no doubt about the bargain he has made:

> The husband should provide for his wife as liberally as his circumstances allow, and without grudging, for the wife has given up her person, her liberty, and all the possible opportunities which might have been hers, to share his life and fortune. These considerations should make him just and generous.[120]

Here, morals and manners combined with economics; four years earlier Mrs Ward managed to make her demand more exacting: in 1878 she had argued for teaching women 'the meaning of the words capital, profit, price, value, labour, wages, and of the relation between these last two', and claimed that they would benefit as housekeepers from a practical knowledge of political economy.[121]

This marked the beginning of professional motherhood in America, where women gathered the skills and expertise unique to any profession. The manners books recognised that the American woman, isolated from the infrastructure which helped to support and confine her English sister, needed to acquire an astonishing range of expertise merely to function as a partner.

The frequency of female pseudonyms – 'Daphne Dale', 'Marion Leroy' or 'Mrs Manners' – among American writers on manners indicated that the imparting and absorbing of manners had become an increasingly female province: market forcés had orchestrated an advantage based on perceived gender.

Among the centres of etiquette Washington was paramount, a domestic city to be proud of which was, by nature of its diplomatic status, always on show to foreigners. Washington etiquette occupied an obligatory chapter or two in many of the manners books, written with the recognition that the capital's etiquette differed from that observed elsewhere . . . less democratic, more formal and perhaps less worthy of imitation than that prevailing in ordinary society'.[122] The same year produced Katherine Thomas's dull little book *Official, Diplomatic, and Social Etiquette of Washington*, which recognised the connection and the distinctness of all three while putting the reader through a rigorous training in how to have tea with the wife of a newly elected Chief Justice, and the length of time to remain after a luncheon with the wife of the Speaker of the House.

Katherine Thomas left nothing to chance. Her book set out the rules clearly and laboriously, and was aimed at visitors to Washington intimidated by metropolitan behaviour: 'The formal season begins in Washington immediately after the New Year morning reception at the White House, and practically closes on Ash Wednesday',[123] although the winter gaieties began somewhat in advance of this, when Congress convened on the first Monday in December. The President, unlike Victoria, was always on public show; an envelope of propriety surrounded his progress – carriage seating, presentations, diplomatic breakfasts and Saturday afternoon White House receptions. In essence, the rules translated directly from the Victorian society of ten years earlier, but they were reapplied to enable Washington participants to communicate on an equable basis, rather than to exclude from London an insistent, vulgar Manchester or Birmingham middle class.

The latter part of the century found an America on easier terms with its own forms of behaviour. By 1898 *Etiquette for Americans* was able to pronounce that, though at one time there might have been an excuse for borrowing from England, 'there is certainly none now. American ways are running in well-oiled grooves; American customs, American hours are the arbiters, of America's code of manners.'[124] Mary Sherwood's *Manners and Social Usages* (a substantial 500 pages, reaching four editions from 1884 to 1897) incorporated the best in English manners into its latest edition by adopting a conservative, retrospective principle, nostalgic for a golden age of manners:

A well-bred lady who entered society with Queen Victoria fifty-three years ago, could she have been put into a Rip-Van-Winkle sleep and suddenly awakened in the most fashionable circles of to-day, would not find herself *rococo* as to her cards, her note-paper, her acceptance of invitations, or her manner of entertaining. Indeed, she would be more *au fait* . . . than many of her *nouveaux riches* entertainers, for she would have learned the language of etiquette in a thorough school . . .[125]

Manners created and maintained an established society. Changes in them became asymptotically more subtle as general patterns of behaviour diminished the scope for dissent. Just as the aesthetes and decadents of the Victorian 1880s and 1890s had begun to dismantle and undermine the carefully established codes of manners by flaunting certain forms of behaviour and flouting others, American etiquette had arrived at the point where it was confident enough to be retrospective about itself.

The growing self-confidence of American manners spilt into the twentieth century in the form of growing assertiveness; in 1915: 'Republican manners ought surely to be the best; we have no privileged class which must be deferred to, we all have an equal right to courteous treatment from each other.'[126] And manners books themselves became more prescriptive and arbitrary towards the end of the century, arriving at a position occupied by their English counterparts fifteen years before. They created a sense of community by defining what the community's sense is: '*Genteel* is an extremely vulgar word, and is never used in good society', or, 'Colored note-paper, so common a few years ago, is no longer in use . . . at present no color that is appreciable is considered stylish.'[127]

In 1895 'Daphne Dale' started the hefty *Our Manners and Social Customs* with an anthropological excursion which belied the book's prescriptive indulgences. The investigation returned upon itself, finding within the newly created history of manners the origins of its own being, the descent of its own manners and the survival of its species. When the American book drew on its own heroes, Washington, Greeley and Franklin, it showed the manners culture keeping faith with itself by collating a litany of temperance, resolution, frugality, industry, sincerity, moderation and tranquillity.[128]

The vital concept in American manners was 'ease' – facility and achievability. In the expressive subtitle of the *American Book of Genteel Behavior* lay the archaeology of American manners in the nineteenth century. Here was their comprehensive go-anywhere,

suit-anyone attitude, their usefulness for the socially mobile on
the threshold of new success, and their ease:

> *American Book of Genteel Behavior*: A Complete Hand Book of
> Modern Etiquette for Ladies and Gentlemen. Embracing the
> Customs and Usages of Polite Society in all places and at all times.
> Being a perfect guide to all about to enter either public or private
> life, showing how to act under all circumstances with ease, elegance
> and freedom.

It could never have happened in England.

5
Money – 'The Time for Panic is at Hand'

On Sunday 17 February 1856, a suicide was discovered on Hampstead Heath; with the body, this note:

> Saturday Night I can not live – I have ruined too many – I could not live and see their agony – I have committed diabolical crimes unknown to any human being. They will now appear, bringing my family and others to distress – causing to all shame and grief that they should ever have known me.
> I blame no one, but attribute all to my own infamous villainy . . . I could go through any torture as a punishment for my crimes. No torture could be too much for such crimes, but I can not live to *see* the tortures I inflict upon others.[1]

The body, and the note (written on the evening of Saturday 16 February), belonged to John Sadleir, MP for Carlow, Junior Lord of the Treasury, Chairman of the Royal Swedish Railway Company and of the London & County Joint-Stock Banking Company. His crime was fraud. He did not name it, nor had he, at his death, been convicted of it.

Sadleir probably issued £150,000 in false shares from the Royal Swedish, and probably defrauded the Tipperary Joint-Stock Bank (which he and his brother James controlled) of £200,000. Monday's *Times* reported that Sadleir had purchased land sold in the Irish Encumbered Estates Court, and that he was 'extensively connected with various commercial undertakings of magnitude' but under no heavy liabilities to the London & County bank. Sadleir was a smart Dublin solicitor with a talent for public relations and a modest lifestyle thought incompatible with vast fraudulence. The paper described him as a 'national calamity'. No one knew how the money was dissipated; there was nothing ostentatious in his habits, nothing extravagant in his mode of living. His gift to posterity was the character for Dickens's Mr Merdle in *Little Dorrit*;[2] Dickens told his biographer that he 'shaped Mr. Merdle himself out of that precious rascality'.[3] Merdle left no letter as Sadleir had, but 'he had left a letter at the Baths addressed to his physician, and his physician had got the letter, and the letter would be produced at the Inquest on the morrow, and it would fall like a thunderbolt upon the multitude that he had deluded'.[4]

Sadleir's offence was to break the rules of conduct imposed throughout the 1850s, 1860s and 1870s which governed confidence in each other and confidence in the future. Breaking them meant transgressing two codes: the legal and the social. Fraud combined the two. Flanked by the Scylla of loss on one side and the Charybdis of failure on the other, commercial crime took a median course piloted by the desire to make money easily, quickly and securely.

Sadleir's story was really a story of how money shaped behaviour. For financial behaviour and money manners combined values of worth, credibility and trust with those of commerce and the palpable realities of wealth, ownership or debt. The rule of manners, and the mid-Victorian thinking which lay behind it, stretched into finance, where financial frauds like Sadleir knew how manners and behaviour within the financial community operated to allow scope for the social and financial entrepreneur. Victorian financial thinking was bounded on the one side by the imperatives of the divines, and on the other by the small solicitations of commercial circumstance.

Fraud was simple misbehaviour, bad manners of the worst kind. Yet the etiquette which surrounded the use of money, the allure of philanthropy or the tactical deployment of largess was precise, robust. Here was where behaviour in the form of manners often found itself at odds with behaviour in the form of self interest or commercial imperative. New money, for the mid-Victorians, the age of capital, produced the need for new codes of behaviour. Raw power was tempered and fitted for everyday commerce by the agency of manners: business forms and patterns of workday repetition made a map of ritualised behaviour. Fraudsters knew the system, how to work it, and how to break the rules without being seen to. That is why in looking at financial manners, the frauds have most to tell.

Fraud and over-speculation were bad behaviour, breaking rules
in a market which, ideally at least, ran on probity. Speculation
was the supreme sin, charity the supreme virtue. Money behaviour
formed an arena in which attitude, behaviour and actuality drew
together to form an environment of manners: this consisted of
beliefs about riches, poverty, trust, fraud, success, failure, decency
and probity. Money meant the practical implementation of
religious beliefs; and financial dealings, like social relations, had
their own cast of etiquette. Codes of money manners encouraged
individuals to live both a public and a private life.

I Trust and Frauds

Trollope was always sensitive to money. His mother was forced
to make it later in life, and Trollope famously dwelt on the money-
making side of his writing in his *Autobiography*. But he also
included this curious incident from his time at the Post Office:

On one occasion in the performance of my duty, I had to put a
private letter containing bank-notes on my secretary's table –
which letter I had duly opened, as it was not marked private. The
letter was seen by the Colonel, but had not been moved by him
when he left the room. On his return it was gone. In the meantime
I had returned to the room, again for the performance of some
duty. When the letter was missed I was sent for, and there I found
the Colonel much moved about his letter, and a certain chief
clerk, who, with a long face, was making suggestions as to the
probable fate of the money. 'The letter has been taken,' said the
Colonel, 'and, by G – ! you have taken it.' As he spoke, he
thundered his fist down upon the table. 'Then,' said I, 'you have
taken it.' And I also thundered my first down, – but, accidentally,
not upon the table. There was a standing movable desk, at which,
I presume, it was the Colonel's habit to write, and on this movable
desk was a large bottle full of ink. My fist unfortunately came
on the desk, and the ink at once flew up, covering the Colonel's
face and shirt front. Then it was a sight to see that senior clerk,
as he seized a quire of blotting-paper, and rushed to the aid of his
superior officer, striving to mop up the ink; and a sight also to
see the Colonel, in his agony, hit right through the blotting-paper

at that senior clerk's unoffending stomach. At that moment there came the Colonel's private secretary, with the letter and the money, and I was desired to go back to my room.

Trollope's outrage was that he had been thought untrustworthy. The farce of the situation derived from closeness to slapstick; the seriousness derived from the realisation that a breach of trust was somehow a fall in character. Since the idea of trust underpinned the City foundations, and since it was seen as vital to City transactions, the financial community made it portable and transferrable.

Trust easily translated into credit,[5] and, in financial circles, into creditworthiness and credibility. W. M. Ellis in *A Chart of Industrial Life* (1869) was emphatic that rules of conduct obliged all who used credit 'never to do so unless sure of having the means to discharge those obligations when called upon to do so'.[6] Favours and credibility were current, too, and money was not the only commodity in which the markets traded.

There was such a danger as over-speculating on oneself. 'If in private life,' mused D. Morier Evans, the great City writer, *à propos* the career of Walter Watts, 'a man live in a mansion, maintain a large establishment – servants – an equipage, and all the outward appearances of wealth, few people care much to inquire whether or not he possesses the reality – credit, almost without limit, is at his command, and without question.'[7] The City figure had to strike a balance between wasteful extravagance and liberal expenditure commensurate with maintaining a station in society. Evans warned against 'the gay, fascinating spendthrift, who gives grand parties, who invites his friends to a trip in his yacht, or a seat in his well-appointed vehicle', suggesting that such a character was too often accepted 'just for what he is worth, without the least reflection as to the means by which his wealth is acquired'.[8]

Manner was essential to the maintenance of credibility and the fostering of trust:

A passable address – an adequate stock of cool assurance – a tolerable knowledge of figures – and an aptitude for ringing the changes in matters of finance – are all that is necessary. With these a man may start as a millionaire, and for a time vie with the wealthiest in expenditure, and possibly – though, happily, for the sake of morality, this is the very rare exception – by some grand *coup*, in the end establish himself in the position he has been assuming. This is the goal which the general class of adventurers have probably always in view when they enter upon their career; but how few of them ever reach it![9]

In fiction, Catherine Gore in *The Banker's Wife, Or Court and City* (1843) realised how social appearances could influence perceived financial standing:

A London banker, having a handsome establishment in town, is held bound to re-assemble his domesticities about him, as soon as may be after the meeting of parliament. It would 'look odd' were his wife to be without an opera-box during the season . . . It would 'look odd', were his pew in Mary-le-bone Church to be empty . . . and a banker is bound to eschew all and any thing that 'looks odd'. Everything about him, both in public and private life, should be as even as the balance of his books.[10]

Dickens too knew this, and was quick to show the process of status, image and vicarious trust at work in the markets. In *Little Dorrit* he cast Mr Merdle as 'immensely rich; a man of prodigious enterprise; a midas without the ears, who turned all he touched to gold':

He was in everything good, from banking to building. He was in Parliament, of course. He was in the City, necessarily. He was the Chairman of this, Trustee of that, President of the other. The weightiest of men had said to projectors, 'Now, what name have you got? Have you got Merdle?' and, the reply being in the negative, had said, 'Then I won't look at you.'[11]

Trollope's archetypal financier, Augustus Melmotte in *The Way We Live Now* (1874–5), also lived on reputation: 'Gentlemen who don't know the nature of credit, how strong it is, – as the air – to buoy you up; how slight it is, – as a mere vapour, – when roughly touched, can do an amount of mischief which they themselves don't in the least understand the extent.'[12] Trollope showed that he knew the system and the structure, the form of behaviour which made it work.

Trollope's depiction of Melmotte's end was also instructive. Just before his description of the Member for Westminster, inebriated in the House on the evening of his suicide, Trollope fashioned a rare self-conscious insight for him:

> Never once, not for a moment; did it occur to him that he should repent of the fraud in which his whole life had been passed. No idea ever crossed his mind of what might have been the result had he lived the life of an honest man. Though he was inquiring into himself as closely as he could, he never even told himself that he had been dishonest. Fraud and dishonesty had been the very principle of his life, and had so become a part of his blood and bones that even in this extremity of his misery he made no question within himself as to his right judgement in regard to them. Not to cheat, not to be a scoundrel, not to live more luxuriously than others by cheating more brilliantly, was a condition of things to which his mind had never turned itself.[13]

Trollope made Melmotte's final hours a painful epitaph to the world of commercial and political power. On the evening of his suicide Melmotte enters the House for a second time, after a bibulous dinner, a hefty cigar and a trio of brandies. He attempts to catch the Speaker's eye during a debate on game laws; eventually he succeeds and has the floor, but is too drunk to speak. This is the fall of Melmotte: 'He stumbled forward, recovered himself, then looked once more round the House with a glance of anger, and after that toppled headlong over the shoulders of Mr. Beauchamp Beauclerk, who was sitting in front of him.' He recovers, and makes his way out of the chamber for the last time: 'Had he fallen some one, – or rather some two or three, – must have picked him up and carried him out. But he did not fall either there or in the lobbies, or on his way down to Palace Yard.'[14]

Trollope found a physical image for the moral state: a fall. The word, according the *OED* (it records 101 uses), inhabits the space between 'dropping down', 'succumbing to temptation; a lapse into sin or folly; moral ruin' and the theological sense of the fall. When figuratively applied to women, 'fall' invariably meant a lapse in chastity or continence, and was therefore of a sexual nature, as in Byron's 'The once fall'n woman must for ever fall.'[15] Matters were decently complicated, since 'fall' also meant 'the fact of being struck down by calamity or disease'.[16] The word straddled responsibility, was either folly or lapse, or a calamity.

Mid-Victorian markets grappled with that notion of responsibility, notably in the attention paid to the matter in the 1855–62 Limited Liability legislation. Or, as Trollope put it in *The Way We Live Now*, 'A man cannot always restrain his own doings and keep them within the limits which he had himself planned for them. They will very often fall short of the magnitude to which his ambition has aspired. They will sometimes soar higher than his own imagination.'[17] The issue of agency and responsibility implicit in 'fall' centred on the extent of individual responsibility.[18] Melmotte's literal fall was delicately placed between the market conditions which brought about his demise, and the imprudence which left him short of time. He was destroyed by lack of credit, the inability to raise instant cash, undone not by lack of money but by lack of time.

The mid-Victorians felt the ambiguity in 'fall' to the extent of evolving a special term to signify a demise associated with a breach of trust: 1846 saw the arrival of the word 'defalcation' to denote 'a monetary deficiency, through breach of trust by one who has the management or charge of funds; a fraudulent deficiency in money matters'.[19] The word still had something of the tint of 'fall' about it when Morier Evans, over a decade later, catalogued the close of Leopold Redpath's career:

> From the moment when the news of Redpath's defalcation burst upon the town, the utmost excitement prevailed. It was not only the talk of City circles, but the topic of clubs and drawing-rooms. The effect of the announcement at the Stock Exchange was similar to that which occurred when the discovery of Robson's fraud was made; the shares dropped, and were for some time after subject to fluctuation.[20]

Evans, writing in the late 1850s, was compiling a taxonomy of deceivers in response to the increased fraud offered by the booms and commercial crises of 1847 and 1857.

Morier Evans's purpose in the incomparable and wholly fascinating *Facts, Failures and Frauds* (1859) was to bring together 'a complete record of the astounding frauds and forgeries, with other attendant circumstances, which have of late so frequently startled the commercial community from their propriety'. Evans tilted at an interesting readership; his 700 pages on fraud, and two substantial books on the crises of 1847–8 and 1857–8 were to be available 'either for the publicist, moralist, or statist'.[21] The frauds, like Smiles's engineers, were exemplars of a kind, ready packaged for the homily industry to work over.

The significance of fraud lay in its breach of the implicit compact, between individuals presupposed by any contractual agreement. Frauds (the Victorians coined the usage, in Dickens's *Reprinted Pieces*[22]) were reprehensible because they violated trust, and damaged the possibility of open relations between people. The likelihood of fraud compelled financiers to deal fairly in order to limit the damage that could be done them. Fraud diminished confidence, which Alfred Russel Wallace saw as fundamental:

> The utilitarian sanction for truthfulness is by no means very powerful and universal. Few laws enforce it. No very severe reprobation follows untruthfulness. In all ages and countries falsehood has been thought allowable in love, and laudable in war; while, at the present day, it is held to be venial by the majority of mankind in trade, commerce, and speculation.[23]

At the time, Wallace was discussing the origin of the moral sense; commerce provided him with the readiest illustration of its lack.

That same lack was noted and capitalised upon by Morier Evans. He opened *Facts, Failures and Frauds* by defining 'High Art' crime in the career of Walter Watts, as much a victim of failure in *savoir faire* as in *savoir acheter*:

> From time immemorial, clerks have been discovered embezzling the property of their employers; but when, save in the middle of the nineteenth century, could it be supposed a case such as that of Walter Watts would occur, who, not content with trifling

peccadillos, successively opened two theatres with money surreptitiously obtained from the Globe Insurance Company, and managed them in a style of undisputed magnificence in the face of empty treasuries. The career of Watts and his melancholy end in Newgate – death by his own hand – may, in fact, be regarded as a symbol of that taste for luxury, and that recklessness in the choice of means to a desired end, which so singularly distinguishes the present age.[24]

The financial suicide – like John Sadleir's – was the last act of departure, a gracious and tidy leaving of the room; as Sadleir and Watts in life, so Merdle the reputed fraud in *Little Dorrit*, or Ralph Nickleby in *Nicholas Nickleby*.

The kinds of calculated crime available or imaginable to the mid-Victorians reflected their sense not only of the possible but of the achievable. And vital, here, was the decision on how to spend it, the first social task of the successful fraud. Evans allots case studies to a variety of financial frauds and tricksters, but levies particular scrutiny on four men: Walter Watts, William Robson, George 'Railway King' Hudson and Leopold Redpath.

Redpath was the last and greatest of the frauds in the 1850s, the most anomalous of all the fraudsters. An insurance broker, late of the Peninsula and Oriental Steam Navigation Company, he perpetrated the Great Northern Railway Frauds:

> One of the most extraordinary instances of successful swindling, combined with a high moral reputation and a truly benevolent career . . . Never was money obtained with more wicked subtlety; never was it spent more charitably. The thief and the desperate criminal were so intertwined with the philanthropist, that his character presents an admirable study for the metaphysician. A greater rogue, so far as robbery is concerned, it were difficult to find; nor a more amiable and polished benefactor to the poor and the friendless.[25]

Redpath used patronage and philanthropy to buy acclaim and consolidate his social position; he became a governor of the children's St Anne's Society (for children of those once in prosperity), and of Christ's Hospital. Charity was a source of amusement and patronage, just as much as the pleasures of the table and refined company. Evans described Redpath's charity as 'spurious . . . a hollow mockery of benevolence; and yet it is hard to suspect that the genuine warmth of true benevolence did not sometimes actuate his movements'.[26] He was ambitious to be talked of as a kind-hearted, benevolent, charitable gentleman, whose hand, heart and purse were ever open.[27] He regarded behaviour as the key to success, and social insider-dealing as the way to hop the Chinese walls within their industry. Like his fellow miscreants from the mid-century, Redpath succeeded by being plausible in the society into which his new money propelled him.

The fraud, like the *arriviste*, needed to know the social codes by which more could be gained; ignorance of them courted loss and, if conviction followed, loss of liberty. Redpath was remarkable for deploying his fraudulent gains across a range of philanthropic causes. He lived discreetly, keeping his crimes from his wife. Morier Evans recounted the moments of his arrest; a messenger had been accidentally encountered, and the papers in his possession led the authorities to Redpath's house in Weybridge:

> At this delicious retreat – one of the loveliest spots in a country remarkable for its scenes of quiet loveliness – a horrible surprise was destined for Mrs. Redpath. She was sitting in her home, surrounded by all the refinements which art can add to nature, expecting her husband's return. Instead, however, of her husband, whose kindness and affection to her was a bright feature in his character, a detective suddenly made his appearance, with news which burst upon her like a thunderbolt, that her husband was discovered to be a forger and a thief. The intelligence, though quietly broken, was too much for her, and in grief she swooned, to be restored only to a more painful and deeply oppressive sense of her misery.[28]

Redpath was deported for life in 1857 for using his position as company clerk for insider dealing in Great Northern Railway shares. On 16 January 1857, Justice Willes summed up:

> You are therefore a person who has forged on a large scale; you have played for heavy stakes, and you must have been aware all along that if your iniquities were discovered, you would be called

to a heavy account. That account it is my duty to close by pronouncing upon you the sentence of the Court, which is, that you be transported beyond the seas for the term of your natural life.[29]

Even after his conviction, many beneficiaries of Redpath's charity refused to believe him guilty.

Revelations of Redpath's dishonesty, his fall from the codes of behaviour which the City was seen to uphold, followed closely on the frauds of John Sadleir and of the great Crystal Palace forger, William Robson. The latter presented a different version of Redpath's anxiety to belong. While Redpath took the philanthropic route to acceptability, Robson took the thespian way.

William James Robson was born in 1820 or 1821, and early on showed acuity in everyday business and a leaning towards creative work. These two components in his character made the ideal fraudster: the sense to know what to do and the wit to carry it out. Until 1854 he was a clerk in the Great Northern Railway; then he joined the Crystal Palace Company as chief clerk in the transfer department, reporting directly to the treasurer and registrar of the company, who noted Robson's aptness in official duties, and 'his engaging and agreeable manners'. Robson sold shares in the name of Johnson (his brother-in-law), 'witnessing' the signature himself. By this means he defrauded £27,000 from 1854 until his arrest in 1856. Evans recalled, 'at the time, no cloud of distrust had dimmed his reputation, to say nothing of his plausible manners and his clever, business-like tact in his pursuits'.[30]

Robson harboured theatrical ambition. The green-room and the ballroom made the everyday duties of desk and transfer book into a drudgery. Evans's account of his psychology reads like a salutary warning in a behaviour manual from the 1850s:

He had drunk deeply of the cup of pleasure till he had become intoxicated with excitement; the glare and glitter of the stage, the gossip of the greenroom, the tinsel friendship of gay associates, unsettled a mind never trained to the steady routine of everyday business, and then the fatal facility of an escape from apparent toil to the assumed refinements of fashionable life was presented to him with a force he was unable to resist.[31]

Robson's theatrical hopes grew with his capacity to fund them. He even wrote poetry:

The Dreams of Youth

We all have dreams in early youth,
    Ere life hath gathered elder dross,
And thought lies buried in its truth,
    Like violet hidden in its moss:
Those times ere fancy leap'd to speech,
    And tear-drops then, unclouded bows,
When hope and love throbb'd each in each,
    And every blossom bloomed a rose.
We backward gaze in after years,
    To view the scenes of early days;
While in the eyes the unbidden tear
    The heart's emotion oft betrays.
And thus old age with childhood meets,
    Until the soul can dream no more;
The past is then a grave of sweets,
    And flowers blossom all before.

His quirky schemes included a literary clearing-house to bring authors into contact with publishers via an expert panel. He wrote the middling *Love and Loyalty* while defrauding the Crystal Palace Company, Robson partied and sailed with his friends, bought and lavishly furnished Kilburn Priory, and lived the part of the *distingué* London gentleman. He was finally revealed, fled to Scandinavia, but was caught in Copenhagen: ('The machinery of the law and the aid of the telegraph proved too much for him. The heads of the continental police were made acquainted with his figure, appearance, manners, etc., and in every city and town their subordinates were keenly on the look-out').[32] He was arraigned at the Central Criminal Court, and in November 1856 was sentenced to twenty years' transportation for forgery, and fourteen (concurrent) for larceny.

The prosecuting attorney, Serjeant Ballantine, felt the occasion called for a homiletic digression:

he [Robson] was one of those persons of whom . . . there were

many in this country – men who, if they were honest and
straightforward in their conduct, might, with the opportunities
given them in this great commercial country, rise, as many had
risen, to the highest positions in society. The prisoner at the bar,
however, having those opportunities, and possessing those
talents, and an entrance into life which most persons would have
grasped at with avidity, was not content with a fair course of
honest industry, but sought to obtain wealth speedily, and was
betrayed from fraud to fraud, until he now stood at the bar a
felon, convicted on his own confession . . .[33]

Ballatine could not decide whether Robson's crime lay in wasted
opportunity or fraudulent activity; the one was a moral, the other
a behaviour offence. Robson was remembered for three things:
his fraudulence, his theatrical life and his interiors, for as Evans
said, 'his style of living was of a kind that upholsterers still speak
of him with admiration for his taste and powers of arrangement'.[34]
The archetype for Robson was the brilliant and briefly famous
Walter Watts, a cheque clerk in the office of the Globe Assurance
Company. He came to prominence in 1844, appearing suddenly
from obscurity. At first he looked like a dangerous outsider, a
figure from Disraeli or Catherine Gore. No one knew where he
came from, nor where he made the money sufficient to meet an
extravagant lifestyle. Watts bought and managed the Marylebone
Theatre (1847) and the New Olympic (1849), and seemed 'a
kindly, free-hearted gentleman, who having an infinite quantity
of money at his command, applied it to the laudable purpose of
patronising art and making his friends happy'.[35] If wealth was the
possession of riches by the good, then all appeared well with
Watts.
City opinion later supposed that Watts's theatrical speculations
were the cause of his crimes; they were the result. Watts was
eventually found to be taking advantage of an antiquated share-
dealing and accounting system at the Globe Insurance Company,
which based the Company accounts on its banker's pass-book, a
form of outdated company etiquette. It cost Globe Insurance
£700,000 (laundered through Watts's own bankers) between 1844
and 1850, when Watts was first investigated. When arraigned,

Watts displayed the usual coolness in face of the inevitable, and conducted himself like the model bankrupt:

> His conduct in the affair was extremely haughty, and when first charged with his crimes by Mr Tite, the then deputy-chairman of the company, boldly declared his innocence; and having been informed that his books and papers had been placed under seal, and would be subjected to investigation, he still showed little or no concern, his *sang froid* never forsaking him throughout the whole proceeding.[36]

Watts was tried on 10 May 1850 at the Old Bailey. He was accused of stealing a £1,400 cheque; a great many technical objections clogged the case, so Watts was eventually convicted of stealing 'a piece of paper of the value of 1d.'[37] In July 1850 he was sentenced to ten years' transportation; but he never left, for he killed himself at Newgate.

Evans felt the celerity with which one crime followed another, and the consistency of motive showed that these crimes were not examples of individual avarice and perversity, but rather indices of a depreciated moral atmosphere pervading the commercial world. He warned that unless the extravagant and pretentious habits of the age were brought within restrained limits, his volume of *Facts, Failures and Frauds*, 'full as it is of the painful records of dishonesty, will be only as a single page in a vast and ever increasing history of the decline and fall of mercantile morality throughout the civilised world'.[38]

The fluctuation of mercantile morality could be traced through money manners in general throughout the century. John Maskelyne's 1894 *Sharps and Flats: the Secrets of Cheating* recognised the ubiquity of gambling subterfuge without actually admitting that cheating at cards was *the* upper-class crime *par excellence*, a mixed deck of money, power, etiquette and nerve. Maskelyne turned native by recasting his book as 'The Sharp's Vade Mecum, or a Theoretical and Practical Treatise on the Art and Practice of Cheating', a kind of 'coney-catching' pamphlet or *Gul's Hornebooke* for the late nineteenth century. A footnote urged, 'The terms "good man" and "cunning cheat" must here be considered as synonymous.'[39]

The book contained a breviary of boxes, sleeve-machines,

mirrors, marked cards, sleights of hand with occasional examples (Kepplinger, the great Californian sharp, perfected the sleeve-machine in 1888) and a range of etiquette for their employement. Maskelyne managed to be snobbish about cheating:

> The rule is . . . that mere sleight of hand is to a great extent obsolete; at least, among those who seek to swindle really good card-players. The methods of legerdemain are more the common property of the multitude than formerly, and this fact tends to operate very largely to the detriment of the sharp. With the legitimate *prestidigitateur* it is otherwise.[40]

Maskelyne thought all gambling essentially dishonest, and stressed 'the absolute immorality of gambling – the desire to obtain money to which one has no right'.[41] There was a strict etiquette of gambling:

> . . . a friend of mine, who belongs to a West End Club, was discusing the subject of gambling with a fellow member. In course of conversation he put the query, 'If you detected a man cheating at the Club, what should you do?' To this the other replied, 'I should back his play; and then, after the game was over, I should make him give me half his winnings.' This is what gambling had done for a presumably honest 'Club man'.[42]

Gambling itself required only nerve and money; it flaunted the capacity for conspicuous consumption. Victorian novels teemed with fortunes squandered and won, across the classes. The gambling scene in *Daniel Deronda* posed personal and social upset in moral and ethical terms.

Cheating at cards featured in poems of the mid-Victorian period. Browning's 'Clive' and *The Inn Album* attended to the matter. Browning probably based *The Inn Album* on the exploits of Henry William, nineteenth Baron de Ros, whose career as a society roué emerged in the 1874 *Greville Memoirs* by court insider Charles Greville. In July of 1836, de Ros allegedly cheated at Graham's Club; the accusation emerged, de Ros fled the country, returned to sue for libel, and lost.[43] *The Inn Album* catalogues the failure of smooth social intercourse between decent people. Its origins lay in reputations lost and decencies forsaken.[44]

Browning's best poem about cheating was the 1864 'Mr Sludge, "The Medium"' (from *Dramatis Personae*), heavily rewritten in manuscript,[45] and subject of the only major disagreement between Browning and Elizabeth Barrett, over the probity of the American spiritualist Daniel D. Home. Perhaps Maskelyne sensed that cheating, whether at cards or in a seance, was an activity of the same moral dimension, for his book stretches to consider other forms of trickery, spritualism among them, taking a dim professional view of those whose incompetence came to light even in darkened rooms. Sludge extricates himself with a series of counter-accusations aimed at the man who has exposed him, followed by a defence of cheating based on the principle ignorance is bliss.

It all came down to how the cheat and how those cheated behaved. The money markets had strict rules for business intercourse, more formal but no less binding than the rules of decency around the card table. Ruskin knew the importance of the state of a community's manners:

> The customs and manners of a sensitive and highly-trained race
> are always Vital: that is to say, they are orderly manifestations
> of intense life, like the habitual action of the fingers of a musician.
> The customs and manners of a vile and rude race, on the contrary,
> are conditions of decay: they are not, properly speaking, habits,
> but incrustations; not restraints, or forms, of life; but gangrenes,
> noisome, and the beginnings of death.[46]

II The City Environment

Morier Evans opened his *Speculative Notes and Notes on Speculation* with this lyrical description of the City:

> It is a beautiful afternoon in March, crisp, clear weather, and the
> sun in shining throws his bright rays over the façade of the Royal
> Exchange, the frontage of the Bank, and the surrounding buildings.
> The reflection is caught by the upper stories of the Globe
> Insurance Office, in the heavily glazed windows of which floods
> of light dance. The busy throng is streaming past Mansion House
> – the great, stern hall of Justice – up the Poultry and Cheapside,
> either westward or in other directions.

The whirlpool of traffic near this spot is, as usual exhausting itself through the assistance of all classes of vehicles, from the neatly-appointed brougham taking up some City magnate, to the fully-freighted omnibus which, laden inside and out, rolls ponderously along, or the adventurous hansom which, driven at furious speed, threads the intricacies of the maze with apparently hazardous, but almost recognized certainty of success.[47]

Evans's rapture was mediated by the thought that the 'maze' was not only one of traffic, but also moral and commercial. He went on to describe a conversation with a City figure whom he later found out to be a fraud.

Here was the mid-Victorian fascination with the City: a love of its appearance, power and style coupled with a quick moral sense and a clear notion of what correct behaviour – financial and moral – looked like. The City continued to engage the Victorians throughout the fluctuations of the market between 1825 and 1875 (one a market crisis, and the other a depression) because it represented a world of possibility, an environment subject to new rules and new modes of behaviour. Technical names imposed themselves on the City bedlam: financiers, bankers, merchants, brokers, dealers, jobbers, insurers.

What absorbed the mid-Victorians most was the behaviour of individuals – successes and frauds – and of the market itself. John Laing's *Theory of Business* looked back with relief in 1867:

For some years past trade has exhibited a gradual transition from stagnation to feverish excitement, embracing cycles of about ten years. These crisis occurred in 1837, 1847, 1857, and in 1866, with pressures of varying intensity between. This sequence has continued long enough to afford ground for the presentiment that it represents what will be the order of events for some time to come.[48]

Eight years before, on 9 November 1859, Evans had charted his own view of market activity:

Within the last sixty years, at comparatively short intervals, the commercial world has been disturbed by a succession of those terrible convulsions that are now but too familiar to every ear by the expressive name, 'panic'. Each separate panic has had its own distinctive features, but all have resembled each other in occurring immediately after a period of apparent prosperity, the hollowness of which it has exposed. So uniform is this sequence, that whenever we find ourselves under circumstances that enable the acquisition of rapid fortunes, otherwise than by the road of plodding industry, we may almost be justified in arguing that the time for panic is at hand.[49]

Evans wrote from a clear perspective. The first great banking crisis of the century had come in 1825; between 1815 and 1830, over 200 country banks had failed (Dinah Craik's John Halifax saved Jessops Bank from a 'run' in December 1825 by depositing £5,000 in gold). Twenty insurance companies were floated on the Stock Exchange in 1825, three survived. Fox Bourne recalled in *The Romance of Trade*, 'Old men lay down to die under the load of disgrace they had brought on themselves . . . and the silent wretchedness of widows and orphans, robbed of their all, furnished a strong contrast to the gratulations of those who had prompted the mania and made money out of the panic.'[50] For Dickens, the City environment, from high finance down to poor housing, schools and individual money habits, provided the foundations for a series of moral fictions.[51] Everyone in Dickens has a job: washerwomen, engineers, watermen, wet-nurses, schoolteachers, glove-cleaners, undertakers and lawyers.

Dickens was apt and sharp in 1865 with *Our Mutual Friend*; the gospel of investment was unseating the gospel of work:

All is well known to the wise in their generation, traffic in Shares is one thing to have to do with in this world. Have no antecedents, no established character, no cultivation, no ideas, no manners; have Shares. Have Shares enough to be on the Boards of direction in capital letters, oscillate on mysterious business between London and Paris, and be great. Where does he come from? Shares. Where is he going to? Shares. What are his tastes? Shares. Has he any principles? Shares. What squeezes him into Parliament? Shares. Perhaps he never of himself achieved success in anything, never originated anything, never produced anything! Sufficient answer to all: Shares. O mighty Shares! To set those blaring images so high, and to cause us smaller vermin, as under the influence of henbane or opium, to cry out night and day, 'Relieve us of our money, scatter it for us, buy us and sell us, ruin us, only we beseech ye take rank among the powers of the earth, and fatten on us!'[52]

Here, in a novel about miserliness and largesse, Dickens allowed himself the luxury of depicting the Harmon fortune, built from dust, detritus and excrement.

For writers like Bulwer-Lytton in *The Disowned* (1828), *Money* (1840) and *The Caxtons* (1849), or Catherine Gore, doyenne of the 'silver fork' school of writing in *The Banker's Wife, or Court and City* (1843), *Men of Capital* (1846) and *Mammon, or The Hardships of an Heiress* (1855), the market crashes were never far from the surface. Gore's preface to *Men of Capital* distilled the essence of the age: 'Few will deny that we live in the age of Money-worship; or that, foremost among the votaries of Mammon, are our own country-people. In Great Britain, however vehement the disputes between High Church and Low, the Molten Calf remains the predominant idol.'[53]

Catherine Gore herself was to suffer at the hands of a fraud. She had a long and difficult life as a writer and mother (only two of her ten children survived her), but in 1850, at fifty-one, she inherited substantial property. She deposited her assets with Straham, Paul & Bates, a reputable seventeenth-century banking house. The bank declared bankrupt on 11 June 1855. Gore, ward to Sir John Dean Paul (senior), lost £20,000. But this was more than mismanagement. Strahan, Paul & Bates had resorted to Overend, Gurney & Co, 'the banker's bankers', and a great discount house (which notwithstanding was to fall in the 1866 crash). Strahan, Paul & Bates had been driven to seek funds from the discounter because the bank had still failed to shake off troubles which dated back to 1816.

When Sir John Dean Paul (junior) became partner in 1852, the partners owed £72,000 to the bank. Imprudent speculations followed during the early 1850s in mining and railway drainage. At the time of the bank's fall one engineering firm, Gandell & Co., owed the bank £289,000. On 8 June 1855 news of the bank's recourse to Overend, Gurney & Co. became public, and there was a run on the bank. On 11 June the *Gazette* listed the bank with liabilities of £750,000. One creditor, the Revd Dr Griffiths, Prebendary of Rochester (he lost £22,000), had the partners arraigned under the Fraudulent Trustees Act at the Central Criminal Court, on 26 October. Morier Evans wrote of their trial with the zest of a novelist:

> [Sir John Dean Paul's] eye wandered among the crowd, until it
> fell upon the countenance of the prosecutor [Revd Dr Griffiths],
> and having attracted his attention, he gazed upon him with a look
> which, had the reverend doctor not been upheld by the self-
> consciousness of imperative duty, might have raised regretful
> feelings in his mind.[54]

All three partners were found guilty, and each was sentenced to fourteen years' transportation. Their reputations ran down the century: for every Joseph Sturge, Hugh Miller or Carl Joachim Hambro who succeeded, a Strahan or Dean Paul fell. Blanchard Jerrold, in *London, a Pilgrimage* (1872):

> the brave men who have handled an office broom in the beginning,
> and ended the possessors of enormous wealth, are the objects of
> general respect. In the list opposite . . . are the names of men who
> began with wealth and ended in disgrace and rags . . . the Sir
> John Dean Pauls, the Redpaths, and the Roupells.[55]

William Strahan himself was well regarded in the City: 'to breathe a word of suspicion against his honesty would have been thought as unreasonable as to dispute the credit of the Bank of England'.[56] Sir John Dean Paul died on 7 December 1868. The single paragraph *Times* obituary cast him as 'a once notorious character' now forgotten. The Strahan, Paul & Bates *débâcle* was all the more remarkable because these men were now the confrères of Magwitch on the prison hulks, awaiting transportation.

The behaviour of City individuals was matched by the behaviour of the market itself. The 1847–8 crisis was caused by circumstances similar to those which had obtained in 1825–6. A mania for the formation of Joint Stock companies in every imaginable branch of trade had involved the whole community; in 1845 the speculation was directed to the construction of railways in every possible locality at home and abroad. The 1847 crash was caused by the bad harvest, by speculation in corn and railways, by the fall in corn prices (from 96s. to 56s. per quarter) because of French imports, by the bankruptcy of the corn houses, and by the ensuing money panic.[57] The 1846 irish potato famine and the disturbances that shook Europe (with the Chartist demonstrations at home) in 1848 were special causes peculiar to this period of commercial depression, and from which, for a protracted period, there was no recovery.

The 1857 crash was begun by the merchants who traded with America, and who had borrowed from British banks. On 27 October the Liverpool Borough Bank failed, and on 17 November the Wolverhampton & Staffordshire Bank, the Western Bank of Scotland, the Northumberland & Durham District Bank. Abroad, tension rose with the Chinese War, the Indian Mutiny and the looming Franco-Austrian War which broke out in 1859. The money panic, begun in the autumn,[58] culminated in the introduction of the Bank Indemnity Bill on 4 December 1857. Evans reflected, balancing moral with procedural questions:

> . . . in an age, like the present, of great luxury and ostentation, mere moral warnings will prove weak in their effect, when the desires that necessitate wealth are many, and riches appear accessible without toil. A revision of the law that will cause the miseries of the panic to fall most heavily on the parties who have most deserved to suffer them, can alone prevent a recurrence of those terrible events that constitute, in the record of the last sixty years, such a chequered and unclean page in the history of the progress of modern commerce.[59]

Moral warnings fell short in face of a society devoted to getting and spending.

Successful operation within the environment depended on forms of behaviour which increased and maintained the standing of the financier. The *Commercial Register* of 1849 reflected on the practice of the great Railway King, George Hudson: 'Whether Mr Hudson did speculate on the issue of his own character, has never been satisfactorily proved; but, at all events, it is clear that the bargains transacted involved an enormous amount of differences to be settled on the various account-days . . .'[60] Hudson knew well enough how to make steady and permanent encroachments to compel others to concede 'the absolute influence necessary for that free individual action on which he felt the very existence of the organisations he brought about, and the success of the negotiations into which he entered, depended . . . He further knew how to make "capital" out of[61] the feelings of reverence and admiration he excited.'[62] He treated shareholders as deluded victims, issued more shares than he said he would, and apportioned shares on unproductive railway lines.

Hudson believed his own publicity, content in the belief that the profitable railway lines would subsidise the unprofitable. He was let down eventually by his manipulation of the market and split-second speculation on the time value of the bargains he struck:

> . . . even when regarded only in a speculative point of view, in
> relation to a character whose scheming propensities would seem
> to have been based upon desperate eventualities. If such were the
> case, it would be difficult to conclude otherwise than that his
> higher qualities had stagnated, and that his paramount principle of
> action did little to honour his heart.[63]

The fall came in 1849. The City seemed glad, and gloated at the 'degradation of a purse-proud, vulgar upstart, who had nothing to recommend him but his ill-gotten wealth'.[64] Hudson fell through lack of time and money rather than through fraudulence. Throughout his difficulties he kept up appearances, and 'sustained himself with an apparent amount of fortitude which was truly astonishing, and, except to those personally acquainted with him, almost passing belief'.[65] Later, Dickens saw the 'Railway King' at Boulogne, shabby and desolate, talking to Dickens's friend Charles Manby, who told Dickens who Hudson was.

Hudson, as old as the century, died on 14 December 1871; the *Times* obituary took the long view and, while far from reinstating Hudson in the public mind, found him a man 'who united largeness of view with wonderful speculative courage'.[66] Hudson's final journey, from York Station to Scrayingham churchyard, was a cortège led by the Mayor of York and accompanied by the great bell of the Minister. He had come home.

Social and commercial buccaneers like Hudson prospered in no way from mid-Victorian England so much as from the railway fervour of the 1840s.[67] From the start, the railway fired the Victorian investment imagination in a world hurtling towards an improved future. Eliot in *Adam Bede* and Thackeray in 'De Juventute' believed those who had lived before railways belonged to another world; Dickens lamented the intrusion of the railroad in Stagg's garden in *Dombey and Son*; and at Sleepy Hollow on 27 July 1844, Concord, Massachusetts, Nathaniel Hawthorne heard the long shriek, harsh above all other harshness, of the locomotive; Thoreau heard it in *Walden*. It was to change both nations.

The pre–1847 boom showed how investment could change everyday behaviour by directly affecting the lives people lived. The mid-Victorian railways spelled class mobility and proximity, and etiquette guides wrestled with luggage behaviour, awkward meetings and the railway reading famously supplied by W. H. Smith. Looking back, A. R. Wallace crooned over the railways as one of the century's great cultural developments. The railways were first and foremost a financial phenomenon.

The railway boom introduced new procedures and new forms of money. New money required new forms of behaviour, of spending, saving, investing. The late 1850s put boundless capital from lenders ripe to invest into the hands of equally avid speculators, greedy for gain. A change in conditions of life could occur through financial disaster; for the Victorians the financial crash represented the economic equivalent of social upheaval, earthquake, religious schism or shipwreck at sea. The system ran, as Morier Evans[68] pointed out, on confidence.

Limited liability was a concept which allowed individuals to be seen to be unaccountable for their actions. Limited liability legislation began with the 1720 Bubble Act and its repeal – with a view to encouraging domestic rather than overseas investment – in 1825; it increased between 1855 and 1862.[69] Gladstone's 1844 Joint-Stock Company Registration and Regulation Act distinguished between joint stock companies and ordinary partnerships, but without granting limited liability. The USA and the Continent (except Sweden) had limited liability legislation in force, but this form of business was open in England only to the rich and to the railway company.

The 1855 Limited Liability Bill (18 & 19 *Vict.*)[70] and 1856 Joint-Stock Companies Act granted limited liability to groups of seven or more in almost any field, with banks and insurance companies coming under the same umbrella in 1858 and 1862. Neither individual investors nor individual creditors were, in practical terms, able to sue. In the midst of debate about the Acts the City chronicler J. R. McCulloch commented:

> In the scheme laid down by Providence for the government of the world, there is no shifting or narrowing of responsibilities, every man being personally answerable to the utmost extent for all his actions. But the advocates of limited liability proclaim in their superior wisdom that the scheme of Providence may be advantageously modified, and that debts and contracts may be contracted which the debtors, though they have the means, shall not be bound to discharge.[71]

Responsibility – and probity – were therefore seen to be undermined by the introduction of limited liability. Charlotte Riddell,[72] one of the City's finest chroniclers, wrote in 1866, ten years after the Acts had been in force:

> The days of 'limited Liability' are not all spent yet – but there were worse days in the early period of its history even than those in which our present lot is cast – when the devil of speculation was loosed in order to deceive the nations; when small capitalists were snuffed out by great companies; when only honest men were ever again to be poor; when the rogues had entered into their temporal heaven; when every body one met was going to make his fortune either by shares, by promoting, by selling his inventions, by lending his name, by procuring noblemen as directors, by starting projects, by advertising the company, or by helping to float it off the stocks.[73]

While individual responsibility waited on questions of limited liability, other mid-Victorian commentators, accustomed from advances in scientific method to seek for origins and cyclic explanations, searched for a logic of fluctuation in the market. What Carlyle had dubbed the 'Dismal Science' in 1850[74] was still young enough to be vigorous. Adam Smith, Thomas Malthus, David Ricardo and James Mill were still fresh in the memory; the intellectual discipline they created hungered for new areas of life to explain; the Political Economy Club (1821) was followed by the first Chair of Political Economy (Oxford, 1825).

Political economy came of age with John Stuart Mill's 1848 *Principles of Political Economy*, and matured in 1890 with the arrival of Alfred Marshall's rigorous *Principles of Economics* (Marshall's pupil J. M. Keynes thought the footnotes more instructive reading than the text). The accumulated experience of the mid-Victorian era allowed Marshall to claim that political economy or economics was 'a study of mankind in the ordinary business of life'.[75] For the mid-Victorians it was much more a study of mankind and the ordinary life of business.

The mid-Victorians, coming to terms with the new environment of money-making and getting in the 1840s, the great prosperity crossed by the crashes of the 1850s and 1860s, and the relative prosperity of the early 1870s, evolved a tradition of market commentary accounts which combined soothsaying with religious fervour and personal moralising. John Laing's useful *Theory of Business* married mid-Victorian greed to piety. He preached to his contemporaries in 1867, just after the fourth crash shook the markets:

> It seems as if we were now deriving a full measure of advantage
> from the introduction of the railway, the telegraph, and free
> trade. An augmented mass of products is placed within reach of
> consumers, as wages, profits, and rent . . . All persons, whether
> they save or not, depend for future revenue upon the continued
> fruitfulness of the earth, and the uninterrupted operation of the
> forces of nature.[76]

Laing's prose hovers between commercial greed and a socially necessary observance of piety. He urged the difficulty in predicting 'the immediate future of the money market',[77] but ventured his opinion on the basis of the behaviour of the economic environment in an assertive attempt to lay hold of something he could not define. It was in these areas of uncertainty that fraud, based on a prediction of how individuals would behave with their money, was able to prosper.

Thackeray sniffed the climate around the 1847 crash in 'Great City Snobs', who were commonly most difficult to see: 'Unless you are a capitalist, you cannot visit him in the recesses of his bank parlour in Lombard Street. Unless you are a sprig of nobility there is little hope of seeing him at home. In a great City Snob firm there is generally one partner whose name is down for charities.'[78] This gave the social impetus to money-making which featured in Disraeli's *Sybil*, where 'capitalist' shared both financial and social connotations. Thackeray revelled in the changes in social behaviour which having money entailed for his straw-man financier, Mr Pump:

> We can imagine the weary life this poor Pump, this martyr to
> Mammon, is compelled to undergo. Fancy the domestic
> enjoyments of a man who has a wife who scorns him; who cannot
> see his friends in his own house; who, having deserted the middle
> rank of life, is not yet admitted to the higher; but who is resigned
> to rebuffs and delay and humiliation, contented to think that his
> son will be more fortunate.[79]

For the Thackeray of *Snobs*, money had cash value and social value. But sometimes social standing alone, irrespective of money, signified power. Catherine Gore's hero in *The Moneylender*, Basil Annesley, went in search of a famous London financier; he encountered him first through the staff:

> 'And where am I to find him in the city?' demanded young
> Annesley; a query that appeared to excite as much amazement
> in the rotund pantler as though he had demanded in what quarter
> of the town he was to look for Westminster Abbey. – Mr Osalez,
> Sir, will be on the Stock Exchange,' said he, conceiving that the
> handsome young gentleman . . . must be infirm of intellect. – 'If
> off 'Change, you will find him at his house of business.' 'And
> where is that?' incautiously inquired Basil. The man seemed to
> draw largely upon the decorum of his calling, in order to refrain
> from a laugh. 'In the Old Jewry, Sir. – But you need only mention

the name of Mr. Osalez in the City, sir, for anyone to shew you
the way. The first cab-man or orange-boy you meet will inform
you.'[80]

Disraeli managed the manoeuvre more elliptically in *Tancred*
with this brief exchange: ' "Do you happen to know, sir, a place
called Sequin Court?" "I should think I did," said the man, smiling. "So you are going to Sidonia's?" '[81]

The path from Samuel Warren's 1839 *Ten Thousand a Year* to
Zola's last word, *Argent* (1891), and Shaw's *Mrs Warren's Profession* (1902) was one of increasing sophistication over money
matters and money behaviour. Thackeray's *The History of Samuel
Titmarsh and the Great Hoggarty Diamond* (1841) dealt with
banking and insurance. Thackeray, like Dickens and Trollope, had
lived in the shadow of debt, and like many writers of the period,
such as the Brownings, Tennyson, Meredith and Catherine Gore,
had intimate first-hand knowledge of the vagaries of the City.
Thackeray shared with them an assiduous attention to money in
all its forms. *The Newcomes* (1854–5) tells of bankruptcy, fraudulence and greed; Bulwer-Lytton's plays, of course, address the
same themes, but still without inside sophistication.

The spectre of failure haunted every Victorian activity; life itself
failed in face of the divine. Failure and public exposure uncovered
the negotiations in personal life between individual and social
principles. Carlyle knew the offence of Sadleir and those like him;
he wrote in *Past and Present*, 'What is it that the modern English
soul does, in very truth, dread infinitely, and contemplate with
entire despair? What *is* his Hell?' and continued, 'With hesitation,
and astonishment, I pronounce it to be: The terror of "Not Succeeding".'[82]

One of the most successful books on failure was by W. H. D. Adams;
his *Wrecked Lives: or Men Who Have Failed* mapped the distinction between failure from the Christian moralist's point of view
and failure from the point of view of the man of the world:

In an age which evinces a fatal disposition to make much of
material success, to glorify the successful general or fortunate
statesman, the opulent trader or the lucky speculator, the lesson
of failure can hardly be too strongly enforced.[83]

Adams's list of wrecked lives in the first and second series (also 1880) included Burns, Chatterton, Heine, Poe, Robespierre and Wolsey, testimony to the scope of his project. Swift qualified as a failure 'if failure is to be reckoned by the extent to which a man makes use of his capabilities and opportunities',[84] the more so because he 'wallowed in filth' and wrote 'whole pages of unpardonable bestiality'.[85]

Writers of fiction were quick to find emblems of reprehensible life in instances of failure. Thackeray in *The Newcomes* and Trollope in *The Way We Live Now* showed social sympathy at odds with the commercial spirit; everywhere in Dickens the shadow of debt made money a darkly held commodity, particularly in *Little Dorrit* and *Bleak House*; bankruptcy glowered over *Dombey and Son*, and fraud over *Nicholas Nickleby*; financial failure haunted *The Mill on the Floss*, and even cast an ever-familiar cloud over *Cranford*.

Fiction colluded in the popular money fascination born of the 1840s. Charles Reade's disappointing *Hard Cash* of 1863 manipulated vast sums, but sold itself short in a rising market of financial books, notably by Thackeray, Trollope and Gore, which tackled the psychology of money-making, the implications of having money, and the ways money could be created socially. In the boardroom, gambling world of *The Way We Live Now*, the right kind of behaviour promised prodigious wealth.

1857 saw the third Victorian market crash, and the publication of *Little Dorrit* which, through Dorrit, Merdle, Clennam and Doyce made money its hero, always bearing on the behaviour of those who once had, now had, or hoped to have it. The same year saw Ruskin moving to an economic view of art in his lectures 'The Political Economy of Art'. The influence of financial matters on cultural behaviour was becoming more apparent.

III Money Manners

The tenth chapter of Samuel Smiles's *Self-help* covered 'Money – it's use and abuse':

How a man uses money – makes it, saves it, and spends it – is

perhaps one of the best tests of practical wisdom. Although
money ought by no means to be regarded as a chief end of man's
life, neither is it a trifling matter, to be held in philosophic
contempt, representing as it does to so large an extent, the means
of physical comfort and social well-being. Indeed, some of the
finest qualities of human nature are intimately related to the right
use of money; such as generosity, honesty, justice, and self-
sacrifice; as well as the practical virtues of economy and
providence.[86]

The mid-Victorians applied ready-made standards to money-
making. Books of morals like Smiles's *Self-help* or *Thrift* presented
consistent moral attitudes amounting to a philosophy of money,
while those in the genre of William Ellis's financial investigations
(*A Chart of Industrial Life*, 1869; *Outlines of Social Economy*,
1846 [1860]) carried specific investment chapters disguised as
moral discourse.

The 1840s had yet to develop a sophisticated language for dealing not only with fraud, but with financial success and failure.
Everyday manners codes forbade the discussion of money, and
the subject was excluded from the home, the one place where
moral codes worked strongly within a defined environment. The
breaking of this taboo made Clough's Spirits Song in *Dipsychus*
(III); the unusual rhyme on 'self-pelf' made money both personal
in the rhyme and strangely unfamiliar in the terminology:

> As I sat at the café, I said to myself,
> They may talk as they please about what they call pelf,
> They may sneer as they like about eating and drinking,
> But help it I cannot, I cannot help thinking
> How pleasant it is to have money, heigh ho!
> How pleasant it is to have money.[87]

Money, like sex, presented new problems as well as new opportunities. The equivalent of the Contagious Diseases Acts were, in
the financial community, the vast 230 sections of the Insolvency
Act of 1861. Until then the 1849 Insolvency Act had precisely
defined bankruptcy and the bankrupt. Private individuals were
still imprisoned for debts over £20 until 1861, and imprisonment

for debt was not formally abolished until 1869. M'Culloch's dictionary explained succinctly: 'The bankrupt, unless convicted of fraud, was secured not only from arrest, but in the possession of property acquired after his bankruptcy, while the insolvent was never discharged from his liability until every creditor had been discharged in full, though he was assured from arrest.[88]

The 1861 Act increased debtors' facilities in escaping unfulfilled obligations; it protected bankrupts from creditors; and it removed the distinction between traders and non-traders, a commercial and a social distinction. After 1861 debtors could discharge debts and liabilities by giving up their property if they had it, or going though the form of relinquishment if they had none. The Acts of 1868 and 1869 followed; and by the time the depression set in the 5,002 bankruptcies in 1870 had increased to the 1879 figure of 13,132.[89] Gladstone proudly pronounced that the economy of the early 1870s had advanced 'by leaps and bounds'; but looking back on the period the social commentator A. R. Wallace saw manners and customs as *the* material of industrial history:

In every case in which we have traced out the efficient causes of the present depression, we have found it to originate in customs, laws, or modes of action which are ethically unsound, if not positively immoral.[90]

An etiquette of business forms existed both in England and in America, and, as Hill's long-selling *Manual of Social and Business Forms* showed, necessarily mixed business and social behaviour: 'in a business, social and artistic view,' wrote Hill, 'it is of very great advantage to most people to be possessed of ease and grace of manner'.[91] This was how J. E. M'Conaughy saw the issue of etiquette in business from 1884:

A young man who finds himself in a new social plane is often greatly perplexed and puzzled as to how he shall carry himself. Etiquette he imagines to be some kind of a system of torture; or, at best, a series of 'shibboleths' which shall make him a marked man in company. It is better defined as 'a high-road on which people once familiar with it travel with infinite ease'; as 'a wall which protects the well bred from those who would make themselves offensive'.

Text-books are abundant, and no young man need feel ashamed of reading over a book of good manners, with a view to self-improvement.[92]

A breach of socio-financial etiquette implied more serious consequences within a particular environment than a simple social solecism, if such a thing existed.

One writer took on the perceived conflict between money-making and morals and made a book of it. William Ellis's *A Layman's Contribution to the Knowledge and Practice of Religion in Common Life* started at first some way from a discussion of commerce, but that was exactly what he produced. He billed his 500 pages as a course in conversation lessons introducing the study of moral philosophy. By this he meant a discussion of favoured Victorian abstracts. Following Smiles, his prose rang with exhortations to sagacity, vigilance, punctuality and zeal; and with admonishments against wastefulness and laxity. First, Smiles from *Self-help*:

> ... the man who is always hovering on the verge of want is in a state not far removed from that of slavery. He is in no sense his own master, but is in constant peril of falling under the bondage of others, and accepting the terms which they dictate to him. He cannot help being, in a measure, servile, for he dares not look the world boldly in the face; and in adverse times he must look either to alms or the poor's rates. If work fails him altogether, he has not the means of moving to another field of employment; he is fixed to his parish like a limpet to its rock, and can neither migrate nor emigrate.
>
> To secure independence, the practice of simple economy is all that is necessary. Economy requires neither superior courage nor eminent virtue; it is satisfied with ordinary energy, and the capacity of average minds.[93]

Now Ellis, whose voice sounded the same, but whose moralisings ushered him down the strange but clearly marked path toward discussing the morality of expenditure. He started from here:

Ought I to do this? Ought I to do that? or, in one question, What ought to be my conduct? The thoughtful, conscientious man is anxious about his own conduct. Why is he anxious? Because he knows that certain lines of conduct are followed by certain consequences, and other lines of conduct by other consequences.[94]

Ellis's concerns put him in the forefront of Victorian thinking on the practical application of philosophy to life. His work amounted to a popular, bastardised but recognisable version of Mill's thinking in the *System of Logic*.[95] Principles for Ellis existed only when put into practice. This was a pattern in books of money advice and on general behaviour. The tension between inner culture and outward behaviour had made itself clear in the 1840s. In 1845 the barrister George Long hinted at the lack of internal attention in his criticism of popular morals books:

Many moral writers seem to consider morality as nothing but a series of acts, and of habits resulting from a repetition of those acts, and which are valuable only on account of their consequences.[96]

Then, in 1852, Binney's immensely popular *Is It Possible to Make the Best of Both Worlds?* took on the question of external appearances by tackling the subject of reputation:

Living in society, another important element in making the best of life is REPUTATION. We are so constituted that, as a general rule, we really cannot get on without this. It makes no matter what a man believes or disbelieves; whether he thinks there is a God or not, or a futuriety or not; nor, indeed, whether there really be either the one or the other. The *fact* of the importance of character in the present life, does not depend either on there being another, or on a man's particular belief about it. Independently of all this, the laws of our nature and the constitution of our society are such, that there is no securing or accomplishing anything without reputation.[97]

This surprising piece of socialpolitik appeared confident and candid about the task required of the individual, and took an exacting detour into theological debate.

Binney and Long represent the two sides of a division which Victorian morals and social conduct both encouraged and endorsed. Writers like Smiles tried to rise above it, and writers like Ellis tried to work the gaps the debate held open. In his *Layman's Contribution* Ellis neither issued instructions nor set out moral absolutes; the complications of modern life disallowed the applicability of simple rules. Where principle met practice, fascinating manoeuvres took place to enable Ellis to maintain a clear grasp on both.

Ellis had been engaged in ascertaining, under all circumstances, what *ought* to be the rule of conduct – what his reader *ought* to do, and he leant towards moral exhortation and away from practical instruction as far as possible. But when he faced the thought that others might not be playing the same game, his advice to the reader necessarily altered. He advised the putative spender, saver and investor to be informed – to be deeply convinced of what constituted good conduct, so that, being virtuously disposed, he could strive earnestly and devoutly to make thought and character cleave to the conviction in practice. He wrote on credit, the crux of commercial honesty:

> We have seen that it is not enough, in this very matter of paper-money, to say to bankers, to statesmen, to legislators, to sovereigns – 'Be honest.' Can it be enough, then, to say so little to the young from among whom these administrators, functionaries, and dignitaries are to be drawn? Ought we not rather to say 'Be well-informed as well as honest, for otherwise you will be liable, through ignorance, to incur for yourselves and to inflict upon others all the mischiefs of dishonesty short of its guilt.'[98]

The extra ingredient of putative guilt felt by the wrongdoers was pure Victorian: the crime stretched out to settle in all its aspects – social, personal, legal, spiritual – on the individual. Ellis went on to integrate 'moral and religious considerations' with 'questions of money'[99] and the workings of the monetary system. This led him to suggest that 'the foundation of all security against the dangers of credit, while enjoying its fruits, is the religious sense of responsibility felt by those who use it'.[100]

The point here was Ellis's belief in the bridgeability of the gaps he constructed between practice and principle, precisely where the two diverged furthest. Haunted by the market crashes of 1837 and 1847, and on the eve of another, Ellis saw no escape from commercial panic except through instruction in 'morals' of credit. Since some had benefited from instruction and others not, Ellis faced the problem of individual probity wasting away in a desert of fraud:

> ... we ought – all men who aspire to take part in some active
> duty, or to become integers of the great sum total of sound public
> opinion, ought to look out for instruction leading to a thorough
> comprehension of the general principles, in obedience to which
> the decision upon all such matters should be formed. At the same
> time, they ought to have present to their minds the consequences
> of a departure from, or inattention to those principles, not merely
> to the culprits themselves, but to society at large.[101]

Ellis's bifurcated view held with Victorian thinking about fraud. Crimes and miscreants were seen as outstanding individual examples of a sub-species, uneasily representative of larger tendencies in the commercial species. The terms of prevention and avoidance were both personal and moral. Corporate scandal in its modern form had not yet evolved.

Given Ellis's interest in the moral principles governing the disposition of money, the abstract qualities which best delivered practical progress and yet cleaved to moral considerations were the habits of prudence, forethought and industry. Ellis everywhere worked from the notion that these qualities mediated between the two worlds of principle and practice. He disapproved of taxation on insurance because he considered that to be an affront to prudence and forethought.[102] Industry was one of his favourites:

> Men who are observed to work diligently and continuously are
> called 'industrious'; and to men who neglect work, or evince a
> reluctance to work, we apply the epithet, 'idle', 'lazy', or
> 'indolent'; and from these terms applied to the men, names have
> also been formed for the qualities we assume them to possess.
> Industry is a quality of the industrious man, as idleness, laziness,
> or indolence is a quality of the idle man.[103]

Ellis believed that no society could function properly without the industrious, and so made his assertions about individual conduct resonate with social implication.

The same turn of mind directed his discussion of speculation and saving. He argued that the young were encouraged by the earliest efforts of their religious instructor to save; and that saving money under the 'improved industrial arrangements of modern times' amounted to lending money. In a nineteenth-century version of the Christian parable of the talents (advocating good stewardship of resources), Ellis's saver lent money to those better able to administer and gain profit from it:

> The young man, entering upon life with his understanding
> enlightened by such teaching, will see in capitalists and
> administrators of capital the trustees of the results of that past
> labour which has made this earth the improved residence of man,
> as he has inherited it, and the directors of their application, so as
> to add still more to the delights of his inheritance. Under them,
> sheltered from the vicissitudes inseparable from the adoption of
> division of labour and the use of credit, he enjoys the opportunity
> of qualifying himself to participate in works which will enable him
> to say in his old age, 'I have done more than profit by the labours
> of others. I have contributed somewhat to improve for my children
> the comfortable abode which I inherited.'[104]

This selective view of what it was to profit from others' work, and the increasingly biblical tone, prepared the way for the resounding, 'Is not this a thought befitting a religious man?'[105] Much was claimed for the role of the religious outlook in matters of political economy.

When Ellis wrote his 1872 *Helps for the Young* he put in practical terms for the individual what theorists like Arnold, Ruskin and Carlyle had advocated for society:

> The application of great principles to the details of practice needs
> to be made with the utmost care and caution, and we educators
> of the present day seem specially bound to teach our children how
> to apply these laws to the details of their own lives, and so to
> arm against those base maxims and those baneful deceptions which
> are now left to spread with far too little check.[106]

The anxiety here to make principles stick found Ellis making laws of them, making them absolute. *Helps for the Young* aided by providing theoretical case studies for the would-be entrepreneur. Selling labour to the highest bidder benefited the worker who strove for efficiency and the employer who gave scope for it. Saving money (or in Ellis's terms, lending to the bank) added to the wages-fund. Using money for investment increased productivity and encouraged the employment of more efficient workers.

Ellis advocated buying cheap and selling dear on the ground that 'we are really offering ourselves as buyers to those who most want to sell, and as sellers to those who most want to buy'.[107] Likewise buying at home and profiting abroad assisted 'the producers of that merchandise to direct their labour in the manner most profitable to themselves and most beneficial to the world in general'.[108] Undercutting home markets with cheap foreign produce, according to Ellis, supplied the things needful for growth at lower costs than could be bought at home; and hoarding merchandise presented no problem, 'for such doings help to guard the community against privation and suffering from bad harvests or other calamities'.[109] Borrowing low and lending dear redirected the capital to those who could best use it.

Beneath this analysis ran tough individualism, and a sense that decisions were always informed and rational. Ellis tried to alter the connotations of money: in economic discussion it was all process; in social, all meaning:

> Ought you to be ashamed because money is showered upon you
> in proportion to your success? or ought you not rather to be
> proud of the distinction conferred upon you – of the estimate
> formed of your usefulness in producing what is longed for by
> others.[110]

Dickens's later satire was directed against people who thought just that, who believed that genteel territory could be entered with no passport but wealth.

IV Inner Life, City Life, Afterlife

In his inaugural lecture at Oxford in 1859, the political economist Goldwin Smith offered this insight on contemporary commerce:

> To buy in the cheapest and sell in the dearest market, the supposed concentration of economical selfishness, is simply to fulfil the command of the Creator, who provides for all the wants of His creatures through each other's help; to take from those who have abundance, and to carry to those who have need. It would be an exaggeration to erect trade into a moral agency; but it does unwittingly serve agencies higher than itself, and make one heart as well as one harvest for the world.[111]

City life and the inner life coalesced in the prevailing mid-Victorian doctrines of self-help, *laissez-faire*, free trade, individualism and evangelical zeal. Outward behaviour had to match inner belief, for the economy was a forum for temporal and spiritual trial and suspense. Gladstone typically worried about matching the worldly to the divine:

> The more we have of system and fixity in nature, the better. For, in the method of natural second causes, God as it were takes the map of His own counsels out of the recesses of His own idea, and graciously lays it near our own view; condescendingly, as it were, to make us partakers of His thought.[112]

How was this to work with money? Gladstone had the answer there, too:

> Where there is real interest and desire, as there certainly is in the pursuit of money, men proceed with activity, with earnestness, with precision: they apply all their powers, what-ever they may be: they do not make much of small difficulties but little of great ones: they venture the present for the sake of the future: they thrust aside out of their path every thing that is frivolous and trivial with reference to the main object: their whole life falls into order and discipline, all the movements of it have a purpose, and the consciousness of that purpose shapes and governs all those movements either sensibly or insensibly yet not less truly.[113]

'They venture the present for the sake of the future' mediates between religious observance and market speculation. Moralists and commentators had been worrying at the relation between devotion and riches, sensing that an affection for riches, beyond what Christianity prescribed, was not essential to any valuable or legitimate extension of commerce. Far from the spirit of enterprise being the soul of commercial prosperity, many felt:

> the excess of this spirit beyond the moderation of the New
> Testament, which, pressing on the natural boundaries of trade,
> is sure, at length, to visit every country, where it operates with
> the recoil of those calamities, which, in the shape of beggared
> capitalists, and unemployed operatives, and dreary intervals of
> bankruptcy and alarm, are observed to follow a season of
> overdone speculation.[114]

The mid-Victorians equipped themselves morally and behaviourally for a world in which technology and economics quickened the changes propelling them from an industrial into a financial society in the 1860s and 1870s. 'Speculation now-a-days,' wrote Morier Evans in 1864, 'is not what it was some twenty years ago. True it is that great advances have been made in all descriptions of scientific and other improvements'; investment changed with them.[115] This situation contrasted with money-making in the 1840s and 1850s, risky and dazzling, which favoured individual rather than collective effort. Nonconformity was the rule for the entrepreneurs.

Speculation was the word which ministered to commercial and religious uses.[116] Over-trading on the market was referred to as 'speculation', a nineteenth-century pejorative combining economic recklessness with a sense of philosophic doubt and atheism. Speculation was what the model, sensible, merchants and financiers of mid-Victorian homily and fiction avoided:

> Typically, Victorian moralists envisaged successive phases of
> business life. The manly honest trader is tempted, falls, is
> terrorized, and then smashed, and in the process he may or may
> not achieve a state of grace. Ideal merchants and financiers, who
> never succumbed to temptation, were a staple of contemporary

biography and widely advertised, especially perhaps in nonconformist circles.[117]

The activity which united thinking about money and the afterlife with matters of everyday prudence was life assurance. This was another word, like 'speculation', mediating between the financial and the theological (Tennyson's 'The doubt would rest, I dare not solve, Assurance only brings resolve'[118]). Assurance in God meant promise of the afterlife; assurance between people meant trust; life assurance meant something between the two.

The 1850s and 1860s saw heated debate about the morality and usefulness of life assurance. On the one hand, why provide for an eventuality which was already divinely plotted, why play God? On the other, why leave needy dependants with no support when prudence could store up earthly treasures and pass them on? John Scoffern's *The Philosophy of Common Life* (1857), written in the thick of market activity, included a chapter on the 'The Nature, Objects and Tendencies of Life Assurance'. It was a prominent feature of the age; important to the individual, and powerful in moulding the characteristics of the family.

For Scoffern, all who believed in the possibility of human moral and material advancement were called upon to map out the principles on which it was based:

> When the practice of life assurance was first established, religious
> objections were urged against it. The argument was used that the
> bargaining, during life, for a sum of money, payable at death,
> partook of irreligion, if not immorality; that it was impious to
> attach a pecuniary value to so portentous an event in the existence
> of man, as death. That feeling, happily, has long since given way
> to a more rational faith; and the practice of life assurance is now
> advocated by members of every Christian religious
> denomination.[119]

Another popular objection urged against life assurance rested on the belief that the insurance companies' data for compiling contracts were inaccurate; this compromised the standing of the institutions, and reduced safety for the insured. Scoffern had a rebuff:

No mistake can be greater than this. Undoubtedly life assurance is founded upon a consideration of chances, or probabilities. But these words convey a very inadequate meaning to such as have not reflected on the matter. Chances, when investigated, over a sufficiently large extent and through the necessary ramifications, are found to be subjected to the operation of laws, no less certain and immutable than the laws of gravitation, or electricity; and if, owing to the incompleteness of records, the ultimate precision of which these laws are susceptible be not attained – danger and inconvenience from this source can be practically obviated, by leaving a small working margin for contingencies.[120]

The supporters of life assurance lived in the belief that it brought closer a pecuniary benefit to surviving friends, for whom it was a duty that provision should be made; and that it encouraged habits of thought and foresight in early youth, and imparted stability of character to those who would otherwise have felt the want of this quality. The relatively small periodical outlay involved in keeping a life policy in force, thought Scoffern, 'may be not inaptly compared to the effect of the fly-wheel or the governor of a steam engine; contrivances which, though involving the expenditure of a proportionate amount of motive power, so far from wasting force, contribute to it; by equalising that power, controlling it, and rendering it applicable'.[121]

Thirty years later, J. T. Davidson's *Talks With Young Men* (1884) saw the matter as settled and decided, claiming what was now called life insurance to be a good and wholesome discipline for the young:

It would be easy to apply those principles in a practical way to the subject of *life insurance*. It is a good and wholesome discipline for a young man, as well as wise and right in the interest of dear ones whom the future may raise up around him, to set apart a sum out of his yearly income for this purpose, and of course the sooner it is done, the better. Sternly, determinately fight the battle with self. If you conquer this foe, you will be a nobler victor than Alexander, of Caesar, or Bonaparte.[122]

Davidson wrote *The City Youth, Sure to Succeed* and *Forewarned-Forearmed*. His works were a commonplace of the triumph of discipline over chaos, fortitude over fortune. Survival in the financial community was a religious enterprise:

> Come, and find in true godliness the grand secret of a bright,
> active, and energetic life, the key to the highest and best success;
> then you shall be independent of fickle fortune's smile and frown;
> you shall know that the blessing of Almighty God is on all your
> ways, and that in every work that you begin, doing it with all
> your heart, you shall truly prosper.[123]

His method looked back to the writing of Hugh Miller, Martin Tupper and Samuel Smiles. Homilies and biographies intermingled; business life made itself continuous with devotional life. Here, Davidson recalls George Peabody's return home:

> What was it that George Peabody said when visting his native
> village in 1855? He said, 'Though providence has granted me
> unvaried and unusual success in the pursuit of fortune, I am still
> in heart the humble boy who left yonder unpretending dwelling.
> There is not a youth within the sound of my voice, whose early
> opportunities and advantages are not very much greater than my
> own, and I have since achieved nothing that is impossible to the
> most humble youth among you.'[124]

It was significant that Peabody, the founder of Morgan Grenfell, started a housing trust (in March 1862). Peabody's business as a merchant and banker in developing trade with the textile industries or Lancashire required frequent visits from his native Massachusetts; in 1836 he established the London base of George Peabody & Co., a point of contact for visiting Americans, and a model of easy generosity for the English. Peabody supported Anglo-American relations by financing the American Exhibit at the Crystal Palace in that Victorian show of shows, the 1851 Great Exhibition. Victorian philanthropy tended to focus on conditions rather than individuals in the way of its benefactions, and Peabody was acting entirely in the spirit of the age when he wrote the first letter to the Governors in 1862: 'My object is to ameliorate the condition of the poor and needy of this great metropolis.' In practical terms this meant 'the construction of such improved dwellings for the poor as may combine in the utmost possible degree the essentials of healthfulness, comfort, social enjoyment and economy'. He originally donated £150,000 (later augmented to £500,000), from which the first housing development was built at Spitalfields and was soon followed by estates in Islington and Shadwell.[125] Peabody was a great lover of music, and left for the use of the Governors of the Trust a box at the Albert Hall.

Here, finance reached into the community to answer the values which the community itself upheld for success in finance: probity, concern, diligence. Peabody succeeded in bringing ideal behaviour to bear on a far from ideal world. This was the way mid-Victorian problem-solving worked best. John Stuart Mill recognised this process, neatly expressed in the 'divisions among the instructed' which he thought nullified authority and prevented practical advancement:

> The longer anyone observes and meditates, the more clearly he
> will see, that even wise men are apt to mistake the almanac of
> the year for a treatise on chronology; and as in an age of transition
> the source of all improvement is the exercise of private judgement,
> no wonder that mankind should attach themselves to that, as the
> last and only resource of humanity.[126]

Mill compared advances in physical sciences since Newton and Descartes. He stressed the cohesiveness and unanimity of the physical sciences: 'We never hear of the right of private judgement in physical science; yet it exists; for what is there to prevent anyone from denying every proposition in natural philosophy, if he be so minded?' He then put the parallel case of the moral and social sciences, where 'this imposing unanimity among all who had studied the subject does not exist; and every dabbler, consequently, thinks his opinion as good as another's'.[127]

This predicted and explained the proliferation of intellectual 'how-to' books and practical series of lectures throughout the mid-Victorian period. J. E. M'Conaughy's *Capital for Working Boys: Chapters on Character Building* (1884) rested on a long and tried tradition.[128] Character was seen as the boy's best capital, and character in relation to business success was narrowly defined and assiduously nurtured:

It is difficult for a young man, toiling hard for a scanty support, to believe that he can still be laying up valuable capital every day. Yet it is a fact. The character he is building will make or unmake his future fortune. He is, in effect, dropping coins daily into the Savings or the Losings bank. What manner of man he is himself will determine all the long future, far more than the money his father may bequeath him . . . Begin right, and let every day witness some growth of your capital. Every good habit you form is the best of capital. Every repetition strengthens the habit, until it becomes even stronger than natural characteristics.[129]

Sometimes such advice could assume ludicrous proportions:

Learning to handle the axe well in boyhood is no drawback to a man's future success. It never hurt Lincoln, or Horace Greeley, or James Garfield; and Mr. Gladstone takes as much pride in his chopping as Oscar Widle does in his posing. Which is the manlier man it would not be hard to decide.[130]

But the book occupied the space between outright moralising and compromised principle. 'Honesty', for example, appeared 'the best policy', though M'Conaughy realised that this looked out of moral kilter, 'considering the sense in which the word "policy" is generally used. It is very proper to consider whether a course is profitable in the long run, and to act accordingly. But a higher law settles all questions of truth and honesty, beyond any reconsidering.'[131] M'Conaughy warned against the dangers of working on Sunday; to do so was to court certain failure. He recommended home ownership on the grounds that it settles a workman, 'and makes him a joint stockholder in public morality and good order'.[132] A religious conclusion looked forward to the afterlife, and a tender and sentimental peroration to write home rounded off the advice:

Write Them a Letter To-Night

Don't go to the theatre, concert or ball,
    But stay in your room to-night;
Deny yourself to the friends that call,
    And a good, long letter write, –

The Descent of Manners

Write to the sad old folks at home,
    Who sit, when the day is done,
With folded hands and downcast eyes,
    And think of the absent one.

Don't selfishly scribble, 'Excuse my haste;
    I've scarcely the time to write,'
Lest their drooping thoughts go wandering back
    To many a by-gone night,
When they lost their needed sleep and rest,
    And every breath was a prayer
That God would leave their delicate babe
    To their tender love and care.

Don't let them feel that you've no more need
    Of their love, or counsel wise;
For the heart grows strongly sensitive
    When age has dimmed the eyes.
It might be well to let them believe
    You never forget them quite;
That you deem it a pleasure, when far away,
    Long letters home to write.

Don't think that the young and giddy friends,
    That make your pastime gay,
Have half the anxious thought for you
    That the old folks have to-day.
The duty of writing do not put off;
    Let sleep or pleasure wait,
Lest the letter, for which they looked and longed,
    Be a day or an hour *too late*.

For the sad old folks at home,
    With the locks fast turning white,
Are longing to hear from the absent ones, –
    Write them a letter to-night.[133]

Sentiment offered one way of controlling an uncontrollable world. The growing power and complexity of commerce, investment and financial practice found the Victorians constantly adjusting an established institution to conform to new procedures. There were those like Ruskin or Carlyle who stood outside received opinion, looking on it as a stranger might; and there were those like Morier Evans who were able to contemplate from inside, looking with a believer's eyes. The former missed the truths inherent in traditional opinion, the latter those outside them.

William Ellis knew that, like it or not, everyone was involved in the City, and found a vision commensurate with his sense of the scope of trade:

Our lot is cast in a densely peopled part of the earth, dotted over with large towns and villages, besides numerous detached dwellings. There are large stores of food, clothing and other necessaries and comforts, hospitals for the sick and wounded, schools and other public buildings, and accumulations of material ready to be worked up for our use and enjoyment. Beings like ourselves, spread over the land and congregated in the cities, are moving to and fro, in and out, and in all directions. They are mostly intent upon some business – ploughing, sowing, reaping, spinning, weaving, mining, building & c. Few, except infants and the infirm, seem to have nothing to do.[134]

6

Poems and Science: The Cultivation of the Feelings and the Order of Nature

I Poems

Hippolyte Taine knew that creative artists evolved from environments made of manners and behaviour:

> In short, there is a *moral* temperature, consisting of the general state of minds and manners, which acts in the same way as the other. Properly speaking, this temperature does not produce artists; talent and gifts are like seeds; what I mean to say is, that the same country at different epochs probably contains about the same number of men of talent, and of men of mediocrity . . .
> There is a prevailing tendency which constitutes the spirit of the age. Talent seeking to force an outlet in another direction, finds it closed; and the force of the public mind and surrounding habits repress and lead it astray, by imposing on it a fixed growth.[1a]

Culture and environment, social, moral and technical, shaped the individual's capacity to create and to imagine what creativity might be. Nineteenth-century theorists called this phenomenon, as Taine did, 'mental condition' or 'circumstances'. Each new situation evoked a certain state of mind, and a corresponding class or work in the arts.

For John Stuart Mill, this was a personal journey into his own circumstances. The despondency struck during the dry heavy dejection in the winter of 1826–7: 'I was in a dull state of nerves, such as everybody is occasionally liable to; unsusceptible to enjoyment or pleasurable excitement; one of those moods when what is pleasure at other times, becomes insipid or indifferent.'[1] The crisis in John Stuart Mill's mental history found him in the flat, stale and unprofitable regions of thought. He was twenty. 'During this time,' he wrote:

> I was not uncapable of my usual occupations. I went on with them
> mechanically, by the mere force of habit. I had been so drilled
> in a certain sort of mental exercise, that I could still carry it on
> when all the spirit had gone out of it.[2]

Mill typically analysed what he learned from this. Asking himself whether he was happy was to cease to be so; he decided not to think about happiness – still the test of conduct – but to focus on another object as the purpose of life. He tried to let the mind's self-consciousness, scrutiny and interrogation exhaust themselves on that object. The happiness should come 'without dwelling on it or thinking about it, without either forestalling it in imagination, or putting it to flight by fatal questioning'.[3]

That was Mill's first lesson in the affections; from then it became a principle germane to his philosophy of life. The second lesson from his depression was his recognition of internal culture for the individual:

> The cultivation of the feelings became one of the cardinal points
> in my ethical and philosophical creed. And my thoughts and
> inclinations turned in an increasing degree towards whatever
> seemed capable of being instrumental to that object.[4]

Reading and responding to Wordsworth's poems had begun Mill's cultivation of the feelings. He proceeded from then on to prescribe poetry as part of the healthy reader's intellectual diet.

The mid-Victorian environment had evolved two strains of thinking which were linked by manners. First, 'the internal culture of the individual', and second, 'the ordering of outward circumstances, and the training of the human being for speculation and for action'.[5] The former was catered for by imaginative literature, the latter by science.

There are manners in ideas. The mid-Victorians evolved a way of thinking according to rule in society, an instinct to do the right thing. In intellectual, creative and scientific matters, behaviour was less constricted; but there were still worries about what proper intellectual, poetic, or scientific processes might be. The age which produced the sermon and the novel generated that uniquely Victorian poetic procedure, the dramatic monologue. This enabled Victorian thinking to chart new forms of life. The Brownings, A. H. Clough, George Meredith and the Rossettis advanced by using new forms of writing and thinking. Cultivation became a form of mental behaviour, manners for the mind. This cultivation proceeded along two distinct paths: the internal route offered by the poets, and the external route offered by the scientists.

Two movements had been gradually gathering momentum in the 1860s and 1870s: a centripetal movement inward to consider the mind and its affections, and a centrifugal movement outward to consider scientific discovery and man's place in the scheme of nature. Other thinkers were reaching similar conclusions, committing themselves to similar processes. On inward cultivation, Carlyle's *Signs of the Times* (1829) had concluded with the same thought as Mill:

> To reform a world, to reform a nation, no wise man will undertake; and all but foolish men know, that the only solid, though a far slower reformation, is what each begins and perfects on *himself*.[6]

And on outward cultivation, G. H. Lewes remarked on the difference between philosophy and science in 1857:

> Philosophy has been ever in movement, but the movement has been circular; and this fact is thrown into stronger relief by the contrast with the linear progress of Science. Instead of perpetually finding itself, after years of gigantic endeavour, returned to the precise point from which it started, Science finds itself year by year, and almost day by day, advancing step by step, each accumulation of power adding to the momentum of its progress . . .[7]

Internal cultivation proceeded through the humanities, external cultivation through the natural sciences. These two habits of thought produced two archetypal questions of manners: how should an individual behave? and how does the species behave? Mill had probed at these issues in *On Liberty*:

... first ... the individual is not accountable to society for his actions, in so far as these concern the interests of no person but himself. Advice, instruction, persuasion and avoidance by other people if thought necessary by them for their own good, are the only measures by which society can justifiably express its dislike or disapprobation of his conduct ... Secondly ... for such actions as are prejudicial to the interests of others, the individual is accountable, and may be subjected either to social or to legal punishment, if society is of the opinion that the one or the other is requisite for its protection.[8]

What bonded the individual to society were systems of manners, morals, customs, conventions and traditions, forces which worked for the collective and against the individual spirit. Mill knew that to do anything because it was the custom was to make no choice. He observed in 'Civilization':

As civilization advances, every person becomes dependent, for more and more of what most nearly concerns him, not upon his own exertions, but upon the general arrangements of society. In a rude state, each man's personal security, the protection of his family, his property, his liberty itself, depend greatly upon his bodily strength and his mental energy or cunning: in a civilized state, all this is secured to him by causes extrinsic to himself. The growing mildness of manners is a protection to him against much that he was before exposed to, while for the remainder he may rely with constantly increasing assurance upon the soldier, the policeman, and the judge; and (where the efficiency or purity of those instruments, as is usually the case, lags behind the general march of civilization) upon the advancing strength of public opinion.[9]

The mid-Victorian period, between 1832 and 1884, had seen an inordinate growth in the power of public opinion, the expression of which was not purely political. The 1832 Reform Bill had addressed the industrial middle class, and the 1867 Bill the working men of the growing towns; but even the 1884 Bill, which spread the franchise to the country, added barely 2 million voters to an electorate of 3 million. The population of England and Wales in the 1880s was well over 25 million. In England, public opinion was synonymous with middle-class opinion,[10] which itself operated through the medium of manners and morals. The ideals spread through the available Victorian technology of communication, the written word. Literacy had increased from 67.3 per cent (men) and 51.1 per cent (women) in 1841, to 93.6 per cent (men) and 92.7 per cent (women) in 1891. The lifestyle legislation of the 1840s (Ashley's Factory Act, Fielden's Factory Act, the Public Health Act, the Free Libraries Committee), together with the 1861 Elementary Education Revised Code and Forster's 1870 Education Act, had begun to bear fruit. A healthier and more literate population, growing in number, was beginning to ask questions about its constituency as a species and its constituency as individuals. Mill had anticipated this in *On Liberty*:

> In politics it is almost a triviality to say that public opinion now
> rules the world. The only power deserving the name is that of
> the masses, and of governments while they make themselves the
> organ of the tendencies and instincts of the masses. This is as
> true in the moral and social relations of private life as in public
> transactions.[11]

Manners were social control internalised, conduct the reflex of character, and the chief purpose of society was to preserve society.

Science, increasingly popular and influential, continued to have an impact on the intellectual scene after Darwin and his accolytes, William Fox, John Henslow, William Hooker, Thomas Huxley, Ernst Krause, Charles Lyell, George Romanes, Herbert Spencer and Alfred Wallace. Throughout the period between 1832 and 1884, the two centripetal and centrifugal forces, of internal and external enquiry, remained in balance. External advances in health, education, the franchise, communication and prosperity improved the prospects for each individual. The social alliance of religion, conduct and custom kept the mid-Victorians apprised of their relative social positions. A letter to *The Times* of 17 July 1896 showed exactly how that balance had been maintained; the correspondent praised Dr Thomas Arnold of Rugby and his contribution to the common weal:

> No one made a deeper change in education, a change which

profited those who had never been at a public school. As much
as any one who could be named, Arnold helped to form the
standard of manly worth by which Englishmen judge and submit
to be judged. A man of action himself, he sent out from Rugby
men fit to do the work of the world. The virtues which his
favourite Aristotle extolled – courage, justice, and temperance –
were his, and the influence of his character and teaching was
calculated to make brave, high-minded soldiers, zealous
enlightened clergymen, lawyers with a just sense of the nature of
their vocation, and useful and public-spirited members of the State.
The width and range of his teaching are apt to be forgotten by
those who dwell on his personal influence. If he offered no large
interpretation of life, if in his writings there are rarely 'thoughts
beyond the reaches of the soul', if as an historian he seems more
at home in dealing with the geographical aspects of his subject,
or in clear delineation of events, than in discovering the hidden
springs of action, if he never or rarely let fall a pregnant or
unforgettable word, he had conceptions, new in his time, first and
foremost his lofty conception of education, his conception of the
Church as a great agency of social amelioration, his idea of each
citizen's duty to the State, his view of history as a whole, with
no real division between ancient and modern, the interest, new in
his time, which he felt in the elevation of the masses. One must
have been at Rugby or Oxford in the thirties to appreciate the
effect of Arnold's sermons on generous, susceptible youth. Even
in the volume of national life as it flows today, there may be
detected the effect of the pure, bracing stream which long ago
joined it.[12]

In the prayer that Arnold read every morning to the sixth form
were the words, 'O Lord, strengthen the faculties of our minds
and dispose us to exert them.' Mental cultivation as a religious
duty was just as important a part of Arnold's teaching as the moral
earnestness increasingly associated with his name in the 1830s.[13]
While Mill and Arnold turned to inward cultivation, either from
philosophical necessity for Mill or from religious injunction for
Arnold, the scientists of the period cultivated their subjects and
their disciplines by looking outward. Scientific mid-Victorian
thinking about nature, natural behaviour, and morals sought more
and more in the 1870s and 1880s to account for behaviour. As if

in response, the behaviour book reacted by turning scientific with such titles as *The Science of Dress* (1885) or *The Science and the Art of Adjustment Between the Producing and Reflecting Vocal Apparatus* (1897), both trying to be scientific. What evolved after Lyell and Darwin, particularly through the impact of Huxley and Spencer, was the sense that there was a scientific manner.

In 1852 two prolific Victorian problem-solvers discussed their intellectual technique. Herbert Spencer recalled the incident in his autobiography; at thirty-two, he had just published *Social Statics*. His friend George Eliot considered that, given how much thinking Spencer must have done, there were, surprisingly, no lines on his forehead:

> 'I suppose it is because I am never puzzled,' I said. This called
> forth the exclamation – 'O! that's the most arrogant thing I ever
> heard uttered.' To which I rejoined – 'Not at all, when you know
> what I mean.' And I then proceeded to explain that my mode of
> thinking did not involve that concentrated effort which is
> commonly accompanied by wrinkling of the brows.[14]

Spencer claimed it was never his way to set before himself a problem and puzzle out an answer: 'The conclusions at which I have from time to time arrived, have not been arrived at as solutions to questions raised; but have been arrived at unawares – each as the ultimate outcome of a body of thoughts which slowly grew from a germ.'[15]

Spencer's thinking fitted the evolutionary models he developed; gradually, in unobtrusive ways, without conscious intention or appreciable effort, a coherent and organised theory emerged.[16] The process was slow, unforced development, often extending over years in an incremental but spontaneous way. There was none of the strain that would have yielded the wrinkles missed by Eliot. Spencer's physiological musings pointed to profounder truths: his own area, natural science and social theory, advanced inordinately from the 1830s to the 1880s. Spencer's method adapted itself to its environmental conditions and fitted itself for survival. The garnering of facts, instances or quiddities, and making notes and queries, represented the best way to proceed.

As an independent thinker relying on some discoveries made

by others, Spencer prospered from the luxury of having time to germinate his ideas. Science in general turned its investigations on to the process of investigation itself. As scientists such as Lamarck, Lyell, Chambers, and after them Wallace, Darwin, Huxley, Spencer and Bain, discovered discovery, they developed new processes to help them mollify the shock of the new.

i The Buried Life

> Great poets are often proverbially ignorant of life. What they know has come by observation of themselves; they have found *there* one highly delicate, and sensitive, and refined specimen of human nature, on which the laws of human emotion are written in large characters, such as can be read off without much study: and other knowledge of mankind, such as comes to men of the world by outward experience, is not indispensable to them as poets: but to the novelist such knowledge is all in all; he has to describe outward things not the inward man; actions and events, not feelings; and it will not do for him to be numbered among those who, as Madame Roland said of Brissot, know man but not *men*.[17]

Mill's 1833 essay 'What is Poetry?' mapped out a space for individualism which he was to occupy in *On Liberty* twenty-five years later, when he warned against the homogenising effects of custom and social censure.

Throughout the 1850s and 1860s three poets colonised new areas of mid-Victorian experience. While manners books, self-help books and homilies urged patterns of behaviour throughout society, the poets Robert Browning, Arthur Hugh Clough and George Meredith had looked at the behaviour of the feelings in case studies from mid-Victorian social and domestic life. Their subjects habitually began from a conversation, a letter home or a domestic connubial dinner. Browning spoke for a movement in poetry which held that the behaviour which really mattered was the behaviour within:

> Our interest's on the dangerous edge of things.
> The honest thief, the tender murderer,

The superstitious atheist, demirep
That loves and saves her soul in new French books –
We watch while these in equilibrium keep
The giddy line midway: one step aside
They're classed and done with.[18]

Browning's rationale is expressed in an early letter to Elizabeth Barrett from 1845:

My inner power, which lives in me like the light of these crazy Mediterranean phares I have watched from at sea, wherein the light is ever revolving in a dark gallery, bright and alive, and only after a weary interval leaps out, for a moment, from the one narrow chink, and then goes on with the blind wall between it and you.[19]

This predated the more mainstream expression of the same feeling, from Walter Pater in *The Renaissance* (1873):

Experience, already reduced to a swarm of impressions, is ringed round for each one of us by that thick wall of personality through which no real voice has ever pierced on its way to us, or from us to that, which we can only conjecture to be without. Every one of these impressions is the impression of an individual in his isolation, each mind keeping as a solitary prisoner its own dream of a world.[20]

Browning's contribution to English poetry, the dramatic monologue, witnessed a series of incidents of personality breaking out of the mould of habit. W. L. Courtney in the *Fortnightly Review* (1 June 1883) shaped this disjunction into social comment: 'It is Browning, more than any one else, who makes us realise the volcano of dangerous forces which simmers beneath the smiling commonplaces of ordinary life and established social usage.'[21] This was poetry about how people behaved without the constraint of social convention.

The new form sat neatly with Mill's definition of poetry as *overheard* rather than *heard*. Mill's distinction of eloquence as *heard* and poetry as *overheard*[22] came alive with the question, 'Who can imagine "Dove sono" *heard*? We imagine it *over*heard.'[23]

Mill and Carlyle, later joined by Arnold, Ruskin and Pater, called for a language of the feelings which mid-Victorian social intercourse was refining out of existence. In Browning's work, the wish for frank communion between people took two courses. First, Browning created a speaking voice in the poems distinct from the author's; and second, he sought out situations in which the rules of polite interchange were being challenged or questioned.

In the light of Mill's divisions between heard eloquence produced by society and overheard poetry born of solitude, the dramatic monologues of Browning's worldly talkers compromised by making themselves overheard. Mill had wounded Browning in 1833 with his stinging marginalia in a copy of *Pauline*, which reached Browning through John Forster. Browning recast the poem as an early attempt at a dramatic monologue; in 1842 he prefaced *Dramatic Lyrics* with the disclaimer: 'Such poems as the majority in this volume might also come properly enough, I suppose, under the head of "Dramatic Pieces"; being, though often Lyric in expression, always Dramatic in principle, and so many utterances of so many imaginary persons, not mine. – R. B.'[24]

To be oneself and not oneself was the opportunity offered by the dramatic monologue and developed by Browning, enabled by an environment which was, as Mill pointed out, changing the balance between the individual and society. In literary terms, mid-Victorian poets found themselves caught between the continuities suggested by the Romantic project and the discontinuities offered by the new age of the novel and of the scientific account.

The new tradition of poems mobilised by the dramatic monologue did not change what or how the Victorians thought; it changed their world structure. Mid-Victorian readers found in the dramatic monologue the ultimate way of behaving like themselves and not themselves, of allowing the mind to take a vacation without vacating, or speaking without being heard as themselves. The monologues of Browning and Tennyson were staples for public and private readings in the 1860s and 1870s. When J. A. Symonds thought that to imagine that Clough was expressing his own view would be to mistake the artist's nature altogether, the Victorians had begun to register the formal, technical message of the dramatic monologue.[25]

The dramatic monologue searched the relation between public strength and private weakness. As Browning wrote to Elizabeth Barrett, 'I have been all my life asking what connection there is between the satisfaction at the display of power, and the sympathy with – ever increasing sympathy with – all imaginable weakness.'[26] The dramatic monologue allowed Browning to pursue that question. It also allowed Tennyson, Clough and the Rossettis to put many views and to be held to none, risking nothing and exposing nothing. But the form also put the speaker into an area where normal mid-Victorian rules for social relations were invoked, only to be flouted. They started from situations which the etiquette books coveted. Browning's garrulous Bishop begins:

> No more wine? then we'll push back chairs and talk.
> A final glass for me, though: cool, i'faith.[27]

and his murdering Duke with a gentle observation about a painting; and his frustrated artist with a marital squall: 'But do not let us quarrel any more, / No, my Lucrezia; bear with me for once.'[28]

For Browning, minute circumstances denoted character, each piece of information about another, palpable and true. The monologue mediated between situations governed by codes of etiquette, and situations free of convention and custom. When the social form of the dramatic monologue failed Browning's purpose, he evolved a lyric genre in which the action took place tangentially, away from the situation described. Behind every Browning poem lay this truth from the 1887 collection, *Parleyings With Certain People of Importance in their day*:

> Suppose his act
> Be to o'erarch a gulf: he digs, transports,
> Shapes and, through enginery – all sizes, sorts
> Lays stone by stone until a floor compact
> Proves our bridged causeway. So works Mind – by stress
> Of faculty, with loose facts, more or less,
> Builds up our solid knowledge: all the same,
> Underneath rolls what Mind may hide not tame,
> An element which works beyond our guess,
> Soul, the unsounded sea . . .[29]

Browning recognised and approved 'An element which works beyond our guess' – the same processes which Carlyle had categorised at the start of his *French Revolution*. Browning wrote to Julia Wedgwood on 19 August 1864: 'All the enviable moments of this life seem when we push out of it into the other, to fall back again fast enough.'[30] And this calls up Arnold's haunting lines from 'The Buried Life':

> Ah! well for us, if even we,
> Even for a moment, can get free
> Our heart, and have our lips unchained;
> For that which seals them hath been deep-ordained![31]

The repeated 'even', the flickering 'free' and the counter-suggestion of 'unchained' gather round 'moment', making it more fragile and therefore more valuable.

Images of depth in Victorian poems invariably referred to the inward or buried life in what some considered a veneered age. Poetry for Browning constituted an escape from the conventional into the real. His skill upheld a disdain for the everyday, either by making the mundane say something more than it promised at first, the task of the dramatic monologue; or second by rejecting 'conventional habits',[32] everyday manners and norms by transcending them. The first produced the social dramatic monologues which open after dinner, or in court, or in a salon; the second the wild descriptions of blasted heath, Italian countryside or imaginative reverie, the last of which involved imagining two places at once.[33] For Browning, Carlyle, and for T. H. Green (Mill's voice after Mill's death), to situate oneself outside consciousness or outside the ways in which knowledge was developed was to imagine an untenable ecstasy.[34] Browning's poems depended on moments of being ecstatic, or beside oneself.

The imagination moved towards frank interchanges which transcended the ordinary limits of custom

> There is something fascinating to me in that Bohemian way of living . . . all the conventions of society cut so close and thin, that the soul can see through . . . beyond . . . above.[35]

The Descent of Manners

In his poems, particularly 'By the Fire-side' and 'Two in the Campagna', the search for a frankness beyond social convention led Browning into moments of intimacy:

> A moment after, and hands unseen
>> Were hanging the night around us fast;
> But we knew that a bar was broken between
>> Life and life: we were mixed at last
> In spite of the mortal screen.
>
> The forests had done it; there they stood;
>> We had caught for a moment the powers at play:
> They had mingled us so, for once and good,
>> Their work was done – we might go or stay,
> They relapsed to their ancient mood.
>
> How the world is made for each of us!
>> How all we perceive and know in it
> Tends to some moment's product thus,
>> When a soul declares itself – to wit,
> By its fruit, the thing it does![36]

Hopkins's 'Late I fell in ecstacy' [sic] depended on this divinity of here and everywhere; Barrett Browning recognised this, too: 'A poet, know him by / His ecstasy-dilated eye'. This looked back to John Donne, whom Browning and Barrett Browning quoted throughout their correspondence.[37] Browning's poems fell short of Donne in 'The Extasie' by being reticent about the physical. Occasionally his scene-setting produced the unutterable in pursuit of the unsayable:

> For the drop of the woodland's fruit's begun,
> These early November hours,
>
> That crimson the creeper's leaf across
>> Like a splash of blood, intense, abrupt,
> O'er a shield else gold from rim to boss,
>> And lay it for show on the fairy-cupped
> Elf-needled mat of moss,
>
> By the rose-flesh mushrooms, undivulged
>> Last evening – nay, in today's first dew

238

Yon sudden coral nipple bulged,
       Where a freaked fawn-coloured flaky crew
Of toadstools peep indulged.[38]

Moments of escape, like Browning's final mismanged flight to
Italy in 1846, left the rest of life flat. Moreover, such revelations
risked embarrassing others by revealing too much. Browning's
wish to frame a moment out of time, a 'moment, one and infinite!'
to break with everyday life, contrasted with the restrained,
resigned ending of Arnold's 'The Buried Life' (1848–52):

And there arrives a lull in the hot race
Wherein he doth forever chase
That flying and elusive shadow, rest.
An air of coolness plays upon his face,
And an unwonted calm pervades his breast.
And then he thinks he knows
The hills where his life rose,
And the sea where it goes.

ii Amours, Modern Lust and Sacred Wantons

Arnold and Clough were more rational than Browning in tackling
the conventions in thinking and behaviour of the 1860s. Arnold's
'Stanza from the Grande Chartreuse' sounds a misery of inactivity,
of thwarted thought. His line 'we stand mute and watch the waves'
looks out to the 'darkling plain' and bleak horizon off 'Dover
Beach'. The power to think unconventionally, or to avoid thinking
rationally, was hard won by the Victorians in the Gradgrind fac-
tual school. The dissent from Gradgrindery, from facts and scientific method, took the form of a Victorian scepticism. This turned
itself initially into an emotional state rather than the intellectual
position it later became; it consisted not of propositions up for
discussion, but in crisis and constituted in minds like Mill's or
Newman's, a history of the understanding's sorrows and conflicts.

Clough found the voice for the sceptic in society, and transformed doubting into a social creed. Against the certainties fixed
in hundreds of homiletic books and sermons, the agonies of
A. H. Clough's poems about social exchange stood out as acts of

uncertain dissent. The final entry in Clough's *Prose Remains* found him walking with Tennyson (who had visited with Hallam thirty-one years before) in *le Midi:*

> Today is heavy brouillard down to the feet, or at any rate ankles, of the hills, and little to be done. I have been out for a walk with A. T. to a sort of island between two waterfalls, with pines on it, of which he retained a recollection from his visit of thirty-one years ago . . .[39]

Clough wrote that on 7 September 1861. He died on 13 November. His life, lived adjacent to others, like his poems, resembled an 'island between two waterfalls' in its commitment to indecision. Clough's friend Arnold thought him too introspective, too eager to learn, never willing to emerge with a truth. Clough's life modelled the morbid self-consciousness Mill found characteristic of the age. His poems watched themselves carefully; his self-reflexive thinking put him into a soliloquy addressed to the culture; and his doubts about everything – belief, relationships, politics and doubt itself – patterned the poems.

Clough's thinking represented the intellectual anarchy which Mill diagnosed in *The Spirit of the Age:* 'We have not yet advanced beyond the unsettled state, in which the mind is, when it has recently found itself out in a grievous error, and has not yet satisfied itself of the truth.'[40] Clough's perplexities flickered between errors and truth; he built a life in the synaptic gap between them. But Clough criticised the age's social and religious norms by challenging the familiar, as he did in 1847 with 'The Lastest Decalogue':

> Thou shalt have one God only; who
> Would be at the expense of two?
> No graven images may be
> Worshipped, except the currency:
> Swear not at all; for for thy curse
> Thine enemy is none the worse:
> At church on Sunday to attend
> Will serve to keep the world thy friend:
> Honour they parents, that is, all
> From whom advancement may befall:

Thou shalt not kill; but needst not strive
Officiously to keep alive:
Do not adultery commit;
Advantage rarely comes of it:
Thou shalt not steal; an empty feat,
When it's so lucrative to cheat:
Bear not false witness; let the lie
Have time on its own wings to fly:
Thou shalt not covet; but tradition
Approves all forms of competition.

The sum of all is, thou shalt love,
If any body, God above:
At any rate shall never labour
More than thyself to love they neighbour.

Because their own age was familiar to the mid-Victorians, Mill thought them prepared to know it by nature: Clough's poems challenged that nature. His finest situations started adjacent to the forms of social intercourse which the etiquette book upheld. Lecturing on Wordsworth, Clough made the crucial point: 'It may really be affirmed that some of the highest truths are only expressible to us by style, – only appreciable as indicated by manner.'[41]

In Clough's greatest poem, *Amours de Voyage*, Claude writes to Eustace on marriage:

Which of three Misses Trevellyn it is that Vernon shall marry
Is not a thing to be known; for our friend is one of those natures
Which have their perfect delight in the general tender-domestic,
So that he trifles with Mary's shawl, ties Susan's bonnet,
Dances with all, but at home is most, they say, with Georgina,
Who is, however, *too* silly in my apprehension for Vernon.[42]

The tug of 'general tender-domestic' toward tenders of affection, and the drift of 'at home is most' toward familiarity and domesticity make this into finely worked social comment.

Clough continued by peeling back the etiquette of mid-Victorian expatriates abroad, as Landor and the Brownings were, for example, in Italy:

> I, as before when I wrote, continue to see them a little;
> Not that I like them much or care a *bajocco* for Vernon,
> But I am slow at Italian, have not many English acquaintance,
> And I am asked, in short, and am not good at excuses.
> Middle-class people these, bankers very likely, not wholly
> Pure of the taint of the shop; will at table d'hôte and restaurant
> Have their shilling's worth, their penny's pennyworth even:
> Neither man's aristocracy this, not God's, God knoweth![43]

The wit depended on slight social adjustments in a stable society where trying too hard, as the Trevellyns did, could undo you: 'Yet they are fairly descended, they give you to know, well connected.' Clough made Claude snobbishly amused at their efforts to 'perform the old ritual service of manners', as if behaving in a particular way were the only alternative to his life of thought. Without the agreed and settled social codes underwritten by popular etiquette books, the Trevellyns would be ill at ease. Although Clough's Claude invoked a world of politics and action, little tarnished his image as a creature of Murray's *Guide;* he affirmed the life of the intellect at the expense of self-esteem and communication with others. Claude could well have fathered Prufrock.[44]

Arnold was tepid about 'the Italian poem';[45] but J. A. Symonds enjoyed Clough by hearing what his work spoke of the age: he felt Clough a victim of the *maladie du siècle* – the nondescript cachexy which mixed aspiration with disenchantment, or satire and scepticism with a childlike desire for the tranquillity of reverence and belief, 'in which self-analysis has been pushed to the verge of monomania, and all springs of action are clogged and impeded by the cobwebs of speculation.'[46]

But this was private and not social behaviour. Manners books offered no advice on inner brooding, on losing the capacity for action in the energies of resolve. *Amours* was published in 1858 in America, where James Russell Lowell predicted that Clough would emerge one hundred years on as the truest mid-Victorian expression of the moral and intellectual tendencies, doubts and struggles toward settled conviction. The English edition appeared in *Poems* after Clough's death. Walter Bagehot reviewed it and found there the conversation for which Clough was most remarkable, giving *Amours* to those who knew him in life a peculiar

charm. Clough saw what it was considered cynicism to see –
personal absurdities, religious pomposities, missionary zeal to
teach what they did not know and 'the earnestness with which
most incomplete solutions of the universe are thrust upon us as
complete and satisfying'.[47] Clough's poems ran counter to social
codes. Because they traded in the same currency, manners and
social values, they became more dissident with matters of nuance,
style and manner in play. *Amours* offered the measured delight in
changes of direction which did not change direction, and in polite
clearings of the throat which cleared nothing more:

> These are the facts. The uncle, the elder brother, the squire
> (a Little embarrassed, I fancy), resides in the family place in
> Cornwall, of course; 'Papa is in business,' Mary informs me;
> He's a good sensible man, whatever his trade is. The mother
> Is – shall I call it fine? – herself would tell you refined, and
> Greatly, I fear me, looks down on my bookish and maladroit
>   manners;
> Somewhat affecteth the blue; would talk to me often of poets;
> Quotes, which I hate, Childe Harold; but also appreciates
>   Wordsworth;
> Sometimes adventures on Schiller; and then to religion diverges;
> Questions me much about Oxford; and yet, in her loftiest flights
>   still
> Grates the fastidious ear with the slightly mercantile accent.[48]

Here 'slightly' and not the obvious 'fastidious' does the damage.
Clough could not be understood without sensing the etiquette and
manners norms which he wrote against.

His 1862 editor, F. T. Palgrave, felt that he 'rather lived than
wrote his poem',[49] witnessing the continuity of life and work.
Clough refused to treat his own life with the right seriousness;
writing on the single life, he considered its superiority as 'that
of being more *painful*, which, in a state of things that offers but
little opportunity for elevated *action*, may be considered a temptation for the aspiring spirit'.[50] And in response to criticism of
Amours' depiction of inactivity, he wrote to a friend on 19 June
1850:

> Let us not sit in a corner and mope, and think ourselves clever,

for our comfort, while the room is full of dancing and
cheerfulness . . . When you get to the end of this life, you won't
find another ready-made, in which you can do without effort
what you were meant to do with effort here.[51]

Clough's friends included Arnold, Emerson, Nightingale,
Charles Eliot Norton, Palgrave; respected by reviewers like
Bagehot, Hutton and Lowell, he never achieved the wide popularity which lay open to him by means of connection and reputation. His enterprise came from his worried disregard for social
forms, and his countervailing recognition that most people could
not function without them. In *Amours*, he reduced the profound-
est cries of the heart to matters of 'juxtaposition': a chance encounter and – '*pour passer le temps*' – a conversation on a tedious
journey put two people in love:[52]

> Well, I know there are thousands as pretty and hundreds as
>   pleasant,
> Girls by the dozen as good, and girls in abundance with polish
> Higher and manners more perfect than Susan or Mary Trevellyn.
> Well, I know, after all, it is only juxtaposition, –
> Juxtaposition, in short; and what is juxtaposition?[53]

Later, in *Dipsychus*, Clough revelled in social set-pieces: 'The
Public Garden', 'At the Hotel', 'On the Piazza'. Casual moments
broke free from the situations which he described in both an
overplayed Shelleyan voice and an excruciatingly bland tone. The
indulgent rhetoric of *Dipsychus* plays off the half-serious asides of
the Spirit:

> *Dipsychus*
> We see the Palace and the Place,
> And the White dome. Beauteous but hot.
> Where in the meantime is the spot,
> My favourite, where by masses blue
> And white cloud-folds, I follow true
> The great Alps, rounding grandly o'er,
> Huge arc, to the Dalmatian shore?

> *Spirit*
> This rather stupid place to-day,
> It's true, is most extremely gay;
> And rightly – the Assunzione
> Was always a *gran' funzione.*

This matched the Brownings' letters for social pretension, redeemed by taking itself lightly. Clough's neatest social disruption in *Dipsychus* as we have seen, allowed 'pelf' to intrude where no discussion of money should happen; the word's connotations (booty, goods, money, filthy lucre, trash, frippery and refuse[54]) cling, like the rhyme, to the self. The poem asked the mid-Victorian reader for a momentary anaesthesia of the heart, a laugh which rejected money used to excess, but which nonetheless urged the usefulness of money.

This social technique in Clough resurfaced from 'There is no God' and 'The latest Decalogue', an ironic catalogue still taken seriously ('Thou shalt not kill; but needst not strive/Officiously to keep alive'). Clough toyed with the Victorian solution to uncertainty, the dramatic monologue, with '*Sa Majesté Très Chrétienne*', but the form lacked the fixed point he needed for delicate irony.

No poet used irony less delicately than George Meredith in *Modern Love*. These fifty sonnets threw vitriol at the Victorian household gods: marriage, the home, woman, and polite social life. Meredith mastered everything but language; as a novelist he could, as Wilde said, do anything but tell a story; as a poet he was anything but articulate. Virginia Woolf thought he flattered people by showing them as they really were.

Meredith's succes sprang from personal and social failure – his marriage to Mary Nicholls in 1849. It was a blunder. In April 1858 Nicholls gave birth to a son: she had not had intercourse with Meredith for over a year. She left Meredith for Capri and the artist Henry Wallis (famous for his painting *The Death of Chatterton*) in 1858; she returned to England and died in 1861. The following year saw *Modern Love*, an anatomy of failed marriage which broke several mid-Victorian taboos and stood comparison with Eliot's speaking of the same woes that are in marriages in *Middlemarch*. Meredith depicted the manners of marriage

in verse. The 1862 *Saturday Review* found in it the scattered leaves
of a stranger's diary, a remark which prefigured T. S. Eliot's
comments on *In Memoriam* having a diary's unity and continuity.

The marriage in *Modern Love*, all passion spent, was against
Victorian type; it anatomised the break-up differently from the
social encounters of Meredith's novels, *Diana of the Crossways* in
particular. Diana Merion knew her position relative to the Dun-
stanes, Redworths and Warwicks of the world. Difficulties in
Diana took syntactical form; Diana, who later, of course, becomes
a writer, says:

> We women are the verbs passive of the alliance, we have to learn,
> and if we take to activity, with the best intentions, we conjugate
> a frightful disturbance. We are to run on lines, like steam-trains,
> or we come to no station, dash to fragments. I have the
> misfortune to know I was born an active. I take my chance.[55]

Modern Love broke with Victorian social manner by being
emotionally messy and outspoken; it found an uninhibited, unre-
pressed voice. Far from the sliding into the pleasureless yielding
to the small solicitations of circumstance which disrupt the marriage of Lydgate and Rosamund in *Middlemarch*, Meredith
showed pain and hurtfulness, 'that fatal knife,/Deep questioning,
which probes to endless dole' (sonnet 50). And Meredith reworked
'Our inmost hearts had opened, each to each./We drank the pure
daylight of honest speech' (sonnet 48) to make opening the heart
look more like a haemorrhage than confession.

Two forces impinged on *Modern Love*. The first was evolutionary science. Lyell, Chambers and Darwin had become well enough
established for the question 'What are we first? First animals, and
next / Intelligences at a leap' (sonnet 30) to have radical import.
The second was a broader social view of relationships. Personal
responsibility broadened into collective guilt (sonnet 43):

> The wrong is mixed. In tragic life, God wot,
> No villain need be. Passions spin the plot:
> We are betrayed by what is false within.

Meredith applied evolutionary and psychological pressures to recast everyday social exchange. Mid-Victorian manners' advice over handshaking and arm-holding between the sexes came alive here (sonnet 39):

> What two come here to mar this heavenly tune?
> A man is one: the woman bears my name,
> And honour. Their hands touch! Am I still tame?

The hollow rapprochement took the form of a taken arm: 'I . . . made proffer of my arm. / She took it simply, with no rude alarm' (sonnet 46). Earlier, the tender-horror of 'Her moist hand clings mortally to mine' (sonnet 21) called up Donne's 'Extasie', stripped of sensuality. Social gestures, sometimes personal, in Redworth's holding Diana's hand a minute too long for friendship, were the reconciliations for the sake of decency, those hoistings of standards vital to the novels.

Meredith's enterprise contrasted with Coventry Patmore's in *The Angel in the House*. This was published six years before Meredith's poem, socially changed by developments in politics since its writing. It remained a record of idealised sex in the ideal marriage (Book II, canto xiii):

> The love of marriage claims, above
> All other kinds, the name of love,
> As perfectest, though not so high
> As love which heaven with single eye
> Considers.
> . . .
> Loves, once married, deem their bond
> Then perfect, scanning nought beyond
> For love to do but to sustain
> The spousal hour's delighted gain.
> . . .
> By Heaven's kind, impartial plan,
> Well-wived is he that's truly man
> If but the woman's womanly,
> As such a man's is sure to be.

Patmore's kind impartial plan changed into Meredith's unkind, planned impartialities in married life and in *Modern Love*.

Patmore had entitled that section 'The Wedding Sermon'. Titles in literature in general and Meredith in particular upheld an etiquette of literary form. Meredith used the convention to shape the ironic final chapter of *Diana*, 'The Nuptial Chapter'. Convention also allowed Meredith to write knowingly within the sonnet-sequence tradition. He concluded the thirtieth sonnet, which weighed innate qualities against circumstance, with the starkly inapposite, 'Lady this is my sonnet to your eyes', closing just as Shakespeare opened his attack on the love-sonnet tradition.[56]

While the brittleness of the sonnets which constitute *Modern Love* prevented them from conveying dramatic or narrative development, they nonetheless uncovered what R. H. Hutton (who rechristened the poem 'Modern Lust') in the *Spectator* called 'the concealed tragedy of social life'.[57] The poems progress by suggestive, arresting images catching the decent, harsh and tender marital impulses. The nastiest moments draw on apparent domestic concord; the awfulness of 'cheerfuller', a neologism searching for an occasion, shows Meredith tight-lipped and polite, saying the unsayable at dinner (sonnet 17):

> At dinner, she is hostess, I am host.
> Went the feast ever cheerfuller? she keeps
> The Topic over intellectual deeps
> In buoyancy afloat. They see no ghost.
> With sparkling surface-eyes we play the ball:
> It is in truth a most contagious game:
> HIDING THE SKELETON, shall be its name.
> Such play as this, the devils might appall!
> But here's the greater wonder; in that we
> Enamoured of an acting nought can tire,
> Each other, like true hypocrites, admire,
> Warm-hearted looks, Love's ephemerioe,
> Shoot gaily o'er the dishes and the wine.
> We waken envy of our happy lot.
> Fast, sweet, and golden, shows the marriage-knot.
> Dear guests, you now have seen Love's corpse-light shine.

Meredith shocked with *Modern Love*, not by admitting

unpleasant truths about the institution which held mid-Victorian society together, but by broadcasting them.

The 1850s and 1860s saw a broadening in what could be talked about in personal relations, provided nothing was said. The art forms which pushed back the boundaries of the sayable during this period were painting and book illustration: the homilies of Augustus Egg (*Past and Present*) and Holman Hunt (*The Awakening Conscience* or *The Hireling Shepherd*); the social accuracy of Richard Redgrave (*The Poor Governess*), Eyre Crowe (*The Dinner Hour, Wigan*) and William Frith (*Derby Day, The Proposal, The Railway Station* and *Ramsgate Sands: Life at the Seaside*); the historical scenes of Daniel Maclise (*Caxton's Printing Office* or *The Death of Nelson*); and the fantasies of John Everett Millais (*Lorenzo and Isabella, Ophelia* and *Mariana*), John Waterhouse (*The Lady of Shallot*) and the excesses of Dante Gabriel Rossetti (*Beata Beatrix, The Blue Bower* and *How They Met Themselves*) with those of Edward Burne-Jones (particularly *The Beguiling of Merlin*).

Painting or illustrations in the form of William Mulready's work for *The Vicar of Wakefield* touched upon the passions, loves and hates which normal codes of etiquette forbade. Millais dressed them in fantasy, as in *Mariana*, or kept them from sight, as he did with the unpublished *Accepted* of 1853, a tender sketch of two lovers who have stolen from company for a private moment.

Painting, and the literature of the period, filled the desire for those privacies and inwardnesses which Mill felt wanting in his own life and in the earlier years of the century. Imaginative literature represented the Victorians to themselves in ways which set aside everyday decorum and which explored the extent of the unsayable. The impulse translated from art to poetry. The most visually rich poems of the pre-Raphaelites – particularly the Rossettis, Morris and Swinburne – turned artistic apprehension into an act of personal and social dissent from the surrounding norms.

Poets were expected to behave according to their profession – that was, unconventionally. Tennyson acted in every way consistent with others' expectations of how a poet should behave:

Tennyson was very unkempt looking, had long hair, wore a long

Inverness cape and a soft wide-brimmed wide-awake, and,
walking along the street, he looked rather like an old beggar man.[58]

Browning, for his part, made every attempt to maintain his nonconformism by rejecting the image Tennyson had established:
'there were those who complained that Browning looked like a
stockbroker and talked like a man of the world'.[59] But later poets
behaved more flamboyantly, and fitted less snugly with expected
norms by exaggerating them: they lived differently.

Rossetti's well-known background promised an unconventional
life: his father was a political exile from Italy, his mother a devout
Anglican, his sister Maria a nun, and his sister Christina a poet.
The careers of the pre-Raphaelites, the public statements of *The
Germ* and the Pre-Raphaelite Brotherhood, and the personal lives
of Rossetti and Morris – around Elizabeth Siddal and Jane Burden
– suggested a life beyond poems, a dedicated commitment to be
other than Victorian. A social view of the Pre-Raphaelites saw in
their personal lives a continuity with the anti-conjugal bliss of
Eliot and Lewes, of Mill and Taylor; and with the conjugal hiss
of Ruskin and Gray, or Meredith and Nicholl. A literary view
saw similarities with Patmore, the rich descriptive detail in *The
Blessed Damozel*, the sensuous and colourful images, the Paganism
and Medievalism,and the occasionally obscure symbolism. An art
history view linked the movement's origin in 1848 with Millais,
Burne-Jones and Holman Hunt.

The ground-breaking work of the Pre-Raphaelites, and of their
adjacent, Swinburne, was changed and continued by Pater and
Wilde later in the century. Pre-Raphaelitism evolved gradually
into the aestheticism of the 1880s and 1890s. Their commitment
to a transfigured nature reached across the channel to meet the
tradition of Gautier, Baudelaire and Huysmans. They shared the
French sense of what an altered social role for poetry might look
like.

In the important 1872 essay 'The Latest Development in Literary Poetry', W. J. Courthope described the 'antipathy to society'
of Morris, Rossetti and Swinburne.[60] Courthope followed the self-
portrait Morris painted: artist, craftsman, designer, entrepreneur,
poet, politician. His brand of revisionary Pre-Raphaelitism
reworked the cultural and literary past; but also his own past.

Morris's *News from Nowhere* came from and returned to
Kelmscott Manor, at once a withdrawal from and an engagement
with moral, social and political life: his heroine Ellen delighted in
the house which held in it the crumbs of happiness gathered from
a confused and turbulent past.

Courthope omitted Christina Rossetti, whose *Goblin Market*
promised paradise on earth by creating a genuinely disorienting
world. Her occluded relationship with Dante, Petrarch, Plato and
Augustine and her preface to *Monna Innominata* found expression
in sensual and religious images yoked together by her technical
abilities. In 1911 Ford Madox Ford classed her 'the most valuable
poet that the Victorian age produced',[61] echoing the laudatory
1895 *Westminster Review* notice on Rossetti. Her combination of
mysticism and melancholy overlaid with a medieval tint placed
her poems safely distant from everyday life.[62]

Rossetti's *Goblin Market* focused on unsatisfied longings and
the futility of sensual delight. But the poem's ripe images thrilled
rather than warned. The goblins tempt Laura:

> 'You have much gold upon your head,'
> They answered all together:
> 'Buy from us with a golden curl.'
> She clipped a precious golden lock,
> She dropped a tear more rare than pearl,
> Then sucked their fruit globes fair or red:
> Sweeter than honey from the rock,
> Stronger than man-rejoicing wine,
> Clearer than water flowed that juice;
> She never tasted such before,
> How should it cloy with length of use?
> She sucked and sucked and sucked the more
> Fruits which that unknown orchard bore;
> She sucked until her lips were sore;[65]

Laura's sister, Lizzie, after confronting and resisting the goblins'
blandishments, returns to redeem Laura's temptation:

> She cried, 'Laura,' up the garden.
> 'Did you miss me?
> Come and kiss me.

Never mind my bruises,
Hug me, kiss me, suck my juices
Squeezed from goblin fruits for you,
Goblin pulp and goblin dew.
Eat me, drink me, love me;
Laura, make much of me;
For your sake I have braved the glen
And had to do with goblin merchant men.'[64]

The moral sentiment in *Goblin Market* shares the poem with thorough sensuality, itself linked with money in the goblin cry, 'come buy'. The poem explores the nature and price of pleasure, but in an environment divorced from conventional Victorian social interaction. When Rossetti attended to community and environment around her, as in 'An Apple Gathering', she produced cogent, well-behaved lyrics which looked across to Emily Dickinson and forward to Robert Frost:

I plucked pink blossoms from mine apple-tree
    And wore them all that evening in my hair:
Then in due season when I went to see
    I found no apples there.

With dangling basket all along the grass
    As I had come I went the selfsame track:
My neighbours mocked me while they saw me pass
    So empty-handed back.[65]

The moral guide or etiquette book tackled sensual pleasure by insisting on its unpleasantness, urging constant vigilance against it.[66] The possibility of temptation arose as a fall from discipline, a lapse in alertness. Unlike the poem, the moral guide could never say what it was advising against. Even into the 1880s the language either remained coy beyond intelligibility, or developed into hysteria:

Never allow an uncleam or profligate man to cross your threshold.
Whether you reside with a family, of live in a private lodging on
the first, second, or third floor, determine that no bad book, or
pamphlet, or newspaper, shall ever enter your room.[67]

This writer, J. T. Davidson, (*Talks With Young Men, Forwarned – Forearmed*, and *The City Youth*) had also written *Sure to Succeed*, which advised, under The Body to Be Cared For', in veiled terms:

> Let no book be on your shelf which has a corrupting influence. Indulge in no conversation that would offend a pure and holy mind. Wear the white flower of purity always on your breast, and let no one snatch it from you.[68]

While writers like Davidson policed the boundaries of the sayable, Rossetti redrew the boundaries of mid-Victorian sensual and religious experience. Her work, like her brother's, sustained an intensely baffled passion, a report from the front lines of experience and an exploration into the qualities of sensation. Her poetic enterprise pointed the way for the aesthetes and decadents of the 1880s and 1890s. While Christina provided the quiet revolution, her brother Dante Gabriel Rossetti was more public.

Robert Buchanan's 1871 'Fleshly School of Poetry'[69] attacked Swinburne, Morris and D. G. Rossetti by reviewing Rossetti's *Poems* (1870), and was remarkable not for the furore it caused in narrow literary critical circles, nor for reviving the intemperance of Buchanan's less famous, 1866, attack on Swinburne,[70] but because it opened a vein of language as richly coloured as that which nourished it. Buchanan found Rossetti's sensuality 'shooting its ulcerous roots deeper and deeper, blotching the fair surface of things'. The debate over 'Nuptial Sleep', the fifth sonnet from Rossetti's opening twenty-eight in *The House of Life*, wrangled on into Rossetti's complaint that the wrongly described 'whole poem' depicted 'merely animal sensations'. Rossetti did not comment on the poem's content; he satisfied himself with, 'It is no more a whole poem, in reality, than is any single stanza of any poem throughout the book.'[71]

'Animal' and 'fleshy' resurfaced in John Morley's more damaging criticism of Swinburne in the *Saturday Review*. Morley struck an Arnoldian note with the notion that the poet had duties, an attitude which looked back to Arnold's great 1853 Preface. But Morley also bolstered the review with contemporary standards; his criticism of Swinburne was a reprimand for bad manners:

He is so firmly and avowedly fixed in an attitude of revolt against the current notions of decency and dignity and social duty that to beg of him to become a little more decent, to fly a little less persistently and gleefully to the animal side of human nature, is simply to beg him to be something different from Mr. Swinburne. It is a kind of protest which his whole position makes it impossible for him to receive with anything but laughter and contempt. A rebel of his calibre is not to be brought to a better mind by solemn little sermons on the loyalty which a man owes to virtue.[72]

Swinburne's poems made a social statement, a decline from decency. Morley responded by finding 'mixed vileness and child-ishness of depicting the spurious passion of putrescent imagin-ation, the unnamed lusts of sated wantons'. Swinburne's redeem-ing grace, for Morley, lay in the unintelligibility of 'Anactoria' (one of the most notorious of the poems). Morley looked forward ironically to English readers acquiring 'a truly delightful famili-arity with these unspeakable foulnesses'.

Morley knew that to recognise 'a libidinous laureate pack of satyrs', as he did in Swinburne, risked complicity if only in the recognition. So he applied the test of speakability in the drawing room: 'It will be very charming to hear a drawing-room discussion on such verses as these, for example:–

> Stray breaths of Sapphic song that blew
>> Through Mitylene
> Shook the fierce quivering blood in you
>> By night, Faustine.
> The shameless nameless love that makes
>> Hell's iron gin
> Shut on you like a trap that breaks
>> The soul, Faustine.'[73]

Morley's exasperation had sent him grasping for social standards. He had found them at home.

Reading aloud at home had long been a test for well-behaved poems. The *Times* obituary of Charles Dickens praised him in terms of social acceptance: 'our great and genial novelist, the intimate of every household'.[74] Swinburne's emergence from the mid-Victorian milieu was a revolt against it.

The Victorians identified their environment with their moral status, as T. E. Brown showed in *Roman Women*, a Jonsonian agglomeration celebrating the power of clutter:

> But morals – beautiful serenity
> Of social life, the sugar and the tea,
> The flannels and the soup, the coals,
> The patent recipes for saving souls,
> And other things: the chill dead sneer
> Conventional, the abject fear
> Of form-transgressing freedom – I admit
> That you have these.[76]

This trespassed on the social territory of Clough, listening for the heartbeats between the social forms. 'The abject fear / Of form-transgressing freedom' was the ethic of mid-Victorian England.

Disraeli realised that, where change was constant, the question was not whether to resist the inevitable, but whether the change should be carried out in accordance with manners, customs, laws and traditions of the culture, or in deference to abstract principle and arbitrary doctrine. New poetry for the Victorians changed the environmental structure. Rossetti and Swinburne altered the potential balance between the Victorian senses; by writing of sensuality, they indicated the sensuous.

These alterations worked widely and subtly in other poets. The 1870s and 1880s provided the scope and political leisure for these changes to work inwardly. The improved living conditions for the majority in the 1870s and 1880s marked the great material achievement of the Victorian age (what G. M. Trevelyan thought 'parallel to its glories in literature, intellect and science'[77]). In the 1860s and 1870s the rise of Robert Owen's Socialism had empowered movements like the Wholesale Co-operative Movement and the working men's associations which had, in turn, trained the character, intelligence and financial skills of the middle and working class. Abroad, since the 1860s, with peace in Italy, Germany and the United States, the foundation for the Bismarckian peace of the 1870s had been laid.

iii Literature, Manners and Morals

The 1870s began to hear Arnold's buried life. The dramatic monologue had allowed the unsayable ('Porphyria's Lover' or 'My Last Duchess' through to the horrors of *The Ring and the Book*) to be said and heard with impunity; then Meredith, Rossetti and Swinburne had stretched the bounds of the sayable in breaking subject-matter taboos. The process in poetry reflected a loosening in manners which started slowly, but which had begun in the mid-century, as G. M. Young observed:

> . . . both in literature and in manners, the stirring and good-humoured fifties had left a grace and brightness behind them across which the Early Victorian time appeared as a season of construction, heaviness, and gloom.[78]

Literature challenged the conformities of the age, yet continued to uphold them; some conservative forms, such as the sentimental ballad, persisted as patterns of behaviour (singing around the parlour piano).[79] Literary became associated with personal behaviour. The *Saturday Review* for 12 February 1876, on affectation, justified itself: 'When we accuse a writer of having an affected mannerism, we clearly liken him to those who show themselves affected in personal behaviour and in the profession of sentiment.'[80]

The mid-century had realised the importance of the continuity of social forms. G. M. Young's favourite Victorian, Walter Bagehot, worked simultaneously as a banker, editor, economist and cultural critic. He amalgamated a breadth and culture unimaginable in the blinkered professionalism of subsequent years. He knew that during rapid change, preservation of such continuity with the past, with recognised standards and a navigable social world, was essential if transition was to be effected without producing confusion and chaos. Literature and manners provided both continuities and processes for change.

The great poems of the 1860s and 1870s dissented from the time: *Modern Love* (Meredith, 1862), *Goblin Market and Other Poems* (C. Rossetti, 1862), *Dramatis Personae* (Browning, 1864), *Dipsychus* (Clough, 1865), *Poems and Ballads* (Swinburne, 1866), *The Ring and the Book* (Browning, 1868–9), *Red Cotton Night-*

Cap Country (Browning, 1873), *The City of Dreadful Night* (Thomson, 1874, published 1880), 'The Wreck of the Deustsch-land' (Hopkins, and the devotional sonnets, 1875–7). The most penetrating linguistic dissent belonged to G. M. Hopkins. The mid-Victorians' expense of the inner life in a waste of self-conscious morbidity meant that problems received different treatment in Victorian poems and in Victorian homiletic books. Hopkins's bravest *coup* was to publicise emotion, although his poems remained unpublished until his friend Robert Bridges edited them in 1918. 'Carrion Comfort' (1877) opens fiercely and painfully:

> Not, I'll not, carrion comfort, Despair, not feast on thee;
> Not untwist – slack they may be – these last strands of man
> In me or, most weary cry *I can no more*. I can.

Crippling despair was something the homiletic books hid from in ready-made formulas. Lucy Soulsby wrote on 'The Slough of Despond' in *Stray Thoughts on Character:*

> One great element of difficulty is that they [sloughs of despond]
> so often belong to what Miss Williams Wynn called 'the
> illegitimate sorrows of life', which cannot put on crape openly and
> appeal for sympathy.[81]

Soulsby appealed to Bunyan, recommending autobiographies in general on the ground that they changed the climate of both mind and body, and the *Pilgrim's Progress* on the ground that it was 'the personal history of every reader – a cypher to which we each have our own key ... to every person and incident in which we could put name and date in the margin – did we live in a Palace of Truth'.[82]

In the 1860s and 1870s poems concerned themselves increasingly with the unmentionable: death, sex and doubt.[83] The relation of poems to everyday behaviour presented the poet with two tasks: dealing with daily experience of interaction with others, and with the truths of personal experience. This was Mill's dilemma. And this was the dichotomy bridged by the dramatic monologue in the 1860s, evaded by Browning's escapist lyrics in the same decade, insinuated into existence by Clough, confronted by Meredith and flaunted by Swinburne in the 1870s. Progress calibrated against social norm and acceptability in the 1870s and 1880s – a standard that moved with the times – needed to find another measure of its advance. How could poems affect behaviour? The answer came from two quarters: Walter Pater's essays which made up *The Renaissance* (1868, 1873) provided the doctrine; the Pre-Raphaelites the daring. The common fidelity of Pater and the Pre-Raphaelites, not to external nature but to inner experience, notwithstanding its running counter to formal moralities, opened the Decadent routes to the spices of exotica and the new worlds of personal self-culture in the 1890s. Victorian science in the 1860s and 1870s was the catalyst.

The fact rather than the complexity of the interchange between literature and manners was crucial. The content of a medium is always another medium; literature contained social interaction and social interaction literature. As manners changed, so did literature. However, it was not so much the content as the literary forms which bore on behaviour by innovating and sustaining the personal emotional culture which Mill found in Wordsworth. Yet there was a counter-movement, as poems of the 1860s and 1870s fostered another kind of attention: individual emotional cultivation. As mid-Victorian prosperity peaked in the 1870s attention had turned outward to forms of social and economic communication. Marshall McLuhan:

> As the nineteenth century heated up the mechanical and
> dissociative procedures of technical fragmentation, the entire
> attention of men turned to the associative and the corporate.[84]

This process of social communication and inward cultivation has not yet worked itself out; the mid-Victorians continue to speak to the late twentieth century because their dilemmas still obtain. Mid-Victorian England rested on the uncomfortable but workable arrangement that set its practical ideals at odds with its religious professions, and its religious belief at issue with its intelligence.

Mill's *System of Logic*, one of the most influential textbooks of the century's middle years, taught that the character of the propositions assented to by the intellect 'essentially determines

the moral and political state of the community'.[85] By the 1870s
those propositions were increasingly the product of two forces.
First, the religious-humanist school typified by Thomas Arnold's
teaching:

> It was not an attempt merely to give more theological instruction,
> or to introduce sacred words into school admonitions; there may
> have been some occasions for religious advice that might have been
> turned to more advantage, some religious practices which might
> have been more constantly or effectually encouraged. His design
> arose out of the very nature of his office: the relation of an
> instructor to his pupils was to him, like all the other relations of
> human life, only in a healthy state, when subordinate to their
> common relation to God.[86]

In direct religious teaching, or on particular occasions, Christian
principles were expressly introduced by Arnold, but without the
appearance of a rhetorical flourish. 'They were looked upon,'
recalled A. P. Stanley in 1844:

> as the natural expression of what was constantly implied: it was
> felt that he had the power, in which so many teachers had been
> deficient, of saying what he did mean, and of not saying what he
> did not mean, – the power of doing what was right, and speaking
> what was true, and thinking what was good, independently of any
> professional or conventional notions that so to act, speak, or
> think, was becoming or expedient.[87]

However, a second force emerged in the 1860s and 1870s
through the work of Alfred Russel Wallace, Charles Darwin and
Herbert Spencer. Thomas Arnold's son felt its pressure in 1881:

> I have heard it said that the sagacious and admirable naturalist
> whom we lost not very long ago, Mr Darwin, once owned to a
> friend that for his part he did not experience the necessity of two
> things which most men find so necessary to them, – religion and
> poetry; science and the domestic affections, he thought, were
> enough.[88]

Arnold even found himself thinking about the order of nature

around him; instead of looking inward, he was investigating outward:

> The spectacle afforded by the wonderful energies prisoned within
> the compass of the microscopic hair of a plant, which we
> commonly regard as a merely passive organism, is not easily
> forgotten by one who has watched its display, continued hour
> after hour, without pause or sign of weakening. The possible
> complexity of many other organic forms, seemingly as simple as
> the protoplasm of the nettle, dawns upon one; and the comparison
> of such a protoplasm to a body with an internal circulation,
> which has been put forward by an eminent physiologist, loses
> much of its startling character.[89]

Thomas Henry Huxley had known since 1868 'that the order
of nature is ascertainable by our faculties to an extent which is
practically unlimited'.[90] The new debate over how humans behaved
was fought out between the Decadents and the Scientists in the
1880s.

II Science: the Gorilla and the Gentleman

Mill died in May 1873. The *Spectator* published an obituary by
R. H. Hutton:[91]

> Probably very few authors who have exerted so powerful an
> influence over the course of English thought as Mr. John Stuart
> Mill have ever been so wanting in superficially marked personal
> characteristics of style. He has recast our political economy,
> converted almost a whole generation of teachers to his own
> opinions on Logic and Ethics, and materially modified the view
> taken even by democratic thinkers of the machinery of political
> life; moreover, he has been for three eventful years a distinguished
> Member of the House of Commons, where he delivered probably
> the most thoughtful speeches of that Parliament . . .[92]

Mill's style, unrelieved by humour, unpunctuated by fancy and
moral inequality, represented what Hutton called the impersonal

intelligence of the age. His work exuded the calm intellect of a thinker committed, as the *System of Logic* witnessed, to processes and systems derived from consistent principles.

1873 was remarkable for three books in the humanities: Mill's *Autobiography*, Arnold's *Literature and Dogma*, and Walter Pater's *The Renaissance* (1868–73), which reworked essays from the *Fortnightly Review* and the *Westminster Review* over the previous five years. All three showed the diversity of the 1870s in the arts (Stephen produced *Freethinking and Plainspeaking*, and Newman *The Idea of a University*). It was Pater's book which made the impact, because his added conclusion made literature intimate with behaviour and became a touchstone for subsequent arts movements. Its link with science at first seemed tenuous, a fragile tissue of connection. But Pater's book was a form of reaction to what a complete account of human behaviour, remove individual expression, would look like. When all was nature and Science had both confidence and potential to explain all, little remained for Art. Scientific advances presented the Decadent movement with intellectual rather than social demands. The last twenty-five years of the nineteenth century shaped the relations between the arts and the natural sciences ever since.

Walter Pater's secret, like Marshall McLuhan's after him, lay in knowing that the content of one artistic medium was another medium. Art aspired to the condition of music, architecture to art, and poetry to engraving. Pater drained the moral content from the art he criticised. He wrote in 'The School of Giorgione':

> In its primary aspect, a great picture has no more definite message for us than an accidental play of sunlight and shadow for a few moments on the wall or floor: is itself, in truth, a space of such fallen light, caught as the colours are in an Eastern carpet, but refined upon, and dealt with more subtly and exquisitely than by nature itself.[93]

This took art beyond nature, precisely the predicate of Joris-Karl Huysmans's *A Rebours (Against the Grain)* over a decade later. Mill had predicted such a move. His own 'Nature' anticipated Pater and Huysmans, not by advocating a simple Decadent ethic 'against nature', but by refusing to be shocked by the fact – if not the specifics – of anything actual or conceivable.

A Rebours was the ultimate misbehaviour book. It was adored by Oscar Wilde ('the heavy odour of incense seemed to cling about its pages and to trouble the brain'), George Moore ('the prodigious book') and Rémy de Gourmant ('we should never forget what a huge debt we owe to this memorable breviary'). The popular power lay in its synthetic, personal *cauchemar* of individual satisfaction, irrespective of morals and society. The intellectual power was its rejection of naturalism (Zola said it had delivered a 'terrible blow to Naturalism'). This struck at the development of the novel during a time when William James, with *Textbook of Psychology* (1892), *The Will to Believe* (1897) and *Talks to Teachers on Psychology* (1892), was evolving another rival to the novel by developing his 'stream of consciousness' ideas.

Huysmans made an impact because he dramatised the intellectual processes behind his work. While he followed a staid career of clerkship in the French Ministry of the Interior, his writing ethic – from his first work in 1874[94] – was a breathless dissent, a new way of behaving:

> The whole secret is to know how to set about it, to be able to concentrate the mind on a single point, to attain to a sufficient degree of self-abstraction to produce the necessary hallucination and so substitute the vision of the reality for the reality itself.
>
> To tell the truth, artifice was in Des Esseintes' philosophy the distinctive mark of human genius.[95]

The hero of *A Rebours*, Duc Jean Floressas Des Esseintes, is a man who tries to alter the course of nature, delighting in the attempt. In one episode he finds a youth of sixteen on the street and takes him to a brothel in rue Mosnier. He explains to the Madam:

> '. . . The boy is a virgin and has reached the age when the blood begins to boil; he might, of course, run after the little girls of his neighbourhood, and still remain an honest lad while enjoying his bit of amusement; in fact, have his little share of the monotonous happiness open to the poor. On the contrary, by bringing him

here and plunging him in a luxury he had never even suspected
the existence of and which will make a lasting impression on his
memory; by offering him every fortnight a treat like this, I shall
make him acquire the habit of these pleasures which his means
forbid his enjoying; let us grant it will take three months for
them to become absolutely indispensable to him – and by spacing
them out as I do, I avoid all risk of satiating him – well, at the
end of the three months, I stop the little allowance I am going to
pay you in advance for the benevolence you show him. Then he
will take to thieving to pay for his visits here; he will stop at
nothing that he may take his usual diversions on this divan in
this fine gas-lit apartment.'[96]

Later, Des Esseintes is planting out a garden, the ideal forum
(as Shakespeare's *The Winter's Tale*) showed for a confrontation
between art and nature:

The men brought other and fresh varieties, in this case presenting
the appearance of a fictitious skin marked by an imitation
network of veins. Most of them, as if disfigured by syphilis or
leprosy, displayed livid patches of flesh, reddened by measles,
roughened by eruptions; others showed the bright pink of a half-
closed wound or the red brown of the crusts that form over a
scar; others were as if scorched with cauteries blistered with burns;
others again offered hairy surfaces eaten into holes by ulcers and
excavated by chancres.[97]

Everywhere *A Rebours* offered the negative of the behaviour book.
The moment Des Esseintes reads improving literature, in this case
Dickens, it has a negative impact:

. . . the volumes produced an effect just the opposite of what he
looked for; his chaste lovers, his Protestant heroines, modestly
draped to the chin, whose passions were so seraphic, who never
went beyond a coy dropping of the eyes, a blush, a tear of
happiness, a squeezing of hands, exasperated him. This exaggerated
virtue drove him into the opposite extreme; in virtue of the law
of contrasts, he rushed into the contrary excess; thought of
passionate, full-bodied loves; pictured the doings of frail, human
couples; of ardent embraces mouth to mouth; of pigeon kisses, as

ecclesiastical prudery calls them when tongue meets tongue in naughty wantonness.[98]

If Huysmans was writing 'against nature', or 'against the grain', what was natural behaviour in the first place? The question was where decadence, science, philosophy and behaviour met. It was a matter of lifestyle.

Mill was more radical though less spectacular than Huysmans. His scrupulous pluralism sought isolated cases, found the principles which supported them; as a philosopher he promised no system or way of life; as an individual his example was intellectual rather than personal, severe rather than warming. His observations kept an enduring accuracy in politics, logic, economics, social science and religion; he had wider influence than all his contemporaries except Darwin. His *Three Essays on Religion* ('Nature', 'The Utility of Religion' and 'Theism') were the final fruits of the habit of long-thinking and writing between 1850 and 1858. He had intended to publish them in 1873.

The *Essays on Religion* spoke to the latter part of the century and provided matter for social dissidents, Decadents and Aesthetes. They bridged the increasingly wide gap between imaginative literature and science, between their centripetal and centrifugal processes. Both imaginative literature and science had a stake in defining what was natural. Mill's essay 'Nature' rested on what could be classed as natural. This thinking involved the question of what social practice, economics, art, industry and other human endeavour might be classed as natural. Mill reached his typically analytic conclusion.

Mill duly defined the word 'nature'. His initial definition was that the nature of an object 'means its entire capacity of exhibiting phenomena ... Nature in the abstract is the aggregate of the powers and properties of all things.'[99] He continued:

Nature means the sum of all phenomena, together with the causes which produce them; including not only all that happens, but all that is capable of happening; the unused capabilities of causes being as much a part of the idea of Nature, as those which take effect.[100]

Mill's secondary definition puts 'nature' against 'art' and

'natural' against 'artificial', suggesting that 'nature' meant not 'everything which happens, but only what takes place without the agency, or without the voluntary and intentional agency, of man'.[101] The two usages persisted in claims of Stoics and Epicureans alike to derive behaviour from nature, and continue through the twentieth century in environmental, genetic and experimental science.

After defining meticulously, Mill complicated the definitions:

> ... in the sense of the word Nature which has just been defined, and which is the true scientific sense, Art is as much Nature as anything else; and everything which is artificial is natural – Art has no independent powers of its own: Art is but the employment of the powers of Nature for an end.[102]

Phenomena depended on elementary forces and elemental properties; human agency could never produce a new property of matter in general. Nature, for Mill, referred to what is, to the actual. And since for Mill all forms of enquiry were either into what is (history, science) or what ought to be (art, morals, politics), nature fell under the aegis of history and science.

This approach matched Mill's thinking about conduct. *On Liberty* attended to how rulers or citizens imposed opinions as rules of conduct, imposing some of the best and worst feelings 'incident to human nature'. Mill knew that these opinion-givers were restrained by nothing but want of power.[103] The notion of human nature behind Mill's model of society encompassed the best and worst instincts, exactly those which the etiquette book sought to encourage in the former case, and suppress in the latter. While Mill was writing 'Nature' in the 1850s, T. Binney wrote of 'the laws of our nature and the constitution of our society are such, that there is no securing or accomplishing anything without reputation',[104] making social attributes into a law of nature. In 1867 the *Saturday Review* had complained that 'the conduct of society is constantly being brought back to the first principles, not of society, but of a state of nature', finding a real inconsistency in the collation of the two.[105]

Mill realised 'nature' could also be used in ethics, 'in which, Nature does not stand for what is, but for what ought to be; or for the rule or standard of what ought to be'.[106] Hippolyte Taine evolved the notion of 'acting naturally well' where the individual 'acts still better on principle':

> In this you recognise the accomplished chief; add to it the English varieties, empire over self, continuous coolness, perseverance in adversity, natural seriousness, dignity of manner, the shunning of all affectation or boasting; you will have the superior model who, copied closely or vaguely discerned, here rallies all who aspire and all who serve.[107]

Taine floated the term over actual and desirable behaviour. But Mill knew that those who offered nature (in natural behaviour) as a standard were not renaming behaviour as nature, but setting out what a standard of action should be. Mill was at his simplest and best:

> Those who say that we ought to act according to Nature do not mean the mere identical proposition that we ought to do what we ought to do. They think that the word Nature affords some external criterion of what we should do; and if they lay down as a rule for what ought to be, a word which in its proper signification denotes what is, they do so because they have a notion, either clearly or confusedly, that what is, constitutes the rule and standard of what ought to be.[108]

This took the daring out of Huysmans's *A Rebours*.

According to Mill, all action is conformable to nature, and since man has no power but to follow nature, 'all his actions are done through, and in obedience to, some one or many of nature's physical or mental laws'.[109] By Mill's second definition, if the natural course of things were perfect, to act at all would be gratuitous meddling. Mill concluded: 'the doctrine that man ought to follow nature, or in other words, ought to make the spontaneous course of things the model of his voluntary actions, is equally irrational and immoral'.[110]

Mill's social and philosophical concerns placed him in a higher division of seriousness than Pater and Huysmans. His questions concerned all levels of mid-Victorian society. Conformity to nature had no connection with right and wrong, so the idea fitted uneasily into ethical discussions. The notion that a thing might be unnatural, for Mill, would not argue its being culpable: criminality was to some no more unnatural than virtue. The implications for the behaviour book were profound. Was it natural for man to behave well? Where did good behaviour come from? By the 1890s these questions were openly put:

> In our northern country the physical sense seems to be dormant.
> Our educational system too is a perpetual lesson of self-restraint
> and suppression of the emotions. From the earliest age we are
> taught that it is cowardly to cry, improper to laugh aloud,
> unseemly to enjoy eating and feeble to love ease. Our whole nature
> is kept back, possibly guided and possibly controlled, only pent
> up to break out with irresistible force when the real overcomes
> the artificial and we act from instinct and no longer from
> thought . . . Civilization is against nature and we are surprised
> when nature gets the better of the fight.[111]

This was expressing a popular 1890s view, a backlash against the artifice advocated in books like *Manners and Rules of Good Society by a Member of the Aristocracy* (1890).

In practice, Mill's 'Nature' predicted the arguments which the Decadents advanced in the 1880s and 1890s. He did little to shape the Victorians' social sense of themselves as either natural or unnatural. That sense operated differently. When *The Public Speaker's Vade Mecum* advised the intending speaker to study nature, it necessarily found itself making qualifications: 'Another important rule to be observed in elocution is *Study Nature*, that is, study the most easy and natural way of expressing yourself, both as to the tone of voice and the manner of speech.'[112] 'Nature' and 'natural' oscillate between values already supposed to exist in conversational intercourse, and values hinted at in the proximity of 'natural' with terms such as 'just' and 'agreeable'.

The debate about the word 'nature' and natural behaviour continued down other and more profound channels of thought in the 1870s: natural science. This decade and the next altered the mid-Victorians' perception of themselves. The settled social structure of the 1870s allowed more inward contemplation; the mechanisms for achieving this on a grand social scale, however, had begun to change. If Gladstone's Ballot Act (1872) and Disraeli's Public Worship Act (1874) allowed for a more inwardly led life, then developments in technology like the James Staley 1871 'Penny Farthing' bicycle (and John Starley's 'Safety', 1885, with John Dunlop's pneumatic tyres, 1889), Alexander Bell's telephone (1876) and the first electric street-lighting in London (1878) allowed for a life led more outwardly.

i Decadence, Science and Morals

Mill's death coincided with the demise of Victorian non-scientific intellectual life in the 1870s and 1880s. Science and technology advanced, the humanities declined. While this was the period of Morris, Pater, Symonds, Hardy, Henry James and George Moore, it was also a period of loss. In those years many of the great mid-Victorians died: Dickens, Kingsley, Lyell, Wilberforce, Martineau, Bagehot, Gilbert Scott, G. H. Lewes and Clerk-Maxwell in the 1870s; and Eliot, Carlyle, Disraeli, Rossetti, Pusey, Trollope, Wagner, Marx, Pattison, Lear, Arnold, Browning, Tupper and Newman by 1890. Pater, Tennyson, Patmore, Huxley, Morris and Ruskin lived on into the 1890s. The critical mass of intellectuals in reviews like the *Westminster*, or the *Spectator* of R. H. Hutton (who died in 1897), no longer produced the debate on essentials which Carlyle, Mill, Ruskin and Arnold had carried through the middle years of the century. What Pater called 'The ever-increasing intellectual burden of our age'[113] in the 1870s and 1880s, caused talent to direct itself towards the intellectualised life Pattison and Mill had predicted. Critical and translation scholarship flourished with Jowett, Jebb, Verrall and Murray.

G. M. Young found the 1870s a crucial period of Victorian transition, pointing to intellectual life, trade and electoral reform:

> It is a strange world we look out on when we stand on the slope of the Victorian age and watch the great lights setting: a world which would have startled and dismayed many of those who had helped to make it . . . Darwin has gone, Carlyle and George Eliot. Browning, Newman and Tennyson are nearing their term. So long and steadily had they shone that it was not easy to think of the

world under other constellations . . . by successive stages, in 1867
and 1885, the educated class was disenfranchised, while the
advance of the arts and sciences was withdrawing them from the
observation and practice of the individual educated man.
Simultaneously the lead of the great industries was
shortening . . .[114]

The older faiths had been challenged by natural science, geology
and astronomy. But the Victorians' social faith in themselves,
incarnate in the etiquette book, was established: this is, the mid-
Victorian knew where to look to discover how to behave.

In the 1870s the real revolution was in the progress of scientific
thought. Mill's 1867 St Andrews University Inaugural lecture had
recognised the difficulty which science was to address with experimental processes of discovery:

> It is time to speak of the uses of scientific instruction; or rather
> its indispensable necessity, for it is recommended by every
> consideration which pleads for any high order of intellectual
> education at all.
>
> The most obvious part of the value of scientific instruction –
> the mere information that it gives – speaks for itself. We are born
> into a world which we have not made; a world whose phenomena
> take place according to fixed laws, of which we do not bring any
> knowledge into the world with us . . . Our whole working power
> depends on knowing the laws of the world – in other words, the
> properties of the things which we have to work with, and to work
> among, and to work upon.[115]

Mill's idea of knowledge included knowledge of the mind's
workings; this looked toward the psychologists James McCosh
and Alexander Bain (Mill's capable 1882 biographer) in mental
and moral science in the 1880s, and to their fictive equivalent in
Pater's *Marius the Epicurean* (1885). The relationship between
inward and outward, centripetal and centrifugal forces in thought,
was the pattern of the fit between the arts and sciences in 1880s
England. Decadent ideas and behaviour in England depended on
their commerce with the new culture of Lyell and Darwin, then
Spencer, Huxley and Wallace.

The movement in thought was not Darwin's original evolutionism, nor the specific brand of evolutionism which Spencer embraced, nor the evolutionary humanism of Huxley, but the growing belief that science and scientific process accounted for all facts. Through the scientific process, the human species was perfecting and refining into a better version of itself. The hortatory sermon and homiletic book had cajoled the mid-Victorians into compliance with what came to be seen as natural social behaviour; the scientists of the 1870s and 1880s wondered whether this was natural.

The 1870s brought the news that mankind was on a developmental path which began with recognising its descent from a monkey (as Wilberforce famously did). The rule of advancement was refinement. Behaviour books constantly referred to accomplished refinement. Alfred Russel Wallace's *Darwinism: an Exposition of the Theory of Natural Selection with Some of its Applications* (1889) knew the scientific version of this, and Wallace's prose had a mutually informing relation with etiquette books of the period:

> For we know that the noblest faculties of man are strengthened and perfected by struggle and effort; it is by unceasing warfare against physical evils and in the midst of difficulty and danger than energy, courage, self-reliance, and industry have become the common qualities of the northern races; it is by the battle with moral evil in all its hydra-headed forms, that the still nobler qualities of justice and mercy and humanity and self-sacrifice have been steadily increasing in the world. Beings thus trained and strengthened by their surroundings, and possessing latent faculties capable of such noble development, are surely destined for a higher and more permanent existence.[116]

This was a seminal moment in Victorian thought. The process was embedded in the prose: first struggle and warfare are overcome by industry and then by law; then 'beings thus trained and strengthened by their surroundings' applies evolutionary process to man's development; and finally a hint of perfectability surfaces: 'destined for a higher and more permanent existence'. The world of absolute morals remained absolute, and man's asymptotic progress to the final goal slowed.

The embellishment of Darwinism, which followed Darwin's

Descent of Man in 1871, made possible modes of thought and lines of questioning about the function and basis for all forms of conduct. Evolutionist anthropologists like Wallace argued that conduct resulted from the practice of man's moral nature. The natural sciences' notions of adaptive change fitted the project of the etiquette book. Science showed that processes of evolution could apply to man in society, and that the processes of civilisation, as Buckle's great 1857 work showed, were the forces of development.[117]

Dinah Craik's *Sermons out of Church* typified the insurgence of scientific process into moral discussion:

> We are still in the A B C of existence, and many a bitter tear shall
> we have to shed, many an angry fit of resistance to both lessons
> and Teacher, many a cruel craving after sunshiny play and
> rebellious laziness, will be our portion, till we are advanced
> enough to understand why we are thus taught.[118]

Science accounted not only for facts but for processes. When William James's *Varieties of Religious Experience* (1902) followed his *Psychology* by explaining the aesthetics of religion and relating mysticism to alcohol use, the scientific process had met its god. The process was inscribed on the Victorian mind when Wallace confidently introduced *Darwinism* in 1889 with the assurance: ' "descent with modification" is now universally accepted as the order of nature in the organic world'.[119]

The reaction against this was the Decadent movement. It was primarily a reaction, through conduct and ideals, against science; it was secondarily the outgrowth of literary history. This reaction against the march of science through the processes of art and conduct attempted to disrupt the natural course of things in two ways: first by embracing the artificial in all its forms; second by claiming that individual experience measured all things. These two reactions met the social environment of the 1880s and 1890s and translated into an affectation and self-centredness new to the century. When Oscar Wilde wrote of lying (in *Intentions*) as 'an art, a science, and a social pleasure',[120] he felt directly the pressures on serious truth-telling in the 1880s: art, science and society.

The excesses and anti-excesses of the 1880s and 1890s (catalogued by social commentators like Holbrook Jackson, literary critics like Graham Hough, or biographers like Richard Ellman[121]) distracted from the underlying process of events by focusing on bright particular stars. What made the nineties 'naughty' or 'yellow' or 'perfumed' had little to do with the literary movement initiated by Baudelaire's *Fleurs du Mal*, a collection of poems feeding on *ennui*, spleen and *impuissance*; nor with the antics of Lionel Johnson, Ernest Dowson, Oscar Wilde and Aubrey Beardsley gesturing to Rimbaud, Gautier (above all, *Mademoiselle de Maupin*), Rémy de Gourmont and Huysmans.

The novelist Théophile Gautier had set the scene in 1835 by championing 'Art for Art's sake', in Second Empire France, opening the possibility of behaviour free from moral constraint. Gautier felt that nothing could be beautiful unless useless; everything useful expressed the necessarily disgusting and ignoble needs of mankind. Swinburne, much influenced by Gautier, praised him lavishly in *Le Tombeau de Gautier*. Baudelaire had enthused about Gautier's *Mademoiselle de Maupin* in a log-rolling review of 1859 which Gautier repaid with his laudatory notice of *Les Fleurs du Mal* to preface the 1868 edition.

The French 1860s and 1870s produced the figure of the Decadent, cynical and bored, relying on the senses as the only experience worth having. Decadence removed temptation by yielding to it, and abandoned familiar for new pleasures in what Rimbaud in 1871 called '*un long, immense et raisonné dérèglement de tous les sens*'.

This risky fun involved quantities of hashish from French colonial North Africa; and the lethal absinthe (a dangerous cocktail of wormwood oil imported from Switzerland by Henri Pernod in 1797, banned in France in 1915; it later emerged, safer and eponymous, as Pernod). Absinthe drinking obsessed artists and writers down the century, leaving the Picasso absinthe glass (1914), Dégas' *Absinthe Drinkers* (1876) and Corelli's absinthe parody *Wormwood* (1900). Poised between the natural and the artificial, drugs suited the ethic of French Decadence, not so much a report from the front line of experience as a campaign to redraw the boundaries. English Decadence took a more social form, and a less rigorous artistic stance.

The conclusion to Pater's *Renaissance*, the 'golden book' of

Wilde, spoke for an attitude of artistic value and personal conduct. The Decadent poet Lionel Johnson found a 'keeping close to life, a sensitiveness almost in excess' in Pater's synaesthetic *Marius the Epicurean*.[122] But Pater's concerns revealed themselves more readily in other forms of writing which showed his language responding to the culture around him. In the *Guardian*, reviewing Amiel, Pater conceived intellectual process as biological, social and evolutionary:

> You might think him at first sight only an admirable specimen of a thoroughly well-educated man, full, of course, of the modern spirit; stimulated and formed by the influences of the varied intellectual world around him; and competing, in his turn, with many various types of contemporary ability.[123]

This represented Pater more faithfully than *The Renaissance*: here, 'specimen', 'stimulated', 'formed', 'influences', 'varied' and 'many various types' obtrude from the lower strata of the prose to suggest Darwinian bedrock beneath.

Pater admired Amiel, all things to and within one man, for stretching nature to the full: ' "This nature," he observes, of the many phases of character he has discovered in himself, "is, as it were, only one of the men which exist in me. It is one of my departments." '[124] He valued Amiel's ability to carry the idea of the culture of *ennui* to the ideal of negation (as Huysmans does for Durtal in *Là-Bas, En route* and *La Cathédrale*). He also valued Amiel's ability to *define* feeling in an intellectual effort to get at the precise motive of pleasure. Pater dwelt on Amiel's description of Swiss fog, elegiac and religious; the Aesthete had come a long way from Temple Bar, obscured by fog at the start of *Bleak House*. At last, by writing on Edmund Gosse, Pater summoned 'intellectual instincts'[125] and admired the exquisite limitations of the 'over-meditative, susceptible, nervous, modern age'.[126] Pater had finally found words for the malaise of the *fin de siècle* without being complicit with it.

The explanation for the Decadent movement was not literary but scientific in character, although its manifestations were literary. The movement began with writers of the 1860s and 1870s as components in a system, trying to maintain, change, and only as an occasional indulgence to contemplate; above all to experience the moment.[127] The 1880s saw that system of literary interchange begin to disappear. Intellectual interchange lacked a means of talking which was common and acceptable to all social commentators. Mill had called for this interchange; he knew the natural sciences had already achieved it. The extra-concentrated literariness and artiness of Decadent culture, and the fact that its foreign origins placed it uncomfortably in English life at the century's close, guaranteed that it would neither fit in nor belong to English culture.

But English culture did not meet Decadence on literary terms alone, for English culture had already become scientific in ethos. It looked outward for proofs, evidences, facts, principles and developments which literary culture could not provide. Swinburne and Pater introduced the inward culture of the 'sense of the splendour of our experience'[128] to stand against any and every theory. Arthur Symons's analyses of Decadence typically made the movement less accessible and more personalised; he linked personal style, outlook and behaviour with comments like the analysis of Laforgue's *blague* of death 'that is, above all things, gentlemanly'.[129]

However, even Decadence, the evolved style of aged civilisation, the ultimate in maturity, refinement and elaboration, was quasi-scientific in its logic. As Bouret said in the great essay on Baudelaire, Decadence broke down organic society into smaller individual units, books into pages, pages into sentences, and sentences into the independent word preached by Mallarmé.

The question for writers of etiquette books turned on whether advances in behaviour, new forms of refinement, were natural. Science had sanctioned a popular view of general human advancement; and yet had set in motion the process by which nothing could go undiscovered and uncatalogued. By the end of the century the Victorians were starting to look beyond the comforts of religious faith into other systems of belief supporting moral values. Some found it in society itself: 'Our civilisation,' wrote William Lecky in 1899, 'is more than anything else an industrial civilisation, and industrial habits are probably the strongest in forming the moral type to which public opinion aspires.'[130]

The history of behaviour and moral progress became the history of the changes that took place not so much in the Victorian conception of right and wrong as in the proportionate place and prominence assigned to singular virtues and vices. And science had started the Victorians questioning the naturalness of these virtues and vices. This left the moralists searching for fundamentals. Hain Friswell's *The Better Self* delivered an evolutionary answer:

> The greatest argument in respect of the inherence of our feelings
> may be found perhaps by reference to the lower creation.[131]

The idea of natural behaviour had troubled anthropological scientists like Wallace, and social-science theorists like Spencer, who maintained that natural selection worked, or should work, in society as in nature; that the socially and biologically fit emerged from the fight for survival; and that the best society was one that approximated to a state of nature ungoverned – as far as possible – by extraneous forces.

T. H. Huxley, who later argued against Spencer's version of Darwinism, and later still delivered the equivocal 1893 Romanes lecture ('Evolution and Ethics'), put the matter more acutely in 'Science and Morals':

> The safety of morality lies neither in the adoption of this or that
> philosophical speculation, or this or that theological creed, but
> in a real and living belief in that fixed order of nature which sends
> social disorganisation upon the track of immorality, as surely as it
> sends physical disease after physical trespass.[132]

Progress was not always won by suffering. The sacrifice of one generation did not always procure the advance of the next. Huxley's lecture touched critically on the 'fanatical individualism' which applied principles of nature to society.[133] He argued that the practice of that which was ethically best – goodness or virtue – entailed conduct at odds with the cosmic forces for survival. In place of self-assertion, ethical conduct argued self-restraint; instead of thrusting aside others it took them up, helped them. But if nature turned out to be non-moral, evolution could lay claim to no ethical theory.[134]

Until the 1880s the mid-Victorians had placed ethical faith in the hands of homileticists and etiquette writers who provided guidance at the point of impact between ethical theory and everyday behaviour. But the 1880s and 1890s put the whole question of natural behaviour into sway as society began to test the ethical implications of Darwinism.[135] Spencer's ground-breaking *Principles of Ethics* (1892, volumes ix and x of his *Synthetic Philosophy*) exerted an influence by raising questions concerning the establishment of rules of right conduct on a scientific basis. He typified Victorian science in its search for grand theory across a disparate range, in his case the search for a hypothesis of fundamental unity which would find reasons for the simplest inorganic actions and the most complex social processes.

Spencer shifted his thought from evolutionary investigation in 'The Theory of Population' (1852) to the ten-volume social and philosophical *System of Synthetic Philosophy* (1860–96). While the evolutionist might fail to infer history from a single animal, a Victorian social thinker had all manner of subjects to hand; so the latter part of the century saw a turning backward into James Murray's search for linguistic origins through his 1879 *Dictionary* editorship,[136] Leslie Stephen's search for personal origins through the *Dictionary for National Biography*, which he initiated in 1885, or even Cesare Lombroso's *L'uomo delinquente* (*Criminal Man*, 1876), which led to the establishment of criteria for preventive criminology based on anthropological data. Lombroso kept his research in harmony with late nineteenth-century notions of propriety, for according to his associate, Enrico Ferri, criminals did not blush.[137]

Another interdisciplinary venture, the philology lectures of the linguist and philosopher Friedrich Max Müller throughout the 1860s, showed that no student of the science of language could be anything but an evolutionist. Max Müller himself was a study in adaptive change: he left his native Dessau for Leipzig in 1841 when he was eighteen, gained his doctorate in Sanskrit in 1843, moved to Paris in 1845, London in 1846 and Oxford in 1847. In 1860 Max Müller was beaten to the chair of Sanskrit by Monier Monier-Williams. He responded to the disappointment by throwing himself into writing books on philology and philosophy, as well as devoting himself to the discovery and preservation of

Sanskrit manuscripts in India. Throughout his writing in general, and his 1887 *Science of Thought* in particular, Max Müller found evolution at work around him.

If Max Müller brought Darwin's ideas to bear on language, other philologists and scientists were quick to test the new theories. August Schleicher's *Darwinism Tested by the Science of Language* (1869) was typical:

> . . . the development of new forms from preceding forms can be much more easily traced, and this on even a larger scale, in the province of words, than in that of plants and animals.[138]

This attitude affected the way the Victorians thought about themselves as a behavioural species.

George Romanes, a Scot at Cambridge with an eye on holy orders, began to apply the ideas of his friend Darwin to matters closer at hand:

> At all events I think it may be safely promised, that when we come to consider the case of savages, and through them the case of prehistoric man, we shall find that, in the great interval which lies between such grades of mental evolution and our own, we are brought far on the way towards bridging the psychological distance which separates the gorilla from the gentleman.[139]

However, for progress to continue the gentleman and gentlewoman needed to distinguish themselves from their peers; the behavioural version of this separation found Decadents developing an over-refinement of the senses which also had a social outlook. Arthur Symons concluded *Studies in Prose and Verse* with the thought that society was the enemy of man, and that to spend a day without feeling some fine emotion was to waste time.

Out of the primordial swamp came ideas of individualism as a refined adaptation to modern life, of indulgence as a means to greater individuality (no one else could feel what one was feeling), and the refusal to admit of any other moral codes. While the Decadent movement used self-conscious refinement to forge its sense of individuality, Victorian science scoured the physical and psychical ground for traces of man's mental development.

Gradually science staked its claims on the available outbacks of thought. George Romanes:

> In previous chapters I have more than once remarked that the science of historical psychology is destitute of fossils: unlike pre-historic structures, pre-historic ideas leave behind them no trace of their existence. But now a partial exception must be taken to this general statement. For the new science of Comparative Philology has revealed the important fact that, if on the one hand speech gives *ex*pression to ideas, on the other hand it receives *im*pression from them, and that the impressions thus stamped are surprisingly consistent. The consequence is that in philology we possess the same kind of unconscious record of the growth and decay of ideas, as is furnished by paleontology of the growth and decay of species.[140]

This search for origins slowly passed from the Victorian novel, with its acute sense of personal and communal history, through Victorian science to the practice of psychoanalysis, which once more called up notions of natural and normal behaviour. By 1930, in *Civilization and its Discontents*, Freud [141] could write:

> ... it is impossible to overlook the extent to which civilization is built upon a renunciation of instinct, how much it presupposes precisely the non-satisfaction (by suppression, repression or some other means?) of powerful instincts. This 'cultural frustration' dominates the large field of social relations between human beings.[142]

The homiletic novel, the hortatory poem, the sermon and the practical etiquette book mediated between the individual and society, were part of that cultural frustration. The etiquette book tasked the Victorians to behave according to preordained values in a stable moral environment; it helped them to communicate with and judge others, and to advance and position themselves in society.

Mill had commented presciently in 1869, 'So true it is that unnatural generally means only uncustomary, and that everything which is usual appears natural. But how entirely, even in this case, the feeling is dependent on custom, appears by ample experience.'[143] To break social codes as Wilde and Beardsley did was to behave against nature.

Darwin had taught that science, especially historical science, should identify processes that yielded observed results. His brilliance was to regard everything as potential evidence, to incorporate inconsistencies without distorting them, and to suggest the principle that natural selection was the main but not the sole means of modification in species, not excepting the case of man.

The flat doubters remained unconvinced. One of Darwin's staunchest opponents was the Bishop of Oxford, Samuel Wilberforce. The most famous debate in Victorian England took place in Oxford under the aegis of the British Association on 30 June 1860, when Wilberforce faced William Hooker and Thomas Huxley to discuss evolutionism before an audience of nearly a thousand. Most accounts give the Hooker and Huxley version;[144] after the event, Wilberforce's *Essays* ironically reprinted the *Quarterly Review* piece from July 1860 on Darwin's *Origin*:

Indeed, not only do all the laws for the study of nature vanish
when the great principle of order prevailing and regulating all
her processes is given up, but all that imparts the deepest interest
in the investigation of her wonders will have departed too. Under
such influences a man soon goes back to the marvelling stare of
childhood at the centaurs and hippogriffs of fancy, or if his is of a
philosophic turn, he comes like Oken to write a scheme of creation
under 'a sort of inspiration'; but it is the frenzied inspiration of
the inhaler of mephitic gas. The whole world of nature is laid for
such a man under a fantastic law of glamour, and he becomes
capable of believing anything: to him it is just as probable that Dr
Livingstone will find the next tribe of negroes with their heads
growing under their arms as fixed on the summit of the cervical
vertibrae; and he is able, with a continually growing neglect of all
the facts around him, with equal confidence and equal delusion,
to look back to any past and to look on to any future.[145]

Wilberforce put Darwin in the same mental territory as the Decadent or Aesthete, substituting absinthe for mephitic gas. His writing nonetheless shows traces of scientific influence, particularly in the opening. But his criticism of Darwin reveals incidental truths by distorting the theory; and distorting it in exactly the way that Huysmans shapes Des Esseintes' imaginings in the garden or the brothel.

Despite the wailings of Wilberforce and the alternative Decadent sideshow, scientific process continued to examine the basis of instinct and self-consciousness in apprehensible terms. Romanes's 'The Darwinian Theory of Instinct' suggested that instincts were not fixed, but were plastic: the plasticity rendered them capable of improvement or alteration subject to rational control 'according as intelligent observation requires'.[146] That intelligent observation worked in the way that Dorian Gray or Des Esseintes did, by watching the processes of behaviour in their own fictional selves.

The diseased self-consciousness of the Decadent was art's answer to the beautiful, implacable searching of science. This from 'Mind in Men and Animals':

> We have seen, then, that self-consciousness consists in paying the same kind of attention to inward psychical processes that is habitually paid to outward physical processes; that in the mind of animals and infants there is a world of images standing as signs of outward objects; that at this stage of mental evolution we have not merely simple concepts, but also the recognition of an ejective no less than of an objective world; and that here we also have the recognition of personality, as far as this is dependent upon 'outward self-consciousness', or the consciousness of self as a feeling and active agent, apart from self as an object of thought.[147]

Self-consciousness resulted from inward process rather than from the cult of the self which art had made it.

Personality for the mid-Victorians functioned on the public stage, lit by moral certainties and prompted by etiquette books. As the scientific 1870s began to explore the mind's workings, and paid less regard to the manners and customs of good society, the relation of the public acting to the private thinking self began to alter. Alexander Bain, for example, moved from outward expression to inward contemplation in *Darwin on Expression* (1873). Constructing a theory on the relation of the outer senses to the inner intellect, he writes in the Postscript to 'The Senses and the Intellect':

I have discussed at length[148] . . . the process of acting out an idea, or the tendency of ideas, in so far as allowed, to become full realities; as when the idea of some crime that has been perpetrated operates upon weak minds to make them repeat it. This principle embraces the influence of ideas upon mesmerized patients; it also embraces the production of a physical accompaniment of a sensation, by means of the ideas strongly suggested to the mind; as salivation at the sight of food.[149]

Using language of weak-mindedness, influence, mesmerism and suggestion, Decadence tried the frontiers of the sayable and sentient.

As early as 1863, Anne Penny, writing on 'The Decline of Sentiment', noted the excess of writing and speaking about feeling then prevalent in England. For her this was the surest evidence of its decay: 'for feelings habitual to us are seldom consciously dwelt upon; and we all know that if people say very much about their affection being strong, we involuntarily suspect that it is weak'.[150] Alexander Bain, one of Penny's touchstones (she elsewhere cites approvingly his *Study of Character*), brought the inner and outer into normative relation by counselling an outward regard, rather than the self-consuming solipsism of some of the quick, bright things of the 1890s; he thought that the best condition of bodily and mental vigour resulted from outward regard.

Throughout the 1870s and 1880s the language of science began to account particularly for aspects of Victorian experience which had been off limits before. Development met moral advocacy in the work of the psychologist James McCosh. *The Emotions*:

The rising generation, trained in homes where religion and morals have been carefully enforced, are apt to complain of the restrictions which have been laid upon them, and to imagine and argue that, under a more liberal system, the good would have been more attractive to them. But they may find as they advance in life that a greater liberty ends in licentiousness in the generation that follow; and the difficulty then is to get back the high standard which has been lost.

In such circumstances wisdom consists in training the young in
law rigid as the bones of our frame, but with love as its life.[151]

The language and its concerns typify the 1870s and 1880s in their
recognition of the interdependent ideals of making advances and
keeping standards; McCosh linked mental process to social process
in suggesting standards for the young.

In 1894, Wilde wrote his own etiquette book. *Phrases and
Philosophies for the Use of the Young*, originally published in the
Chameleon,[152] made a stand against accepted behaviour, logic and
scientific method in its wilful absurdities. Wilde's brilliance was
to write an etiquette book which was also a profound personal
statement. The same thinking underpinned his defence on 3 April
1895 in face of Edward Carson's leaden advocacy:

> Listen, sir. Here is one of the 'Phrases and Philosophies for the
> Use of the Young' which you contributed [to the *Chameleon*]:
> 'Wickedness is a myth invented by good people to account for the
> curious attractiveness of others.' You think that true? – I rarely
> think that anything I write is true.
> Did you say 'rarely'? – I said 'rarely'. I might have said 'never'
> – not true in the actual sense of the word.[153]

Wilde prospered best in formal atmospheres where rules could
be flouted; the courtroom drama was ideal. The same anti-eti-
quette prefaces *Dorian Gray*. Wilde succeeded in resisting both
the scientific and the moral culture of the age. He was remembered
for his publicly lived private life, or for his calculated solipsisms;
but whether at Magdalen College, Oxford, or in Reading Gaol,
he operated in symbolic relation to Victorian art and culture. In
the sad melodrama of privacy and privation, and in the confusion
of his life, lay his resistance to the investigation and categorisation
with which the scientific method called the world to account.

Decadence was the emotional version of self-surgery, with the
scalpel in one's own hand; J. B. Mayer noted in 1871 that 'decadence' 'came into fashion to *denote* decline, and *connote* a scientific
and enlightened view of that decline on the part of the user'.[154] The
unofficial biographer of the Decadent movement, Arthur Symons,

found Decadent behaviour over-natural, over-refined, an ex-
crescence of nature at the same time continuous with it:

> For its very disease of form, this literature is certainly typical of a
> civilization grown over-luxurious, over-inquiring, too languid for
> relief of action, too uncertain for any emphasis in opinion or in
> conduct. It reflects all the moods, all the manners, of a
> sophisticated society; its very artificiality is a way of being true to
> nature: simplicity, sanity, proportion – the classic qualities – how
> much do we possess them in our life, our surroundings, that we
> should find them in our literature – so evidently the literature of
> a decadence?[155]

Amidst the jungle of orchids, violets and hothouse flowers
which bloomed as the ultimate connivance of man with nature
against itself, writers of science took an integrated view of what
nature meant. George Romanes read Shakespeare:

> 'I know a bank whereon the wild thyme grows,'
>   And there I lay me down to drink anew
> The lyric dream of Midsummer. The woes
>   Of Lear followed next; and last I drew
> Upon the 'sugared sonnets', till methought
>   Their sweetness with a lotus influence
> Had bathed my being in a joy that sought
>   To worship him who held its every sense.
> Then on the page a creature from the grass
>   Leaped forth – a living gem of Italy.
> 'Behold,' it seemed to say, 'how I surpass
>   In wonder all the world of Poetry.'
>   'Twas true. Creative strength to God belongs,
>   And weak its image in our greatest songs.[156]

The literary version of this was already in process with Coventry
Patmore's 'To The Body' from 1877:

> Creation and Creator's crowning good;
> Wall of infinitude;
> Foundation of the sky,
> In Heaven forecast

And longed for from eternity,
Though laid the last;
Reverberating dome,
Of music cunningly built home
Against the void and indolent disgrace
Of unresponsive space;
Little, sequestered pleasure-house
For God and for His Spouse;
Elaborately, yea, past conceiving, fair,
Since, from the graced decorum of the hair,
Even to the tingling, sweet
Soles of the simple, earth-confiding feet,
And from the inmost heart
Outwards unto the thin
Silk curtains of the skin,
Every least part
Astonished hears
And sweet replies to some like region of the spheres . . .

While Romanes's attention moved outwards from detail, Patmore's gathered inwards from generalisation.

Literature taught that personality issued from within; science had found an undiscovered country without. The confident, outward-looking society of the mid-century began to shift in sensibility: the beautiful logic of scientific enquiry and the stupid solipsism of Decadent art had shaped a new consensus not only about the relative value of the two cultures, but about the status of personal behaviour within society.

1886 produced one such moment of dislocation: a scandal and an etiquette book. Lady Colin Campbell, friend of Wilde and model for Whistler's *A Harmony in White and Ivory*, and described by a news reporter as a woman with a diseased passion for every man she met, having 'the unbridled lust of a Messalina and the indelicate readiness of a common harlot',[157] fought her husband in the Campbell vs. Campbell divorce case. This filled the London papers in November and December 1886; it brought sex, voyeurism, venereal disease and the aristocracy into close public proximity. The case also impinged outrageousness on the national, or, rather, the metropolitan psyche. The Campbell divorce case later appeared, heated up, in Campbell's *Darrell Blake: a Study* (1889), which drew on her marriage and on her experience as a prodigiously productive journalist (the *Saturday Review*), art editor (the *World*) and editor-columnist (the *Realm*). That experience also included the writing of an etiquette book, *Etiquette of Good Society* (1886), which sold nearly 100,000 copies. Campbell wrote with no sense of irony, and the book is remarkable for its continuity with other books of the genre, its deft advice on introductions and handshakings, on conversation and courtship. If ever the publication of a book separated the person from the issue, then this was it.

ii The End of Manners

On 30 March 1871, John Morley wrote to Charles Darwin, objecting to *The Descent of Man*:

> The selection by a community, through its current opinion, laws, institutions, traditional usages and so forth, of certain qualities, and ideals of character, for admiration . . . The community is the organism, the unit . . . The transmission is not physical, from father to son, but 'in the air' from generation to generation. That there are physical conditions cannot be doubted. But within the society itself, the characteristic habits of thought, rules of conduct, &c. are acquired through the non-physical medium of opinion, positive law &c.[158]

Disraeli had known this, intuitively, in *Tancred* (1847), where he saw a people as a species, a civilised community as a nation, and a nation gradually created by a variety of influences. This was in tune with T. H. Huxley, who thought species in nature were determined by their relations to the conditions which surrounded them, their mutual harmonies and discordances of structure, the bonds of union with their present and past history.

Science gave the Victorians the long view. Mid-Victorian culture combined political democracy with tempered nationalism and individual economic enterprise; this combination was balanced by a strict moral code and by conventional, churchgoing Christianity.[159] G. M. Young saw the continuities within the period:

. . . a tract of time where men and manners, science and philosophy, the fabric of social life and its directing ideas, changed more swiftly perhaps, and more profoundly, than they have ever changed in an age not sundered by a political or a religious upheaval.[160]

The pattern of formal and informal legislation throughout the period imposed on mid-Victorian England a way of thinking and behaving. Social and legal consensus worked through Acts governing Open Spaces and Agriculture (1833); Criminal Law and Inebriety (1834); Trade Unions (1838); Police (1839); Towns (1840); Factories (1841); Cities (Metropolitan, 1844); Railway Navvies (1846); Universities (1851); Charities (1853); Education (1861); Schools (1864); Housing (1884); and Local Government (1888).

The price for this relative administrative order and organisation was individuality. Mill thought England's greatness had become collective, individually small, and capable of nothing great but by the habit of combining. The circumstances surrounding different classes and individuals were daily becoming more assimilated:

Comparatively speaking, they now read the same things, listen to the same things, see the same things, go to the same places, have their hopes and fears directed to the same objects, have the same rights and liberties, and the same means of asserting them.[161]

Mill everywhere maintained that the 'despotism of custom' was the standing hindrance to advancement, a deterrent from aiming at anything better than customary.

Etiquette books continued to amass sales in the 1880s and 1890s, but by then the writer who opted for the etiquette genre was buying into a tired, if not falling, market. The etiquette book introduced the mid-Victorians to themselves at their ideal best, advising and encouraging them in moral conduct, finance, furnishing, literary consumption or personal hygiene. These books provided self-help and self-therapy for a society which had changed itself beyond recognition in the middle years of the century. As the century aged, the etiquette book felt the pressures which had begun to mould late-Victorian consciousness: social dissent in the form of Decadence, and intellectual change in the form of the revolution brought about by scientific thinking.

The most able of the century's better known writers had touched on manners: Bagehot in the essays, Trollope in the novels, Dickens in both, Thackeray in *Snobs*, George Eliot in her advice on dealing with servants,[162] and Mill above all in *On Liberty*. The etiquette book and its related forms, written by Smiles, Tupper, Reid, Mahaffy or Friswell, kept close contact with forms of behaviour either by helping to create them in the first place, as with Smiles and Tupper, or by reacting to them as a fact of social life, in the case of Reid or Mahaffy. As commentaries on Victorian life, these books covered the widest range of concerns consistent with the position of the mid-Victorian middle classes: how to eat, love, dress, sleep, die; what to talk about, what not to talk about. In effect, the history of the etiquette book, of the relations between various types of behaviour, is the history of a civilising process.

The civilising process seen through the etiquette book opens long perspectives on local historical problems: individual moral growth and its practical application, class mobility and class imitation, the formation of character as social value, and the political processes of social cohesion around shared values. The moral world of the advice book put abstract belief in touch with practical behaviour for thousands of people for the first time. The counsel of Adams or Ellis or Tupper opened a view of the ideal which made the ideal worth striving for. Such writers provided a universe policed with simple rules of work and reward which made social virtues of moral necessities. In them, the Victorians had found a way of talking about what was happening to their society, and had fashioned a barometer to measure the social and ethical changes which actually altered the way they behaved.

Over the century the message of the homiletic book was that life could be better here, now, if only one tried. The means at hand were not money or status or talent, but simple practical behaviour. The mid-Victorians evolved behaving well into a process of life, a way of living which carried them down the road to improvement by offering fixity in a shifting world. The behaviour book provided, above all, a system for life.

Walter Bagehot typified the period, in G. M. Young's words, 'always experiencing, and always working its observation into pattern, into system, but – and here we touch on his central excellence or virtue – into a system open towards the future'.[163] Searching for answers at the close of the *System of Logic*, John Stuart Mill paused with the notion that the Art of Life concerning Right, Expedient and Beautiful human conduct subordinated all other arts, since its principles were 'those which must determine whether the special aim of any particular art is worthy and desirable, and what is its place in the scale of desirable things'. He continued to search for an ultimate standard:

> Every art is thus a joint result of nature disclosed by science, and of the general principles of what has been called Teleology, or the Doctrine of Ends.[164]

Mill concluded that every art consists in truths of Science arranged in an order suitable for some practical use, according to the standard of what he calls the principle of practical Reason. His thinking here, as elsewhere, was elegant and ordered when dealing with practical problems. Despite a footnote offering 'the little volume entitled *Utilitarianism* as further elucidation', he rounded off with an uncharacteristic unwillingness to qualify:

> Without attempting in this place to justify my opinion, or even to define the kind of justification which it admits of, I merely declare my conviction, that the general principle to which all rules of practice ought to conform, and the test by which they should be tried, is that of conduciveness to the happiness of mankind, or rather, of all sentient beings: in other words, that the promotion of happiness is the ultimate principle of Teleology.[165]

What Mill was looking for, the principle which would govern the practical reason, beliefs and values which constitute the Art of Life, came close to Bagehot's notion of pattern and system. Both thinkers lived in the processes they created, and both searched for new ways of explaining the world that might enhance an individual life. Mill knew that in the conduct of human beings towards one another general rules should be observed, so that people could know what to expect. He also knew that, in each person's own concerns, individual spontaneity was entitled to free exercise. This was fundamental, and ran through the nineteenth century to prove Mill's instincts almost true. He wrote this in *On Liberty* in 1859:

> It is desirable, in short, that in things which do not primarily concern others, individuality should assert itself. Where, not the person's own character, but the traditions or customs of other people are the rule of conduct, there is wanting one of the principal ingredients of human happiness, and quite the chief ingredient of individual and social progress.[166]

Notes

Introduction

1 John Stuart Mill, *The Subjection of Women* (London 1929 [1869]), 283.
2 Ibid.
3 *The Nineteenth-Century Constitution*, ed. H. J. Hanham (London 1969), 37.
4 Ibid., 39.
5 Mill, op. cit., 283.
6 Walter Bagehot, *The English Constitution*, 2nd edn (London 1872), Introduction.
7 T. H. S. Escott, *England: her People, Polity and Pursuits* (London 1885 [1879]), 22ff.
8 Ibid.
9 Henry James, 'The Question of Our Speech' (New York 1905), 10.
10 Nancy Armstrong, 'The Rise of the Domestic Woman', in *The Ideology of Conduct*, ed. Nancy Armstrong and Leonard Tenninghouse (London 1987), 97.
11 Henry Maine, *The Reign of Queen Victoria*, ed. H. Ward (London 1887), vol. i, 170.
12 In Alan Bullock and Maurice Shock, *The Liberal Tradition from Fox to Keynes* (London 1956), 147.
13 See John Burrow, *Whigs and Liberals* (Oxford 1988), 35.
14 Ibid.
15 Arthur Hugh Clough, *Amours de Voyages*.
16 Behind Mill's *Civilization* lie Rousseau's *Discourses* and Adam Ferguson's *History of Civil Society*.
17 Boyd Hilton, *The Age of Atonement* (Oxford 1988), 5.
18 Dates of these Acts: 1834, 1834, 1840, 1842, 1848.
19 J. F. C. Harrison, *Early Victorian Britain* (London 1988 [1971]), 134.
20 See Walter Houghton's *The Victorian Frame of Mind* (New Haven, Conn., 1957), 1n. Houghton finds Arnold, Brown, Carlyle, Disraeli, Mallock, Martineau, Mill, Morley, Morris, Spencer, Symonds, Tennyson, 'and no doubt many others'.
21 E. Bulwer-Lytton, *England and the English* (London 1833), 281.
22 Thomas Carlyle, 'Signs of the Times' (London 1971 [1829]), 64.

Notes

23 Mill, *System of Logic* 1843 [London 8th edn 1872]), Book VI, Ch. 12, 616.

Chapter 1

1 Mill, *On Liberty* (London 1859), 73.
2 William Makepeace Thackeray, *The Book of Snobs* (London 1848 [1989]), 7.
3 John Locke, 'Some Thoughts Concerning Education', *Works* (London 1812), ix, 50.
4 For a critique of Elias, see Anna Bryson, *From Courtesy to Civility: Concepts of Civility in England, 1560–1685* (D. Phil. Thesis, Bodleian Library, Oxford).
5 See ibid. See also F. J. Furnivall's *Meals and Manners in Olden Time* (London 1868, 1894) for a selection of fifteenth-, sixteenth- and seventeenth-century courtesy books.
6 John E. Mason, *Gentlefolk in the Making* (Philadelphia, 1935), 56–7.
7 Specific advice on education appeared in Roger Ascham's *Schoolmaster* (1570); on travel in John Stradling's version of Justus Lipsius's *A Direction for Travailers* (1592); on talk in Thomas Wilson's *Institutio Oratorica* (1553); on swearing in Thomas Becon's *Invectyve Agenst Swearing* (1543); on letter-writing in Gabriel Harvey's *Letter-Book* (1573–80) and Geoffrey Fenton's *Golden Epistles* (1575); and on warfare in the 1590 *The Booke of Honor and Armes*, itself an unacknowledged translation of *Vincentio Saviolo His Practice* (1565).
8 Richard Alstree, *The Gentleman's Calling* (London 1660), 48.
9 Thomas Wright, *The Passions of the Minde* (1601), 54.
10 Jean Gailhard, *The Compleat Gentleman* (1678), Book II, 66.
11 Cited in a review of Stuart Hampshire's *Innocence and Experience* (London 1990) by Andrew St George in the *Independent*, 22 January 1990.
12 In *Hartleian Miscellany*, ed. Park, ix, 86.
13 William Gouge, *Of Domestical Duties* (1622), 539.
14 Abbé Bellegarde, *Reflexions Upon Ridicule* and *Reflexions Upon the Politeness of Manners*, trans. 1706–7.
15 Mason, op. cit., 289.
16 Hilton, *The Age of Atonement*, 204.
17 Numbers: 166, 173, 278.
18 In R. S. Fitton and A. P. Wadsworth, *The Strutts and the Arkwrights 1758–1830* (Manchester 1958), 145.
19 Hannah More, *Christian Morals* (London 1813), vol. i, 69.
20 See S. Collini, 'The Idea of "Character" in Victorian Political Thought', *Transactions of the Royal Historical Society*, 5 (1985), 39.
21 Thomas Tupper, (London, 1853): 'Come, I will show thee an afflic-

tion, unnumbered among this world's sorrows, / Yet real and weari-
some and constant, embittering the cup of life.' ('Of Speaking',
p. 154).

22 Derek Hudson, *Martin Tupper, his Rise and Fall* (London 1949),
59–61.
23 Thomas Tusser (1524?–80); see *Hundreth good pointes of husbandrie*
(1557) on gardening, farming and conduct in general.
24 Tupper, 1–2.
25 Tupper, *Proverbial Philosophy* (London 1882), 'Of the Smaller
Morals', 283.
26 Hudson, op. cit., 6.
27 Ibid., 19.
28 Tupper, *Proverbial Philosophy*, vi.
29 Ibid., 'Of Anticipation', 2.
30 *Short Essays from the Saturday Review: Studies in Conduct* (London
1867), 27.
31 Oliver Wendell Holmes, *Autocrat of the Breakfast Table* (1891; 1st
edn, Boston 1858), 271: 'Whether I dipped them from the ocean of
Tupperian wisdom . . . I cannot say.'
32 Tupper, *Proverbial Philosophy*, 'Of Society', 223–4.
33 Ibid., 226.
34 Tennyson, *In Memoriam*, XCV, lines 42–3.
35 Tupper, *Proverbial Philosophy*, 'Of Circumstance', 249.
36 Ibid.
37 Ibid., 'Of Scripture and Science', 258.
38 Ibid., 260–1.
39 Ibid., 'Of Success', 279.
40 Ibid., 280.
41 W. H. D. Adams, *The Secret of Success: or How to get on in the
world* (London 1879), 18.
42 Tupper, *Proverbial Philosophy*, 281.
43 In Hudson, op. cit., 178.
44 In ibid., 179.
45 In ibid., 180–2.
46 *Daily News*, 24 January 1870.
47 Samuel Smiles, *Self-help* (London 1894 [1859]), Introduction to the
1859 edn, ix.
48 *Short Essays from the Saturday Review*, 31.
49 Ibid., 12.
50 Ibid., 18.
51 Published in 1859, 1861–3, 1871, 1875, 1880, respectively.
52 Samuel Smiles, *Duty: with Illustrations of Courage, Patience and
Endurance* (London 1880), Preface, i.
53 T. Binney: *Is It Possible to Make the Best of Both Worlds? A Book
for Young Men* (2nd edn, London 1853), 30–41.
54 *Saturday Review*, 69–70.

55 Smiles, *Self-help*, Introduction to the 1859 edn, ix.
56 Ibid., 337 (*Macbeth* II. ii. 54).
57 Ibid.
58 Ibid., 388.
59 Ibid.; 1866 Preface, iv.
60 Mill, *Diary*, 13 January 1854.
61 Arnold-Clough *Letters*, 134.
62 Adams, *Plain Living and High Thinking or Practical Self-culture: Moral, Mental and Physical* (London 1880), 57.
63 Ibid., 183.
64 Ibid., 65.
65 Ibid., 183.
66 Ibid., 249.
67 Ibid., 290.
68 Ibid.
69 By Professors Tait and Balfour Stewart.
70 Adams, *Plain Living*, 293.
71 Adams, *The Boy Makes the Man: Anecdotes and Examples for the Use of Youth* (London 1867), 206.
72 Adams, *Plain Living*, xvii.
73 See: Blake, R. *Disraeli* (London 1966), 95, 97.
74 Hughenden Papers, Bodleian Library, A/XI/A/8.
75 Ibid.
76 *Saturday Review*, 21.
77 George Eliot, *Adam Bede*, Ch. 52.
78 Charles Bray, 'The Reign of Law' in Mind as in Matter, and its Bearing upon Christian dogma and Moral Responsibility (1874), vol. ii, 23.
79 William Edward Lecky, *The Map of Life* (London 1899).
80 Roosevelt, *The Strenuous Life* (London 1902), 91. Roosevelt's views, gathered in 1902, apply the dicta of self-help, duty and self-reliance to national and international politics. So the Colorado springs address (2 August 1901), 'Manhood and Statehood', equates American success with the American character; while foreign policy in the Philippines turns on the need to encourage nations to be self-sufficient.
81 Lecky, op. cit., 3.
82 Ibid., 286, 'No more probable explanation has yet been given of the manner in which human nature has been built up, and of the various instincts and tastes with which we are born, than the doctrine that habits and modes of thought and feeling indulged in and produced by circumstances in former generations have gradually become innate in the race, and exhibit themselves spontaneously and instinctively and quite independently of the circumstances that originally produced them. According to this theory the same process is continually going on'.

83 Ibid., 287.
84 Thackeray, *The Book of Snobs* 270.
85 Ibid.
86 Hippolyte Taine, *Notes on England* (London 1874), 175–6. This translation is more contemporary than the more readily available translation by Edward Hyams (London 1957).
87 Ibid., 173.
88 Ibid.
89 Ibid.
90 *OED* use 3.
91 *OED* use 4.
92 1862, vol. v, 330.
93 G. P. Marsh, *Lectures on the English Language* (London 1862), 175, 6.
94 J. A. Hessey, *Moral Difficulties of the Bible (2nd series)* (London 1873), 101.
95 *Cornhill*, 1862, vol. v, 330.
96 W. R. Brown, 'The English Gentleman', *National Review*, April 1886, 261.
97 Montaigne, after all, thought falsehood one of our ordinary vices (treachery, disloyalty, cruelty and tyranny). See *Of the Canibales* and Judith Shklar's *Ordinary Vices* (Harvard 1984).
98 John Ruskin, *Modern Painters* (London 1888), vol. v, 266–7.
99 Ibid., 267.
100 J. H. Newman, *Idea of a University* (London 1852 [1881]), 209.
101 Ibid.
102 Charles Kingsley, *Sermons for the Times* (London 1855), 315.
103 1881 edn; vol. i, 13.
104 *Quite a Gentleman* (1878), 16.
105 *Great Expectations*, Ch. 22, 104.
106 Mrs Craik, *John Halifax, Gentleman* (London 1878), 167.
107 Lieber, *Character of the Gentleman* (London 1847), 14.
108 *The English Gentleman* (London 1849) [anon.], 6.
109 Mill, *On Liberty*, 125.
110 Tupper, *About in the World* (London 1864); Smiles, *A Man's Thoughts* (London 1872); Adams, *The Better Self* (London 1875); Hain Friswell, *The Gentle Life* (the 1864 1st series had reached its 21st edn by 1875, the 1866 2nd series its 6th).
111 Peter Bayne, *The Christian Life* (London 1859); *Lessons from my Masters* (London 1879).

Chapter 2

1 Roger Boswell, *The Art of Conversation* (London, 1867), 12.
2 Carlyle, *Sartor Resartus* (Boston, Mass., 1836).

3 Taine, *Notes on England*, 92–3.

4 Ibid., 95.

5 *Modern Etiquette in Private and Public* (London 1871) [anon.], 1.

6 See Richard Sennet, *The Fall of Public Man* (London 1986), 125–255.

7 Charles Darwin, *The Expression of the Emotions*, 375.

8 *Manners and Rules of Good Society* (32nd edn, London 1910), ix.

9 *OED* use 4, figurative.

10 The *OED* quotes Carlyle, *Critical Miscellany*, 193.

11 *OED* use 7 (a).

12 *OED* use 3. See also Rosaline Mason in *Poets, Patriots, and Lovers*, writing naturally enough in 1933 about an event in 1884: 'At a conversazione held in the Museum of Science and Art [Edinburgh University] it became apparent that Browning was drawing the crowd as a magnet draws steel shavings' (p. 33).

13 *OED* use 4.

14 Nathaniel Hawthorne, *The English Notebooks* (1879 edn), vol. ii, 24.

15 Journal of Benjamin Moran, 6 February 1873 (Library of Congress, Washington, DC).

16 F. Arnold *Three-cornered Essays* (London 1886) 276.

17 See also *Talking & Debating . . . A Handbook of Conversation and Debate* (London 1856), 4–5 ff., for a professional sense of the word 'conversationalist'.

18 G. S. Bowes, *Conversation: Why Don't We Do More Good By It?* (London 1886), 124–5.

19 *Memories of Victorian London* (London 1912), 64.

20 *Memoir of the Rev. Sydney Smith*, by his daughter, Lady Holland (London 1869), 234.

21 Stuart J. Reid, *The Life and Times of Sydney Smith* (London 1896, 4th edn).

22 Lady Holland, op. cit., 236–7.

23 Sydney Smith was born on 3 June 1771; he died on 22 February 1845. Reid, op. cit., 1, 364.

24 G. W. E. Russell, *Collections and Recollections* (London 1898), 129.

25 De Tocqueville, *Journeys to England and Ireland*, ed. J. R. Meyer (London 1958), 108.

26 G. M. Young, ed., *Early Victorian England*, vol. i, 201.

27 *The Times*, 22 April 1859.

28 J. P. Mahaffy, *Principles of the Art of Conversation* (London 1887), 99.

29 Boswell, op. cit., 23.

30 Ibid., v-vi.

31 Ibid., 9.

32 Ibid., 16.

33 Ibid., 17–18.

34 Ibid., 10.

35 Ibid., 13.
36 *Talking & Debating*, 4.
37 In *Logic and Conversation* Paul Grice outlines the principle which he believes operates in conversation: 'We might then formulate a rough general principle which participants will be expected (ceteris paribus) to observe, namely: Make your conversational contribution such as is required, at the stage at which it occurs, by the accepted purpose or direction of the talk exchange in which you are engaged. One might label this the COOPERATIVE PRINCIPLE' (p. 45). He distinguishes four constituent categories which will, he claims, 'in general, yield results in accordance with the Cooperative Principle'. He calls these categories Quantity, Quality, Relation and Manner.
38 Edwin Drew, *The Public Speaker's Vade Mecum. Elocution: its Principles Reduced to Practice*(London 1857), 7. See also Mahaffy, op. cit.: 'All people are supposed to study literature, and a good knowledge of either familiar or fashionable books can hardly fail to tell in any gathering of cultivated men and women' (p. 29).
39 Boswell, op. cit., 24.
40 *Talking & Debating*, 8.
41 Boswell, op. cit., 31.
42 Ibid., 33.
43 Ibid., 36–7.
44 Ibid., 37, 42, 45, 46.
45 *Talk and Talkers*, (London 1859), 7.
46 *How to Shine*, (London 1867), 78.
47 Ibid., 82.
48 *Talking & Debating*, 4.
49 Ibid., 5.
50 Ibid., 7.
51 Charles L. Graves, *Mr Punch's History of Modern England* (London 1921), 211–12.
52 Boswell, op. cit., 49.
53 Beatrice Knollys, *The Gentle Art of Good Talking* (London 1899), 33.
54 *Talk and Talkers*, 10–11.
55 Mahaffy, op. cit., 1.
56 Ibid., 5.
57 Ibid., 173–4.
58 *Modern Etiquette* (London 1859) [anon.], 24.
59 Mahaffy, op. cit., 175.
60 Ibid., 54.
61 Lady Greville, *The Gentlewoman in Society* (London 1892), 86.
62 Mahaffy, op. cit., 2.
63 Ibid., 44.
64 Ibid., 30.
65 Ibid., 82–3.

66 Boswell, op. cit., 40.
67 Mahaffy op. cit., 40–1.
68 Hain Friswell, *The Gentle Life*, 154.
69 Graves, op. cit., vol. ii, 198.
70 Mahaffy, op. cit., 19.
71 John Honey, *Does Accent Matter?* (Faber 1989), 29.
72 Mahaffy, op. cit., 16–17.
73 Ibid., 21–2.
74 G. M. Young, *Portrait of an Age* (Oxford 1936), 2.
75 *Talking & Debating*, 8–9, 13.
76 'After some laborious research, the writer came to the conclusion, that no complete work on this subject exclusively has ever been published in any country, not even in France [my emphasis], where Conversation is deservedly ranked among the arts' (ibid., i).
77 W. H. Griffiths, *The Human Voice, its Cultivation and Preservation, a Manual for Singers and Speakers* (London 1892), 62.
78 Revd J. P. Sandlands, *The Voice and Public Speaking, Third Edition* (London 1885 [1880]): 'There is a peculiar charm in a good voice, even in conversation, which few other things can inspire' (p. 22).
79 Ibid., 14–15.
80 Ibid.
81 L. A. Tollemache, *Safe Studies* (London 1884), 79.
82 Ibid., 87.
83 Boswell, op. cit., 31.
84 Mahaffy, op. cit., 170–1.
85 *Spectator* (5 August 1882), no. 2823, p. 1019.
86 Mrs Humphry Ward, *A Writer's Recollections* (London 1918), 223–4.
87 Hain Friswell, op. cit., 163.
88 Bowes, op. cit., 84.
89 *The Rhetoric of Conversation*, xv-xvi.
90 See ibid., v: 'The Rhetoric of Conversation is an American work; but though an American work, we may learn much from it – perhaps all the more for its being American.'
91 Ibid., xvii.
92 Bowes, op. cit., x.
93 Ibid., xi.
94 *The Rhetoric of Conversation*, v.
95 Ibid., ii.
96 Ibid., 227.
97 Bowes, op. cit., xii.
98 Ibid., 132.
99 Ibid., 57, 58, 59.
100 Ibid., 65.
101 *The Habits of Good Society*, [anon] (London, 1859) 264–5.
102 Knollys, op. cit., 4.

103 Sandlands, *How To Develop General Vocal Power* (London 1886), vi-vii.
104 Edwin Drew, ed., *The Elocutionist Annual* (London 1889), 23. Drew was also responsible for a number of one shilling guides, among them: *Elocutionary Studies, Reciting and Reading, Speech Studies, How to Recite.*
105 Sandlands: 'It is true that nothing yields so readily to training as the voice' (*The Art of Healing*, 'The Relation Between the Principles of Voice Production and Health'), 92.
106 Drew, ed., *The Elocutionist Annual*, 45.
107 Drew, *The Public Speaker's Vade Mecum.*
108 George Vandenhoff, *The Art of Reading Aloud* (London 1878), 195.
109 For example, Frederic Maccabe offers this advice to public speakers: 'Speak with calmness and confidence, as though you were conversing with a friend' (*Voice Production, the Arts of Speaking, Singing, Acting and Ventriloquism*, London 1893, p. 108).
110 Charles Lunn, *The Philosophy of Voice* (London 1878, 4th edn), 57. The 1st edn of 1874 sold well: 'the entire edition has become exhausted in the brief space of two months' (Lunn's Preface to the 2nd edn, 1875); and the 2nd too: 'Now that in the briefest time a third edition is required, it would be idle in me to pretend not to know that I have been accepted by the public as an authority upon these questions' (Preface to the 3rd edn, 1875).
111 Lunn, *Vox Populi* (London 1880), 1. Lunn points out in his Preface that the work reprints articles from *The Orchestra.*
112 Ibid., Preface.
113 For example, in addition to those already cited: *Correct Voice Production* by Frank Quatremayne (1888); *Voice and Health* by Henry Sidon (1890); *Voice Production* by Theodore W. Barth (1890); *Voice Cultivation* by Josiah Richardson (1892); *Voice Production* by H. Fell (1893); *The Pocket Voice Gymnasium* (anon., 1893); *Voice Production and Vowel Enunciation* by J. J. Mewburn Levien (1895); *Voice Production* (1896) and *Science and the Art of Adjustment Between the Producing and Reflecting Vocal Apparatus* (1897) by Paul Mahlendorff; *Practical Guide to Articulation* by Joseph Clarkson (1903); *The First Principles of Voice Production* by Thomas Kelly; and the familiar Sandlands, *The True Theory of Voice Production* (1903).
114 'To public speakers, vocalists, &c., much pains have been taken to make the book a kind of Medical Guide or Companion – a sort of Vocal Vade Mecum, to which reference may be made for information relation to the minor troubles, and some of the graver diseases, to which the vocal organs are liable' (*The Human Voice* by J. Farrar, London 1881, pp. iii-iv).
115 Ralph Dunstan, in *Exercises in Voice-Production and Enunciation for Speakers and Readers* (London 1896, p. 19), refers to Max Müller's

Lectures on the Science of Language (2 vols, London 1864) in discussing the correct articulation of vowels.

116 *Athenaeum*, Saturday, 22 July 1876, 101.

117 '. . . the best of the many works on the subject I have seen . . . stands quite alone in its comprehensive and practical exposition of the technique of the art of elocution.' These comments came from Ernest Pertwee, Richard Temple and Allen Beaumont in 'A Selection from the Recent Publications of Charles William Deacon & Co.' (London 1898).

118 F. Harrison, ed., *Voice, Speech, and Gesture* (London 1898), 188–9.

119 Ibid., 175.

120 The dates, respectively: November-December 1876; April 1877; May 1877; June 1877-February 1878; Summer and Autumn 1878; January 1879; Winter 1880–81; Winter-December 1881. *The Letters of Anthony Trollope*, ed. N. J. Hall (2 vols, Stanford 1983), appendix to vol. ii.

121 F. T. Palgrave writes to a friend, 17 March 1869: 'I have just finished reading *The Ring and the Book* through to my wife' (*His Journals and Memories of his Life*, ed. G. F. Palgrave, London 1899, p. 103).

122 Trollope, *Diaries*, October 1876.

123 Mrs W. W. Story read Milnes's *Life of Keats*, lent her by Browning, aloud to her husband as he worked in his studio in Florence (E. P. Gould, *The Brownings and America*, Boston 1904, p. 84.

124 Ibid., 36–7.

125 James Stuart, *Reminiscences* (London 1911), 203.

126 *Baylor Browning Interests*, 1960.

127 Palgrave, Journal for July 1889 (op. cit., p. 218).

128 'I am reminded by one or two American friends . . . that he also read often to our own little family circle' (Fannie Barrett Browning, *Some Memories of Robert Browning*, Boston 1928, p. 16).

129 Elizabeth Porter Gould, 66–7.

130 Ibid., 22.

131 *Cornhill Magazine* LXXXV, 1902, 161. Browning's interest in newspaper reports is noted in a newspaper report on *The Inn Album* by the *Guardian* of 1 December 1875, 1538.

132 Ibid., 22. 'He and his sister used to hear Melville preach in Camberwell I believe, when they were young and thought him a fine preacher'.

133 George Howard, MP for East Cumberland, tabled the Bill of 19 May, 1882 to open all National Museums and Galleries on Sundays; the Bill was opposed principally by Henry Broadhurst, MP for Stoke.

134 Browning's Preface to *The Divine Order* by Thomas Jones, ed. Brynmor Jones (London 1884), v.

135 *Voice, Speech, and Gesture*, 190.

136 Henry James, *The Question of our Speech* (New York 1905), 10.

Chapter 3

1 *Illustrated London News*, 8 October 1853.
2 Mill, *The Subjection of Women*, 290.
3 Monseigneur Dupanloup, *Studious Women*, trans. R. M. Phillimore (London 1868), 7.
4 Ibid., 19.
5 George Augustus Sala, *Twice Around the Clock: or the hours of day and night in London* (London n.d.).
6 Mrs H. R. Haweis, *The Art of Beauty* (London 1878),
7 *Letters of Charles Dickens*, ed. Walter Dexter, vol. ii, 327; letter of 11 July 1851.
8 Ibid., vol. xix, 183.
9 John Davidson, *The Crystal Palace* (London 1851).
10 Robert Ellis, Preface to the *Official Catalogue* (1851).
11 See John Steegman, *Victorian Taste* (London 1970), 17.
12 J. L. Stevenson, *House Architecture*, 2 vols (London 1880), vol. i, 84.
13 Supplement to the *Official Catalogue*, advertisement to vol. iv, 3.
14 R. W. Emerson, *English Traits* (London 1908) [1847], Chapters VI, VII, VIII passim.
15 A. Trollope, *Barchester Towers* (London 1857).
16 In Asa Briggs, *1851* (Historical Association, 1951), 6. Porter began the *Progress* in 1837.
17 Robert Browning, *Dramatis Personae*, 'A Likeness', lines 1–7, 11–24.
18 See Gillian Avery, *Nineteenth Century Children: Heroes and Heroines in English Children's Stories, 1780–1900* (London 1968).
19 Class XXVI, Jennens and Bettridge of Birmingham exhibit.
20 Class XXVI, item 2a.
21 Class XXVI, item 6.
22 Class XXVI, item 27.
23 Class XXVI, item 28.
24 Class XXVI, item 187.
25 Class XXVI, item 54.
26 Class XXVI, item 78 number 4.
27 Class XXVI, item 192.
28 John Mitchell, *The Art of Conversation: with remarks on fashion and address* (London 1842), 67.
29 Section XXX, item 110, Cookes & Sons, Warwick.
30 Class XXVI, item 204.
31 Class XXVI, item 261.
32 Class XXVI, item 386.
33 Lady Barker, *Bedroom and Boudoir* (London 1878), 14.
34 Ibid., 31.
35 Kerr, *The Gentleman's House: or How to Plan English Residences,*

from the Parsonage to the Palace, cited in Stevenson, op. cit., vol.
i, 8.

36 Mrs Loftie, *The Dining-Room* (London 1878), 78–9.

37 Stevenson, op. cit., vol. ii, 47–8.

38 Taine, (1870), 91.

39 Mrs Haweis, *Beautiful Houses* (London 1882 [originally a series of articles in the *Queen*, 1880–1]), 23, 106.

40 Orrinsmith *The Drawing-room, it's decorations and furniture* (1877), 6.

41 Ibid., 145.

42 In Loftie, op. cit., 12.

43 Orrinsmith, op. cit., 4–5.

44 In Loftie, op. cit., 21.

45 Taine, 87.

46 John Ruskin, *Sesame and Lilies* (London 1865), 128.

47 Ibid., 143–4.

48 Millett, (1979), 79: 'The Victorian belief in marriage – nearly an article of faith – is an attempt to beautify the traditional confinement of women at any cost.'

49 Ruskin, op cit., 144.

50 Ibid., 144–5.

51 In J. Laver, *Victorian Vista* (London 1954), 29.

52 *Old Jonathan; or, the District and Parish Helper* (London 1867) in Laver, op. cit.

53 Mrs W. Fison, *Hints for the Earnest Student* (London 1850).

54 [Mrs Warren ed.,] *The Ladies' Treasury* (London 1867).

55 In Laver, op. cit., 41.

56 Charlotte Mason, *Home Education* (London 1886), 272. See also Loftie, op. cit., 7: 'To boys intending to emigrate even a slight acquaintance with the elementary principles of cooking would be found invaluable.'

57 Mason, op. cit., 6.

58 Ibid., 52.

59 Ibid., 68.

60 Ibid., 60.

61 Ibid., 75.

62 Ibid., 94.

63 Ibid., 96.

64 Ibid., 102.

65 Although this looks like a Hopkins coinage, Mason's usage calls up the *OED* citation of Donne (1651): 'all our moralities are but our outworks'; here, Mason pushes the military – architectural metaphor through the sieve of character.

66 Mason, op. cit., 123.

67 Ibid., 168.

68 Thomas Higginson, *Women and Men* (New York 1888), 58.

69 Taine, 87.
70 In Robin Kent, *Agony Aunt Advises* (London 1979), 52.
71 Margaret Dodd, *Cookery Book* (London 1830).
72 Table etiquette also gave scope to Victorian xenophobia, for example, *Hints on Etiquette* (1834): 'Wet a corner of your napkin, and wipe your mouth, then rinse your fingers; do not practise the *filthy* custom of gargling your mouth at table, albeit the usage prevails among the few, who think *because* it is a foreign habit, it cannot be disgusting.'
73 Thackeray, *The Book of Snobs*, 371–2.
74 Loftie, op. cit., 63.
75 Ibid., 67.
76 Warne, *Modern Etiquette*, ([Warne's Guides] London, 1871), 22.
77 Carlyle, *Anecdotes*, 417.
78 Mitchell, op. cit., 181.
79 Mahaffy, *Principles of the Art of Conversation*, 99.
80 *Studies in Conduct [Short Essays from the Saturday Review]* (1867), 139.
81 Maggie Lane, *Literary Daughters* (London 1989),
82 Letter of 25 August 1845 to Robert Browning.
83 Edmund Gosse, *Father and Son*; Samuel Butler, *The Way of All Flesh.*
84 Elizabeth Sewell, *Principles of Education, drawn from nature and revelation, and applied to female education in the upper classes* (London 1865), vol. ii, 237.
85 Elizabeth Eastlake, 'Vanity Fair, Jane Eyre and the Governesses' Benevolent Institution', *Quarterly Review* 84 (December 1848), 176.
86 Sarah Stickley Ellis, *The Wives of England* (London 1843), 219.
87 Eastlake, op. cit., 177.
88 *Governess Life: its Trials, Duties and Encouragements* (London 1849), 127. See also Sewell, op. cit., vol. ii, 259, 275; Eastlake, op. cit., 179–80; Ellis, op. cit., 209–10.
89 Warne, op. cit., 1.
90 Loftie, op. cit., 89.
91 Warne, op. cit., 1.
92 Charles Kingsley, *Letters and Memories* ed. F. Kingsley (London 1877), vol. i, 431 (unabridged).
93 In Leonore Davidoff, *The Best Circles* (London 1986), 43. Davidoff's fine discussion of calls and calling-cards can be found in Warne, op. cit., 5–10.
94 Oliphant, (1899), 71.
95 *Manners and Rules of Good Society* (32nd edn, 1910).
96 Ibid.
97 Warne, op. cit., 6.
98 Ibid.
99 The Carlyles dined at six. As dinner became later, the aristocrat's

afternoon tea from the 1830s became a larger affair; it reached the wider public in the 1860s and 1870s.

100 W. S. Rockstro and H. Scott Holland, *Memoir of Madame Jenny Lind-Goldschmidt* (London 1891), vol. i, 80.

101 Ibid., 75.

102 Ibid., 77–8.

103 *Useful Toil: Autobiographies of Working People from the 1820s to the 1920s* (London 1984),

104 Julian Charles Young, *A Memoir of Charles Mayne Young* (London 1871), 20 October 1834.

105 Warne, op. cit., 4.

106 Ibid.

107 Ibid., 5.

108 M. Oliphant *Dress* (London 1878), 2.

109 Ibid., 2.

110 Ibid.

111 Ibid., 62.

112 Ibid., 40.

113 Ibid., 83.

114 Ibid., 85. The cost of dress-making may have been reduced by the introduction of the sewing-machine, invented by Barthélemy Thimmonier and first exhibited at the Great Exhibition in 1851; the machine came into general use in the mid–1860s. He died in 1857.

115 Ada S. Balin, *The Science of Dress in Theory and Practice* (London 1885), 122.

116 Ibid., 221.

117 In 1851 *Punch* ridiculed 'The Bloomer Ball'; and the popular ballad 'I'll be a Bloomer' runs: 'Ladies do declare / A change should have been sooner, / The women, one and all, / Are going to join the Bloomers.'

118 C. G. Harper's *Revolted Woman* (1896) blames the bicycle for a return to Bloomerism in the 1890s.

119 *The Times*, 21 October 1851.

120 See W. P. Frith's famous 'The Fair Toxophilites'.

121 Bloomers were worn for tennis in the 1880s.

122 'Until we can find some means of lightening the draperies of the female toilette or distributing their weight better, it is always possible that it [the crinoline] may appear again'; in Balin, op. cit., 263.

123 Ibid.

124 Ibid., 9.

125 Ibid., 263.

126 Ibid., 258.

127 Ibid.

128 *Books and Portraits*, ed. M. Lyon (London 1979), 38.

129 *Sessional Papers, House of Commons 1871*, vol. xix, 327.

130 These Acts were 'calculated to prevent the spread of certain Con-

tagious Diseases in the Place to which this Act applies' (Portsmouth, Plymouth, Woolwich, Chatham, Sheerness, Aldershot, Colchester, Shorncliffe, The Curragh, Cork and Queenstown, and, in 1866, Windsor). Any woman living in these areas could be informed against on oath by the superintendant of police as being a prostitute. She was required to present herself for examination at a certified hospital, and – if found to be carrying a disease – could be detained for three months' treatment in hospital (see *27 & 28 Victoriæ*, C A P 85, 711–15). 'If any Person, being the Owner or Occupier of any House, Room, or Place within the Limits of any Place to which this Act applies, or being a Manager or Assistant in the Management thereof, knowing or having reasonable Cause to believe any common Prostitute to have a Contagious Disease, induces or suffers such common Prostitute to resort to or be in such House, Room, or Place for the Purpose of Prostitution, every person shall be guilty of an Offence against this Act, and on summary Conviction thereof before Two or more Justices of the Peace shall be liable to a Penalty not exceeding Ten Pounds, or, at the Discretion of the Justices, to be imprisoned for any Term not exceeding Three Months, with or without Hard Labour' (see *27 & 28 Victoriæ*, 712, article 18).

131 See *27 & 28 Victoriæ*, and Mayhew (1851–62); Booth (1899–1903); Stephen Marcus, *The Other Victorians* (London 1969 [1966]; Pearsall (1971 [1969]).

132 Parliament Papers (1871), vol. xix, 728.

133 Ibid.; question 19, 994.

134 On 1 January 1870, Butler, Mary Carpenter, Harriet Martineau, Florence Nightingale and 2,000 others wrote to the *Daily News* attacking the Acts on eight counts: the Acts removed legal safeguards from women; they removed personal security from women; they failed to define the offence which they punished; they punished the victims and not the cause of vice; they facilitated moral cupidity; they brutalised the women they affected; the disease the Acts set out to limit had never been removed by any legislation; and finally the conditions of the disease were not physical but moral. The protest concluded: 'The moral evil through which the disease makes its way separates the case entirely from that of the plague, or other scourges, which have been placed under police or sanitary care. We hold that we are bound, before rushing into experiments of legalising a revolting vice, to try to deal with the *causes* of the evil, and we dare to believe that with wiser teaching and more capable legislation, those causes would not be beyond control.' (*Daily News*, 1 January 1870).

135 *49 Victoriæ*, 16 April 1886.

136 Josephine Butler, *The Hour Before the Dawn: an Appeal to Men* (London 1876), 1.

137 Ibid., Preface.
138 Marcus, op. cit., 94.
139 The Acts' advocates emphasised four achievements: the Acts reduced the number of women falling ostensibly within their intent; they reduced the extent and virulence of contagious disease in women who did fall within their operation; they would halt the downward moral course of some women through the shock of alarm; and they fostered an overall sense of outward decency and order in the places of the Acts' legislation. The Acts' opposers claimed that the Acts encouraged clandestine prostitution (and tended to make the real offence seem to be transgression of the Acts rather than breach of moral codes); that while the protected districts were left for others by some prostitutes, married men tended to resort to protected districts in the belief that the Acts made intercourse less of a health risk; that the system of local inspectorships encouraged corruption and venality in the local police; and that the decorous surface burnished by the Acts merely concealed an increasing amount of irregular and unobtrusive prostitution. Evidence from committees of enquiry into the Acts shows that the grim details of the private medical examination became street gossip, and that small crowds frequently gathered around the examination room to count the women in and count them out safe (See W. T. Stead, *Josephine Butler: a Life Sketch* (London 1888), 75).

Opposers claimed that the Acts made disease a crime in one sex, not the other, and in order to discover it the Acts sanctioned this arrest and 'compulsory outrage' of women, illegal on suspicion of felony; and that the Acts created a class of 'Queen's women', virtually licensed, 'guaranteed by the state, as safe to sin with, who had the last remnant of womanhood destroyed by the supreme degradation of periodical official violation'. (See Stead, op. cit., 67, 68.)

In practice, a suspected woman might have to submit to a bimonthly examination throughout the year, or disprove the accusation of prostitution brought against her by the appointed local officials. Moreover, one opponent in the 1866 Commons debate on the extension of the Acts made plain the fear which the legislation had uncovered in the mid-Victorian psyche: 'It's object was to preserve the health of Her Majesty's troops, and its endeavour was to remove all penalties which a higher Power had imposed upon sin, and to give the opportunity of sin without the punishment.' (House of Commons, 22 March 1866, 815).

Other opponents claimed the Acts encouraged immoral behaviour by taking prostitution as a fact of life, and making using prostitutes safer: 'Now, no sophistical excuses about "sanitary measures", "protection of the community", "stamping out disease", and the like can get rid of the patent fact that by the Acts in question prostitution is recognised by the State as a permanent and necessary fact, the only concern of the State being the diminution and restriction of the diseases which that fact carries in its train.' (See S. Amos, *The Policy of the Contagious Diseases Acts* (London 1870), 13.)

140 Amos, op. cit., 31.

141 William Cobbett, Henry Ward Beecher and Timothy Titcomb, *The Friendly Counsellor: or Advice to Young Men and Young Women* (London 1876), 129.

142 Dinah Craik, *Mistress and Maid* (London 1863), vol. i, 104.

143 Butler embarked on her first media tour in 1870. Between then and 1881 she organised, directly or indirectly, 18,068 petitions for repeal to Parliament signed by 2,657,348 persons. Evidence to the 1880 Parliamentary Commission shows 83 petitions in favour (3,883 signatures, of which 1,112 were women registered under the Acts). Butler combined her efforts with those of other women's groups, including the Association for the Defence of Personal Rights, Wolstenhome Elmy's association for the vital Married Women's Property Act and her organisation for the reform of the Mutiny Act (which released married and single soldiers from all responsibility for legitimate and illegitimate children) and the Women's Suffrage Movement; the 'Society of which Elizabeth Fry was a distinguished member was ... among the first to welcome the public action of women in this matter'. Butler, 238

144 The 1870 election at a garrison town under the Acts, Colchester (Liberal 1,467; Conservative 1,284), provided the ideal platform. The luckless Liberal candidate, Sir Henry Storks, whose Newark campaign failed when he was tailed in a cart by pro-repeal activists distributing leaflets, continued to believe prostitution a necessity, and advocated fortnightly testing of prostitutes and soldiers' wives. This tepid stand helped neither the working women (by establishing standards for their care free of government intervention), nor addressed the social causes of prostitution, nor tackled the health issue by testing soldiers. In a brilliant manipulation of press and opinion, Butler helped the London Radical Dr Baxter Langley (pro-repeal) unseat the Liberal (853 votes) and disrupt the vote to return the pro-repeal Tory, Colonel Learmouth (1,364). Colchester was a riot of meetings, hustings and sandwich-boarders; and Butler had to return to Liverpool on polling day.

145 Stead, op. cit., Preface.

146 Butler, epigraph.

147 Ibid., 37.

148 Ibid.

149 Ibid., 41.

150 'She approached them from the "mother" side of her nature; and she brought to her work a sense of the dignity and even the divinity of womanhood, which in itself was a great inspiration. Other labour-

ers in this most difficult and most dangerous field have been impelled
thither by a desire to save souls, or to rescue women. Mrs Butler
always wanted to save DAUGHTERS. Motherhood is to her the sacred-
est thing in the world.' (Stead, op. cit., 18).

151 Ibid., 19–21.
152 She was also a biographer: she wrote *Catherine of Siena, John Grey
of Dilson* (a biography of her father), and the religious meditation
John Frederic Oberlin. She was a polemicist, opening the 1868 anti-
Acts campaign with *The Education and Employment of Women*.
1870 saw *An Appeal to the People of England on the Recognition
and Superintendence of Prostitution by Governments*, by an English
Mother (Nottingham).
153 Stead, op. cit., 41.
154 Stead, op. cit., 85.
155 J. Butler, *The Education and Employment of Women* (Liverpool
1868), 3.
156 Ibid., 17.
157 Butler, (1898), 71.
158 *The New Abolitionists* (London 1875), 228–9.
159 Butler, *The Hour Before Dawn*, 63.
160 Ibid., 70.
161 Stead, op. cit., 100.
162 Mill, *The Subjection of Women*, 304.
163 In *Victorian Studies* (December 1972), 189.
164 Ibid.
165 In Laver, op. cit., 32.
166 Taine, 81–2.
167 Ibid., 82.
168 George Eliot, *Scenes of Clerical Life*, 'Janet's Repentance'.
169 Taine, 88.
170 In Gertrude Himmelfarb, *Marriage and Morals among the Victorians* (New York 1987 [1975]), 61.
171 Mathild Blind, *George Eliot* (London 1883).
172 Mrs H. Coghill, ed., *The Autobiography and Letters of Mrs. M. O.
W. Oliphant* (London 1899), 5–6.
173 Oliphant, (1899), 163.

Chapter 4

1 In Boorstein, *The Americans: the National Experience*, London 1988
[1865]), 68–9.
2 See ibid., 72
3 See ibid., 79
4 In J. D. Unruh, *The Plains Across* (London 1992 [1979]), 11.
5 In ibid., 27

6 M. Arnold, 'Civilization in the United States,' in *Arnold*, ed., R. H. Soper (Michigan 1977), vol xi, p 361–2.
7 The sea journey from New York via Panama to San Francisco took six weeks in the 1840s, three or four weeks in the 1850s.
8 In Boorstein, op. cit., 66.
9 W. A. Alcott, *Young Man's Guide* (Boston 1836).
10 John Wentworth of Illinois. In Unruh, op. cit., 23.
11 In Boorstein, op. cit., 293–4.
12 In Unruh, op. cit., 120.
13 Fanny Trollope, *Domestic Manners of the Americans* (New York 1832).
14 Fanny Kemble, *American Journal* (London 1835).
15 Fanny Kemble, *Plantation Journal* (London 1863).
16 See Christopher Hibbert, *Redcoats and Rebels* (London 1990), 184.
17 Trollope, op. cit., iii.
18 Ibid.
19 Ibid., Introduction by Donald Smalley, ix.
20 Ibid., 324.
21 *Illustrated London News*, 17 May 1851.
22 Trollope, op. cit., 197.
23 Ibid., 224.
24 Ibid., 109.
25 Ibid., 131.
26 Ibid., 243.
27 Ibid., 242.
28 Ibid., 132, 75, 177.
29 Ibid., 202.
30 Ibid., 262–3.
31 Ibid., 263–4.
32 Basil Hall, *Travels in North America* (London 1830).
33 Russell Conwell, *Acres of Diamonds* (New York 1890), 19.
34 Trollope, op. cit., 321.
35 *Illustrated Manners Book and Manual of Good Behaviour and Polite Accomplishments* (New York 1857), 247.
36 Charles Dickens, *American Notes* (New York 1842), 23.
37 Ibid., 47.
38 Ibid., 55.
39 E. Cooley, *A Description of Etiquette at Washington City* (Philadelphia 1829), 1.
40 Dickens, op. cit., 111–12.
41 Ibid., 112.
42 Ibid., 131.
43 See U. Pope-Hennessy, *Charles Dickens* (London 1945), 182.
44 Michel Chevalier, *Society Manners and Politics in the United States* (New York 1966 [Boston 1839]), 348.
45 Chevalier, op. cit., 415.

46 Tupper's *Diary*, in Hudson, *Martin Tupper*, 127.
47 Ibid., 117.
48 Ibid., 120.
49 Ibid., 134.
50 A. Cleveland Coxe, *Impressions of England* (Philadelphia 1855), 125.
51 Ibid., 129.
52 S. J. Ransone, *'Good Form' in England* (New York 1888), 279.
53 Ibid., 280–1.
54 Ibid., 281n.
55 Ibid., 282.
56 Price Collier, *England and the English from an American Point of View* (New York 1911), 379.
57 Fredrika Bremer, *England in 1851* (Boulogne 1853), 27.
58 *Illustrated Manners*, 488.
59 Ibid.
60 Thomas Higginson, *Women and Men* (New York 1888), 22.
61 Ibid., 23.
62 Ibid., 25.
63 Dickens, op. cit., 244.
64 Lionel Tollemache, *Talks with Mr Gladstone* (London 1898), 178.
65 *A Victorian Vintage*, from the Diaries of Sir Mountstuart Grant Duff, ed. A. T. Bassett (London 1930), 16.
66 Tollemache, op. cit. (London 1898), 59.
67 G. M. Trevelyan *British History in the Nineteenth Century (1782–1901)*, (London 1934), 333.
68 George Washington, *Rules of Conduct* (Boston 1887), 8.
69 Cecil B. Hartley, *Gentlemen's Book of Etiquette and Manual of Politeness* (Boston 1876), 56.
70 Ibid., 57.
71 Emily Thornwell, *Lady's Guide to Perfect Gentility* (Cincinnati 1857).
72 Hartley, op. cit., 296.
73 Samuel Wells, *Book of Republican Etiquette* (New York 1857), 57, 124.
74 See Boorstein, op. cit., 307.
75 M. C. Conkling, *The American Gentleman's Guide to Politeness and Fashion ... Illustrated by sketches from life, of the men and manners of our times* (New York 1857), 73.
76 *The Bazar Book of Decorum* (New York 1870), 251.
77 *Laws of Etiquette* (Chicago 1878), 165.
78 Charles Day, *Etiquette; or, a Guide to the Usages of Society* (New York 1844 [London 1836]), 18–19.
79 *The Bazar Book of Decorum*, 148.
80 A. Trollope *North America*: ed. D. Smalley and B. Boothy (New York 1951) [1862], 483–4.
81 Ibid.

82 Isaac Peebles, *Politeness on Railroads* (Nashville 1899), 9–10, 11, 20, 23.
83 Ibid., 25.
84 Cooley *Etiquette* (1829), 109
85 [anon.] *American Etiquette and Rules of Politeness* (Chicago 1882), 99.
86 Mrs Ward, *Sensible Etiquette of the Best Society, Customs, Manners, Morals and Home Culture* (20th edn, Philadelphia 1889 [1878]), 230–5.
87 Ibid., 231.
88 Ibid., 231–32.
89 Ibid., 232.
90 Ibid.
91 Anonymous citation in Hartley, op. cit., 73.
92 [anon.], *Ladies Pocket Book of Etiquette* (Liverpool 1838), 57
93 Day, *Hints on Etiquette* (New York 1844), 3
94 Day (1843), 36.
95 J. Hazazer, *Guide for Young Beginners* (Baltimore 1880), 41.
96 Mary Sherwood, *The Art of Entertaining* (New York 1892), 392.
97 *Ladies Pocket Book of Etiquette*, 3, 47.
98 [anon.], *The Art of Good Behaviour and Letter-Writer* (New York 1850), 7.
99 *Ladies Pocket Book of Etiquette*, 147.
100 'We worked through spring and winter, through summer and through fall/But the mortgage worked the hardest and steadiest of them all;/It worked on nights and Sundays, it worked each holiday; It settled down among us and never went away . . .' (*Alliance Herald*, Stafford, Kansas, 29 May 1890).
101 Charles Leland, *The Art of Conversation* (New York 1864), 8.
102 T. S. Arthur, *Advice to Young Men on their Duties and Conduct in Life* (Philadelphia 1860), 86.
103 G. W. Hervey, *Principles of Courtesy* (New York 1852).
104 For example, Day, *Hints on Etiquette*; Jane Swisshelm, *Letters to Country Girls* (New York 1853); Revd J. B. Waterbury, *Considerations for Young Men* (New York 1851); *The Illustrated Manners Book and Manual of Good Behaviour and Polite Accomplishments* (New York 1855); *A Manual of Politeness* (Philadelphia 1851).
105 Louis Fitzgerald Tasistro, *Etiquette of Washington* (Washington 1866), 9.
106 James Parton, *Topics of the Time* (Boston 1871), 254.
107 Cooley, op. cit., 63.
108 Tasistro, op. cit., 6.
109 Abby Longstreet, *Social Life* (New York 1889).
110 Wells (1857), 37.
111 'Mrs Manners', (New York 1854 [1853]).
112 Ibid., 159.

113 *Illustrated Manners*, 229.
114 Ibid., 14.
115 Alcott, op. cit., 229.
116 Mrs F. Armstrong, *On Habits and Manners* (Virginia 1888), Ch.20, 133–43.
117 Ibid., 150.
118 Daphne Dale (C. F. Beezeley), *Our Manners and Social Customs: a Practical Guide to Deportment, Easy Manners, and Social Etiquette* (Chicago 1895), 45.
119 Marie Corelli, *Free Opinions* (London 1905), 117.
120 Marion Leroy, *Good Manners* (Springfield, Ohio, 1882). 12.
121 Mrs Ward, op. cit., 429–30.
122 Daphne Dale, op. cit., 317.
123 Katherine Thomas, *Official, Diplomatic, and Social Etiquette of Washington* (New Jersey 1895), 143.
124 *Etiquette for Americans* (New York 1909 [1898], 5.
125 Sherwood, *Manners and Social Usages* (1897 [1884]), Preface to 4th edn, 8.
126 Anne Seymour, *An A-B-C of Good Form* (New York 1915), 2.
127 Frances Stevens and Frances M. Smith, *Etiquette, Health and Beauty*, comprising 'The Usages of the Best Society' and 'Talks With Homely Girls on Health and Beauty' (New York 1889), 188, 193.
128 Anon., *The American Book of Genteel Behavior* (New York 1875), 12 (Franklin's maxims).

Chapter 5

1 According to D. M. Evans in *Facts, Failures and Frauds* (London 1859), this letter was found with the body. However, the solicitor Anthony Norris received it, posted on the evening of Sadleir's suicide, and produced it at the second inquest (25 February 1856).
2 See G. Smith, *Dickens, Money, and Society* (Berkeley, CA, 1968), 154ff.; E. T. Powell, *The Evolution of the Money Market, 1385–1915* (London 1966), 365.
3 Humphry House, *The Dickens World* (Oxford 1971 [1942]), 29.
4 Charles Dickens, *Little Dorrit*, Book II, Ch. 25.
5 W. M. Ellis, *A Chart of Industrial Life* (London 1869), 28: 'The rule of conduct suggested to all who use credit or come under obligations of any kind, is never to do so unless sure of having the means to discharge those obligations when called upon to do so.'
6 Ibid.
7 Evans, op. cit., 74.
8 Ibid., 403.
9 Ibid., 74–5.

10 Catherine Gore, *The Banker's Wife* (London 1843), Book II, Ch. 6, 203.
11 Dickens, op. cit., Ch. 21.
12 Anthony Trollope, *The Way We Live Now* (London 1874–5), Book I, Ch. 40, 379–80.
13 Ibid., Book II, Ch. 81, 295.
14 Ibid., Ch. 83, 318–19.
15 Lord Byron, *Marino Faliero, Doge of Venice* (London 1820), II, i.
16 *OED* uses 1, 16a & b, 18.
17 Trollope, op. cit., Book I, Ch. 35, 323.
18 First was, 'to get into a low state, physically or morally; to decline'. Second, when applied to persons, 'to pass (usually with suddenness) in, into or to some specified condition, bodily or mental, or some external condition or relation'. And third, at the same time as the first two, the word carried with it the sense of an occurrence or happening, 'to come to pass, befall, result' (as in 'to fall into a rage' or 'fall asleep'). *OED*, uses 7b, VII, VIII, 38a.
19 J. E. Worcester's 1846 *Universal and Critical Dictionary of the English Language*.
20 Evans, op. cit., 446.
21 Ibid., iv.
22 'The Begging-Letter Writer' in the *Centenary Edition* (London 1911), 15.
23 Alfred Russel Wallace, *Natural Selection and Tropical Nature* (London 1891), 200.
24 Evans, op. cit., 3.
25 Ibid., 432.
26 Ibid., 441.
27 Ibid., 434.
28 Ibid., 445.
29 Ibid., 483.
30 Ibid., 402.
31 Ibid.
32 Ibid., 409.
33 Ibid., 423.
34 Ibid., 4.
35 Ibid., 83.
36 Ibid., 89.
37 Ibid., 93.
38 Ibid., 3, 5.
39 John Maskelyne, *Sharps and Flats, the Secrets of Chanting* (London, 1894), 125.
40 Ibid., 112–13.
41 Ibid., 323.
42 Ibid., 324.
43 *The Times*, 11, 12, 14 (editorial), 1837.

Notes

44 The unlikely plot broke several Victorian taboos: a woman's past loves, gambling (and cheating), blackmail and suicide. The characters are unnamed: a Lord and a Youth have been gambling overnight at an inn; the Lord has hoped to dupe the younger man, but has failed, and now owes him ten thousand pounds. The Youth has chosen this inn because there he plans to meet his fiancée, the Girl, who owns an adjacent estate. While the Youth waits for her, he talks with the Lord and they discover they have both loved, the Youth an older, the Lord a younger, woman, four years ago. When the Youth's fiancée arrives, she has brought with her an older married friend for a second opinion on the Youth. This friend turns out to be the one and the same woman loved by the Youth and the Lord. The Lord presses the woman to accept him; she refuses; and he decides to blackmail her into a liaison with the Youth to clear the ten thousand pound debt. When the Youth discovers the Lord's plot, he kills him. The Woman kills herself. The Girl discovers her fiancée and two corpses.

45 Pierpont Morgan Library, New York.
46 John Ruskin, *Works*, vol. xvii, 282–3.
47 Evans, *Speculative Notes and Notes on Speculation* (London 1864), 1.
  48 John Laing, *Theory of Business* (London 1867), 236.
49 Evans, *The History of the Commerical Crisis, 1857–58* and *The Stock Exchange Panic 1859* (both in one vol., London 1859), vi.
50 In Norman Russell, *The Novelist and Mammon* (Oxford 1986), 48.
51 See Henry Maine, *Law and Opinion in England* (2nd edn), 419.
52 Dickens, *Our Mutual Friend*, Book I, Ch. x.
53 Gore, *Men of Capital* (London 1846).
54 Evans, *Facts, Failures and Frauds* (London, 1859) 123.
55 In Russell, op. cit., 73–4.
56 Evans, op. cit., 109–10.
57 In 1847 gold reserves stood at £8m., with £1.5m. in notes. The price of funded and other properties fell by £400m., and the loss to the funded and other interests was £60m.
58 In 1857 there was £6.5m. in gold reserves and £957,000 notes reserves; the panic lowered the prices of funded and other properties by £400m., and cost fund-holders and other interests £80m.
59 Evans, *The History of the Commercial Crisis, 1857–58*, 12.
60 *Commercial Register* (London 1849).
61 See *OED*, 'He tried to make . . . political capital out of the desolation of his house' (Macaulay, *History of England* (1869 [1855]), vol. iv, 314 and *1865*, Make capital out of. The inverted commas round Evans's 1859 usage indicate a word making its way into more common usage.
62 Evans, (1859), 25.
63 Evans, (1859), 67.

64 Charles Greville in J. W. Dodds, *The Age of Paradox* (London 1952), 386.
65 Evans (1859), 66–7.
66 *The Times*, Friday 22 December 1871.
67 Evans cites company formations through 1845 and 1846 in *The Commercial Crisis 1847–48* (London 1848), 3–52.
68 In Evans, *The History of the Commercial Crisis 1857–58*.
69 See H. A. Shannon, 'The Coming of General Limited Liability', *Economic History (Economic Journal Supplement)*, 2 (1930–33), 267–91.
70 See *Hansard* 1855, Ser. III, cxxxix, 358.
71 J. R. McCulloch: *Considerations on Partnerships with Limited Liability* (London 1856), 10–11.
72 See John Sutherland, *Victorian Fiction* (London 1990 [1988]), 535–6.
73 Mrs J. H. Riddell [Charlotte Elizabeth Lawson Riddell], 'F. G. Trafford', *The Race for Wealth* (New York 1866), Ch. 39.
74 Carlyle, *Latter-Day Pamphlets, 1* (London 1899 [1850]), 44.
75 Alfred Marshall, *Principles of Economics* (London 1920 [1890]), vol. i, 1.
76 John Laing, *Theory of Business* (London 1867), 196, 199.
77 Ibid., 236.
78 Thackeray, *The Book of Snobs*, 296.
79 Ibid., 298.
80 Gore, *The Moneylender* (London 1843), Book II, Ch. 7, 279–80.
81 Benjamin Disraeli, *Tancred* (London 1847), 118.
82 Carlyle, *Past and Present* (1843, Book 2.), vol. 2, 146.
83 W. H. D. Adams, *Wrecked Lives: or Men Who Have Failed* (London 1880, 1st series), v.
84 Ibid., 225.
85 Ibid.
86 Smiles, *Self-help*, 290.
87 *Poems of A. H. Clough*, ed. A. L. P. Norrington (Oxford 1986 [1968]), 242.
88 M'Culloch, *A Dictionary, Practical, Theoretical and Historical, of Commerce and Commercial Navigation* [London 1832], Final edn. 1882, ed. A. J. Wilson , 723.
89 The depression dates from the mid–1870s: 'The industrial depression is generally thought to have commenced in the closing months of 1874' (Professor Fawcett, *Free Trade and Protection*, 151, cited by A. R. Wallace in *Bad Times* (London 1885).
90 Wallace, op. cit., 117.
91 Hill, 'The Laws of Etiquette in Business Life', *Manual of Social and Business Forms* (Chicago 1893, 27th edn), 144.
92 J. E. M'Conaughy, *Capital for Working Boys: Chapters on Character Building* (London 1884), 78–9.
93 Smiles, op. cit., 290, 295.

94 William Ellis, *A Layman's Contribution to the Knowledge and Practice of Religion in Common Life* (London 1857), 17.
95 Mill, *System of Logic* (8th edn), Book VI, Ch. 12, para. 6.
96 George Long, *The Conduct of Life* (London 1845), Ch. 6, 'Moral Life', 142–3.
97 Binney, *Is it Possible to Make the Best of Both Worlds?* (London 1853), 36.
98 Ellis, op. cit., 366.
99 Ibid., 367.
100 Ibid., 342.
101 Ibid., 394–5.
102 See *Outlines of Social Economy* (London 1860 [1846]), 117.
103 Ellis, *Religion in Common Life*, 28.
104 Ibid., 346–7.
105 Ibid.
106 *Helps for the Young*, vii.
107 Ibid., 83.
108 Ibid., 84.
109 Ibid., 84–5.
110 Ibid., 87.
111 Goldwin Smith, *An Inaugural Lecture* (Oxford 1859), 33.
112 Gladstone, *Studies Subsidiary to Butler* (London), 306–9.
113 Gladstone, 'Memorandum on theology', 1 January 1855, *The Gladstone Diaries*, ed. M. R. D. Foot and H. C. G. Matthew (Oxford 1968-), vol. v, 1.
114 T. Chalmers, *The Application of Christianity to the Commercial and Ordinary Affairs of Life, in a Series of Discourses* (Glasgow 1820), in *Works*, vol. vi, vi-vii.
115 Evans, *Speculative Notes*, 51.
116 See John R. Reed, 'A friend to Mammon: Speculation in Victorian Literature', *Victorian Studies* (Winter 1984), 181–202.
117 Boyd Hilton, *The Age of Atonement* (Oxford 1988), 141.
118 Tennyson, 'The Two Voices', 315.
119 John Scoffern, *The Philosophy of Common Life* (London 1857), 274.
120 Ibid., 274–5.
121 Ibid., 275.
122 J. T. Davidson, *Talks With Young Men* (London 1884), 243.
123 Ibid., 200.
124 Ibid., 180–1.
125 By 1914 the Trust owned and administered over 6,000 homes throughout London; and by 1939, over 8,000. At its centenary, the Peabody Trust had invested £5m. since its foundation. It is, at the time of writing, the biggest housing association in London and has assets of over £1b.
126 Mill (1831), 36.
127 Ibid., 38.

128 The contents pages show familiar concerns: Occupation – small beginnings – the life purpose – the best capital – ingrained working habits – your business education – tent mates – on time – habits of economy – a courteous manner – weights – reefs – second thoughts – success out of hardship – manly independence – a straight course – boys who read – decision of character – conversation – letter writing – the best praise – the rest day – power to work – the tree by the river – by-path meadow – enduring riches – home.

129 M'Conaughy, op. cit., 30–1.

130 Ibid., 40.

131 Ibid., 127.

132 Ibid., 228.

133 Ibid., 171–2. The poem was introduced by a Revd. Dr Deems in New York.

134 Ellis, *A Chart of Industrial Life*, 6.

Chapter 6

1 Mill, *Autobiography* (London 1873), 113.

2 Ibid., 118.

3 Ibid., 121.

4 Ibid., 122.

5 Ibid., 121.

6 Carlyle (1829), in *Selected Writings*, ed. A. Shelston (London 1971), 85.

7 In Paul Turner, *English Literature 1832–1890* (Oxford 1989), 10.

8 Mill, *On Liberty*, 292.

9 Mill, 'Civilization' (1836), in *Essays on Literature and Society* ed. J. B. Schneewind (London 1965), 161.

10 Mill, *On Liberty*, 268: 'Those whose opinions go by the name of public opinion, are not always the same sort of public: in America they are the whole white population; in England chiefly the middle class. But they are always a mass, that is to say, collective mediocrity.'

11 Ibid.

12 In Joshua Fitch, *Thomas and Matthew Arnold and their Influence on English Education* (London 1905), 156. Fitch was HM Inspector of training colleges.

13 See Arnold Whitridge, *Dr Arnold of Rugby* (London 1928), 111.

14 Herbert Spencer, *Autobiography* (London 1904, 2 vols), vol. i, 399–400.

15 Ibid., 400.

16 Newman had dogmatically said in his famous St Peter's Day sermon of 1840 that the mind ranges, spreads and advances with a celerity which defies investigation; he likens its progress to the ascent of a climber up a crag.

17 Mill, 'What is Poetry?' (1833), in Schneewind, op. cit., 106.
18 *Robert Browning: The Poems*, ed. J. Pettigrew (London 1981), vol. i, 627: lines 395–401.
19 *The Letters of Robert Browning and Elizabeth Barrett Browning, 1845–1846*, ed. Elvan Kintner (Cambridge, Mass., 1969), vol. i, 17.
20 *The Renaissance* (Oxford 1986 [1873]), 151.
21 *Fortnightly Review*, vol. xxxiii, 1 June 1883, 889.
22 Mill, 'What is Poetry?', 109.
23 Ibid., 111.
24 Browning, *Poems*, vol. i, 347.
25 *Fortnightly Review*, December 1868.
26 Kintner, op. cit., vol. i, 19.
27 Browning, *Poems*, vol. i, 617: lines 1–2.
28 Ibid., 643.
29 Browning, 'Parleying With Charles Avison', 152ff.
30 *Robert Browning and Julia Wedgwood: a Broken Friendship as Revealed in their Letters*, ed. R. Curle (London 1937), 64.
31 Arnold, *Poems*, ed. K. Allott (London 1965), 272: 'The Buried Life', lines 26–9.
32 Kintner, op. cit., vol. ii, 802.
33 In any one place or atmosphere or mental climate, Empson urges, life is intolerable, 'in any two it is an ecstasy'. *Seven Types of Ambiguity* (London 1961 [1930], 131.
34 Johnson, *Dictionary* (4th edn, London 1773), use 1; Murray's *Dictionary*, uses 1, 3b, 5.
35 Kintner, op. cit., vol. ii, 585.
36 Browning, *Poems*, 560: 'By the Fire-side', lines 231–45.
37 Kintner, op. cit., vol. i, 26, 141, 189, 405; vol. ii, 667, 1038.
38 Browning, *Poems*, 554: 'By the Fire-side', lines 54–65.
39 Clough, *Prose Remains* (London 1888), 279.
40 Mill, *The Spirit of the Age* (1831), in Schneewind, op. cit., 34.
41 *Selected Prose Works of A. H. Clough*, ed. B. B. Trawick (Alabama 1964), 114.
42 Clough, *Poems*, 180–1: *Amours de Voyage*, lines 115–20.
43 Ibid., lines 121–9.
44 Michael Roberts, in *The Faber Book of Modern Verse* (London 1936), 11–14, points out the affinities between Eliot and Clough.
45 R. K. Biswas, *Arthur Hugh Clough* (Oxford 1972), 308.
46 J. A. Symonds, 'Arthur Hugh Clough', in *Last and First*, ed. A. Morrell (New York 1919), 602.
47 *National Review*, October 1862.
48 Clough, *Amours de Voyage*, lines 202–12.
49 Clough, *Poems*, xxi.
50 Letter of January 1852, in Clough, *Prose Remains*, 178.
51 Ibid., 174.
52 'As for your making the marriage, I trust it was made elsewhere,

where they say all true marriages are made.' Letter of June 1847, anonymous addressee, in ibid., 116.

53 Clough, *Poems*, 184: *Amours de Voyage*, lines 222–6.

54 *OED* uses 1–5.

55 George Meredith, *Diana of the Crossways* (London 1889), 61.

56 'My mistress' eyes are nothing like the sun' (Shakespeare, sonnet 130).

57 *Spectator*, September 1862.

58 James Stuart, *Reminiscences* (London 1911), 213. Stuart described a breakfast at Gladstone's, at which Browning was 'quite different from Tennyson' (p. 214).

59 Margaret L. Woods, 'Poets of the 'Eighties', in *The Eighteen Eighties: Essays by Fellows of the Royal Society of Literature*, ed. Walter de la Mare (Cambridge 1930), 2–3.

60 W. J. Courthope, 'The Latest Development in Literary Poetry', *Quarterly Review*, January 1872, 63.

61 Ford Madox Ford, *Critical Attitude* (London 1911), 179.

62 See A. H. Harrison, *Christina Rossetti in Context* (London 1988), 89–187.

63 Christina Rossetti, *Poems* (London 1890), 5: *Goblin Market*.

64 Ibid., 17.

65 Ibid., 143: 'An Apple Gathering'.

66 *Studies in Conduct* (1867), 29, 43–4.

67 J. T. Davidson, *Talks with Young Men*, 285. The tradition of mid-Victorian fear of city life dates from John Todd's *The Moral Influence, Dangers, and Duties Connected With Great Cities* (1841), which explained the possibilities of transgression and enumerated them exactly.

68 Davidson, *Sure to Succeed* (London 1888), 71.

69 Robert Buchanan, 'Fleshly School of Poetry', *Contemporary Review*, October 1871.

70 Buchanan, *Athenaeum*, 4 August 1866.

71 D. G. Rossetti, *Works*, 617.

72 John Morley, 'Mr. Swinburne's New Poems: *Poems and Ballads*', *Saturday Review*, 4 August 1866.

73 Ibid.

74 *The Times*, obituary for Charles Dickens, 10 June 1870.

75 Taine, *Lectures on Art* (1865), trans. J. Durand (New York 1875) in *Nineteenth-Century theories of Art*, ed. J. C. Taylor (California 1987), 373.

76 T. E. Brown, *Roman Women* (1895), in *The New Oxford Book of Victorian Verse*, ed. C. B. Ricks (Oxford 1987), 486: XIII, lines 41–50.

77 G. M. Trevelyan, *British History in the Nineteenth Century (1782–1901)* (London 1922), 367.

78 G. M. Young, *Daylight and Champagne* (London 1948 [1937]), 166.

79 *Parlour Poetry: a Hundred and One Improving Gems* (London 1967), ed. M. Turner, 10–17.
80 *Saturday Review*, vol. xli, 12 February 1876, 198.
81 Lucy Soulsby, *Stray Thoughts on Character* (London 1900), 142.
82 Ibid., 136.
83 The popular *Christian Life* by Peter Bayne, a panegyric to the certainties offered by Carlyle, arrived in 'Modern Doubt' at the sense that those early accustomed to dispute first principles rarely acquired sufficient sincerity and earnestness, nor the love of truth and 'conscientious solicitude for the formation of just opinions, which are not the least virtues of men, but of which the cultivation is the more especial duty of all who call themselves philosophers' (*The Christian Life* [London 1859], p. 2730).
84 Marshall McLuhan, *Understanding Media* (Toronto 1965), 39.
85 Mill, *System of Logic*, 605 (Book VI, Ch. 10, section 7).
86 A. P. Stanley, *Life and Correspondence of Thomas Arnold* (London 1844), 62.
87 Ibid., 63.
88 'Literature and Science', the 1881 Rede Lecture at Cambridge University.
89 Matthew Arnold (1881), Rede Lecture, Cambridge.
90 T. H. Huxley, 'On the Physical Basis of Life' (1868), lecture, Edinburgh University.
91 *Spectator*, obituary for John Stuart Mill, 17 May 1873. Mill died on 8 May 1873.
92 In *A Victorian Spectator: Uncollected Writings of R. H. Hutton*, ed. R. H. Tener and M. Woodfield (Bristol 1989), 203.
93 Walter Pater, *The Renaissance* (Oxford 1986 [1873]), ed. A. Phillips, 84–5.
94 Joris-Karl Huysmans, *Le Drageoir à Epices* (1874), *Marthe* (1876), *Les Soeurs Vatard* (1879), *En Ménage* (1881) and *A Vau-l'Eau* (1882).
95 Huysmans, *A. Rebours* (1884), trans. as *Against the Grain* (New York 1969 [tr. 1931]), 21–2.
96 Ibid., 69–9.
97 Ibid., 85.
98 Ibid., 96.
99 Mill, *Three Essays on Religion*, ed. H. Taylor (London 1874), 5.
100 Ibid.
101 Ibid., 8.
102 Ibid., 7.
103 Mill, *On Liberty*, 73.
104 T. Binney (1853), 36.
105 *Short Essays from the Saturday Review: Studies in Conduct* (London 1867), 31.
106 Mill, *Three Essays on Religion*. 12.

107 Taine, *Notes on England*, 175–6. This translation is more contemporary than the more readily available translation by Edward Hyams (London 1957).

108 Mill, *Three Essays on Religion*, 13.

109 Ibid., 64.

110 Ibid.

111 Harley Rodney, in *Voices 1870–1914*, ed. P. Vansittart (New York 1985), 148.

112 Edwin Drew, *The Public Speaker's Vade Mecum. Elocution: its Principles Reduced to Practice* (John Farquhar Shaw, London, July 1857). Third thousand printed.

113 In *Essays from 'The Guardian'* (London 1910), 14.

114 G. M. Young: *Portrait of an Age* (London 1960 [1953]), 157, 159.

115 Mill (1867), St Andrews University inaugural lecture, in Schneewind, op. cit., 375–6.

116 Alfred Russel Wallace, *Darwinism: an Exposition of the Theory of Natural Selection with some of its Applications* (London 1889), 477–8.
    117 Buckle's *History of Civilization in England* (London 1857, 2 vols): 'what makes the history of England so eminently valuable is, that no where else has the national progress been so little interfered with, either for good or for evil' (vol. i, p. 231).

118 Dinah Craik, *Sermons out of Church* (London 1875), 217–18.

119 Wallace, op. cit., v.

120 Oscar Wilde, *Intentions* in *The Artist as Critic*, ed. R. Ellman (Chicago 1982 [1968]), 293.

121 Holbrook Jackson, *The Eighteen Nineties* (London 1913); Graham Hough, *The Last Romantics* (London 1893 [1949]); Ellman, *Oscar Wilde* (London 1987).

122 *Post Liminum: Essays and Critical Papers by Lionel Johnson*, ed. T. Whittlemore (London 1912), 25, reprints the 1894 *Fortnightly Review* piece on Pater.

123 Pater (1910), 21–2.

124 Ibid., 23.

125 Ibid., 113.

126 Ibid., 117–118.

127 See Hough, op. cit., xiii.

128 Pater: *The Renaissance* (Oxford 1896 [1873], 152.

129 Arthur Symons, *The Symbolist Movement* (London 1899), 109; see also Havelock Ellis, 'Introduction' to Huysmans, *Against the Grain*.

130 William Lecky, *The Map of Life*, (London 1899), 50.

131 Friswell, *The Better Self* (London 1875), 155.

132 T. H. Huxley, *Evolution and Ethics and Other Essays* (New York 1898), 146.

133 Ibid., 82.

134 See S. J. Gould, *Hen's Teeth and Horse's Toes* (London 1984 [1983]), 44.

Notes

135 Henry Sidgewick's *Lectures on the Ethics of T. H. Green, Mr. Herbert Spencer, and J. Martineau* (London 1902) appeared in *Mind* throughout the 1880s.

136 The *Oxford English Dictionary*, conceived in 1858, first appeared in 1884 and ran to 1828 until the completion of the first edition.

137 See S. J. Gould, *Ever Since Darwin: Reflections in Natural History* (London 1980 [1978]), 225.

138 August Schleicher, *Darwinism Tested by the Science of Language* (London 1869), 41.

139 George Romanes, (London 1888), 439.

140 Ibid., *Mental Evolution in Man: Origin of Mental Faculty* 238.

141 For Darwin and Freud, see L. B. Ritvo, *Darwin's Influence on Freud* (Yale 1990).

142 Freud, *Civilization and its Discontents*, trans. J. Strachey (New York 1961), 49.

143 Mill, *The Subjection of Women*, 230.

144 John Bowlby, *Charles Darwin* (London 1990), 354ff.

145 Samuel Wilberforce, *Essays* (London 1874), 2 vols, vol. i. 102–3.

146 Romanes, *Essays* (London 1897), 37.

147 Ibid., 81–2.

148 See Bain, *Darwin on Expression* (London 1873), 336ff.

149 Ibid., 712.

150 Anne Judith Penny, *Problems in Human Nature* (London 1863), 50. This had been put in literary terms, with Charlotte Brontë's comment on *In Memoriam*.

151 James McCosh, *The Emotions* (London 1880), 250–1.

152 Wilde, *Phrases and Philosophies for the Use of the Young*, in *Chameleon*, December 1894.

153 Ellman, *The Artist as Critic*, 436.

154 J. B. Mayer, *Journal of Philosophy* (London 1871), 348.

155 Arthur Symons, 'The Decadent Movement in Literature', in *Aesthetes and Decadents*, ed. K. Beckson (New York 1966), 136.

156 Romanes, *Poems*, selected and ed. T. H. Warren (London 1896), 33.

157 G. H. Fleming, *Victorian 'Sex Goddess'* (Oxford 1990 [1989]), 1–2.

158 Cambridge University Library, Darwin Papers, 87 fo., 187.

159 See Crane Brinton, *The Shaping of Modern Thought* (Prentice Hall 1963 [1950]), 201.

160 Young, *Portrait of an Age*, 181.

161 Mill, *On Liberty*, 274.

162 George Eliot, 'Servants' Logic', in *Pall Mall Gazette*, 17 March 1865.

163 G. M. Young, *To-day and Yesterday* (London 1948), 243.

164 Mill, *System of Logic*, Ch. xii, section 7, 620.

165 Ibid., 621.

166 Mill, *On Liberty*, 261.

Index

Index

Index

Index

Fox, William, 230
fraud, 181ff., 205–6
Freud, Sigmund: *Civilization and its Discontents*, 278
Friswell, J. Hain, 22, 44
  The Better Self, 275
  The Gentle Life, 22, 68, 69, 73
Frith, William, 249
furniture and furnishings, 54, 87, 88, 90, 92–4, 98–100, 107, 108, 109, 115

Gailhard, Jean: *The Compleat Gentleman*, 5
Galaxy, The, 168
gambling, 194–5
Garcia, Manuel, 79
Garrett, Agnes and Rhoda, 99–100
Gaskell, Elizabeth, 58, 72
Gates, William, 143
Gautier, Theophile, 250, 272
  Mademoiselle de Maupin, 272
Gay, John, 7
Gentleman's Magazine, 123
Germ, The, 250
Gisborne, Revd Thomas: *Enquiry into the Duties of Men in the Higher and Middle Classes*, 9
Gladstone, William Ewart, xiv, 14, 15, 32, 69, 81, 72, 111, 159, 203, 210, 217, 223
Goffman, Erving, 5
Gooch, Daniel, 111
Gore, Catherine, 199
  The Bankers Wife, 185, 199
  Mammon. . ., 199
  Men of Capital, 199
  The Moneylender, 206–7
Gosse, Edmund, 273
Gouge, William, 7
Gould, Elizabeth Porter, 81
Gourmont, Rémy de, 262, 272
Governess Life: its Trials, Duties and Encouragements (anon.), 112
governesses, 111–12, 113
Great Exhibition, the (1851), xix, 29, 54, 84, 85, 87–91, 93, 99, 146, 156, 221
Greeley, Horace, 139, 173
Green, T.H., 30, 237
Green a Jersey Co., 140
Greene, Robert, 7
  Quip for an Upstart Courtier, 4
Greenwood, James: *Seven Curses of London*, 124
Greville, Charles: *Greville Memoirs*, 195
Greville, Lady: *The Gentlewoman in Society*, 66
Grice, Paul, 57

Griffiths, W.J.: *The Human Voice*, 71, 79
Grote, George, 107
Grote, Mrs George, 107, 108

Habits of Good Society, The (anon.), 76
Hall, Basil, 149
Hall, John: *A Christian Home. . .*, 134
Harberton, Lady, 122
Hardy, E.J.: *Manners Makeyth Man*, 101
Harper's Monthly, 27
Harrington, William: Commendations of Matrimony, 3
Harrison, Clifford, 80
  Reciting and Recitative, 83
Harrison, J.F.C., xvi
Hartley, C.B.: *Gentlemen's Book of Etiquette and Manual of Politeness*, 161
Haweis, Mrs H.R., 87, 97
  The Art of Beauty, 87
Hawthorne, Nathaniel, 203
  The English Notebooks, 49
Heathcote, John, 31
Henslow, John, 230
Hervey, G.W.: *Principles of Courtesy*, 172–3
  The Rhetoric of Conversation. . ., 74–5
Hessey, J.A., 40
Higginson, Thomas: *Women and Men*, 104, 157–8
Hill: *Manual of Social and Business Forms*, 210
Hoby, Thomas (trs.): *Boke of the Courtier*, 4
Home, Daniel D., 196
Home Journal, 12
Hooker, Herman, 12
Hooker, William, 230, 279
Hopkins, Gerard Manley, 238, 257
  'Carrion Comfort', 257
  'The Wreck of the *Deutschland*', 257
hotels, American, 163–5
Hough, Graham, 272
house design, 95–7, 99
How To Shine in Society. . . (anon.), 60
Hudson, George, MP ('The Railway King'), 166, 189, 201–2
Hugo, Victor: *Les Misérables*, 6
Hunt, William, Holman, 18, 249, 250
Hutton, R.H., 244, 248, 268
  Mill's obituary, 260
Huxley, Thomas Henry, xvi, 17, 58, 59, 230, 232, 260, 268, 269, 270, 279, 285
  Man's Place in Nature, 34
  'Science and Morals', 275
Huysmans, Joris-Karl, 123, 250, 266, 273
  À Rebours, 261, 262–4, 280

Index

Index

Marsh, G.P., 40
Marshall, Alfred: *Principles of Economics*, 205
Maskelyne, John: *Sharps and Flats: the Secrets of Cheating*, 194–5, 196
Mason, Charlotte: *Home Education*, 103–4
Massey, Rt Hon. William N., 125
Maurice, F.D., 34
Mayer, J.B.: *Journal of Philosophy*, 282
Mayhew, Henry, 58
Meredith, George, xx, 59, 228, 233, 245, 256, 257
   Diana of the Crossways, 246, 248
   Modern Love, 100, 245–7, 248–9, 256
Michelet, Jules, 166
Mill, John Stuart, xvi, xx, 29, 30, 31, 42, 45, 111, 112, 119, 125–6, 132, 137, 222, 231, 235, 237, 249, 257, 258, 260–1, 264, 268, 274
   Autobiography, 226–7, 261
   Civilization, xv, 229
   On Liberty, xv, 1, 18, 26, 28, 41, 43, 44, 228–9, 230, 233, 265, 286, 287, 289
   Principles of Political Economy, 205
   Representative Government, xiv–xv
   St Andrews University Inaugural Lecture, 269
   The Spirit of the Age, 240, 241
   The Subjection of Women, xi, xii, 86, 100, 132–3, 278–9
   System of Logic, xx, 212, 258–9, 261, 288–9
   Three Essays on Religion, 264–7
   'What is Poetry?', 233, 234
Millais, Sir John Everett, 50, 249, 250
Miller, Hugh, 31, 221
Mitchell, John: *The Art of Conversation. . .*, 94, 108
Mivart, St George: *Contemporary Evolution*, 34
Modern Etiquette (anon., 1859), 65
Modern Etiquette in Private and Public (anon., 1871), 46–7
Moore, George, 262
More, Hannah: *Christian Morals*, 10
   Thoughts on the Importance of the Manners of the Great to General Society, 9
Morgan Grenfell, 221
Morley of Blackburn, John Morley, 1st Viscount, 49, 58, 285
   'Mr Swinburne's New Poems. . .', 253–4
Morris, William, 58, 85, 94, 99, 249, 250, 253, 268
   News from Nowhere, 251
Morton, Charles, 68
Mottram, R.H., 53

Moxon (publishers), 23
Müller, Friedrich Max, 48, 79, 142, 276–7
   Science of Thought, 277
Mulready, William, 249
Murray, James, 276
Museums Act (1845), 54
music hall, the, 68

Nash, Beau, 7
Nation, The, 168
National Review, The, 31, 41
National (later Rational) Dress Society, 122
Newman, J.H., 24, 42, 102, 268
   The Danger of Riches, 9
   The Idea of a University, 42, 261
Norton, Charles Eliot, 244

OED, see Oxford English Dictionary
Oliphant, Margaret, 114, 136–7
   Dress, 119–21
Orrinsmith, Lucy, 97, 98
Osborne, Francis: *Advice to a Son*, 4
Overend, Gurney & Co., 199
Owen, Robert, 255
Oxford English Dictionary (OED), 11, 16, 39–40, 49, 133, 186

painting and illustration, 249
Palgrave, Francis, T., 81, 90, 243, 244
Pall Mall Gazette, 27, 128
Palmerston, Henry Temple, 3rd Viscount, 111, 159, 160
Parton, James: *Topics of the Time*, 173
Pater, Walter, 123, 235, 250, 266, 268, 274
   Essays from 'The Guardian', 268, 273
   Marius the Epicurean, 269, 273
   The Renaissance, 234, 258, 261, 273
Patmore, Coventry, 250, 268
   The Angel in the House, 18, 247–8
   'To the Body', 283–4
Pattison, Mark, 31, 268
Paul, Sir John Dean (senior), 199
Paul, Sir John Dean (junior), 199–200
Paxton, Joseph: Crystal Palace, 88
Peabody, George, and the Peabody Trust, 221–2
Peacham, Henry: *Art of Living in London*, 6
   The Compleat Gentleman, 4
Peebles, Isac: *Politeness on Railroads*, 165
Peel, Sir Robert, 69, 159
Pennell, Cholmondeley: sonnets, 23–4
Penny, Anne: 'The Decline of Sentiment', 281
Pernod, Henri, 272
Plumptre, Professor, 70

327

Index

population statistics, *see* demographic statistics
Porter, G.R.: *Progress of the Nation*, 91
Pre-Raphaelite Brotherhood, the, 249, 250, 258
prostitution, 124–33 *passim*
Public Libraries Act (1850), 54
public speaking, 77–8
Punch, 23, 62, 69, 88

Quarterly Review, 31, 279
Quite a Gentleman (anon.), 42

railways (railroads): in America, 163–4, 165, 166
in England, 163, 165–6, 200, 203
Ransone, S.J.: *'Good Form' in England*, 156
Rational Dress Society, 122
Reade, Charles: *Hard Cash*, 208
reading habits, 79–82
Record (magazine), 25
Redgrave, Richard, 249
Redpath, Leopold, 189–91
Reform Acts and Bills, xiii, xiv, 15, 36, 45, 47, 99, 229
Reid, Hugo, 55, 287
(under pseudonym Roger Boswell) *The Art of Conversation*, 45, 55–7
Ricketts, Charles, 90
Riddell, Charlotte, 204
Robson, William James, 189, 191–3
Rogers, Samuel, 50, 51
Romanes, George, 230, 277, 278, 280, 283
Roosevelt, Theodore, 37
Rose, Elizabeth, 93
Rossetti, Christina, xx, 228, 236, 250, 253
'An Apple Gathering', 252
Goblin Market, 128, 251–2, 256
Rossetti, Dante Gabriel, xx, 228, 236, 249, 250, 253, 255, 256, 268
Poems, 253
Rossetti, William, 23
Rundell, Mrs: *New System of Domestic Cookery...*, 106
Ruskin, John, 30, 58, 88, 121, 166, 196, 208, 224, 235, 268
Modern Painters, 41
Sesame and Lilies, 100–1
Russell, G.W.E., 51, 72–3
Russell, John: *Boke of Nurture*, 3

Sadleir, John, MP, 181–2
Sala, George Augustus, 87
Sandlands, Revd J.P.:
How to Develop General Vocal Power, 76–7

The Voice and Public Speaking, 71
Saturday Review, 16, 26–7, 28, 36, 102, 109, 246, 253, 256, 265, 285
Schleicher, August: *Darwinism Tested by the Science of Language*, 277
Scoffern, John: *The Philosophy of Common Life*, 219–20
Searle, John, 57
sermons, reading of, 82
Sewell, Elizabeth, 111
Shadwell, Thomas, 7
Shannon, Charles, 90
Shaw, G. Bernard: *Mrs Warren's Profession* 132, 207
Sherwood, Mary, 171
Manners and Social Usages, 178
Sidgwick, Henry, 136
Sidney, Sir Philip, 3
slang, 68–9, 73
Smiles, Samuel, xviii, 11, 13, 18, 19, 20, 26, 44, 110, 166, 213, 287
Character, 26, 27
Duty..., 26, 27e
Industrial Biography, 27
Life and Labour, 26
Lives of the Engineers, 27
Self-Help, xvi, 12, 18, 26, 27, 28–31, 208–9, 211
Thrift, 26, 27, 209
Smith, Adam, 9
Smith, Goldwin: *An Inaugural Lecture*, 217
Smith, Sydney, 50–1, 108
Smollett, Tobias, 7
Soulsby, Lucy: *Stray Thoughts on Character*, 257
Sowerby & Castle, 94
Spectator, 23, 72, 248, 260, 268
speculation and overspeculation, 183, 184, 218
speech, *see* accents, regional; conversation; slang
Spencer, Herbert, 58, 230, 232, 259, 269, 270, 275
Principles of Ethics, 276
Social Statics, 17, 232
System of Synthetic Philosophy, 276
Stanley, A.P., Dean of Westminster, 117, 259
Stead, W.T., 128, 130
Stebbing, Revd Dr Henry, 15
Stephen, Leslie, xv, 261, 276
Stephenson, Robert, 88
Stevenson, George, 110
Stevenson, J.L.: *House Architecture*, 90, 96–7
Stevenson, Robert Louis, 63

Index

Index

Wilde, Oscar, 64, 90, 223, 245, 250, 262,
272, 279, 282, 284
Dorian Gray, 68, 282
Intentions, 271
*Phrases and Philosophies for the Use of
the Young*, 282
Wilde, Mrs Oscar, 122
Wilson, Thomas: *Institutio Oratorica*, 3
Wither, George, 12
women: in America, 148–9, 150, 176–7
in England, 86–8, 91, 92, 93, 97, 109–14,
134–7, 176
see also dress; education; prostitution

Woolf, Virginia, 245
'Modes and Manners of the Nineteenth
Century', 123–4
Wordsworth, William, 227, 241, 258
Wright, Thomas: *The Passions of the
Minde*, 5
Wyatt, Sir Thomas, 3

Young, G.M., 70, 256 (*bis*), 268–9, 286, 287
Young, Julian Charles, 118

Zola, Émile, 262
Argent, 207

330